RISE UP

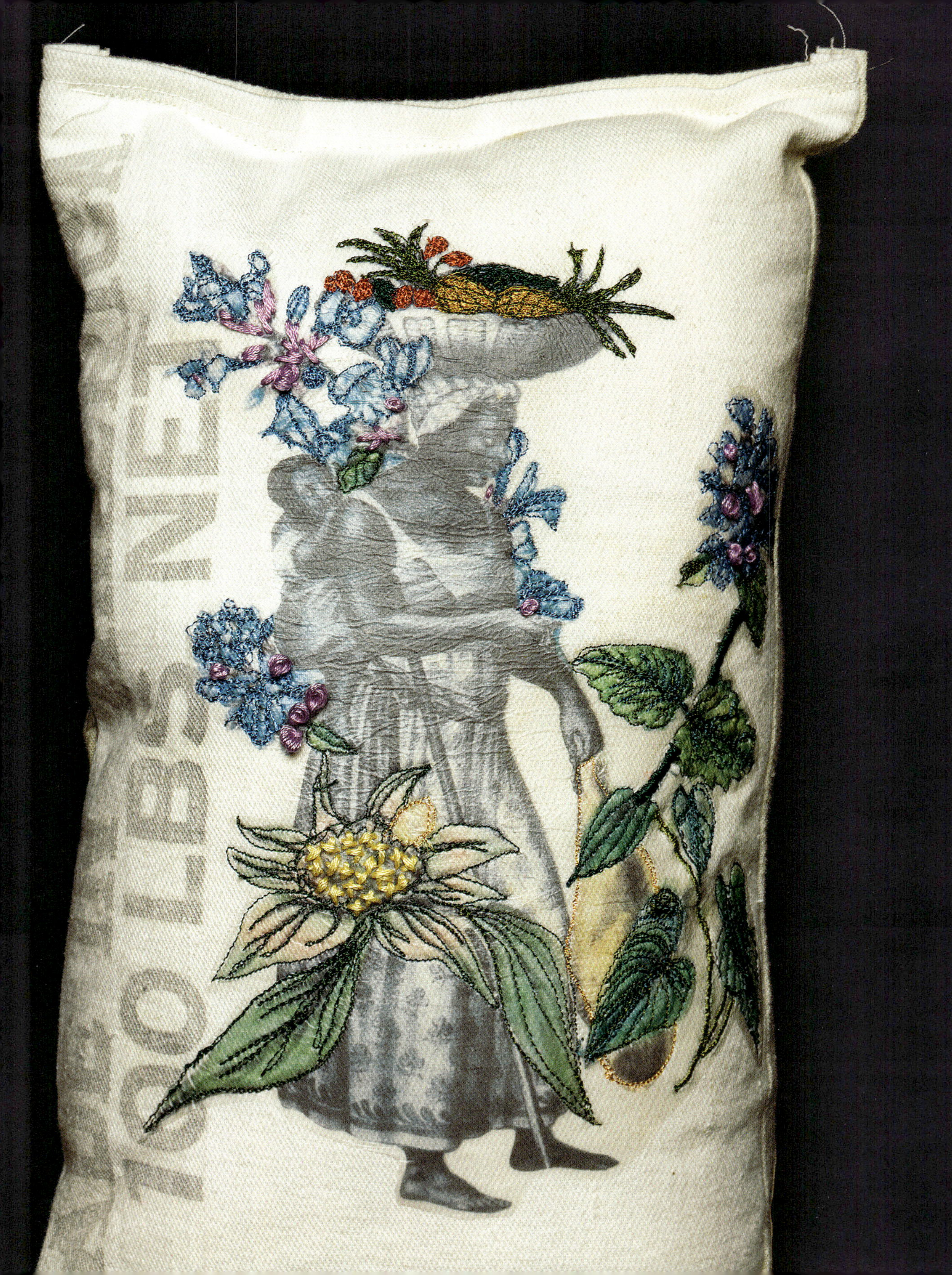

RISE UP

RESISTANCE REVOLUTION ABOLITION

Edited by **Victoria Avery** and **Wanja Kimani**

with contributions by
Victoria Avery · Jacqueline Bishop
Sabine F. Cadeau · Kimathi Donkor · Jahnavi Inniss
Wanja Kimani · Joy Labinjo · Mathelinda Nabugodi
Temi Odumosu · Lila O'Leary Chambers · Keith Piper
Niru Ratnam · Orlando Reade · Steven Swaby

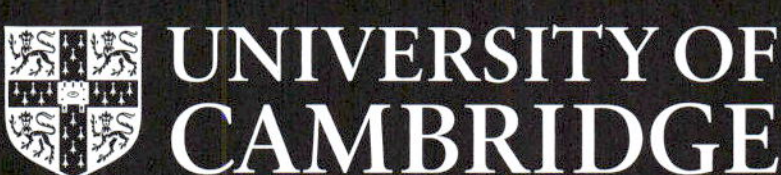

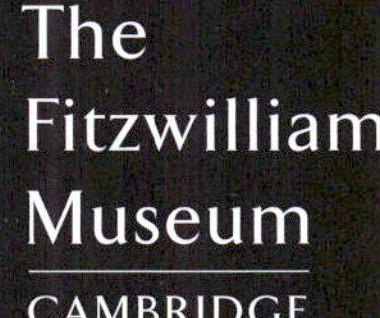

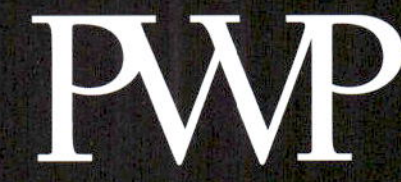

PHILIP WILSON PUBLISHERS
Bloomsbury Publishing Plc
50 Bedford Square, London, WC1B 3DP, UK
29 Earlsfort Terrace, Dublin 2, Ireland

BLOOMSBURY, PHILIP WILSON PUBLISHERS and the PHILIP WILSON
logo are trademarks of Bloomsbury Publishing Plc

First published in Great Britain in 2025

Published on the occasion of the exhibition:
Rise Up: Resistance, Revolution, Abolition
The Fitzwilliam Museum, Cambridge, 21 February — 1 June 2025

A catalogue record for this book is available from the British Library
Library of Congress Cataloguing-in-Publication data has been applied for

ISBN: 978 1 78130 135 7

Frontispiece: Detail of 42 (see page 72)

Designed and typeset in Roc and Macklin
Printed and bound by DZS Grafik, Slovenia

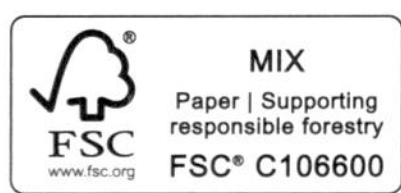

To find out more about our authors and books visit www.bloomsbury.com
and sign up for our newsletters

Contents

Foreword 7

Introduction 11

Dark finance: the intertwined history of slavery and abolition at the University of Cambridge 13
Sabine F. Cadeau

Introducing Olaudah Equiano, or Gustavus Vassa, The African 21
Victoria Avery

1 | Oppression and resistance 35

Seeing against the grain 37
Mathelinda Nabugodi

Olaudah Equiano's roots 48

The 'Africa Trade' 50

Life on British Caribbean plantations 54

Forms of resistance 60

2 | The British anti-slave trade campaign 75

Breaking through: Black Georgian voices 76

Cambridge connections 84

Olaudah Equiano and Cambridge 87
Victoria Avery

Ongoing abolition campaigning 108

3 | Britain's colonies in Nova Scotia and Sierra Leone 113

Nova Scotia: northern exposure 114

Sierra Leone: the 'province of freedom'? 119

4 | Revolutions in the Caribbean 123

Creation of Haiti: republic and kingdom 124

Cambridge and Haiti: slavery, the Haitian Revolution and British abolitionism 131
Sabine F. Cadeau

Tipping points: Barbados, Guyana and Jamaica 144

5 | Ending British slavery 153

Women's activism 154

Freedom at last? 161

Celebrating Black Cambridge history 164

Moving forward 175

I'll think of a title after I write 177
Wanja Kimani

Touching the void: on becoming an art historian and reckoning with slavery at Cambridge 190
Temi Odumosu

Contributors 200
Acknowledgements 202
Picture credits 204
Index 205

Content notice: This book explores enslavement and racism. It includes objects linked to violence against Black people and their exploitation. To call attention to historic and ongoing racialised inequalities, the collective terms 'Black' and 'Indigenous' are capitalised in the section texts and captions while 'white' is not. Individual contributors have made their own decisions regarding preferred terminology, capitalisation, and the redaction of certain historic racist words.

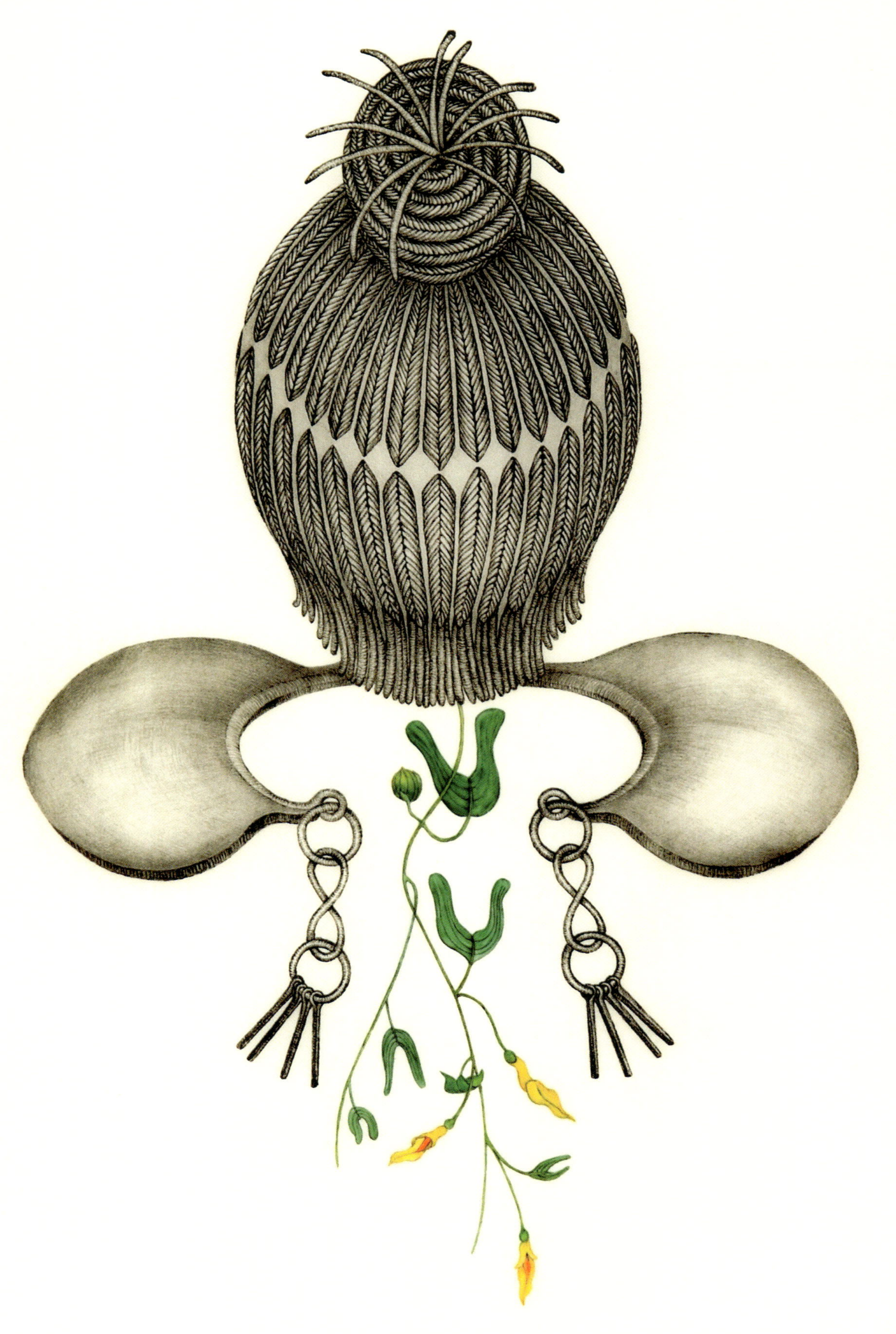

Foreword

Two histories play out in this book. One from the past, one from this moment. Histories of individuals and movements, places, communities and institutions. The Black Atlantic history of enslavement and genocide has a legacy that reaches into today. Acts of resistance by those most directly affected have until recently been neglected in favour of narratives of white abolitionism, and this book explores how even those convinced of the abhorrence of enslavement did not always notice how racist injustices were enshrined in power structures — a reality that continues to shape our present world.

These histories come together in the evolution of the Fitzwilliam Museum, founded in 1816 using funds derived from the trading of enslaved people and of commodities produced using slave labour. The University of Cambridge is much older with a larger, even more entangled history. The Fitzwilliam still relies on an endowment that came originally from shares in the South Sea Company. We still display works purchased by the 7th Viscount Fitzwilliam and the Museum continues to bear his name. Thus, his founding gift remains part of our identity, framing the journey of change we're taking.

Our work began in 2019 when the University of Cambridge announced its Legacies of Enslavement inquiry. We've focused first on the development of our collection — to ensure it becomes more representative — and on research-driven exhibitions like this one. There is more we need to do for these projects and acquisitions to help the Museum become a place where more equitable ways of working are embedded and visible in what our visitors experience.

Detail of 12 (see page 39)

The context for Fitzwilliam's bequest was explored in our 2023 exhibition, *Black Atlantic: Power, People, Resistance*. This second exhibition traces the pathways to abolition, celebrates the pivotal contributions of individuals and groups, analyses what happened next and what is happening now. Its curation responds to critiques and discussions of *Black Atlantic* among writers and cultural commentators, and to the many visitor comments thoughtfully and generously shared.

Cambridge and Cambridgeshire figure large — microcosms of an expansive, transatlantic history. Soham was where the extraordinary Black campaigner for abolition Olaudah Equiano chose to live. His wife, Susannah Cullen, was born in Ely, while the Cambridge-educated white abolitionist Thomas Clarkson was native to Wisbech, whose museum later acquired his remarkable campaign chest. Cambridge and its University nurtured strong abolitionist feeling from the mid-1780s onwards and began to welcome students of colour from the early 1800s but continued to benefit financially from the trade in and labour of enslaved people, and to educate members of enslaving families. This exhibition therefore maps a place of complexity, of contradictions. Which stories, hitherto neglected, do we need to know better? Which histories do we need to complicate, to tell more fully? What cultural practices and adherence should be understood as forms of resistance? What, above all, does the exploration and acknowledgement of this complex history mean for our futures?

Rise Up emphasises individual testimony as a powerful tool of resistance, challenging neutral or unpersuaded onlookers to reckon with and confront the harrowing truths of human suffering and stark realities of injustice. The curators have worked to amplify the voices of its key figures, ensuring their stories leave an indelible impact. Simultaneously, they and other contributors have described their own experiences — accounts that are potent because they are personal. Feelings are more evident in this book than our last, and there are inevitably going to be many perspectives. Facts continue to matter, and interpretation of motives and consequences can differ, but anger, frustration and sadness — historic and present — are also important considerations.

Only by paying proper attention to the words of figures such as Olaudah Equiano and Phillis Wheatley, and by open and frank conversations now, can we hope that our efforts are genuinely collaborative, no longer undermined by enshrined assumptions or by unaltered power structures.

Our journey is just beginning and while our commitment remains unwavering, we will sometimes make mistakes. We all need our passion, patience and resilience, our support and care for one another, if we are to effect lasting change.

Realising a project of this kind is a huge group effort. I am enormously grateful to the contemporary artists whose work is presented here. Yours are voices — objects and images — that ensure the link between past and present and whose creativity is inspirational. We are indebted to every author for your wisdom and courage. My thanks also to Sophia Patel for your outstanding logistical work in delivering this exhibition. Finally, I want to express my gratitude to the exhibition's co-curators and co-editors of this volume, Victoria Avery and Wanja Kimani. Your work not only illuminates and honours vital histories but will inform and inspire present and future generations.

Luke Syson
Director and Marlay Curator
The Fitzwilliam Museum

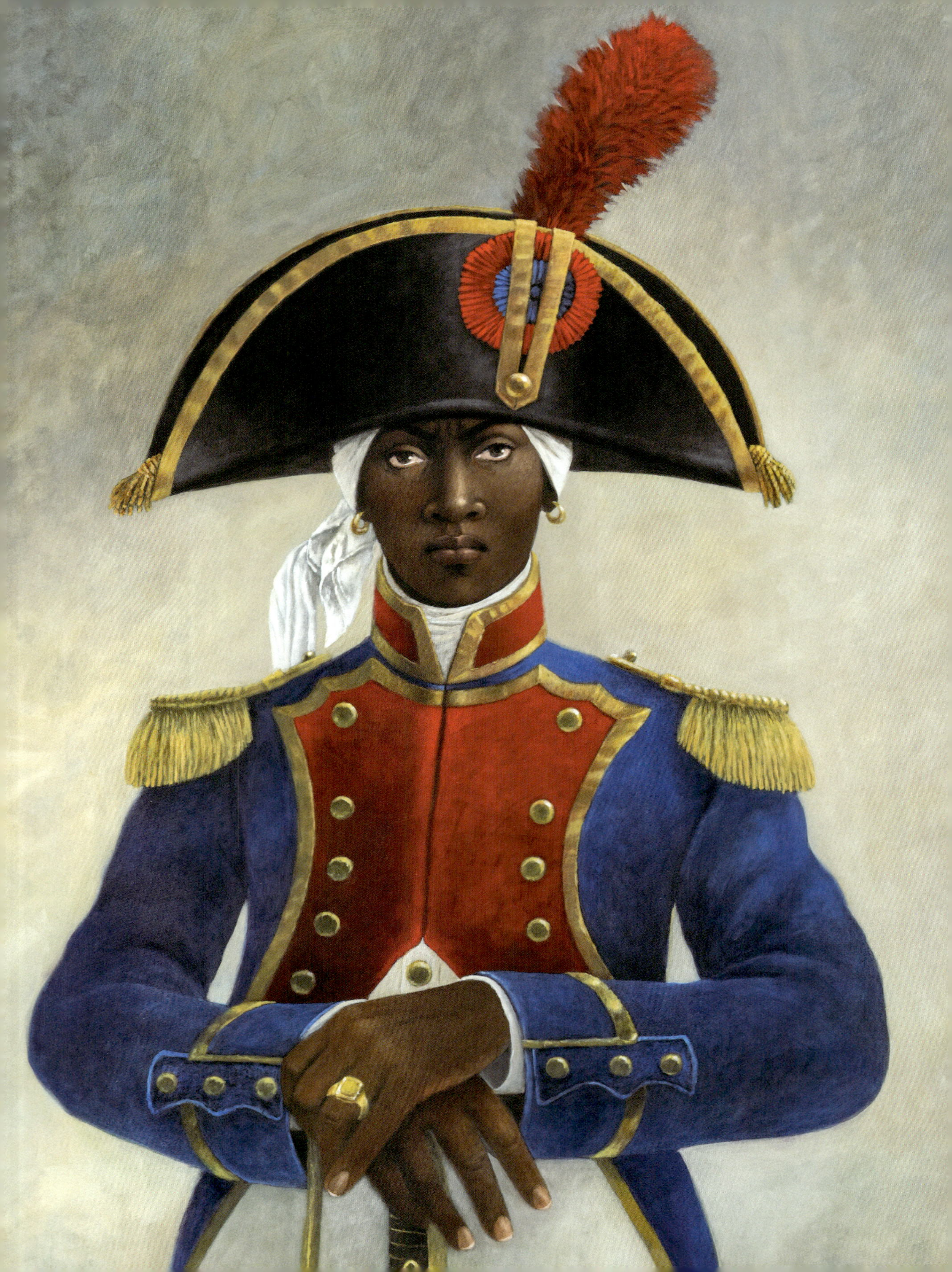

Introduction

This book focuses on the period between 1750 and 1850, when Britain played a central role in the Atlantic slave trade, trafficking more captive African people to plantations in the Caribbean and the Americas than any other European power until Parliament abolished the trade in 1807. This was one of the largest forced migrations in history.

The institution of slavery attempted to silence Black voices and cultural practices. Enslaved women, men and children resisted at every stage but often paid with their lives. In Britain, Black and white anti-slavery groups and individuals campaigned for abolition. Controlled and filtered through a white colonial perspective, countless Black lives have been marginalised or erased from both historical narratives and the mainstream art and culture of subsequent periods into the present. Through celebrating these individual and group biographies and interrogating texts, artworks and objects from Cambridge collections and beyond, this book shows how prevailing racist ideologies and stereotypes were repeatedly challenged through the written and spoken word, visual images, material culture and performance. These forms of expression provided outlets for courageous resistance and agency in the active pursuit of liberty.

Works by contemporary artists bring vital new perspectives. They retrieve what was lost and reimagine alternative pasts and futures, honouring these histories of resistance and emancipation while subverting the visual codes of the era. Each life encountered here can teach us about past experience and inspire us as we shape our future. The fight for true equality, justice and repair continues.

Detail of **83** (see page 124)

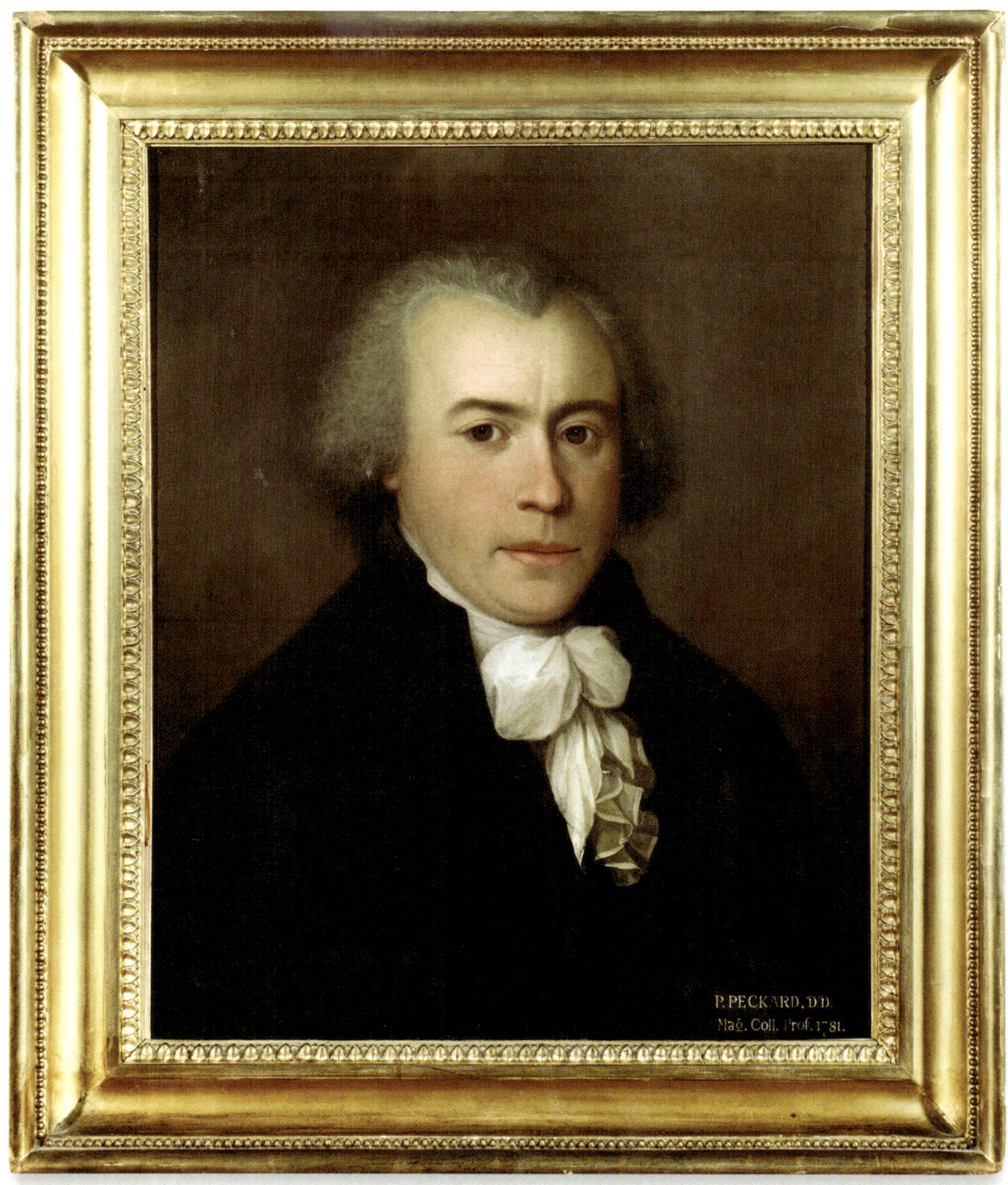

1

Unrecorded artist. *Peter Peckard*, 1781. Oil on canvas, 57 × 45.5 cm

Magdalene College, Cambridge (MCWA/A/83). Commissioned by Magdalene College to commemorate Peckard's appointment as master, 1781

Dark finance: the intertwined history of slavery and abolition at the University of Cambridge

Sabine F. Cadeau

1. The Royal African Company transported an estimated 187,000 slaves, more than any other single slave-trading company. The South Sea Company transported an estimated 64,000. There is some overlap between these two statistics, as the two companies undertook joint voyages. The East India Company also transported a smaller number of the enslaved from Mozambique and Madagascar to its Indian Ocean possessions and to Saint Helena's Island. For further details, see the Trans-Atlantic Slave Trade database https://www.slavevoyages.org/voyage/database (accessed 15 July 2024). There is an enormous literature on these companies and the slave trade, including: Eric Williams, *Capitalism and Slavery*, New York 1964; Colin A. Palmer, *Human Cargoes: The British Slave Trade to Spanish America, 1700–1739*, Chicago 1981; William A. Pettigrew, *Freedom's Debt: The Royal African Company and the Politics of the Atlantic Slave Trade, 1672–1752*, Chapel Hill, NC 2013; and Jennifer L. Morgan, *Reckoning with Slavery: Gender, Kinship, and Capitalism in the Early Black Atlantic*, Durham, NC 2021.

2. In 2019, Stephen Toope, Vice-Chancellor of Cambridge University, commissioned a study into the University's historic connections with Atlantic slavery and other forms of forced labour. For its final report (September 2022), see 'University of Cambridge Advisory Group on Legacies of Enslavement: Final Report', https://www.cam.ac.uk/about-the-university/history/legacies-of-enslavement/advisory-group-on-legacies-of-enslavement-final-report (accessed 17 August 2024). This summarised two forthcoming book manuscripts by Nicolas Bell-Romero, *Preliminary Report*, and Sabine Cadeau, *Bonds and Bondage: Fixed Income and Broken Lives*, submitted to the Chair of the Legacies of Enslavement Advisory Board and Vice-Chancellor's office in April 2022.
Note 2 continued overleaf

From the early sixteenth century through the middle of the nineteenth century, an estimated 12.5 million enslaved Africans were trafficked from Africa to the Americas. An estimated 1.7 million died during the Atlantic crossing. This forced migration was one of the largest and most enduring in history. England was a major participant in this trade. Along with a large proliferation of private merchants, the English slave trade was partially monopolised by publicly traded, crown-chartered joint stock companies. These included the South Sea Company, the Royal African Company and the East India Company, all of which traded in African slaves.[1]

Research I conducted from 2019 to 2024 for the University of Cambridge Legacies of Enslavement inquiry revealed that the most enduring institutional financial legacy of the Atlantic slave trade was the South Sea Company securities.[2] These were owned by the central university as well as most of the older Cambridge colleges, including Magdalene, where the key abolitionist Peter Peckard was master from 1781 until his death in 1797 [1].[3] Initially founded in 1711 to finance the British Navy's war debt, in 1714 the South Sea Company was granted the Asiento contract to supply African slaves to Spain's 'New World' colonies. The South Sea Company is widely known for the 1720 speculative bubble and crash, after which the company was bailed out by Parliament and the Bank of England.[4] The Company continued its slave-trading activity through 1739, when the Asiento trade was interrupted by the outbreak of another war between England and Spain. From 1714 to 1739, the South Sea Company trafficked an estimated 64,000 enslaved Africans. This trade was strategically important for Britain, as it was the country's main means of obtaining silver bullion from the Americas. Called 'South Sea Annuities', the company's repackaged securities paid reliable rates of interest and were traded actively until 1854, when the Bank of England exchanged them for other government

The University of Glasgow published the first UK university report on its link to enslavement. However, they did not explore the South Sea links and other financial instruments. My unpublished report introduces a new dimension to the historiography of universities and slavery. Other reports have been published in the United States and Canada, for example, Georgetown University (2016); Brown University (2021); and Harvard University (2022). This field continues to grow in Europe, the United States and Canada. The University of Wageningen in the Netherlands is currently conducting an investigation into its ties to colonialism. See Craig Steven Wilder's pathbreaking study, *Ebony & Ivy: Race, Slavery, and the Troubled History of America's Universities*, New York 2013.

3. Peter Peckard (c. 1718—1797): Venn Cambridge Alumni online database: unique identifier (hereafter Venn): PKRT753P.

4. See Helen J. Paul, *The South Sea Bubble: An Economic History of Its Origins and Consequences*, London 2013.

5. John Woodward (1665—1728): Venn WDWT695J. For Woodward's will of 2 May 1728: National Archives, Kew: PROB 11/622/25.

6. Robert Smith (1689—1768): Venn SMT708R. For Smith's will of 18 April 1768: National Archives, PRB 11/938/214; for the Plumian Professorship: https://www.hr.admin.cam.ac.uk/files/plumian.pdf; see also Geoffrey Cantor, 'Smith, Robert (bap. 1689, d. 1768)', *Oxford Dictionary of National Biography*, 23 September 2004, https://doi.org/10.1093/ref:odnb/25891 (accessed 15 July 2024). Smith also donated £2,000 in South Sea capital to Trinity College, which paid for a new Combination Room and a new window in the Library, 'depicting George III celebrating [Isaac] Newton'. He also left £2,000 in South Sea capital to his friend Edward Walpole, the son of Robert Walpole.

7. For the present-day Smith's Maths prize, see 'Smith-Knight & Rayleigh-Knight Prizes', *University of Cambridge*, https://www.maths.cam.ac.uk/postgrad/smith-knight-and-rayleigh-knight-prizes (accessed 18 August 2024).

8. Charles Babbage (1791—1871): Venn BBG810; Tim Radford, 'Hawking, Stephen William (1942—2018)', *Oxford Dictionary of National Biography*, 10 March 2022, https://doi.org/10.1093/odnb/9780198614128.013.90000380502 (accessed 18 August 2024); C.W. Kilmister, 'Eddington, Sir Arthur Stanley (1882—1944)', *Oxford Dictionary of National Biography*, 14 April 2022, https://doi.org/10.1093/ref:odnb/32967 (accessed 18 August 2024); and George Darwin (1845—1912): Venn DRWN863GH.

securities. Thus, my work revealed that the university benefited enormously from these investments in multiple, highly visible ways.

These assets never went away, they merely took on new forms. They remain identifiably ensconced in the financial endowments of Cambridge colleges. Many of the landed estates purchased by multiple colleges were bought and maintained with South Sea Company and East India Company capital. Many capital projects, such as the Gibbs Building at King's College, were heavily funded with South Sea capital. South Sea capital also funded major professorships still in existence. In 1728, naturalist John Woodward bequeathed South Sea capital to found the Woodwardian Professorship in Geology.[5] In 1768, Robert Smith, the distinguished mathematician and astronomer who was a Vice-Chancellor of Cambridge (1742—3) and Master of Trinity College (1742—68), bequeathed 'three thousand five hundred pounds stock, being part of my capital stock in the old South Sea Annuities' to further fund the Plumian Professorship of Astronomy and Experimental Philosophy, a post he had held from 1716 until 1760.[6] Smith's bequest also created the Smith's Prizes in Mathematics and added funds to the Lucasian Professorship in Mathematics and the Lowndean Professorship in Astronomy and Geometry.[7] These slave trade financial instruments shaped the intellectual life of the university by supporting the country's most renowned mathematicians and scientists. For example, Charles Babbage and Stephen Hawking both held the Lucasian Professorship, while Arthur Eddington and George Darwin were both Plumian Professors of Astronomy and Experimental Philosophy.[8]

Financial account books that document institutional transactions in slave-trading securities render the enslaved invisible. Collateralised into stocks and bonds, institutional financial ledgers use abbreviations such as 'OSSA' for 'Old South Sea Annuities', 'NSSA' for 'New South Sea Annuities', and 'EIC' for 'East India Company' bonds. The abstract shorthand in the ledgers erases the names, histories and experiences of individual lives that exist in the historical record only in terms of their commodity value. Archival encounters with South Sea Company shares or East India Company bonds do not directly mention or include any trace of these victims. When purchased in Spanish colonial ports such as Cartagena, Havana or Panama, the South Sea Company captives were abstractly identified as '*piezas de indias*' or 'pieces of the Indies'. This was a distinctly impersonal calculation: one '*pieza*' was the notional value of a single high-quality, healthy slave, whereas two less valuable slaves might have been valued at one '*pieza*'. The 'thingification' of the enslaved is also legible in more transparent slavery sources, such as an 1818 plantation record from the island of Dominica that is held in the University Library at Cambridge in the papers of the Royal Commonwealth Society [28].[9] In plantation sources like these, slaves are usually listed by name, but often alongside their cash value and frequently on the same page as livestock.[10]

Stephanie Smallwood describes the process by which the slave trade transformed the enslaved from people into commodities.[11] However, the financialisation processes that knitted together world commodity markets took this process one step further by transforming human commodities into financial instruments, such as stocks and bonds. In the era of the financial revolution, thingification evolved into securitisation. The financial ledgers of the University of Cambridge document this key feature of the financial revolution. Through the process of capture and enslavement, slaves were transformed into bonds. This commodification, and indeed the securitisation of African captives, is the utmost expression of the theory of racial capitalism.[12]

The abstract workings of early colonial trade and the monumental political and military struggles over slavery are made concrete through a proliferation of historical objects. This is clearly seen in the life of Matthew Decker, a Dutch merchant, author and art collector who was a leading share-holder in the South Sea Company, Royal African Company and East India Company. In 1720, Decker owned South Sea Company shares valued at £49,271.[13] Notional modern equivalent estimates of that sum range widely across the multiple metrics employed by the UK Measuring Worth project, from £8.74 million to £1.28 billion.[14] In 1723, Decker held an enormous £31,000 in Royal African Company capital stock, and he was also a director of the East India Company.[15] Interestingly, given that he was a major investor and leading figure in these crown monopoly companies, in his *Essay on the Causes of the Decline of the Foreign Trade,* started in 1739 and published in 1744, Decker emphasised the advantages of free trade nearly two generations before Adam Smith's *Wealth of Nations* was published in 1776.[16] Decker's four daughters, pictured in the 1718 portrait by Jan van Meyer [10], inherited his vast fortune. His eldest daughter, Catherine, third from the left in Van Meyer's portrait, married the 6th Viscount Fitzwilliam. Her son, the 7th Viscount Richard Fitzwilliam, was educated at Trinity Hall, Cambridge. Richard Fitzwilliam used both his grandfather's art collection and a vast sum in South Sea Company assets to found the museum that bears his name.[17]

At the Fitzwilliam Museum, the role of the South Sea Company assets was foundational. Viscount Fitzwilliam died in 1816,

9. On 'thingification', see Arjun Appadurai, 'Introduction: Commodities and the Politics of Value', in A. Appadurai (ed.) *The Social Life of Things: Commodities in Cultural Perspective*, New York 1986, pp. 3–63.
10. Because slaves' names were most often imposed by enslavers, during emancipation and afterwards, people often exercised their freedom by choosing new names.
11. Stephanie E. Smallwood, *Saltwater Slavery: A Middle Passage from Africa to American Diaspora*, Cambridge, MA 2007.
12. For the foundational text on racial capitalism, see W.E.B. DuBois, *Black Reconstruction: An Essay Toward a History of the Part Which Black Folk Played in the Attempt to Reconstruct Democracy in America, 1860–1880*, New York 1935. For three recent seminal texts, see Peter Hudson, *Bankers and Empire. How Wall Street Colonized the Caribbean*, Chicago 2017; Destin Jenkins and Justin Leroy (eds), *Histories of Racial Capitalism*, New York 2021; and Catherine Hall, *Lucky Valley: Edward Long and the History of Racial Capitalism*, Cambridge 2024
13. As Jake Subryan Richards points out, Decker managed to sell all of his South Sea capital before the notorious bursting of the bubble in late 1720. See Jake Subryan Richards, 'Reimagining the Dutch Connection: The Fitzwilliam Museum in a World of Atlantic Enslavement and Empire', in Victoria Avery and Jake Subryan Richards (eds), *Black Atlantic: Power, People, Resistance*, exh. cat., Fitzwilliam Museum, Cambridge 2023, pp. 17–39. This timely sale made Decker, along with Robert Walpole, one of the deftest and most successful investors of that era. Financial investments, then as now, were more fluid than fixed. Constant activity in the exchanges meant that vast fortunes and allocations could constantly move around.
14. The UK Measuring Worth project (https://measuringworth.com) has four financial models for generating estimates of historical monetary equivalencies: 1. 'real price', 2. 'labour value', 3. 'income value', and 4. 'economic share'. The fourth generates by far the largest estimates.
15. Midsummer Dividend 1723, Royal African Company, National Archives, Kew: T/70 180 Matthew Decker £31,000.
16. Anonymous [Matthew Decker], *An Essay on the Causes of the Decline of the Foreign Trade, Consequently of the Value of the Lands of Britain, and on the Means to Restore Both, Begun in the Year 1739*, London 1744; Adam Smith, *An Inquiry into the Nature and Causes of the Wealth of Nations*, 2 vols, London 1776.
17. Richard Fitzwilliam (1743–1816): Venn FTSN761R. For further discussion, see Richards 2023.

Slave-Trade Securities associated with Matthew Decker and Viscount Fitzwilliam

South Sea Trading Stock
Year of documentation: **1720**
Nominal value: **£49,721**
Notional 2023 equivalencies: **£8.74 million to £1.28 billion**

Royal African Company Stock
Year of documentation: **1723**
Nominal value: **£31,000**
Notional 2023 equivalencies: **£5.76 million to £889 million**

South Sea Annuities
Year of documentation: **1816**
Nominal value: **£6,310 and 10 shillings** (sale price of £10,000 face value of New South Sea Annuities at a discount rate of 63.25%)
Notional 2023 equivalencies: **£587,000 to £39.8 million**

18. Will of The Right Honorable Richard Fitzwilliam Viscount Fitzwilliam of Ireland, 22 February 1816, PROB 11/1577/416.
19. See Richards 2023, esp. pp. 25–7. Both the History of Parliament biography of Lord Fitzwilliam and the 1996 *Concise History of the University of Cambridge* have published a figure of '£100,000' for the face value of the New South Sea Annuities in Lord Fitzwilliam's bequest. Here I refer to Jake Subryan Richards's research from the Hoare's bank archive. Further research will hopefully clarify the discrepancy between the two different figures.

and in his will he bequeathed to the University of Cambridge 'all my capital stock in the New South Sea Annuities', for the purpose of establishing the museum.[18] The Fitzwilliam bequest apparently contained £10,000 worth of South Sea annuities, which were sold at a 63.25% discount rate to the face value in 1816 for the sum of £6,310 and 10 shillings. This formed a substantial part of the museum's founding bequest.[19] Based on different metrics employed by the UK Measuring Worth project, the roughly £6,310 worth of South Sea annuities bequeathed in 1816 to found the Fitzwilliam Museum would be worth anywhere between £587,000 and £39.8 million in contemporary money [Table 1]. Colonial wealth proved important during the founding phases of the Fitzwilliam Museum and other Cambridge institutions established during the eighteenth and nineteenth centuries, including Downing College, Newnham College and Girton College.

The older Cambridge colleges, in existence well before Columbus crossed the Atlantic, were clearly not founded with colonial wealth. However, by the eighteenth century and in some cases earlier, slave-trade securities had become part of their financial history, as they received donations and hefty tuition payments from colonial slave-owners. The most significant institutional financial exposure to slavery involved the same kind of colonial securities in which Matthew Decker so heavily invested: South Sea Company securities, East India Company Bonds, Royal African Company shares and investments in Queen Anne's Bounty, a gigantic fund bequeathed by Queen Anne to the Church of England based largely on South Sea securities.[20]

Ironically, Cambridge, a major colonial crossroads and a historic centre of colonial wealth accumulation, would also become perhaps the most significant intellectual cradle of Britain's abolitionist movement.[21] Peter Peckard [1], one of Britain's most influential abolitionists, contributed to the anti-slavery debate in his writings and through his prominent role at Cambridge University, where he served as Master of Magdalene College and University Vice-Chancellor. In 1785, he famously posed the question for the Senior Bachelor's Latin essay prize — 'Is it right to make slaves of others against their will?' — which inspired Thomas Clarkson, then a student at St John's College, to respond with his important essay on slavery. Peckard subsequently became Clarkson's mentor and close collaborator.

The University of Cambridge rightfully celebrates its leading abolitionists and their work to end slavery. However, it is ironic that these abolitionists also helped to justify colonial expansion into Africa. There is a rich historiography that explores the complex and contradictory roles of abolitionists.[22]

20. For Queen Anne's Bounty and the importance of the South Sea annuities, see Arthur Burns and Helen Paul, 'Church Commissioners' Research into Historic Links to Transatlantic Chattel Slavery', *The Church of England*, London 2023, https://www.churchofengland.org/sites/default/files/2023-01/church-commissioners-for-england-research-into-historic-links-to-transatlantic-chattel-slavery-report.pdf (accessed 18 August 2024).

21. See Michael E. Jirik, 'Beyond Clarkson: Cambridge, Black Abolitionists, and the British Anti-Slave Trade Campaign', *Slavery & Abolition*, 41, no. 4 (March 2020), pp. 748–71.

22. For selected recent publications from the now-vast literature on slavery and abolition, see: Nicholas Draper, Catherine Hall and Keith McClelland (eds), *Legacies of British Slave-Ownership: Colonial Slavery and the Formation of Victorian Britain*, Cambridge 2016 [2014]; Manisha Sinha, *The Slave's Cause: A History of Abolition*, New Haven, CT 2016; David W. Blight, *Frederick Douglass: Prophet of Freedom*, London 2018; and Sami Pinarbasi, 'Manchester Antislavery, 1792–1807', *Slavery & Abolition*, 41, no. 2 (2020), pp. 349–76.

23. Nicolas Bell-Romero's forthcoming book, *The University of Cambridge in the Age of Slavery*, discusses the influence of the West India lobby and other pro-slavery phenomena at Cambridge in detail.

24. James Albert Ukawsaw Gronniosaw, *A Narrative of the Most Remarkable Particulars in the Life of James Albert Ukawsaw Gronniosaw*, Bath 1772; Olaudah Equiano, *The Interesting Narrative of the Life of Olaudah Equiano or Gustavus Vassa, The African. Written by Himself*, London 1789.

25. Similarly, in his capacity as University Vice-Chancellor, Peckard also oversaw the use of dividends from South Sea capital held by the central university. I discuss these funds and the associated prizes and professorships at length in my forthcoming book.

26. Arthur Annesley (1678–1737): Venn ANSY696A. His cousin, Francis Annesley, had advanced the bill in Parliament in 1712 for the continuation of the South Sea Company.

27. Magdalene College Audit Book 1733–1803; and Magdalene College Audit Book 1805–95.

28. Samuel Pepys (1633–1703): Venn PPS650S.

29. Phillip Emanuel, '"[A]s Fast as Ships Return he Will Send Everyone a Boy": Enslaved Children as Gifts in the British Atlantic', *Slavery & Abolition*, 44, no. 2 (2022), pp. 334–49.

Nicolas Bell-Romero's important work also challenges the one-sided emphasis on the university's abolitionist history and points out that pro-slavery ideologues were as much part of the university's intellectual tradition as the abolitionists.[23] The contradictory dimensions of the abolitionist movement are worth exploring. A prime example is the 'abolitionist slave-owner' Selina Hastings, Countess of Huntingdon [49], whose vast wealth included a plantation in Georgia and another in South Carolina. Hastings, whose remarkable religious work included legacies at Cambridge's Westminster College, used a great deal of her wealth to support the abolitionist cause and to underwrite the costs of publishing the works of Black poet Phillis Wheatley and Black abolitionists Ukawsaw Gronniosaw and Olaudah Equiano.[24]

Moreover, Magdalene College provides an ideal case for exploring the complex overlapping historical points of contact between wealth accumulated from Atlantic slavery and early abolitionism. South Sea capital was so embedded in the institutional functioning of Magdalene that Peckard, as master, ironically oversaw and managed the interest income from these slave-trade securities. One of the college's South Sea funds was used to maintain Magdalene's Pepys Library and pay the librarian.[25] The Pepys Library exemplifies the essence of Cambridge University's multilayered involvement with slavery and colonialism. Magdalene alumnus Arthur Annesley, 5th Earl of Anglesey, was a major benefactor of the Pepys Library.[26] When he died in 1737, he bequeathed land to support the library's establishment and upkeep. Of this bequest, £100 was spent in helping to establish the Pepys Library, while another £200 was converted in three separate transactions into South Sea annuities, one each in 1738, 1741 and 1747. The relatively consistent £6 in annual interest income from these South Sea annuities was used to pay the Pepysian librarian for the next 150 years.[27]

While children of colonial enslavers were common among the students at Cambridge, Samuel Pepys was probably the institution's most prominent slave-owner and slavery investor.[28] Pepys frequented Africa House in London, where he would check to see if his ship, literally, had come in. Pepys stands out in that he not only owned shares in the slave-trading Royal African Company but also owned his own slaves and was an absentee buyer and seller in the Caribbean.[29] Other notable enslavers connected with Cambridge include Sir Henry Pickering, Baronet, who married Philadelphia Downing of the Downing College dynasty and became a major slave-owner on Barbados; and three of the American signatories to the Declaration of Independence, who had studied at Cambridge: Thomas Nelson Jr (at Christ's College), Arthur Middleton (at Trinity Hall College) and Thomas Lynch Jr (at Gonville and Caius College).[30] Hundreds if not thousands of less prominent future slave-owners likewise attended Cambridge as students but, aside from Pepys, few are well known.

However, the influential masters of many Cambridge colleges frequently invested in South Sea Company capital during the eighteenth century. Moreover, many Cambridge figures such as poet Thomas Gray were active participants in the vibrant market in South Sea securities that operated from South Sea House in the City of London.[31] The complex history of colonial assets at Magdalene College is representative of the older Cambridge colleges, where colonial assets were often folded into other accounts, fellowships, funds and landed holdings, sometimes called stocks. In 1752, Magdalene College decided to purchase an East India bond at the price of £187 and used the dividends for 'beautifying the chapel'.[32] In 1760, Revd John Groome bequeathed Magdalene College £500 in South Sea annuities to provide an annual income for the Vicar of Childerditch (a post he had held since 1709); the remaining amount was 'to be divided each year betwixt the master and resident fellows' of Magdalene.[33] Thus, the dividends from these slave-trade assets flowed directly into the administration of one of history's most prominent abolitionists, Peter Peckard [Table 2]. While the Bank of England converted South Sea annuities into other interest-paying bonds in 1854, Magdalene College kept the designation of 'Old South Sea annuities' in its account books until 1893.[34]

These capital sums of £100, £200 or £500 might appear small to modern readers, and they were indeed small compared to the roughly £6,310 worth of New South Sea annuities used to create the Fitzwilliam Museum. However, the proverbial 'old money' of the early modern era was worth a great deal more than the inflated sums of today. In a world of silver South Sea Company shillings and Royal Africa Company gold guineas, £500 was equal to 122 ounces of gold. Today, a very conservative estimate would value this quantity of gold at more than £220,000. According to the 'economic share' metric employed by the UK Measuring Worth project, the £500 in South Sea annuities donated to Magdalene College in 1760 are equivalent to £10.6 million in today's economy.

The coincidental historical points of contact between South Sea capital and abolitionism demonstrate that both were important to elite institutional life. As a Cambridge student, abolitionist Isaac Milner of Queens' College won the Smith's Maths Prize in 1774 and became the Lucasian Professor of Mathematics in 1798; as mentioned above, both were funded with South Sea Company capital.[35]

30. Sir Henry Pickering, Baronet (1653—1705): Venn PKRN672H; Thomas Nelson (1738—1789): Venn NL758T; Arthur Middleton (1742—1787): Venn MDLN759A; and Thomas Lynch (1749—1847): Venn LNC767T.

31. Thomas Gray (1716—1771): Venn GRY734T2.

32. Magdalene College Register No. 3 1675—1814, June 1752, Disbursement for the Chape , fols 751 and 755. At different points in the account-book, this East India bond is listed with values of £187 and £113. This might reflect a discrepancy between the face value and the market value of the bond, held to be the key 'dynamic' feature of the public market in government securities. For more on the Indian Ocean slave trade, see Pier Larson, *History and Memory in the Age of Enslavement: Becoming Merina in Highland Madagascar, 1770—1822*, Portsmouth, NH 2000; and Richard Blair Allen, *European Slave Trading in the Indian Ocean, 1500—1850*, Athens 2015.

33. John Groome (1679—1760): Venn GRM695J Magdalene College Master's Private Books, C1 Groome's Benefaction, p. 178. Groome's South Sea annuities seem to have been converted to 3% consols by at least 1778.

34. Magdalene College Audit Book 1805—95.

35. Isaac Milner (1750—1820): Venn MLNR77CI.

36. Thomas Chapman (1717—1760): Venn CHPN734T.

37. Agreement Between George Hartlay and the Master and Fellows, 5 December 1775, Pepys Library A/41, MB 430, 3 and Chapman's Estate, 1762, Including Inventory of Master's Lodge, Magdalene, 1760. Magdalene College Archives.

38. Hon. George Neville Grenville (1789—1854): Venn NVL807G.

39. For Grenville's compensation payout, see: 'Hon. George Neville Grenville: Profile & Legacies Summary', *Centre for the Study of the Legacies of British Slavery*, https://www.ucl.ac.uk/lbs/person/view/42697 (accessed 18 August 2024).

40. David Scott, *Irreparable Evil: An Essay in Moral and Reparatory History*, New York 2024.

Slavery in Britain's colonies outlasted Peckard by many decades. Preceding and subsequent masters of Magdalene College include an investor in the South Sea Company and one of Cambridge's most prominent Caribbean plantation owners. At his death in 1760, Magdalene College Master Thomas Chapman owned a massive £4,150 in South Sea annuities.[36] The disposition of his fortune was a complex and lengthy process, but one of Chapman's trustees managed to transfer £400 worth of Chapman's South Sea capital to Magdalene in 1775, where it provided income for both the Pepys Library and the college's Milner Foundation scholarships.[37] A subsequent master of Magdalene College was George Neville-Grenville, chaplain to Queen Victoria.[38] In 1833, Neville-Grenville received part of the compensation paid for the emancipation of 379 enslaved people from the Hope plantation in Jamaica.[39]

Societies are contradictory, and if contradictory forces drive historical change, change surely gives rise in turn to new contradictory predicaments. The abolitionist work of Peter Peckard at Magdalene College is a special lens through which to view many of the wider contradictory historical dynamics surrounding English abolitionism. The French and Haitian Revolutions involved the conscious destruction of age-old social orders in the name of equality and liberty. Standing firmly against the revolutionary tide, Britain nonetheless wrestled with enlightenment notions and witnessed influential movements to end Atlantic slavery through peaceable reform, pious appeals to morality, and elite preferences for gradualism and moderation. The Crown, the Church of England, Parliament, the City of London and the colleges of Cambridge and Oxford were all heavily exposed to the securitised wealth of Atlantic slavery. The irony was intrinsic — the wealth and institutional advancement that was heavily fuelled and financed by colonial slavery gave rise to political movements and a moral discourse that led tens of thousands of British people to decry and campaign against enslavement. Nowhere is the irony more obvious than in the case of Peter Peckard, the abolitionist who headed an institution in which South Sea Company dividends were used to run the library of Royal African Company subscriber and slave-owner Samuel Pepys. England's most influential abolitionists stood atop a powerful edifice of securitised slavery capital that not only predated the abolitionists by many generations, but also survives intact today as a foundation of the Western financial order. As the University of Cambridge and other British institutions are confronted with the idea of historical reparations, David Scott reminds us that conducting serious study of slavery is to grapple with its legacies of 'irreparable evil'.[40]

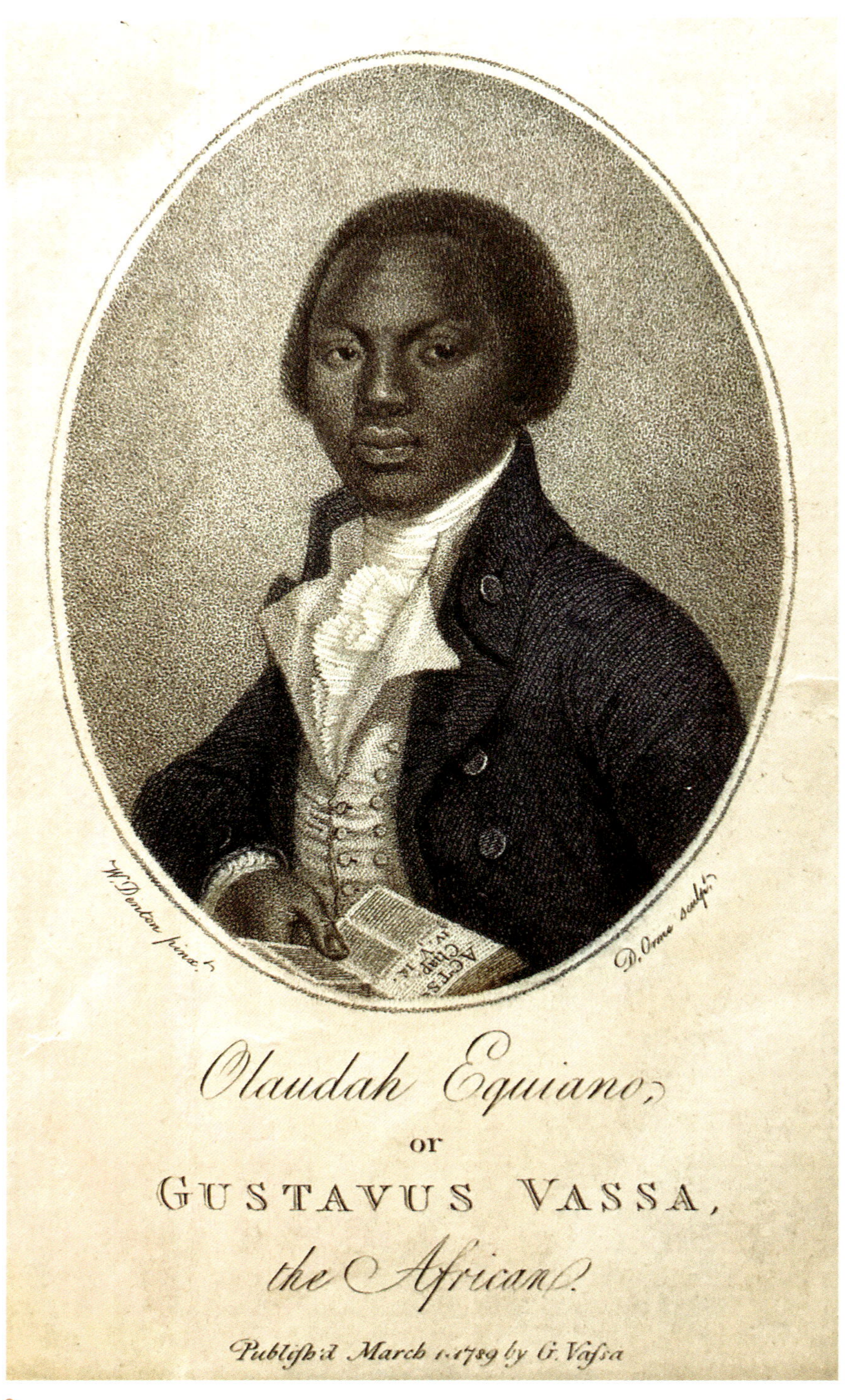

2

Daniel Orme (1766—1837), after William Denton (active 1789—94).
Olaudah Equiano, or Gustavus Vassa, the African, late 1788 to early 1789.
Stipple with etching and colour printing, 15.5 × 9.7 cm

The Card-Reynolds Collection, London. Bought from a dealer, 2016.
Published by Gustavus Vassa, London, 1 March 1789 [not in exhibition]

Introducing Olaudah Equiano, or Gustavus Vassa, The African

Victoria Avery

Olaudah Equiano, also known as Gustavus Vassa, the African (*c.*1745–31 March 1797) was the most famous and influential Black abolitionist writer of his day and, arguably, in British history, whose efforts did so much to promote the abolition of the British slave trade and, eventually, the institution of slavery itself [2].[1] In late March 1789, Equiano published his autobiography, *The Interesting Narrative of the Life of Olaudah Equiano, or Gustavus Vassa, The African. Written by Himself.*[2] From then until autumn 1794, Equiano is documented as having travelled across England (with a very early stop in Cambridge), Scotland and Ireland to sell his book and further the abolitionist cause. Thanks to securing a steady supply of book subscriptions and on-the-spot sales, Equiano became one of the most successful authors of his day: nine lifetime editions were published between March 1789 and September 1794,[3] with an unauthorised reprint (New York 1791), and unauthorised translations in Dutch (Rotterdam 1790), German (Göttingen 1792) and Russian (Moscow 1794).

Equiano's *Interesting Narrative*

When Equiano published his *Interesting Narrative*, he was in his mid-forties and a seasoned anti-slavery lobbyist, having been active since the early 1780s on his own account and, from 1785, as a key spokesman of the grassroots Sons of Africa. A loosely constituted social justice group of formerly enslaved London-based African men, its members included (in addition to Equiano): John Adams, Yahne Aelane (aka Joseph Sanders), Joseph Almaze, Cojoh Ammere (aka George Williams), James Bailey, John Christopher, Thomas Cooper, Ottobah Cugoano (aka John Stuart/Steward), Boughwa Gegansmel (or Broughwar Jogensmel, aka Jasper Goree), William Greek, Bernard Elliot Griffiths, Thomas Jones, George Robert Mandeville (or Mandevil), Thomas Oxford, William Stevens and George Wallace.[4] They disseminated information about the evils of slavery and racial discrimination, wrote letters of thanks to key early abolitionist supporters such as the Quakers [43], and lobbied powerful white establishment

1. Equiano's birth date is unknown but the traditional date of '*c.*1745' is based on his own testimony and documented events. For a selection of the secondary literature on Equiano, see 'Selected reading'.
2. Equiano 1789. For an excellent edited version, see Equiano/Carretta 2003.
3. The eight further lifetime editions were published regularly and in varying print runs: 2nd (London, 24 December 1789); 3rd (London, 30 October 1790); 4th (Dublin, 20 May 1791); 5th (Edinburgh, June 1792); 6th (London, 30 December 1792); 7th (London, August 1793); 8th (Norwich, March 1794); and 9th (London, 27 September 1794).
4. See 'Sons of Africa' on 'Equiano's World' website: https://equianosworld.org/associates-abolition.php?id=2#content (accessed 2 September 2024).

figures demanding 'an Act for the total Abolition of the Slave Trade'.[5] They played a critical role, for example, in the passing of the 1788 Slave Trade Act (known as Dolben's Act), the first British legislation to regulate slave shipping, by limiting the number of captives who could be transported on a single voyage. The year before, Equiano's friend and fellow Son of Africa Ottobah Cugoano had published his radical book of political philosophy, *Thoughts and Sentiments on the Evil and Wicked Traffic of the Slavery and Commerce of the Human Species* (London 1787) that demanded all enslaved people be emancipated immediately [53].

A passionate abolitionist and devout evangelical Christian, Equiano clearly felt the time had come to publish his own narrative of manumission from slavery and Christian conversion to grace. Equiano's *Interesting Narrative* was vital in bringing a personal voice into the deliberately depersonalised global-market system of the Atlantic slave trade. By sharing his own 'freedom story' and 'conversion narrative', Equiano hoped to persuade his readers of the need for radical social and political change that would ultimately give true equality to Black people. Equiano was aware of the power of the printed word and its effectiveness as a lobbying tool for the anti-slavery cause. He knew his book would reach far greater audiences than he could ever meet in person, and that it would far outlast him. Its contents demonstrated his innate intelligence and capacities, infinite resourcefulness and resilience, noble character, moral rectitude and Christian credentials. These characteristics disproved then-popular racist, pseudo-scientific theories and slavery ideologies that claimed African people were intellectually and morally inferior to their European counterparts, lies that helped to justify the dehumanising of Black bodies into chattel commodities to be bought and sold for mainly white profit.

In order to counter frequent claims levelled against Black authors that their work had been ghost-written by white abolitionist allies, Equiano 'The African' made sure to affirm full authorship of his autobiography, stating at the end of its title that it had been 'written by himself'. Equiano's publication can be interpreted as an act of defiance and resistance. It unequivocally asserted the right of a Black man to write, publish, sell and distribute his own autobiography, and that his life was worth reading about. As sole author, Equiano recognised the importance of retaining control of his text, and so registered his book at Stationers' Hall on 25 March 1789, thereby ensuring that his words could not be edited, reworded or redacted by anyone else [3].[6] To quote historian and Equiano biographer Vincent Carretta, 'the story of [Equiano's] life became his own most valuable possession ... Print allowed Equiano to resurrect not only himself publicly from the "social death" enslavement

3

Copyright registration for Equiano's autobiography, Stationers' Hall, London, 25 March 1789

Register of Entries of Copies 1786—92, Stationers' Company Archive, London (TSC/E/06/11), fol. 224 [not in exhibition]

had imposed on him but also the millions of other diasporan Africans he represented.'[7]

Equiano's authorised lifetime portrait

The frontispiece of the *Interesting Narrative* is dominated by a portrait of Equiano in which he presents himself as an enlightened, rational and reasonable man [4]. This is the only known lifetime portrait of Equiano and is significant in being authorised by him and reproduced in all lifetime editions (although the quality deteriorated over time).[8] Equiano's 'official' portrait embraces and promotes his dual identity: an African man clothed like a European, holding forth an English translation of the Bible. This image is reinforced by the title-caption recording his two names: first, 'Olaudah Equiano', his African birth name, given by his parents because it meant in his native tongue 'vicissitude or fortune also, one favoured, and having a loud voice and well spoken';[9] second, 'Gustavus Vasa', the final of three different European names imposed by enslavers, and the one he preferred to go by even after manumission, using it (spelled 'Vassa') to sign his letters and all legal documents, including his marriage certificate and will [61—65].[10] This, too, had deep significance for Equiano given that his namesake was the national hero of Sweden, King Gustavus Vasa, the sixteenth-century founder of the modern Swedish state. Regarded as having led his people out of bondage, Vasa would have been known to eighteenth-century Britons thanks to a 1739 play by Henry Brooke: *Gustavus Vasa, the Deliverer of his Country*.[11] Equiano considered that both his African and English names had predetermined his personal destiny and were thus worth printing twice, in full: once under the frontispiece portrait and once at the top of the title page.[12]

7. Carretta 2005, p. 367.
8. Equiano/Carretta 2003, Appendices A and B, pp. 310—16, makes this point, comparing the portraits in the first edition of 1789 and the New York edition of 1791.
9. Equiano 1789, vol. 1, p. 31.
10. Equiano 1789, vol. 1, p. 96.
11. Lovejoy 2006.
12. For ongoing discussions about Equiano's name, see Lovejoy 2024.

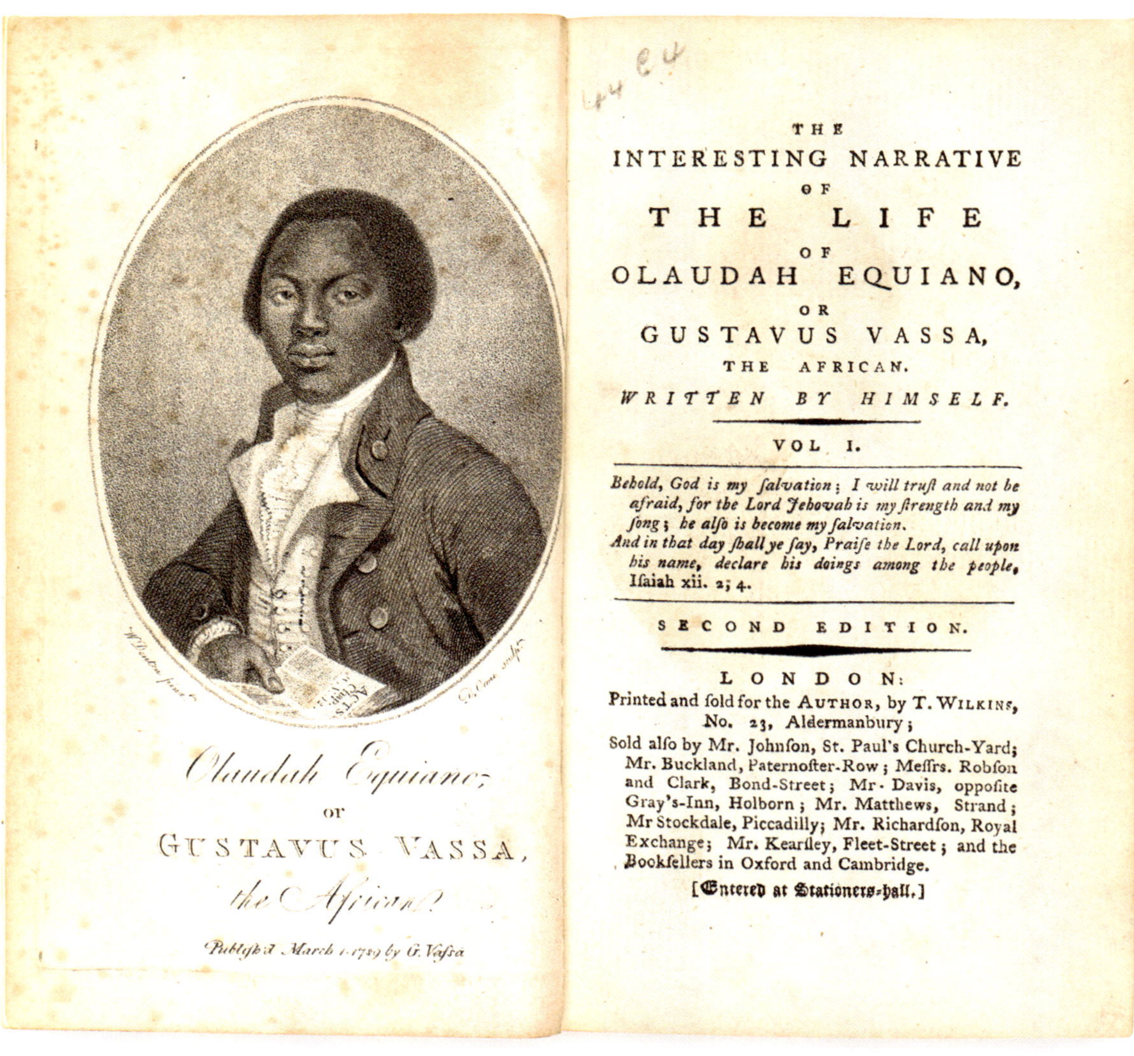

4

Olaudah Equiano
(*c*.1745—1797).
The Interesting Narrative of the Life of Olaudah Equiano, or Gustavus Vassa, The African. Written by Himself,
2nd edn, London, December 1789

Although the details surrounding its commissioning are unrecorded, Equiano's portrait was clearly part of his bibliographic thinking and self-presentation well before his autobiography was published. In his printed solicitation for subscriptions, dated November 1788, Equiano promises: 'In Volume I, will be given an elegant Frontispiece of the Author's Portrait.'[13] Moreover, given that Equiano owned the image rights and assigned these to himself underneath its title: 'Published March 1 1789 by G. Vassa', it is likely that it was he who actually commissioned the (currently untraced) original portrait from William Denton. This probably took the form of a portrait miniature, similar in format to that of an unidentified Officer of the Light Dragoons, which Denton painted in February 1794.[14] Similarly, Equiano almost certainly commissioned Daniel Orme to engrave it for his book. How Equiano met both artists remains unknown, but it may have been through Ottobah Cugoano, who was valet to Richard Cosway, Principal Painter from 1785 to the Prince of Wales, and his wife Maria Hadfield, also a well-known society painter [52]. It is noteworthy that both Denton and Cugoano subscribed to the first three editions of Equiano's autobiography, and Cugoano additionally to the fourth.

Certainly, the image's self-assuredness implies Equiano as ideator: his swanky clothes; his authoritative pose with shoulders back, chest out, and head held high; his direct, unswerving gaze that purposefully meets that of the viewer. Equiano is keen to present himself as the reader's equal and a personification of authority. Like the text it precedes, Equiano's portrait can be read as an act of resistance and a challenge to prevailing artistic norms. In Georgian Britain Black people were regularly included in portraits, not as the main subject, but rather as objects, 'exotic' adornments to and status symbols for their white masters. Indeed, Equiano's powerful portrait stands in stark and deliberate contrast to the unnamed, naked and chained African man who kneels with his hands upheld in a gesture of supplication [5], which had been devised fifteen months earlier, in late November 1787, by the London Committee of the Society for Effecting the Abolition of the Slave Trade (SEAST) as its campaign logo. Its final form was designed in the workshop of potter, industrialist and abolitionist Josiah Wedgwood, who later became a friend of Equiano.[15]

It is a bitter irony that this ultimately racist image was so effective in garnering anti-slavery support and enjoyed such wide circulation across Britain and British North America. In addition to its use in wax form to seal SEAST official correspondence [59] and engraved on the title page of key SEAST-sanctioned publications, it was reproduced as jasperware medallions by Wedgwood's factory, and incorporated into the design of hairpins, brooches and buttons for SEAST supporters to wear, and on all manner of domestic objects from tobacco pots to teapots. Although well-intentioned and intended to elicit empathy and sympathy, the design — in which the generic and anonymised Black man is shown as powerless and helpless — has been interpreted since the 1960s as deeply problematic, demeaning and disempowering, with American Civil Rights protestors converting the question into a statement of fact: 'I AM A MAN' [130]. Indeed, the illustrated title page of Elizabeth Heyrick's influential tract, *Immediate, not Gradual Abolition, or, An Inquiry into the Shortest, Safest, and Most Effectual Means of Getting Rid of West Indian Slavery* of 1824 had already radically reimagined SEAST's logo and motto, showing the enslaved African man as emancipated, free of shackles, standing upright and stating, 'I AM A MAN, YOUR BROTHER' [107].

13. For the copy sent to Josiah Wedgwood, see Carretta 2005, pp. 271—3; and Sapoznik 2013, pp. 105—7. The original is in the Wedgwood Museum, L74/12632.
14. Signed by Denton and dated 1794, this oval watercolour on ivory was set into a gold frame, measuring 6.7 cm high. It was sold by Chiswick Auctions, 30 March 2021, lot 451: https://www.chiswickauctions.co.uk/auction/lot/451-william-denton-british-exh-1792-1795/?lot=143744&sd=1 (accessed 8 August 2024).
15. For the SEAST logo, see, for example, Mary Guyatt, 'The Wedgwood Slave Medallion: Values in Eighteenth-Century Design', *Journal of Design History*, 13, no. 2 (2000), pp. 93—105; and Cynthia S. Hamilton, 'Hercules Subdued: The Visual Rhetoric of the Kneeling Slave', *Slavery & Abolition*, 34, no. 4 (2013), pp. 631—52. See note 13 above for Equiano's November 1788 solicitation of Wedgwood.

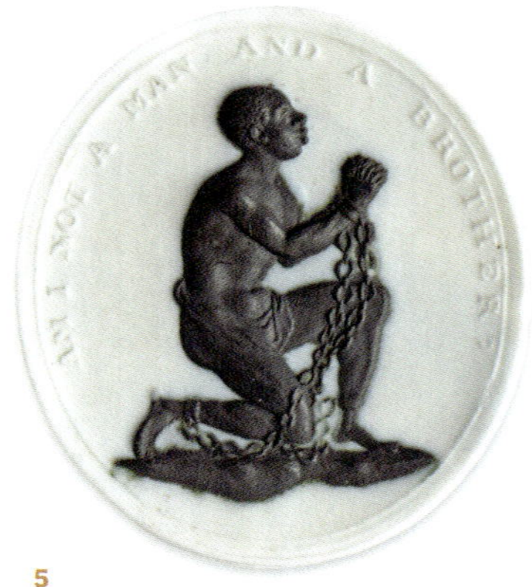

5

Henry Webber
(1754–1826; designer)
and **William Hackwood**
(c.1757–1839; modeller).
**Emancipation badge of the
Society for Effecting the
Abolition of the Slave Trade**
with logo of a kneeling and
chained enslaved African
man and motto, 'AM I NOT
A MAN AND A BROTHER?'
Wedgwood Factory, Etruria,
Staffordshire, about 1788.
White Jasperware with
black relief, 3 × 2.8 cm

Drawing inspiration from similar frontispiece portraits
in recent publications by Black authors, notably those of
Phillis Wheatley and Ignatius Sancho [51 and 46], Equiano
ensured that his portrait was even more authoritative. By
commissioning it himself, Equiano asserted his right to do so,
his personhood, his self-worth in having his features recorded
for posterity, and his equality with his white peers. This un-
equivocal message is reiterated through his use of Scripture
to justify his work, and his worth before God. In his portrait,
the Bible is open at Acts, Chapter 4, verse 12 — the verse he
was reading at the moment of his conversion to Christianity:
'Neither is there salvation in any other: for there is none other
name [Jesus Christ] under heaven given among men, whereby
we must be saved.' Under his autobiography's title, Equiano
inserts two verses from Isaiah to claim parity with his white
brethren as a redeemed son of God: 'I will trust and not be
afraid for the Lord Jehovah is my strength and my song …
[I shall] Praise the Lord, call upon his name, declare his
doings amongst the people.'

Self-promotion by the self-made man

A savvy self-promoter, Equiano used Orme's engraving not
only as the frontispiece to his autobiography but also as a
separate engraving for circulation. Deluxe, colour-printed
versions, in which he is shown wearing a striking blue
jacket, were additionally made in much smaller numbers —
presumably at Equiano's instigation, given the strict control
he maintained over all aspects of his self-fashioning. Was this
in memory of the 'superfine blue clothes' that he had purchased
for himself twenty-three years earlier in anticipation of his
manumission in Montserrat? Certainly, Equiano mentioned
his blue 'freedom suit' twice in his *Interesting Narrative*: first,
noting how 'In this expectation [of purchasing my freedom]
I laid out above eight pounds of my money for a suit of superfine
clothes to dance with at my freedom, which I hoped was then
at hand';[16] and second, as part of his 11 July 1766 freedom-day
narrative, recording how having obtained his manumission,
'the fair as well as black people immediately styled me by a
new appellation, to me the most desirable in the world, which
was Freeman, and at the dances I gave, my Georgia superfine
blue clothes made no indifferent appearance', boasting how
he had turned a number of Black women's heads.[17]

Equiano may have sold copies of his portrait to raise money for
himself, as well as using it as a form of authentication and proof
of identity. He also gifted copies to friends and supporters. On
29 March 1791, for example, Susannah Atkinson, wife of wealthy
Yorkshire industrialist and mill-owner Law Atkinson, wrote
to Equiano after he had experienced some unspecified (likely
racist) 'slights', 'rebuffs' and 'uncivil treatment' that had left

16. Equiano 1789, vol. II, p. 19. I am grateful
to Fr Charles Card-Reynolds for pointing
this out and for generously allowing me
to reproduce the coloured version in his
collection [2].
17. Equiano 1789, vol. II, p. 19.

him feeling 'low'. Susannah reassured her 'much valued friend' of her family's constant and abiding friendship, telling Equiano 'how happy I shall always be to see you' and underlining how much his portrait was valued:

> I thank you for your picture — believe me we shall value it much — we will have it Framed — and hung with our own Family who are doing now — I hope you *may* see it — it wont be done the next time you come — but hope you will see it the time *after* next — till then may God preserve and Guide you — and believe me to be *ever* sincerely your well wisher — and Friend.[18]

For a man forcibly separated from his family at a tender age, this literal and metaphorical welcome into the heart of another family in his adopted country must have meant a great deal, especially a family who were such keen supporters — Law Atkinson purchased one hundred copies of the fourth edition — and explains why Equiano kept this letter until he died.

Re-presenting Equiano

Equiano's 'interesting' life remains a paradox: on the one hand, it was unexceptional, with his lived experiences and acts of resistance being similar to those of millions of enslaved and freed African people across the Black Atlantic. On the other hand, it was exceptional in terms of its accomplishments and achievements. His CV was extraordinary: self-made man who purchased his own freedom; self-educated and highly proficient, self-taught English-speaker; ship's deck-hand, mariner, and able seaman in the Royal Navy; trader, businessman and civil servant with wide experience in the Caribbean and North America; hairdresser; traveller across Europe, the Caribbean and British North America; intrepid Antarctic explorer and scientific assistant; published author of prose, poetry and literary reviews; political activist, lobbyist and public speaker; and husband to an English woman and father of two girls. Equiano's autobiography made him an international celebrity as well as a target for the powerful pro-slavery lobby, primarily led by the West India Committee in London. It also guaranteed Equiano's place in history as one of the key drivers behind the abolition of the slave trade — which, sadly, he did not live to see formalised in law, dying in 1797, a decade before the Abolition of the Slave Trade Act of 1807. That said, his *Interesting Narrative* has had an enduring legacy that Equiano cannot have envisaged with its message reaching and resonating with readers across the globe.[19]

Such a trail-blazing figure in British history deserves to be better known, celebrated and visually commemorated than Equiano has been since his death in 1797. In 2021—2,

18. Sapoznik 2013, pp. 53—4. The original is in the Cambridgeshire Record Office, Ely, in the papers of John Audley, his executor (R. 63/12.2). For a useful summary of the Atkinsons and their relationship to Equiano, see 'Law Atkinson and Susannah Atkinson', *The Equiano Society*, https://equianos world.org/'associates-abolitionphp?id= 22#content (accessed 8 August 2024).
19. For a useful overview of the critical history of Equiano's autobiography, see Lovejoy 2006, pp. 1—3, and 'Editions of The Interesting Narrative' on the Equiano's World database.

British-Nigerian artist and visual storyteller Joy Labinjo decided to rectify this through her *Ode to Olaudah Equiano* project. Drawing on historical archives and collections, this body of paintings centres the lives of pre-twentieth-century Black British individuals, both known and unknown, and their communities, who have been 'largely absent in pictorial accounts of the social and cultural life of the period', seeking 'to piece together some of those missing histories [and] to re-present their stories in the twenty-first century.'[20] Among these is *Olaudah Equiano* [6], in which Labinjo boldly reworks and repurposes Orme's engraving. Aware of all the travails that Equiano experienced in the years after his 1789 portrait, Labinjo has imagined Equiano as older, more careworn and hardened. But, equally aware of Equiano's legacy and impact, Labinjo has transformed the small-scale engraved source into an epic work. Equiano is now re-presented as he should be: a giant of a man with strong shoulders, broad chest, clenched jaw and a penetrating, steely-eyed gaze. It captures both his likeness and his greatness. Both ordinary and extraordinary, Olaudah Equiano/Gustavus Vassa finally has a heroic swagger portrait worthy of his names and his innumerable accomplishments.

My sincere thanks to Matthew Abel, Vincent Carretta, Emma Jones, Dawnanna Kreeger and Paul Lovejoy for insightful feedback on earlier drafts.

Selected reading

- Vincent Carretta, *Equiano, the African. Biography of a Self-Made Man*, London 2005.
- Olaudah Equiano (Gustavus Vassa), *The Interesting Narrative of The Life of Olaudah Equiano, or Gustavus Vassa, The African. Written by Himself*, 1st edn, London, 26 March 1789.
- Olaudah Equiano, *The Interesting Narrative and Other Writings*, Vincent Carretta (ed.), 1st edn, London 1995; revised 2nd edn, London 2003.
- Paul E. Lovejoy, 'Autobiography and Memory: Gustavus Vassa, alias Olaudah Equiano, the African', *Slavery & Abolition*, 27, no. 3 (2006), pp. 317—47.
- Paul E. Lovejoy, 'Olaudah Equiano or Gustavus Vassa — What's in a Name?', *Atlantic Studies*, 9, no. 2 (2024), pp. 165—84.
- Karlee Anne Sapoznik (ed.), *The Letters and Other Writings of Gustavus Vassa (Olaudah Equiano, the African). Documenting Abolition of the Slave Trade*, Princeton, NJ 2013.
- 'Equiano's World', *The Equiano Society*, https://www.equianosworld.org/ (accessed 13 August 2024).
- 'Olaudah Equiano, or, Gustavus Vassa, the African', *Brycchan Carey*, https://www.brycchancarey.com/equiano/index.htm (accessed 13 August 2024).

20. 'Ode to Oluadah Equiano', *Joy Labinjo*, https://www.joylabinjo.com/2022/ode-to-olaudah-equiano-2022 (accessed 13 August 2024). The *Ode to Olaudah Equiano* exhibition was at Chapter Art Gallery, Cardiff, 26 March — 3 July 2022.

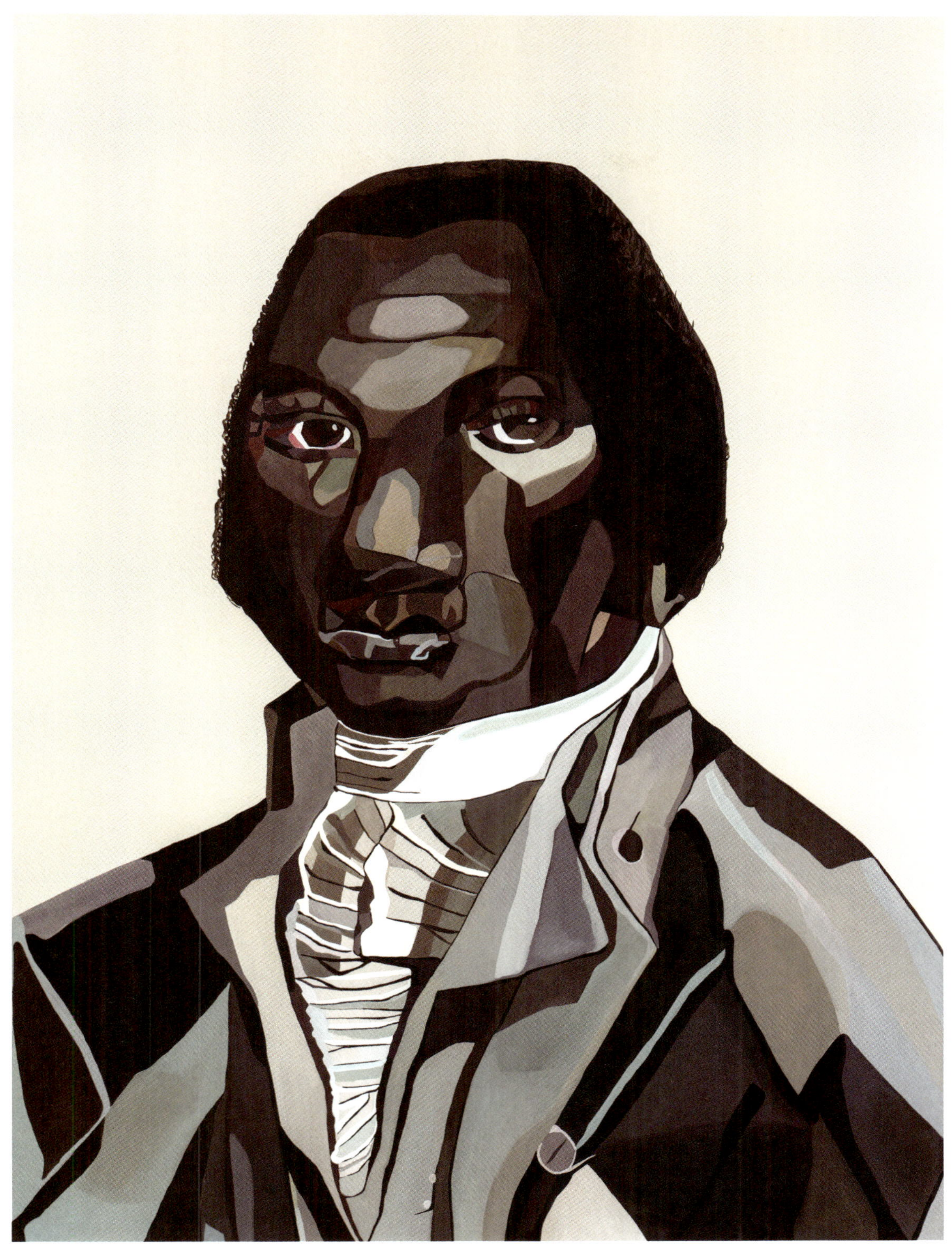

6

Joy Labinjo (born 1994). ***Olaudah Equiano***, 2022. Oil on canvas, 200 × 150 cm
Private collection © Joy Labinjo

Joy Labinjo's portraits of eighteenth-century Black writers

Orlando Reade

These two paintings by Joy Labinjo represent arguably the two most famous Black writers of the eighteenth century: Olaudah Equiano [6 and 8] and Phillis Wheatley [7]. In repainting and reanimating their portraits, Labinjo's work meditates on absences in the archives of Black life and on contemporary desires to repair them.

Olaudah Equiano was born in modern-day Benin, West Africa. As a child, he was abducted and sold into slavery. He was put on a slave ship to Virginia, and later became a sailor on British merchant ships. He eventually bought his own freedom and served in the British Navy during the Seven Years' War (1756—63). Later, he settled in London, where he became instrumental in the movement to abolish slavery. He is most famous as the author of *The Interesting Narrative of the Life of Olaudah Equiano, Or Gustavus Vassa, The African* (1789) [4]. Equiano's *Interesting Narrative* is an autobiography, and a resounding argument against slavery, which includes a rare account of the 'Middle Passage' by someone who was transported as a captive. It also contains the only known image of Equiano: William Denton's engraving of the writer as a fashionable and composed man, with a double-breasted coat and a white scarf fastened round his neck. Labinjo's distinctive brushstrokes, combining elements of cartoon and Cubism, invest the image with a new liveliness, but also a sense of unknowability, discovering new aspects in his face, and new shadows [6].

Labinjo's painting of Phillis Wheatley achieves a similar effect [7]. Wheatley was born in West Africa, likely in modern-day Gambia or Senegal. She was captured as a child and sold into slavery. She was transported to Boston, then part of the British Empire, where she was purchased by a wealthy merchant, John Wheatley, who named her after the ship that had transported her: the *Phillis*. She was taught to read and write by Wheatley's children, and started composing poetry as a teenager. She travelled to London in 1773, and her *Poems on Various Subjects, Religious and Moral* was published there. It is now considered the first published poetry collection by an African American poet. Wheatley's *Poems* contains the only surviving lifetime image of her — an engraving of the poet sitting at her desk, pen in hand, caught in a state of meditation [51]. Included as its frontispiece, the engraving is thought to be by the artist Scipio Moorhead (or after a painting by him), who was, like her, an enslaved Bostonian. In a poem 'To S.M. A Young African Painter, On Seeing His Works', Wheatley praises the 'deathless glories' of Moorhead's paintings: evidence that Black people could master the cultural sophistication prized by white society. Likewise, her sophisticated neoclassical poetry was an enduring argument about the humanity of enslaved people. In repainting Wheatley's portrait, Labinjo has created a doubled meditation on the importance of images — but also their unreliability — as the bearers of arguments about humanity.

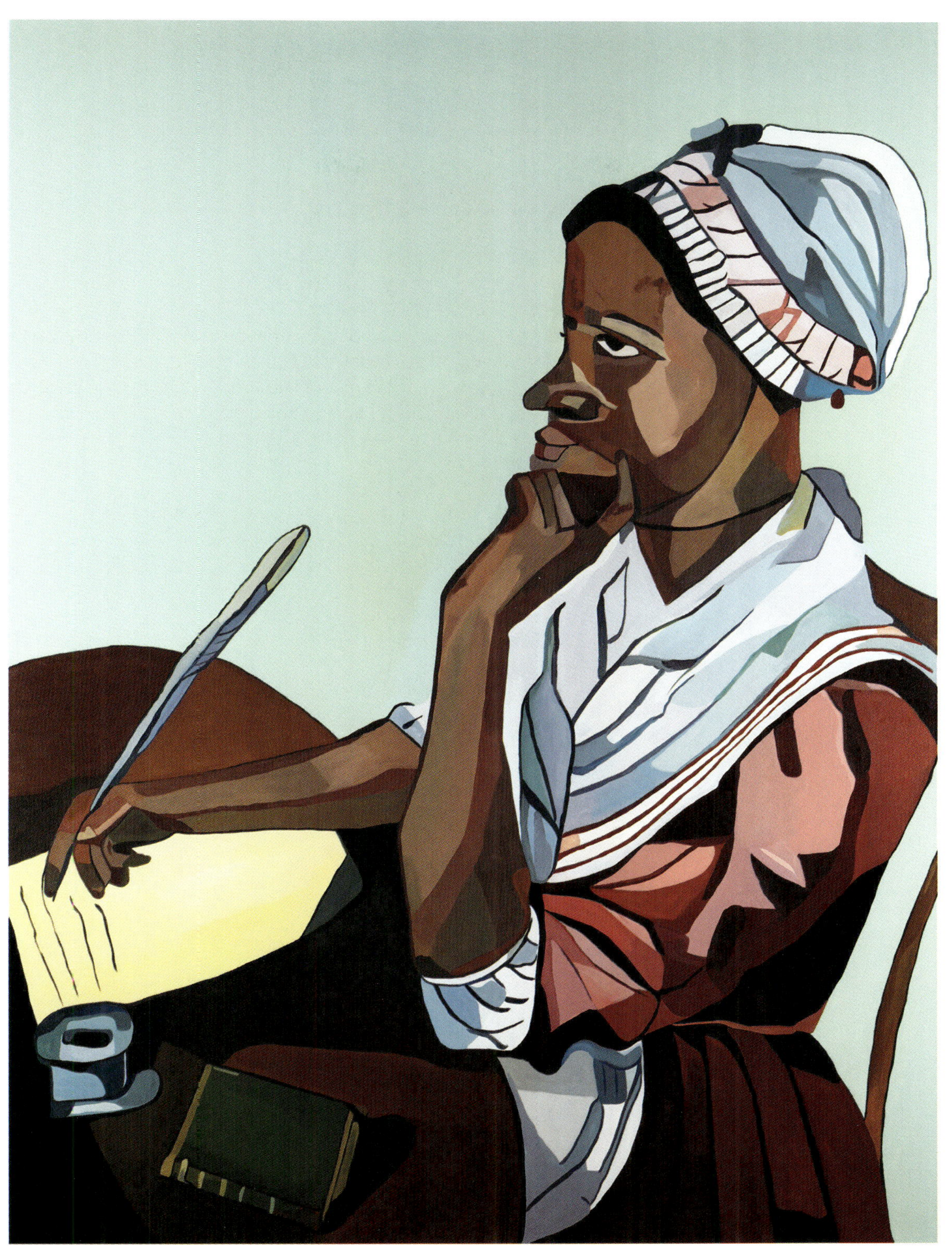

7

Joy Labinjo (born 1994). *Phillis Wheatley*, 2022. Oil on canvas, 200 × 150 cm

Courtesy of the Artist and Tiwani Ltd, London (JLA 118) © Joy Labinjo

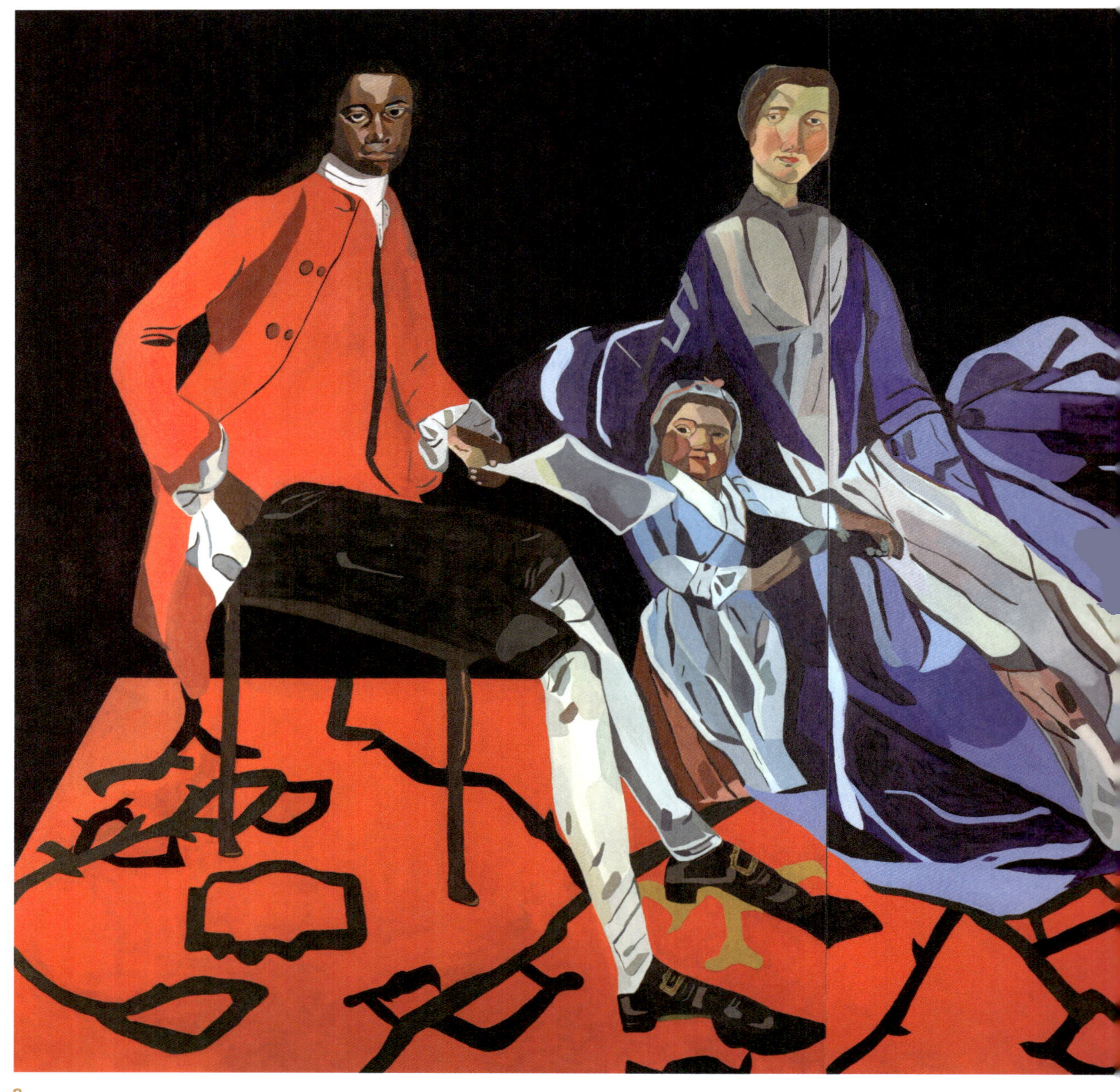

8

Joy Labinjo (born 1994). *An Eighteenth-Century Family*, 2022. Oil on canvas, 200 × 300 cm
Fitzwilliam Museum, Cambridge (PD.74-2022). Bought with the Simms Fund, 2022 © Joy Labinjo

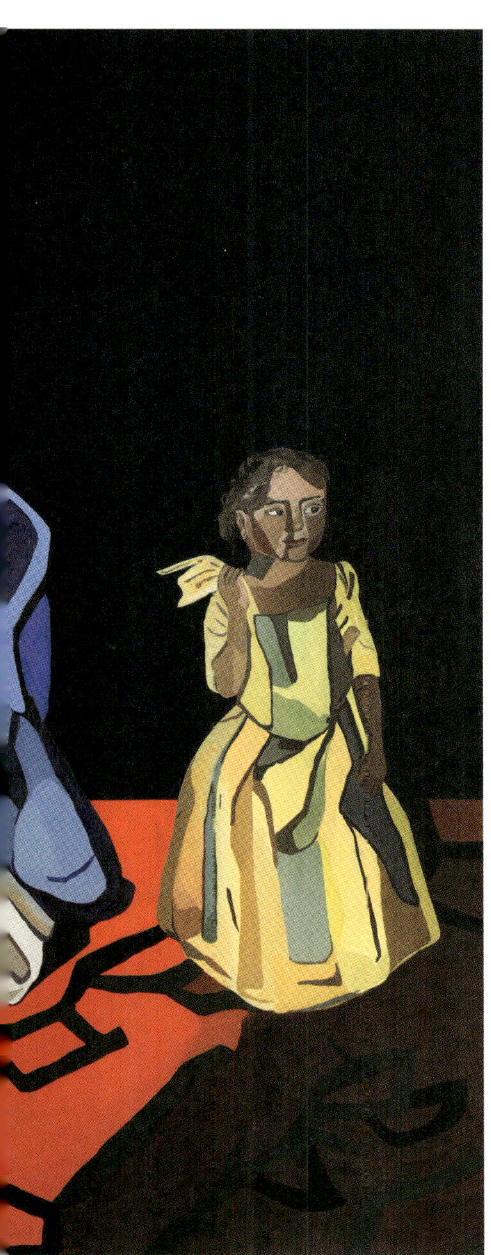

Labinjo's painting, *An Eighteenth-Century Family*, is a second portrait of Equiano, but it makes a deliberate departure from the historical record [8]. In 1792, Equiano married a white Englishwoman, Susannah Cullen, in St Andrew's Church, Soham, in Cambridgeshire. Equiano and his wife had two children together, Anna Maria and Johanna. Labinjo's portrait is based not on the engraving of Equiano but on an anonymous portrait in the Royal Albert Memorial Museum in Exeter, now called *Portrait of a Man in a Red Suit*. It was for a long time held to be of Equiano. This identification is now disputed, but the image still circulates under Equiano's name. Labinjo used this unidentified portrait as the basis for a painting of Equiano with his wife and two children. Her angular lines render their faces strange, almost inhuman, obscuring their identities at the same moment as she imagines them.

Unlike the other two paintings, *An Eighteenth-Century Family* is a speculative portrait. In imagining a wished-for but currently non-existent image, it is of a piece with popular counter-factual fictions such as *Bridgerton*, *Hamilton* and *Inglourious Basterds*, which imagine a more equitable past. However, Labinjo has not invented its facts. There were thousands of Black people living in Britain in the eighteenth century. But few images of them and their families survive. The visual archive — which contains a single image of Equiano, and none of his wife or children — is marked by exclusions based on race, class and gender. Labinjo has not invented a fantasy image of the past, as a substitute for other forms of reparation, but a body of work that holds out for the possibility of a visual culture not organised around the same old exclusions.

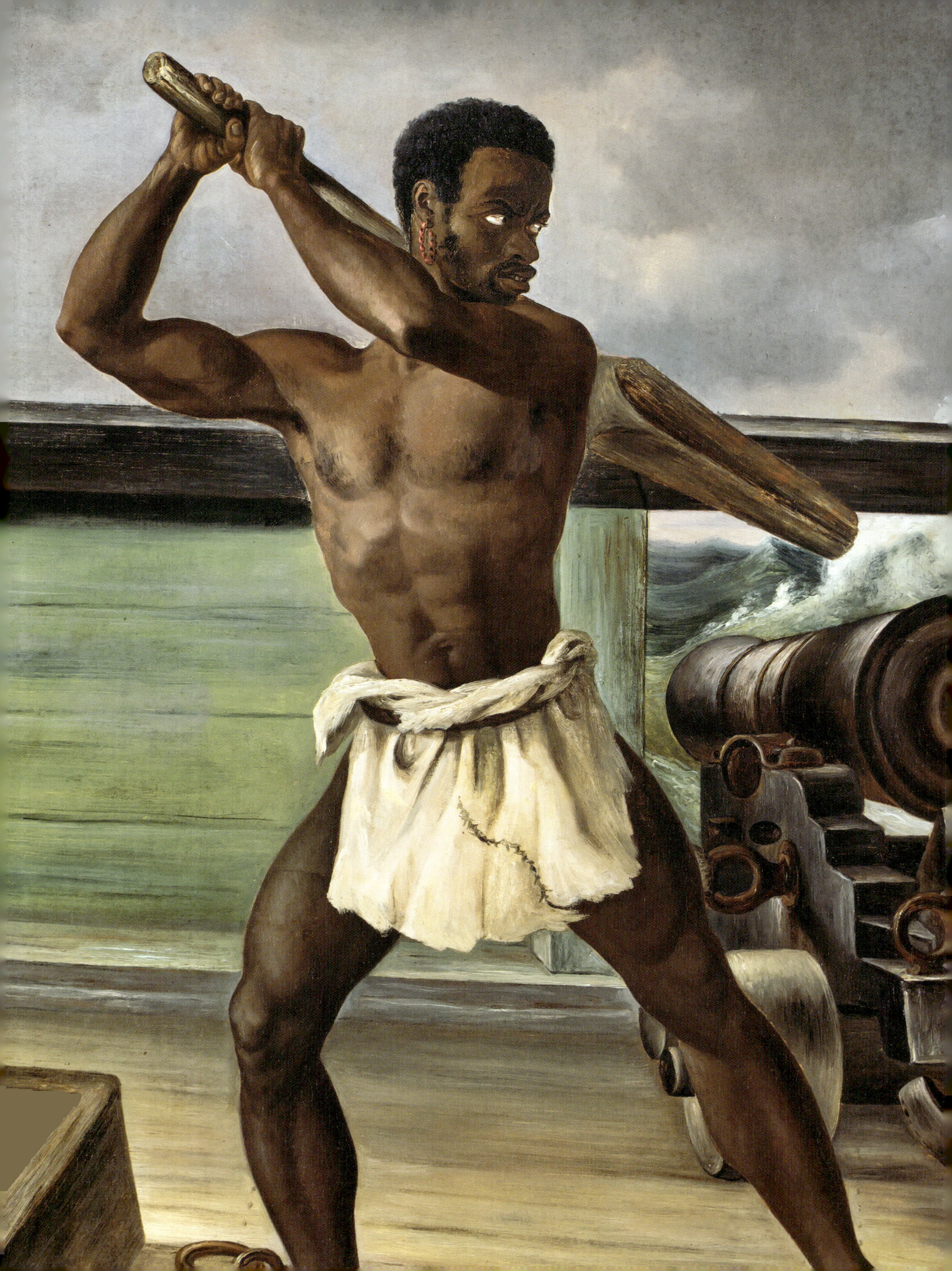

1 Oppression and resistance

The desire of African and African-descended people to preserve their personhood, cultures and kinship ties were seen as threats to the rigid social structures and power hierarchies of Caribbean plantation societies. Such efforts could also provide catalysts for rebellion. Plantation owners and overseers ruthlessly suppressed any signs of resistance.

Despite relentless brutality, enslaved people fought back. Resistance took many forms, individual and collective, non-violent and violent, but had common aims — to regain freedom and self-governance, and to keep dignity, customs and cultures intact.

African dance, music and religious ceremonies from many regions lived on. These varied cultures came together with Indigenous Caribbean and European practices to create new traditions, often shared and handed on secretly. Enslaved people used music and dance, for example, to find joy and connection in community celebration, creating moments of everyday resistance that defied their constant oppression.

Enslaved people also worked together in acts of sabotage and protest. Some escaped bondage. They sometimes formed or joined independent, often remote, communities of maroons who challenged the power of the slaving system. At times, enslaved and formerly enslaved people plotted uprisings and organised rebellions.

Detail of **25** (see page 52)

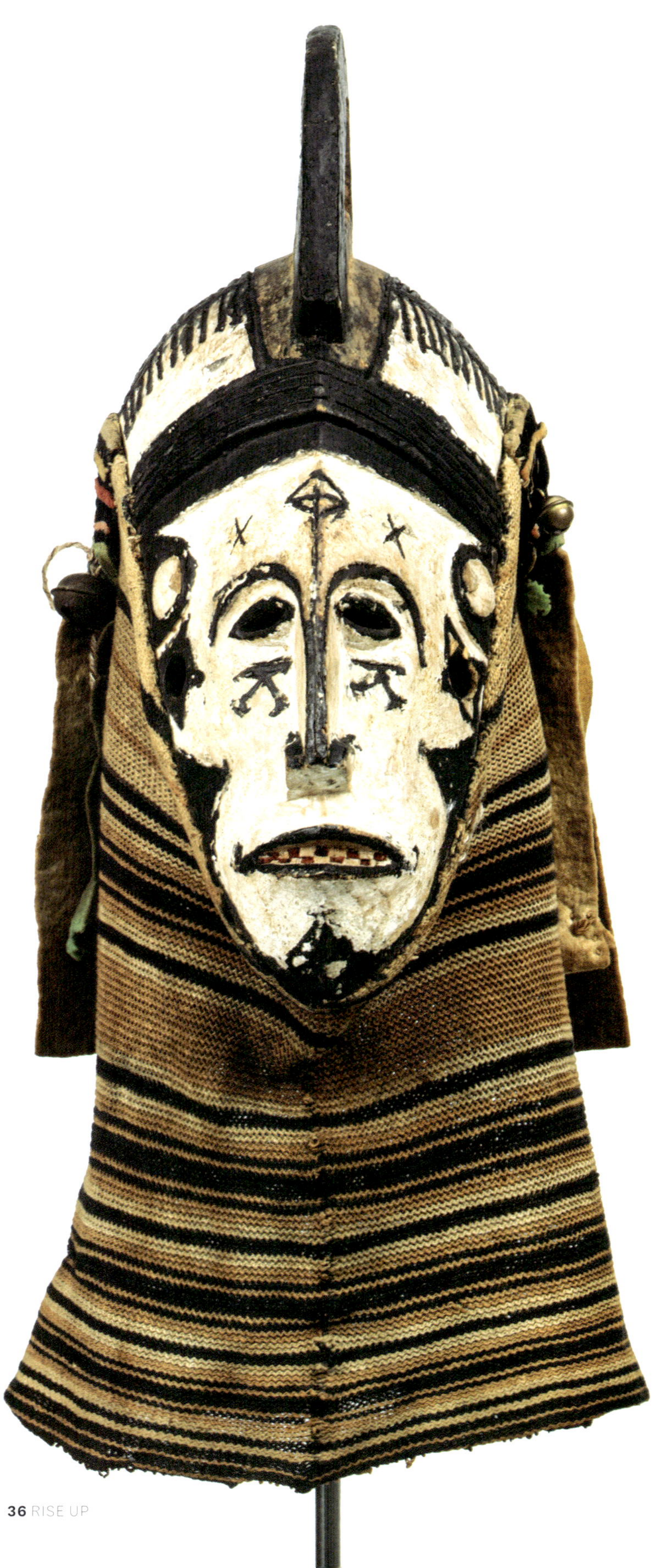

Unrecorded Igbo maker,
Awka, Anambra State, Nigeria.
Agbogho Mmuo
(Maiden Spirit) masquerade
mask, unrecorded date,
probably early 20th century.
Wood, kaolin and other
pigments, plant fibre and
cloth, 36.5 × 14.5 × 17 cm

Museum of Archaeology and Anthropology,
University of Cambridge (2014.300). Bought
from Ursula Jones, widow of Gwilym Iwan
'G.I.' Jones (1904—1995), with donations
from Jesus College, Cambridge, John
Goodliffe, Margaret Risbeth and the
Wenbam-Smith family, 2014. Collected
by G.I. Jones when a colonial District
Officer in Bende, Nigeria, 1926—46

Seeing against the grain

Mathelinda Nabugodi

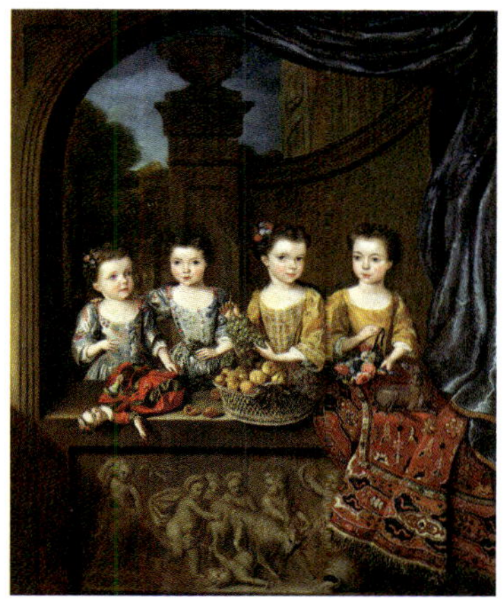

10

Jan van Meyer
(*c*.1681—after 1741).
The Daughters of Sir Matthew Decker, Bart, 1718.
Oil on canvas, 77.5 × 66.1 cm

Fitzwilliam Museum, Cambridge (437).
Bequeathed by Richard, 7th Viscount
Fitzwilliam, 1816

Five maidens. Five white faces, peering out of the artworks [9 and 10]. One African, four European. Looking at you. No, it's not true. None of them looks at you; gazes slightly askance, they all look past you because you do not matter for them. The African face belongs to an Igbo maiden spirit mask, painted white to symbolise beauty and delicacy, now exiled in the Museum of Archaeology and Anthropology (MAA) in Cambridge. She looks disgusted. If it wasn't for the glass vitrine in which she is caged, she would suck her teeth and spit you in the face, right in the left eye. Then she'd spit again, in your right. That's not what the white maidens would do. Elizabeth, Mary, Catherine, Henrietta Maria. Daddy's little girls, who already know how to behave in a 'civilised' manner: how to blush on cue, how to pour a cup of tea, how much sugar to take, how to stir the sugar in a way that shows off the fineness of their wrists. Their cheeks are dappled with red to highlight the 'transparency' of their skin, an epithet used for fair skin that is prone to vivid blushing and revealing the tracery of blue veins beneath its surface. Since these features were deemed to be the unique preserve of white skin, they became particularly prized as contrast to the presumed 'dullness' of darker skin tones. With their pale bosoms and rosy cheeks, the Decker quartet perfectly embodies the white supremacist aesthetic of their time.

This is why, although I noted the similarities between the five white-faced maidens, nothing could be more different from the four little Decker girls than the Igbo maiden spirit mask, who embodies a wholly different conception of beauty. The fact that she resides at the MAA, while the Decker quartet is found in the Fitzwilliam Museum, reflects the racist ordering of the world's artistic heritage. Works from Ancient Egypt, Europe and the Orient are presented in the Fitzwilliam's palatial building with plenty of wall-space and a cool, quiet, reverential atmosphere, while at the nearby MAA, artworks from the rest of the globe are crammed together in the helter-skelter chaos of a flea market. The cacophony of everything in this space bears down on me on the day that I go to visit one of the Igbo maiden spirit masks. I find her pinned up between some beadwork from South Africa and a display on environmental sustainability in the Pacific region. She is still. No, not just 'still', that's too small a word. I should rather say that she is crowned in majestic stillness. Her eyes are empty slots, yet I feel her refusal to meet my gaze. She bides her time. Angry? Resigned? Definitely forlorn.

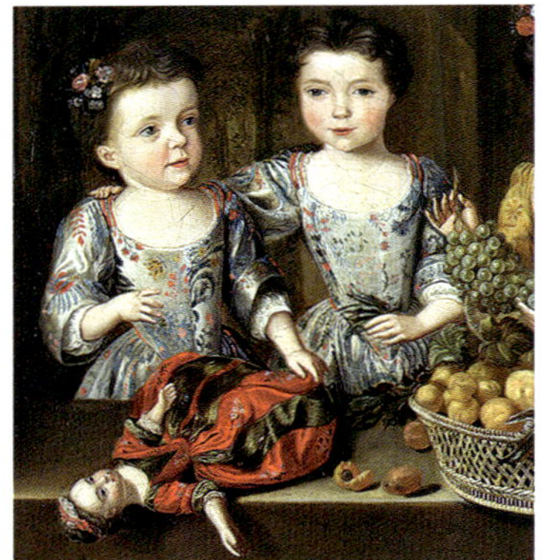

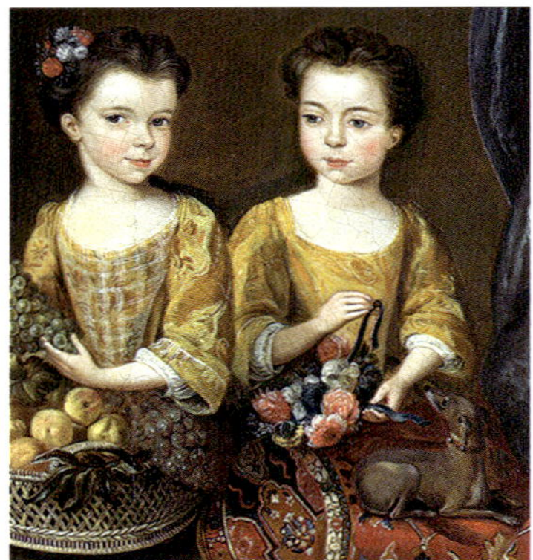

Details of **10** (see page 37)

She should be alive and dancing, not pinned up behind glass like a specimen of some rare insect. Looking into her face I feel awed, and humbled. A trespasser seeing something not meant for my eyes.

In contrast, the Decker girls gave me the creeps the first time I saw them. It was not the painting itself, but a larger-than-life reproduction hanging in an office at the Fitzwilliam Museum, the printed canvas spreading over the wall like a mural or ominous mould patch. It always caught my eye on the way back from the staff tearoom. Even before I learned that they were the daughters of Matthew Decker, and where the Decker fortune came from, I sensed that there was something rotten about the four girls, so similar in size and age, looking more like clones than sisters. It is as if the portrait secretes its own sweet, sultry scent, thick like the folds of sleek fabric framing the image, or the carpet that lies folded over a corner of the table. Picking up the red, blue, white and ochre tones of the girls' dresses, these materials are placed here to signal opulence, though in the context of this exhibition they also call to the colours of the fabrics in Thomas Clarkson's campaign chest [56].[1]

Clarkson's aim in displaying these richly coloured fabrics was to show that Africans were capable of producing cultural artefacts so as to promote trade in goods rather than humans, though in reality the two trades co-existed in symbiosis. It is most likely that some of the dyes in the dress and paraphernalia of the four Decker girls originate in colonial contexts, as do the pigments used by Jan van Meyer to represent them. This is even more true of the fruit that decks the table in the foreground. Do you hear the low yet insistent buzz of fruit flies milling around the basket of apricots and the overripe grapes that Catherine displays with a cheeky wink? Fairly ubiquitous today, in the eighteenth century grapes were a luxury item reserved for the rich; these particular grapes serve as a reminder of the exotic plants cultivated by foreign gardeners in the hothouses on the Decker estate in Richmond-upon-Thames. That explains the young girl's twinkling eye and knowing smile: she may look modest, but she knows the price of the fruit in her hands. Imagine grabbing that bunch of grapes and squeezing it hard: the translucent grape-skin bursting and squirting juice in all directions, the texture of the fruit flesh, the slimy pits slipping between your fingers. The image is not a bad metaphor for this type of portraiture — prod it too closely and you will be left with something sticky and deflated dripping in your hands.

Her sister, Henrietta Maria, looks hard done by. She wanted to clutch the grapes but was stuck with a basket of flowers. Boring English roses. To make matters worse, she also has to pose with the family lap dog. She doesn't like it. It's small, but it's yappy and she's slightly scared of it. Yet Mr van Meyer,

1. For further discussion of the African cloth in the Clarkson chest, see Sarah Coleman, Margarita Gleba and Malika Kraamer, 'From West Africa to Wisbech: analysing 18th-century textiles in Thomas Clarkson's campaign chest', *The Past*, 5 January 2022, https://the-past.com/feature/from-west-africa-to-wisbech-analysing-18th-century-textiles-in-thomas-clarksons-campaign-chest/ (accessed 16 July 2024).

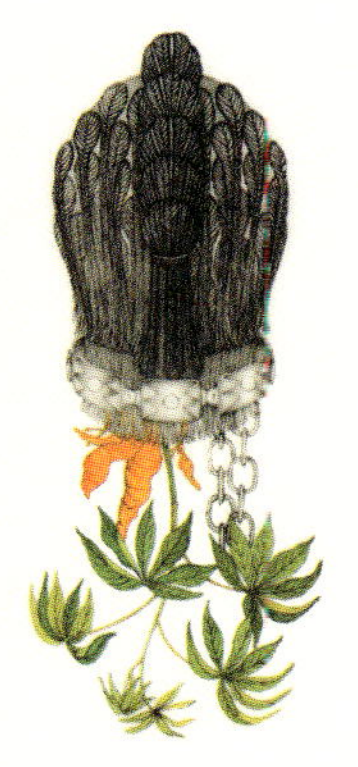

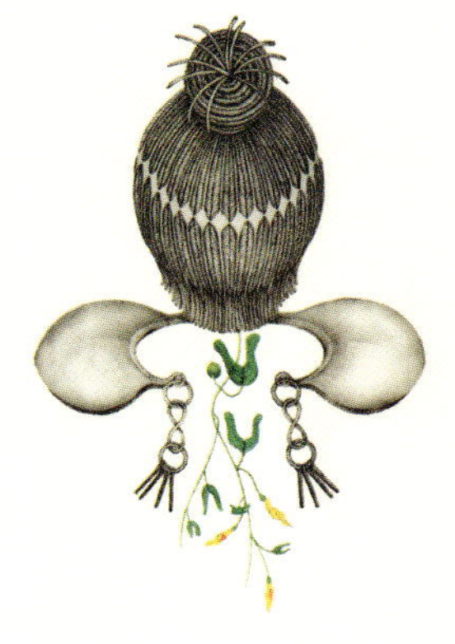

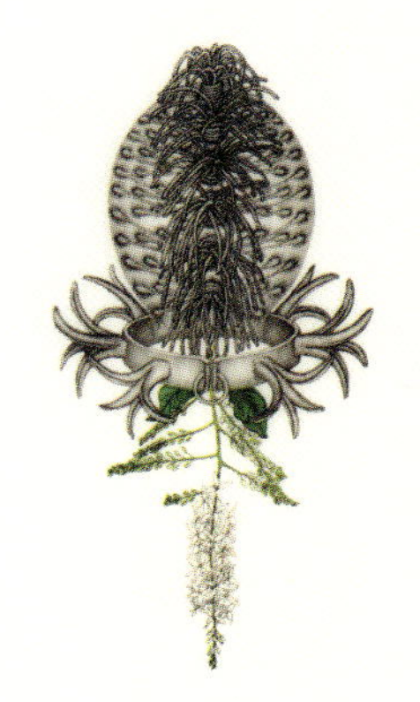

11

12

13

the painter, insisted on putting it there, to counterbalance Elizabeth's doll even though little Lizzie is a dunce and can't even manage to hold the doll, not to mention stand still and pose nicely without poor Mary keeping her in place. Mary is bitter too. She just got landed with some sprigs of asparagus, and clutching Lizzie of course. We all wanted to hold the grapes. They're so lush.

Henrietta Maria absent-mindedly picks at the flowers, strangling them with a piece of ribbon. The bouquet in her hand is matched by posies in her sisters' hair and the floral motifs on their brocade dresses. This association of flowers and femininity directs me towards Joscelyn Gardner's *Creole Portraits III: 'bringing down the flowers …'* [11—13]. The series can be read as a group portrait of women whose names and faces have been lost to history. In contrast to the entitled attitude with which the Decker girls offer themselves to the painter, Gardner's subjects look away in a gesture of refusal. The portraits depict the back of a woman's head, suspended in nebulous blandness, the dirty white of frosted mylar. This could be many different women, or the same woman on different days, but I see her as an archetype: a single woman who represents a multitude of female experience. That's why she compels me to think of her in the plural when I study the crowns of hair on her heads and see in them an echo of the crown worn by the spirit maiden — all of them celebrate the texture and possibilities of shaping Afro hair.

Her intricately braided hairstyles are mirrored in the flowers flowing down her spine — not English roses but the blooms of the Caribbean. *Aristolochia bilobala* (Nimine). *Manihot flabellifolia* (Old Catalina). *Petiveria aliacea* (Mirtilla). They adorn her like living necklaces, or so I think at first.

But that's not true. Look again. Her necks are circled by the contraptions of enslavement: neck-irons with chains to be linked to arms and feet or hooks designed to get stuck in the undergrowth, obstructing any attempt to escape through the bush. It disconcerts me to see adornments extending into neck collars, remembering the continuities between African beauty and enslavement in the transatlantic context. Or is it the other way around: are these instruments of torture sprouting into beauty, like wildflowers will grow over the ruins of a prison?

After all, Gardner's flowers are not entangled in the chains, they are not innocent flora made to ensnare a woman running towards her freedom. They grow inwards from her mouths, flowing with the air down her throats, unfolding their leaves into the capillaries of her lungs. Slowly breathing, choking, transforming exhaled, exhausted carbon dioxide into oxygen, a perfect symbiosis of flower and absent body. These flowers gesture towards a fugitive mode of survival: hidden in the breath, folded within the body where no one can see it. As such, they can be read as allegories of Black survival. The transatlantic crossing was unspeakably horrible, but not so horrible that people lost their culture. While European slave traders intended for the captive Africans to disembark the ships as chattel — items of moveable property — they failed. The people who survived the journey were still human, still carrying their languages, their ancestors, their dreams in their bones. They gave birth to a new Black Atlantic culture in which their ancestors continued to dance in new forms.

Music was a central element in the cultural practices that African people brought with them to the 'New World'. This was manifested in daily life through song — one person took the lead by improvising a line to which others responded in chorus. White observers compared the lead singer to an Italian *improvisatore*, an artist who specialised in extemporising lyric verse to set cues. Most accounts of life in the Caribbean include fragments of song lyrics and even attempts to transcribe the melodies in European musical notation [14]: such attempts testify to the pull that African music culture exercised on white listeners even as they complained about its 'barbaric' and 'primitive' sounds. I am particularly struck by Robert Renny's account of his arrival in Jamaica in 1799 when he met with a group of singing women:

> As soon as the vessel in which the author was passenger arrived near to Port Royal in Jamaica, a canoe, containing three or four black females, came to the side of the ship, for the purpose of selling oranges, and other fruits. When about to depart, they gazed at the passengers, whose number seemed to surprise them; and as soon as the canoe pushed off, one of them sung the following words,

while the other joined in the chorus, clapping their hand regularly while it lasted.

> New-come buckra,
> He get sick,
> He tak fever,
> He be die;
> He be die.
> New come, &c.

The song, as far as we could hear, contained nothing else, and they continued singing it, in the manner just mentioned, as long as they were within hearing.[2]

I am charmed by this vision of a small group of intrepid women plying their canoe through the harbour, a masculine space dominated by seasoned sailors and imposing ships, while singing mocking songs of the men they pass on their way. The word 'buckra' denotes white person — and the women's song alludes to the yellow fever which killed many new arrivals in the Caribbean. Looking at a shipload of white men, the women gleefully anticipate the murderous disease that awaits them on shore. It is a spontaneous and ruthless response to the racial realities of their life in Jamaica.

As this example demonstrates, impromptu songs accompanied the daily labour of Black Caribbeans. They were heard all over the Americas — from rivers and waterways where rowers used them to pace their strokes, to the fields growing sugar cane, coffee, cotton or tobacco and the tropical forests where men were set hewing mahogany trees and clearing land for more plantations [14]. Enslavers saw this incessant singing as evidence of how happy the slaves were with their lot, though in reality many such songs had subversive meanings — they offered a chance to commune with one's origins, they bore witness to the horrors of slavery, and they served to ridicule the whites and incite rebellion.

Sundays provided some relative respite from the gruelling workday on a plantation. The morning was often spent at the provision grounds — areas set off from the plantations where people could grow their own food. Any surplus produce was taken to the market; this is quite possibly what the three or four women selling fruit out of their canoe were doing. In the evening, with the business of the day over, Black Caribbeans would gather for more music-making and dancing. Here the choral songs were accompanied by a variety of drums in different shapes and sizes [15], string instruments and rattles that were either held in the hand or tied to the dancer's body.

Sensing the power of Black music, British Caribbean authorities tried to control it. Hans Sloane, having described African

2. Robert Renny, *An History of Jamaica. With Observations on the Climate, Scenery, Trade, Productions, [redacted], Slave Trade, Diseases of Europeans, Customs, Manners, and Dispositions of the Inhabitants*, London 1807, p. 241.

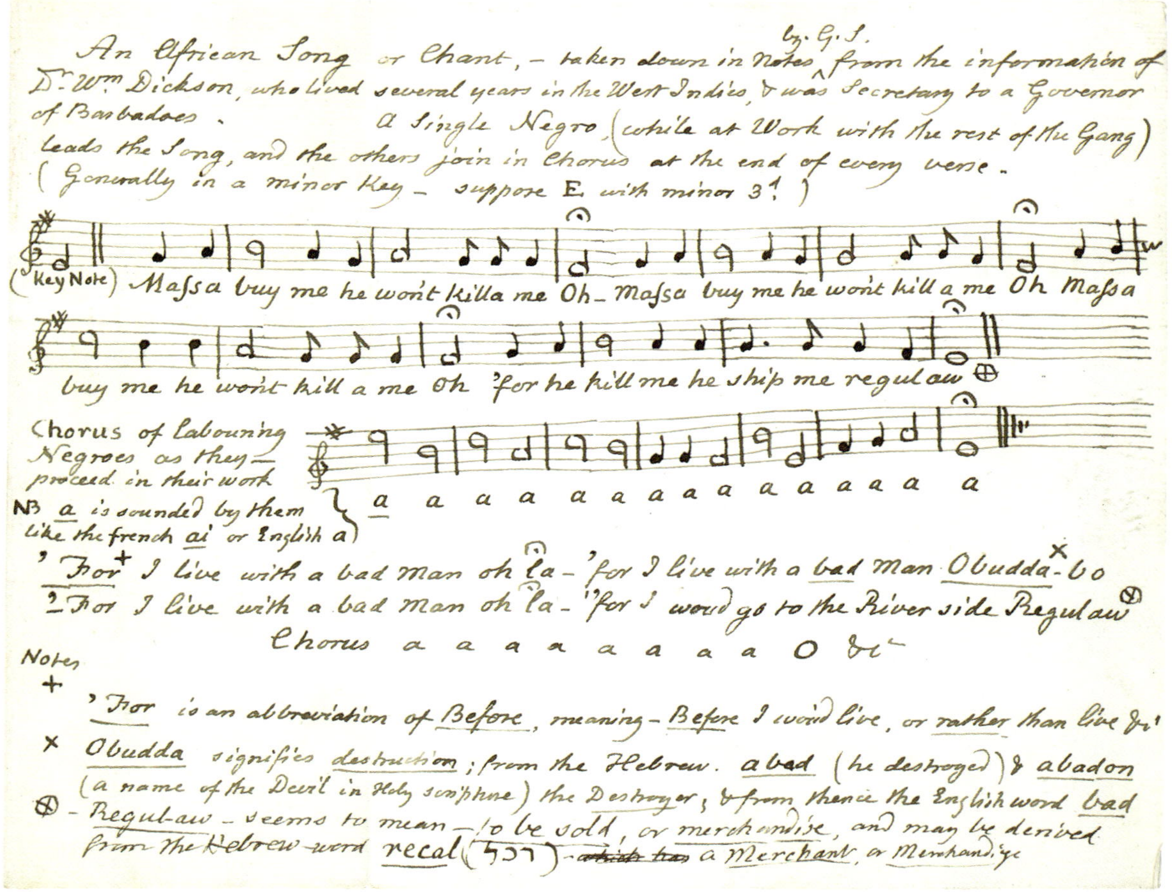

14

Unrecorded British compiler.
'An African Song or Chant …',
about 1772—9. Ink on paper,
19.8 × 25.4 cm

Fair copy manuscript transcription by
Granville Sharp (1735—1813) from notes
by William Dickson (1751—1823) of the lyrics
and music to what is believed to be the oldest
known work song sung in Barbadian Creole
by enslaved labourers. Gloucestershire
Archives, Gloucester (D3549/12/3/27)

drums, added that since drums were used in warfare, 'it was thought too much inciting them to Rebellion, and so they were prohibited by the Customs of the Island'.[3] Sloane visited the Caribbean in the late seventeenth century and the ban that he mentions is one in a long series of attempts to control drumming [16]. Two hundred years later, British Caribbean authorities were still issuing edicts to this end. The reissuing of anti-drum laws bears witness to the futility of these attempts to silence Black music. These prohibitions merely challenged music makers to become more inventive, for example by fashioning new kinds of percussive instruments — this is one reason why steel pans are used in contemporary Caribbean music: they developed from bamboo drums invented to contravene an 1877 drum ban issued by the British authorities in Trinidad and Tobago.

The weekly Sunday dances would build up towards an annual celebration. While Black Caribbeans originated in different parts of the African continent and therefore had different cultural and religious backgrounds, most of them would have grown up with masquerade traditions — ceremonial occasions

3. Hans Sloane, *A Voyage to the Islands of Madera, Barbados, Nieves, S. Christophers and Jamaica*, 2 vols, London 1707, vol. 1, p. lii.

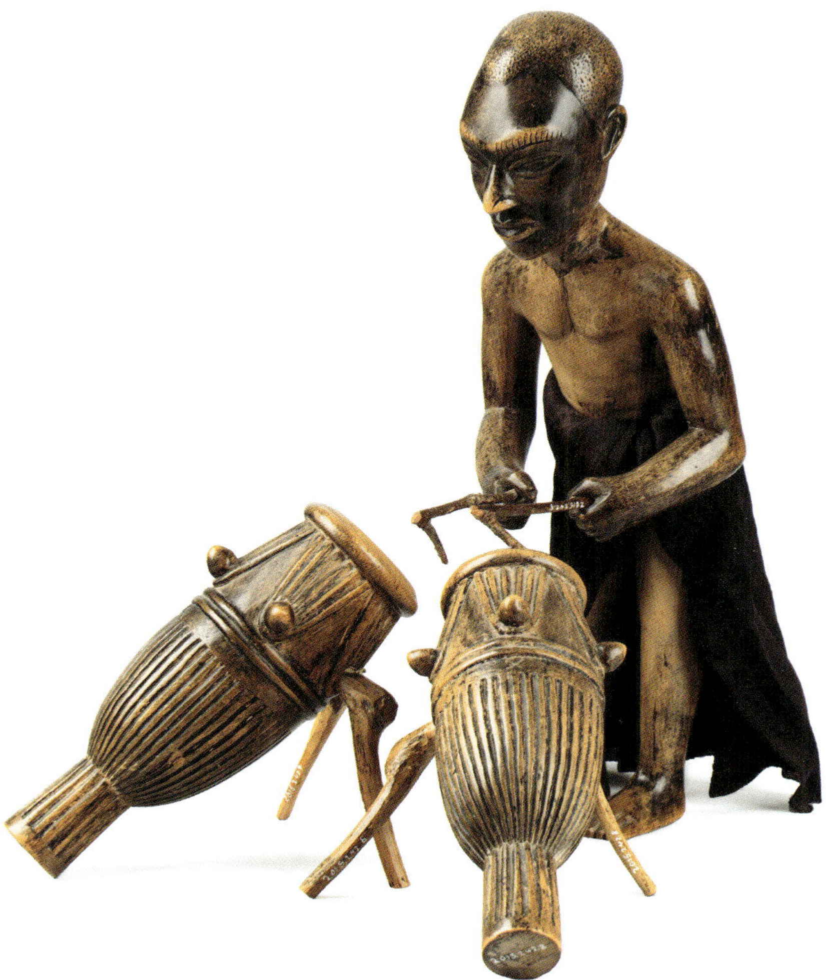

Osei Bonsu (1900—1977).
**Male drummer with
two *ntumpane* drums
of *djembe* shape**,
Goaso, Ahafo Region, Ghana,
1930/31. Wood, cloth,
33 × 10 × 12 cm (drummer)

Museum of Archaeology and Anthropology,
University of Cambridge (2015.242.1-9).
Given by Sylvia Spooner, wife of Arthur
Casswell Spooner (1906—1996), and their
son, Professor Edward T. Spooner, 2015.
Carved by Bonsu for Spooner, about 1930, at
the start of his colonial appointment in West
Africa from 1929 to 1963

when masked dancers representing ancestors, spirits or gods appeared. Their dance served to mark significant events in the life of the community, such as a funeral, the inauguration of a new ruler, or a judicial hearing in which the ancestral spirts or gods passed judgement on criminals and resolved communal conflicts. In French and Spanish islands, these masquerades were performed under the guise of carnival, a Catholic practice of riotous feasting in the period leading up to Lent. In the British islands, African masquerades were performed on Christmas Day, Boxing Day, New Year's Day and during Easter. In Jamaica, these celebrations were known as 'John Canoe', an English mishearing of an African term. Many British observers referred to the masked dancers as 'Mummers', perceiving their Afro-diasporic activities through the European folk tradition of mumming that was widely practised in the British Isles.

The meaning of the 'John Canoe' masquerades was purposefully kept secret from white observers, many of whom concluded that the participants had forgotten the significance of their own cultural practices. The idea is ludicrous and could only seem

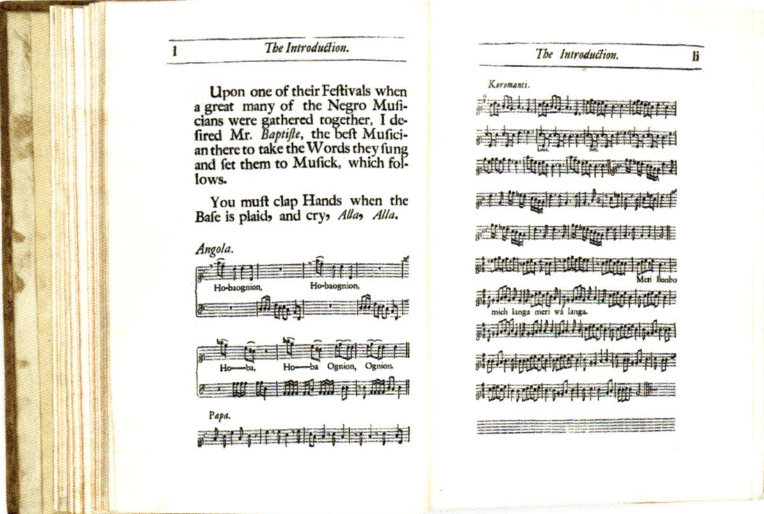

16

Hans Sloane (1660—1753).
A Voyage to the Islands of Madera, Barbados, Nieves, S. Christophers and Jamaica, vol. 1, London 1707, pp. l—li

Fitzwilliam Museum, Cambridge (15.2.l.21-22). Bequeathed by Richard, 7th Viscount Fitzwilliam, 1816. Transcription by Mr Baptiste, likely an enslaved African musician, of songs sung at a gathering of enslaved people in Jamaica, 1688

persuasive to a person already committed to denying the value of African culture. The slave-era British Caribbean was a parallel society, where the white self-proclaimed 'masters' had limited insight into what went on in the life of Black communities. Secret networks burst to the surface in the form of ever larger-scale rebellions; while outwardly pretending to be stupid, or happy, or content, beneath the surface enslaved people were always scheming on how to overthrow their oppressors. The hidden symbolism of carnival and 'John Canoe' helped channel the spirit of resistance by giving it a focused outlet. The same is true of Obeah, a system of spiritual practices based on West African religious traditions [17]. Many practitioners of Obeah acted as nodes in the rebel networks and were therefore singled out for persecution by the whites.

This spirit was by no means confined to Obeah practitioners or a handful of days in the calendar. The women greeting a ship of freshly arrived Europeans with the song 'New-come buckra … He be die' testify to the dissemination of resistance into the most seemingly innocuous contexts. Their song can be read as a direct threat to the white men, warning them not so much of the yellow fever as of the prospect of an impending violent death. The historian Julius Scott has reconstructed some of the Black communication networks that facilitated such resistance across the Caribbean.[4] Since the conspirators did not leave records of the type that entered the official archives, Scott scoured newspapers and legal proclamations in order to map attempts by the authorities to control and limit the movement of dangerous ideas and people. Just like with the futile edicts against drumming, the repeated issuing of laws to control Black communication testifies to the authorities' failure to shut it down.

4. Julius Scott, *The Common Wind: Afro-American Currents in the Age of the Haitian Revolution*, London 2018.
5. My phrasing is indebted to Ann Laura Stoler, *Along the Archival Grain: Epistemic Anxieties and Colonial Common Sense*, Princeton, NJ 2008.
6. Isaac Mendes Belisario, *Sketches of Character. In Illustration of the Habits, Occupation, and Costume of the ▮▮▮▮ Population, in the Island of Jamaica. Drawn after Nature, and in Lithography*, Kingston, Jamaica, 1837. A facsimile reproduction of this publication is found in Tim Barringer, Gillian Forrester and Barbaro Martinez-Ruiz (eds), *Art and Emancipation: Isaac Mendes Belisario and his Worlds*, New Haven, CT 2007.
7. Belisario, 'Koo. Koo. Or Actor-Boy', in Belisario 1837, n.p.
8. See note 7.

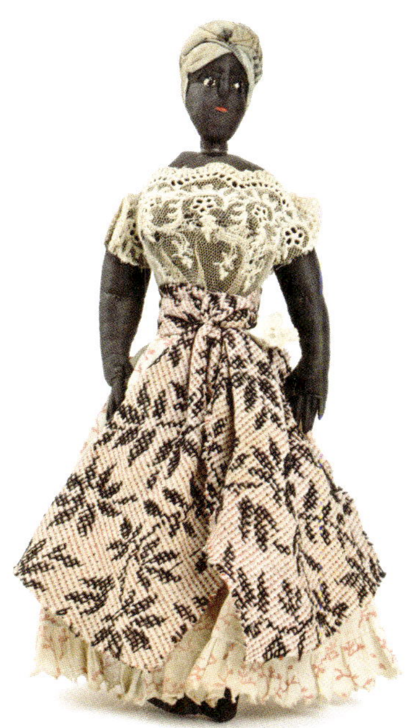

17
Unrecorded maker,
Bahia, Brazil.
**Doll representing a
Baiana (vendor or hawker)
or a practitioner of *Obeah*
or *Camdomblé* carrying a
child on her back**, about 1850.
Cloth, lace, cotton, h. 29.5 cm

Museum of Archaeology and Anthropology,
University of Cambridge (1947.550). Given
by Miss V.M. Curtis (life dates unrecorded),
1947. Bought in Bahia, about 1850

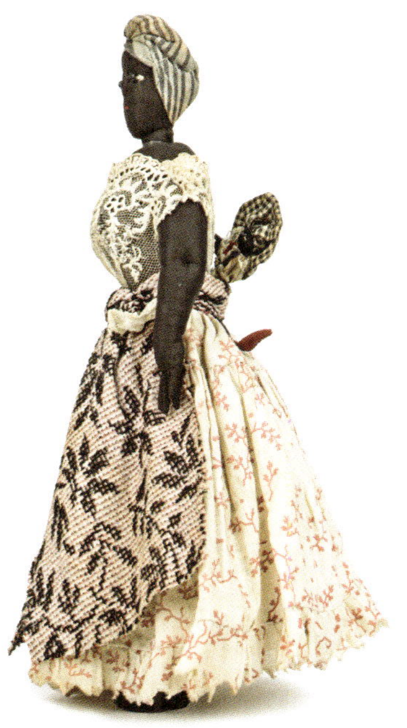

Scott's work is a good example of the unusual methodology that one needs to adopt when studying African/European encounters in the eighteenth and nineteenth centuries. It is a method of reading the archival record 'against the grain', scanning for things inadvertently recorded in passing, often at odds with the writer's racist worldview.[5] This is especially the case when trying to reconstruct Afro-diasporic masking practices which were commonly dismissed in derogatory terms even by those witnesses who clearly admired the spectacular displays, such as the Jamaican Jewish artist Isaac Mendes Belisario.

Belisario attended the 'John Canoe' masquerade held in Kingston during the Christmas holidays of 1836. He came with a sketchbook in hand, intending to draw the maskers 'from life' and 'with great attention to detail' so as to publish a series of prints. His inspiration was the then-popular genre of 'Street Cries' — collections of prints representing different character types found on the streets of a modern city, typically London or Paris. Belisario's unique selling point was that his engravings depicted the streetscape of Kingston, Jamaica, an 'exotic' imperial outpost. It was also topical. Slavery had been formally abolished in 1833—4. This did not yet mean full emancipation: in the first instance, enslavement was replaced by an 'apprenticeship' system of forced labour. The debates preceding abolition and the controversies surrounding the apprenticeship system served to keep Black life in Jamaica a subject of political interest.

Belisario's collection appeared in 1837 under the title *Sketches of Character*.[6] This series of coloured lithographs contains the earliest visual record of Jamaican 'John Canoe' maskers. The sketches were accompanied by short prose essays that contextualised the people and scenes depicted on them. The tone is often snooty and supercilious, yet Belisario does convey snippets of important information about the maskers. In the essay accompanying the Actor Boy print [19], Belisario explains that Actor Boys compete by parading in the central streets of Kingston, inviting passers-by to decide who is 'the smartest dressed'.[7] Each Actor Boy is accompanied by a band that 'consists of drums and fifes only, to which music the Actor stalks most majestically, oftentimes stopping to afford the by-standers a fair opportunity of gazing at him.'[8] Together with the print, this gives a vivid picture of what this performance may have looked like.

Belisario also offers a close depiction of the Actor Boy's towering headdress, helping the person viewing his prints parse it.

The foundation of it is an old hat, affording the wearer the means of sustaining the superstructure, to which it is firmly attached, and composed of various colored beads, bugles, spangles, pieces of looking-glass, tinsel, &c. attached to a pasteboard form trimmed round the edges with silver lace, surmounted with feathers. The garments are of muslin, silk, satin, and ribbons.[9]

Yet something is missing. The problem with these explanatory captions is not that they are inaccurate, but that they are partial and incomplete. Belisario describes the surface appearance but not the spiritual meanings of the performance and the costumes. Kenneth Bilby has remarked that as an effect of Belisario's own cultural ignorance, we get to see the visible surface without any indication as to 'the deeper significance these Christmas rituals almost certainly had for the performers themselves — meanings that, like the rest of the immense background of which they were a part, ended up being 'cropped', unknowingly, from Belisario's images.'[10]

Belisario's eye for detail and his skill as an artist mean that, even in their cropped state, his sketches give a unique insight into how Black Jamaicans performed an annual masquerade. In looking at them, we need to develop a double vision, learning how to scan the surface for the hidden or disguised meanings that the artist could not see. Contemporary scholars like Bilby have connected the details found in Belisario's Actor Boy prints to symbolic elements still present in West African masking traditions. This includes the white face mask itself as well as the magnificent crest, the particular choice of colours, and the incorporation of feathers, fans, bells, birds, stars and diamonds into the costume. The striking similarities between one of Belisario's Actor Boy prints and one of the Igbo maiden spirit masks collected in 1911 from Agukwu-Nri, Southern Nigeria by British colonial anthropologist Northcote Whitridge Thomas [18],[11] are not coincidental; both the spirit masks and the Actor Boy costumes are the products of a greater cultural tradition that encompasses both sides of the Atlantic. We could say that the Igbo spirit maidens are among the gods and ancestors who accompanied some of their charges across the Atlantic to dance on a distant shore. We just need to learn how to see them.

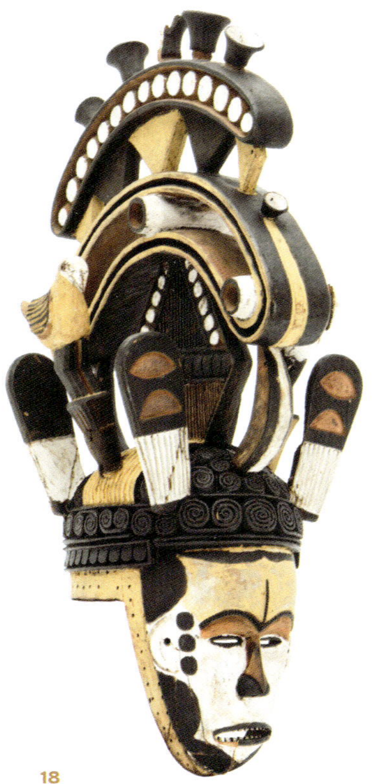

18

Unrecorded Igbo maker, Nibo, Anambra State, Nigeria. ***Isi abogefi***, face mask with headdress including combs, birds and crests, early 20th century. Egbu wood, pigment, metal and copper, h. 71 cm

Museum of Archaeology and Anthropology, University of Cambridge (Z 13689). Bought from Northcote Whitridge Thomas (1868—1936) with Prof. Anthony Ashley Bevan's subscriptions to the Accessions Fund. Collected by N.W. Thomas in 1909—13 while working for the Colonial Office and stationed in Nigeria [not in exhibition]

9. See note 7.
10. Kenneth Bilby, 'More Than Met the Eye: African-Jamaican Festivities in the Time of Belisario', in Barringer et al. 2007, pp. 121—33 (p. 123).
11. For contextualisation of this mask, see Carmen Vida, 'Conservation Notes: Maiden Spirit Mask', [Re:]Entanglements, October 2020, https://re-entanglements.net/maiden-spirit/ (accessed 17 August 2024).

Selected reading
• Émeric Bergeaud, *Stella: A Novel of the Haitian Revolution*, 1859, trans. C. Mucher and L.S. Curtis, New York 2015.
• Erna Brodber, *Nothing's Mat*, Kingston, Jamaica 2014
• William Earle Junior, *Obi: or, The History of Three-Fingered Jack: In a Series of Letters from a Resident in Jamaica to his Friend in England*, London 1800
• Raphael Chijioke Njoku, *West African Masking Traditions and Diaspora Masquerade Carnivals: History, Memory, and Transnationalism*, Rochester, NY 2020
• J.T. Williams, *The Lizzie and Belle Mysteries: Drama and Danger*, London 2022
• J.T. Williams, *The Lizzie and Belle Mysteries: Portraits and Poison*, London 2023

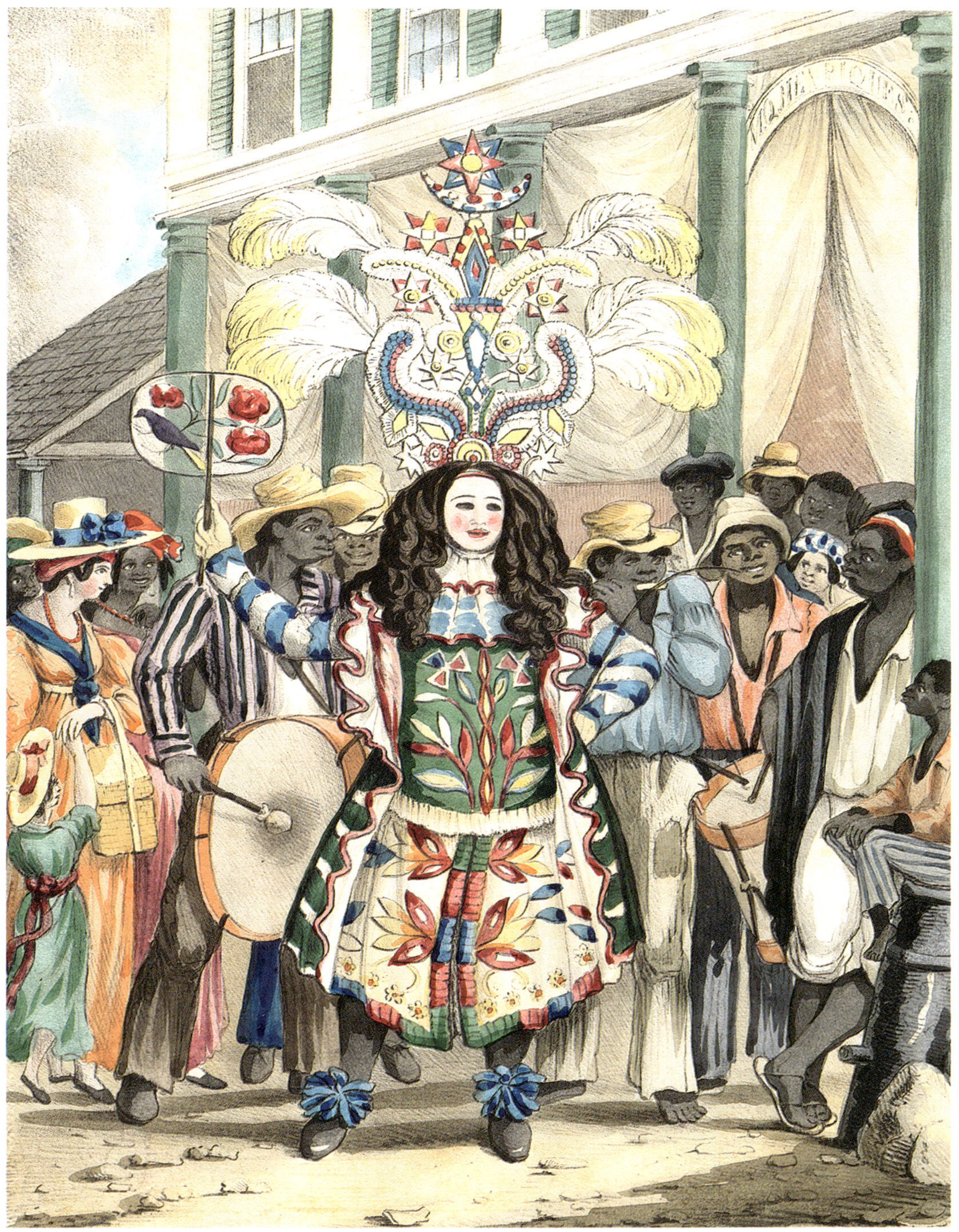

19

Isaac Mendes Belisario (1795—1849).
'Koo, Koo, or Actor-Boy', Kingston, Jamaica, October 1837. Lithograph, 37.5 × 24.5 cm.

Inscribed (above title): 'Drawn from Life, and Lithog[raphe]d by J.M. Belisario' and (below title): 'Printed by A. Duperly'. Plate from *Sketches of Character: In Illustration of the Habits, Occupation, and Costume of the ▨ Population, in the Island of Jamaica. Drawn after Nature, and in Lithography*, Kingston, Jamaica 1837–8. Printed unpaginated book with hand-coloured lithograph. Yale Center for British Art, Paul Mellon Collection, Rare Books and Manuscripts (Folio A 2011 24). [Version in exhibition: The Bodleian Libraries, University of Oxford (RHO) 522.12 t. 1 (v.1)]

Olaudah Equiano's roots

According to his autobiography, Olaudah Equiano (also known as Gustavus Vassa) was born in Isseke, West Africa, in what is now Anambra State, Nigeria. His life story, first published in 1789, offers rich descriptions of his homeland and his people, the Igbo.

Equiano tells us about Igbo society, customs and religious beliefs. Music, dance and ritual played a vital role. Masking and oral tradition were important Igbo cultural tools that ritualised and reinforced complex systems of social belonging and spiritual responsibility. He also wrote devastatingly about the loss of his mother and siblings caused by slave traders capturing him for sale across the Atlantic when he was a small boy.

In the eighteenth century, the Igbo lived in autonomous kinship-based towns governed by senior leaders, judges and council members. Members of Equiano's family held such positions. Communities of farmers, traders and craftspeople generated wealth and expertise by cultivating palm oil, making pottery, spinning and weaving cotton, and producing their own iron tools and weapons.

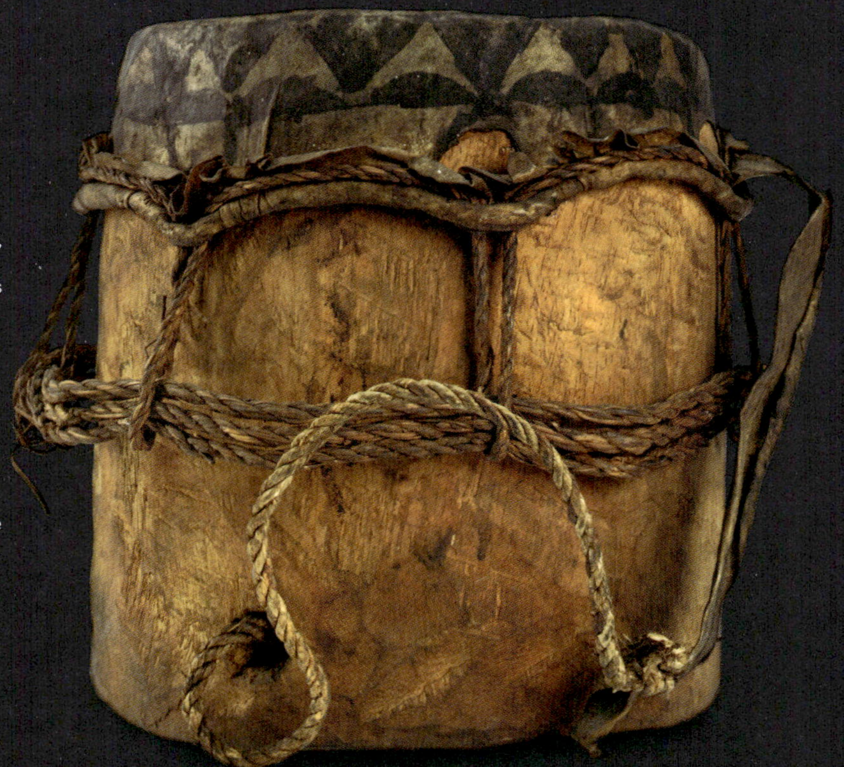

20
Unrecorded Igbo maker, Awgbu (Obu), Anambra State, Nigeria.
***Igba* (drum)**, unrecorded date, probably early 20th century. Wood, skin, pigment and plant fibre, h. 23.5 cm; diam. 24 cm

Museum of Archaeology and Anthropology, University of Cambridge (Z 14200). Bought from Northcote Whitridge Thomas (1868—1936) with Prof. Anthony Ashley Bevan's subscriptions to the Accessions Fund. Collected by N.W. Thomas in 1909—10 while working for the Colonial Office and stationed in Nigeria

Music and dance are vital aspects of Igbo culture. This wooden *igba* (drum) was most likely commissioned by N.W. Thomas and is typical of those made for use in village ceremonial life. The body comprises a carved hollow cylinder open at both ends with a hole at the bottom for a rope handle. The skin cover, decorated with black geometric patterns, is tied onto the drum with rope bound into complex plaits. Wooden pegs may originally have been present to tighten the skin, but these have been lost.

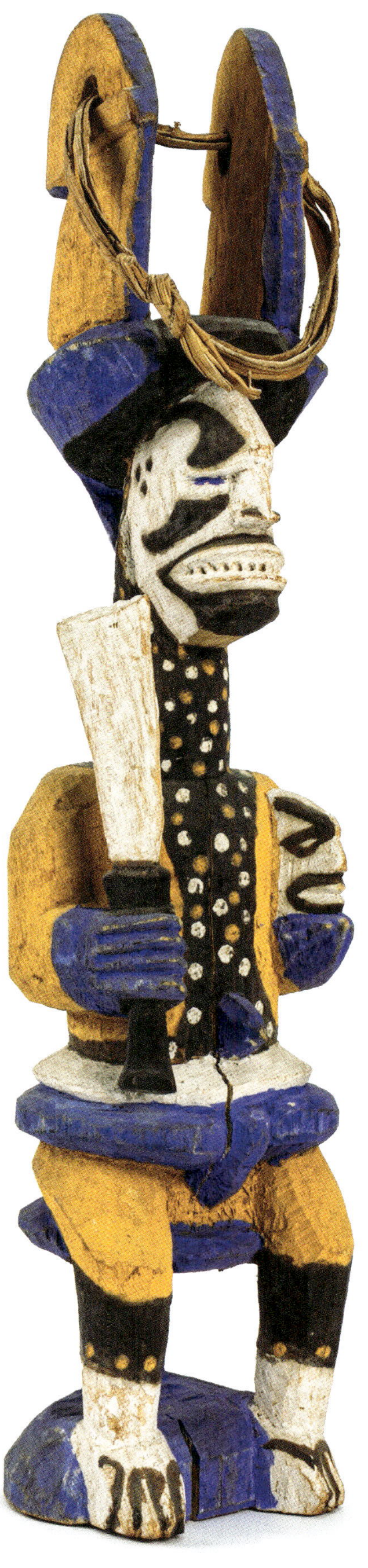

Unrecorded Igbo maker,
Akwa, Anambra State, Nigeria.
Ikenga of *Alusi*, unrecorded date, probably
20th century. Wood, pigments and plant fibre,
h. 48 cm

Museum of Archaeology and Anthropology, University of Cambridge
(1980.1052 A). Given by John Reginald Victor Smyth (1900—1985),
1980. Acquired by Smyth, either brand new or commissioned directly
from the maker, when a Superintendent of Agriculture, Nigeria,
1928—36

This carved figure represents the *Alusi* (spirit) of time, success
and achievement. Usually maintained by men, but sometimes
by women, it symbolises sovereignty and resilience as well as
achievement and industry. A powerful and enduring symbol
of Igbo culture in Nigeria and its diaspora, it still resonates
today, manifesting in examples such as Nnedi Okorafor's
2020 children's novel *Ikenga*. This Nigerian superhero story
about resistance, justice, power and control features a boy who
draws his powers from a magical *Ikenga*, using them for good.

The 'Africa Trade'

Trade in captive African people and natural resources from both Africa and the Caribbean, in exchange for British exports, grew massively throughout the eighteenth century.

Britain was at the centre of this lucrative 'Africa Trade' through the Royal African Company and private investors. Port cities such as London, Bristol and Liverpool boomed. Some African merchants and political leaders participated by exchanging captives (often from outside their communities) for guns, textiles, alcohol and other commodities.

Many British men and women viewed the Atlantic slave trade as essential to the nation's success and an inevitable part of securing a range of fashionable commodities such as African gold, mahogany and ivory, and Caribbean sugar, rum, cacao, tortoiseshell and hardwoods. African lives were deemed expendable in the pursuit of power and profit.

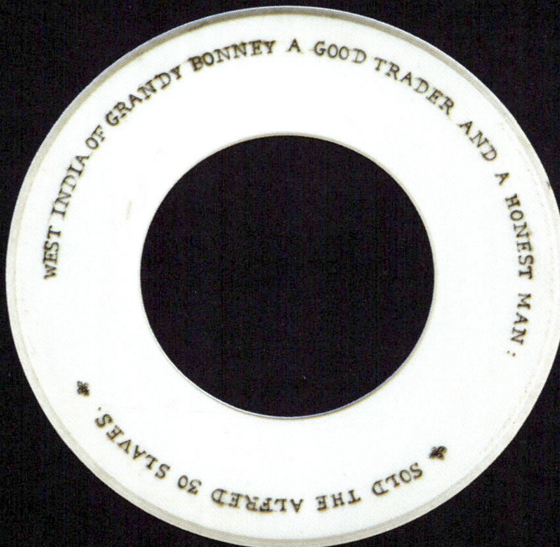

22

Unrecorded maker, probably in Bonny, near Port Harcourt, Nigeria. **Trade token** formed as pierced disc given by John Trousdall to Young West India, 1788. Ivory, black pigment, diam. 12.2 cm

Inscribed (obverse): 'WEST INDIA OF GRANDY BONNEY A GOOD TRADER AND A HONEST MAN SOLD THE ALFRED 30 SLAVES'; (reverse): 'THE GIFT OF CAPTAIN JOHN TROUSDALL TO YOUNG WEST INDIA OF GRANDY BONNEY'. Wisbech & Fenland Museum, Wisbech (WISFM 1870.13.78). Part of Thomas Clarkson's campaign chest. Acquired by Thomas Clarkson in Bristol about 1788

This token was given by English sea-captain John Trousdall (Trousdale) to African trader Young West India of Bonny (near Port Harcourt, Nigeria), following the sale of thirty enslaved African people. European traders in enslaved people gave these tokens to African counterparts to assure future European business partners of their reliability. In this token Trousdall testifies to Young West India as 'a good trader and an honest man'. The Trans-Atlantic Slave Trade Database reveals that Trousdall jointly captained the four-gun, 199-tonnage, Bristol-registered slaving ship *Alfred* on a voyage to purchase 420 captives. Having set sail from Bristol on 21 December 1787, and embarked 359 enslaved people at Bonny (thirty supplied by India), the *Alfred* arrived at St Vincent on 7 August 1788. Only 328 captives disembarked, meaning thirty-one captives had died during the journey, along with four of the thirty-eight-man crew. The *Alfred* returned to Bristol on 19 August 1788.

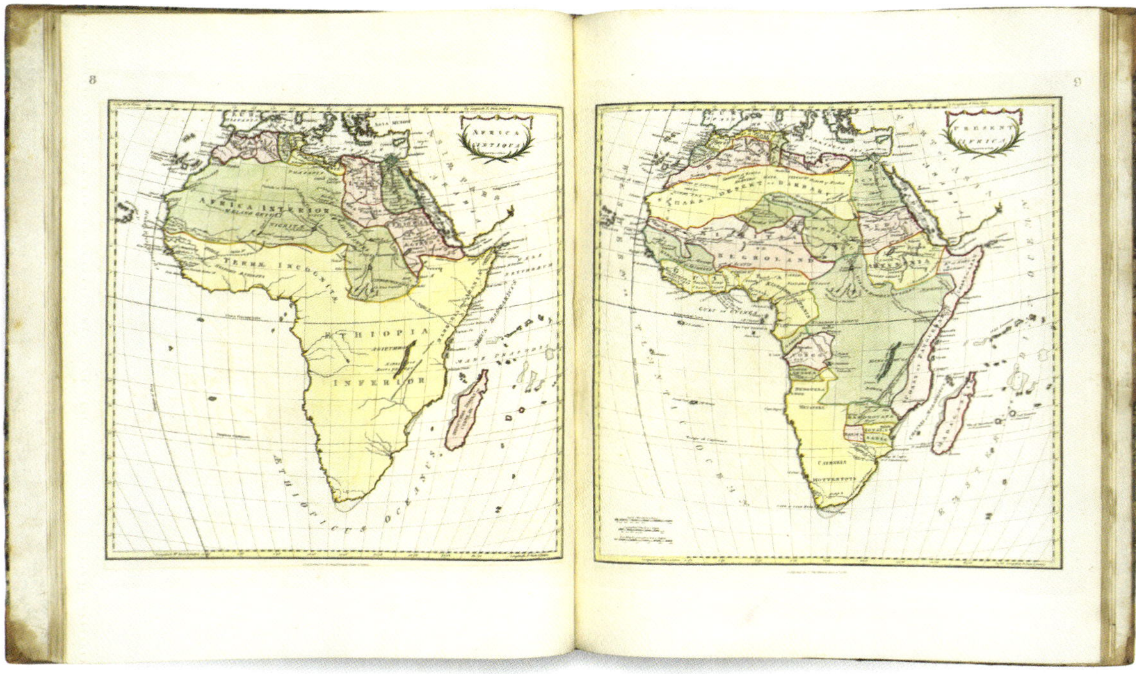

23

Thomas Stackhouse (1756—1836).
'Africa Antiqua' and 'Present Africa'

In Thomas Stackhouse, *The Universal Atlas … to Illustrate and Explain Ancient and Modern Geography*, 2nd edn, London 1786. Fitzwilliam Museum, Cambridge (23.D.10). Bequeathed by Richard, 7th Viscount Fitzwilliam, 1816; purchased by him, 1790

An antiquary and prolific writer on a variety of subjects, including ancient, pre-Christian British history, Quaker Thomas Stackhouse first published his *Universal Atlas* in 1783 to illustrate both ancient and then-modern global geography. Rudimentary past and more detailed present divisions of countries and place names were presented on opposite pages. His representation of 'Present Africa' (right side) depicts the continent reimagined from a colonial perspective. Africa is shown neatly carved up by European colonial powers and with English names assigned, at a time when vast areas were still unknown to European geographers. The complex reality of African polities is erased in Stackhouse's cartographic rendition.

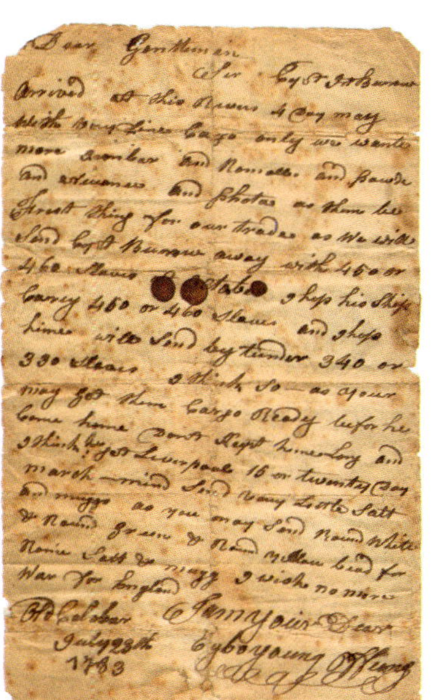

24

Egboyoung Effeong of Old Calabar
(life dates unrecorded, active 1780s).
Letter to Liverpool merchants, 23 July 1783.

Wisbech & Fenland Museum, Wisbech (TCC/273). Possibly originally part of Thomas Clarkson's campaign chest

Egboyoung Effeong was an African — likely Efik — merchant and trader in enslaved people who prospered through trade with European nations, including Britain. This letter details his demands for goods — above all iron bars, 'romalies' and ammunition specified as trading commodities; and salt, mugs and round-shaped, white, green and yellow glass beads as currency — in exchange for 'a very fine cargo' of 460 enslaved people. An important international port since the sixteenth century, Old Calabar (in present-day south-eastern Nigeria) became a major hub during the transatlantic slave trade boom. It was here that more than 62,000 captive African men, women and children were sold to European traders in enslaved people between 1772 and 1775. Many of the people trafficked through Old Calabar and its neighbouring port of Duke Town (Atakpa) were Igbo, like Olaudah Equiano.

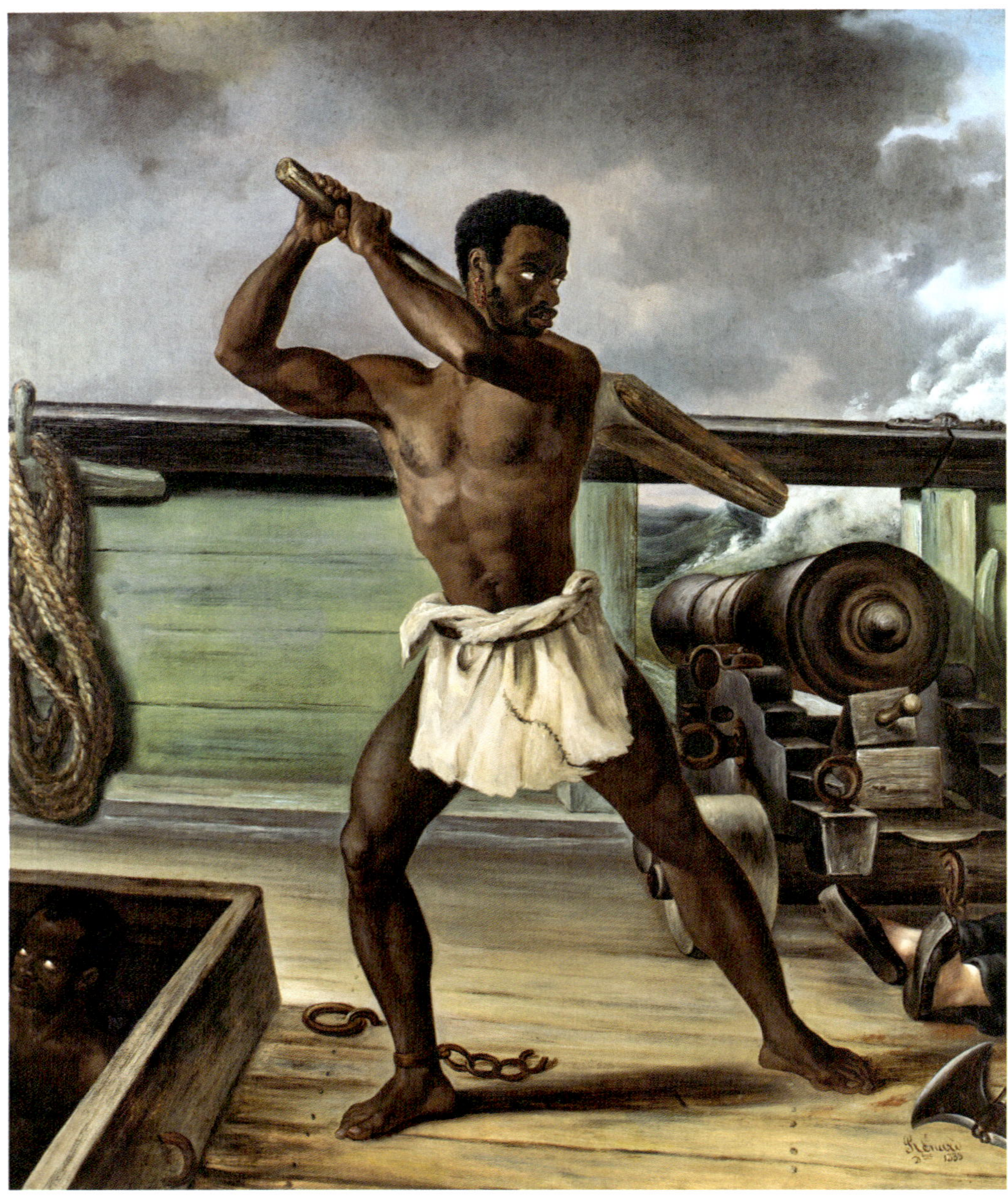

Édouard-Antoine Renard
(1802—1857).
The Rebellion of an Enslaved Man aboard a Slaving Ship, 1839
(*Révolte d'un esclave sur un navire négrier*). Oil on canvas, 99 × 83 cm (unframed)

Collections des musées d'Art et d'Histoire de La Rochelle, France (MNM 1987.1.9). Bought in 1987

Renard's painting debunks European notions of African people passively accepting the inhumane conditions of their enslavement aboard slaving ships during the Atlantic crossing from West African ports to Caribbean ones. An enslaved man has broken free from his shackles, and is shown heroically fighting back, swinging an oar at his unseen captor. A second enslaved man, who has also freed himself, is shown emerging from a hatch in the deck to assist. The prone feet of an already slain enslaver are shown at bottom right. An estimated one in every ten slaving ships experienced onboard resistance, but the true number was likely far higher. Incidents of rebellion during the so-called 'Middle Passage' were often recorded by slaving-ship captains as part of insurance claims but these did not include other forms of resistance by the onboard captives, such as suicide.

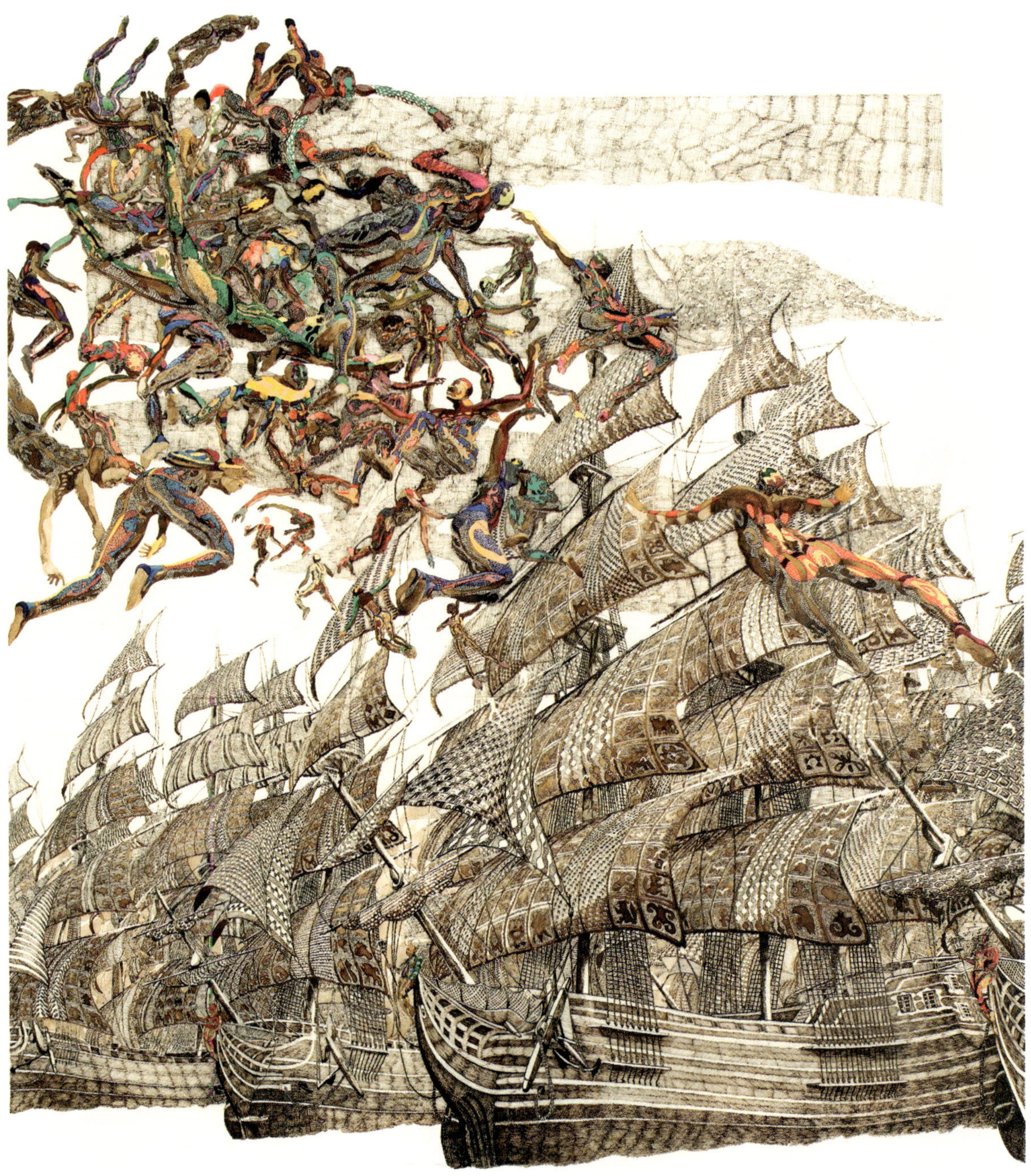

Julien Sinzogan (born 1967). ***Land Ho!***, 2010
(*Terre en vue!*). Coloured inks and acrylic
on paper, 150 × 110 cm

Private collection, London © Julien Sinzogan. Left panel of triptych

Sinzogan's pen-and-ink work references the annual *Egúngún* masquerades of Yorubaland, where returning ancestor-spirits join living descendants in days of communal festivities. Local spirits emblazoned with traditional insignia float down to welcome the phantom galleons bringing home long-lost ancestors from the Diaspora. The sepia-tinted spirits returning to the living world recover the colourful liveries identifying their lineage. Sinzogan employs the Yoruba conception of joyful reunion between humans and their spirit-ancestors to salve the long-standing trauma of the transatlantic slave trade.

Life on British Caribbean plantations

Long, gruelling hours of backbreaking and dangerous work. Extreme heat, poor diet and malnutrition, and rudimentary living conditions. Ever-present threats of physical and sexual violence, injury and disease. This was the daily reality for millions of enslaved people across the Caribbean.

Caribbean plantations operated at an industrial scale, mass-producing sugar, rum, coffee and cacao. They generated vast profits, but their owners saw limited value in improving the conditions endured by enslaved labourers.

When an enslaved woman, man or child died or became disabled through illness or injury, they were replaced by newly arrived captives. Rather than provide better material circumstances for those already trafficked, British enslavers viewed Africa as providing an endless supply of dispensable labour.

Under British Caribbean and American law, children born to enslaved women were automatically the 'property' of their enslavers and were also enslaved.

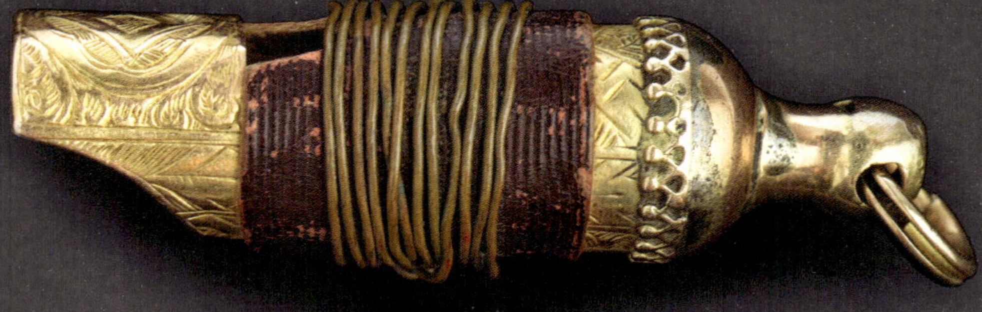

27

Unrecorded maker, probably Bajan goldsmith. **Enslaver or plantation-overseer's whistle**, unrecorded date, probably 18th or early 19th century. Whistle: gold, twine, 4.7 × 1.3 cm

Fitzwilliam Museum, Cambridge (M.4-2008). Purse (not shown): leather. Fitzwilliam Museum, Cambridge (M.5-2008). Given by Jean Ivey Cambell Bruce Austin, 2008. Inherited from the donor's father, Col. J.B.J. Austin, by descent through the Austin family, who had emigrated to Barbados in 1629, becoming plantation owners and enslavers

This whistle may appear insignificant, but its small scale belies the routine role it played in marshalling the exploitation of enslaved labourers. It materialises violent, complex and entangled histories that unite Cambridge and Atlantic enslavement. It was designed as an active instrument in the slavery economy: it was blown by overseers to signal orders and control the enslaved workforce on a British-owned plantation in Barbados. Likely used in conjunction with the cracking of a whip, its sound represented power and authority to the owner or user, but brutal labour, violence and oppression to the captive worker.

28

Unrecorded compiler,
likely Hillsborough plantation manager.
'Inventory of Slaves, Mules, Cattle and plantation ustensils [sic] and & other stores on Hillsborough Estate, the 22nd April 1818'.
Manuscript inventory of the Greg family's Hillsborough plantation, Dominica

Cambridge University Library (RCMS 266(4)). Presented by Mrs Margaret Longden and Miss Natalie Greg (daughters of Robert Philips Greg) to the Royal Commonwealth Society, 1964. RCS collections acquired by Cambridge University Library, 1993

This inventory is typical of ones drawn up across British colonial plantations in the eighteenth and nineteenth centuries to keep an itemised record of property that could then be used in assessing its value for mortgages, probate or lines of credit. Compiled in April 1818, this inventory details the movable assets of the Hillsborough plantation, Dominica, owned by the Greg family. It records the names, role, age and ability of the 139 enslaved African people forced to work on the plantation. The seventy-one adult men and male infants and sixty-eight adult women and infant females are listed immediately above mules and cattle, and the movable property in various buildings. Such lists reveal how human beings were commodified and dehumanised as part of the economic machine of colonial slavery.

Kimathi Donkor: rethinking canonical history paintings through critical fabulation

Niru Ratnam

Kimathi Donkor makes paintings that re-centre Black historical figures who have been ignored by mainstream Western history, or who were victims of state and police brutality. Donkor references and uses the tools of the genre of history painting, evoking that visual language to actively difference the canon. Donkor has been working in this way since the early 2000s, and these works can be seen as prefiguring more recent debates in both art history and wider society. In particular, Donkor's way of working has a strong parallel with the academic Saidiya Hartman's idea of 'critical fabulation', a way of working that Hartman says, 'troubles the line between history and imagination'.[1]

The notion of critical fabulation is a strategy that produces a counter-history of those Black subjects who were enslaved or who fought against slavery or were subject to more contemporary forms of oppression. It adds to the gaps where conventional history in the form of archives or written testimonies are scarce. In this way these Black subjects, who have been either largely erased or at best used as ciphers, are given a fuller agency, rooted in whatever historical record is left but re-thinking the archive through imagined moments and futures. Donkor has produced works that feature figures such as Toussaint L'Ouverture, one of the leaders of the Haitian Revolution against the island's French colonial occupiers, and Nanny of the Maroons, who led a community of former slaves in guerrilla warfare against the British authorities in Jamaica.

In his 2004 *Bacchus and Ariadne* [29], Donkor aimed to provide a pictorial response to the genocidal intentions given by the French General Charles Leclerc, Napoleon's brother-in-law, who was in charge of suppressing the Haitian uprising, to kill all mountain-dwelling Haitians over twelve years of age. In this painting, Donkor draws on Titian's 1523 painting *Bacchus and Ariadne* (National Gallery, London), reimagining the mythical narratives this canonical painting is predicated upon — a strategy he has used throughout his career. Often, as is the case here, Donkor will invert the composition of an earlier painting so that his painting might be understood as answering back to or facing off with the earlier work, reasserting the presence of an erased history in defiance of one that is well-known and taught as part of the Western artistic canon. In Titian's work, the chaos of Bacchus and his followers is initially alarming to Ariadne, who looks startled on the left of the painting, but is ultimately well-meaning. However, in Donkor's painting, the chaos brought by the French troops is linked to their orders to wipe out the Haitians. There is no promise of safety for the figure on the right of Donkor's painting. This is a history painting that stops at the moment before the erasure of its subjects, insisting instead on bringing their presence back.

In a more recent painting, *Mary Prince dictating to Susanna Strickland* [106], and two works on paper, *The Life of Mary Prince (Mary Ingham dictating to Mary Prince)* [30] and *The Life of Mary*

1 Alexis Okeowo, 'How Saidiya Hartman Retells the History of Black Life', *The New Yorker*, 19 October 2020, https://www. newyorker.com/magazine/2020/10/26/ how-saidiya-hartman-retells-the-history-of-black-life (accessed 23 August 2024).

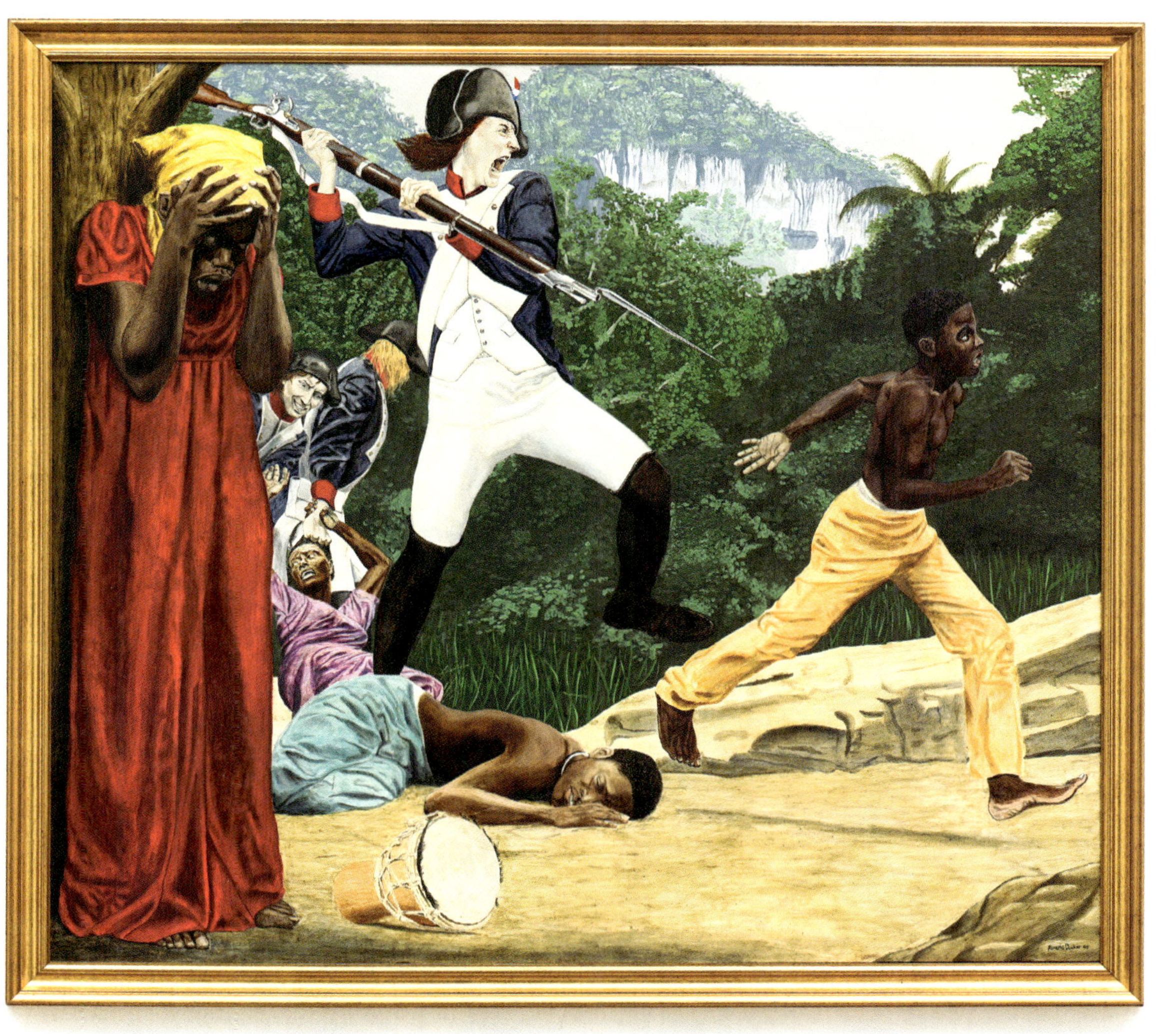

29
Kimathi Donkor (born 1965). *Bacchus and Ariadne*, 2004. Oil on linen, 144 × 164 cm (framed)

Courtesy of the Artist and Niru Ratnam, London © The Artist

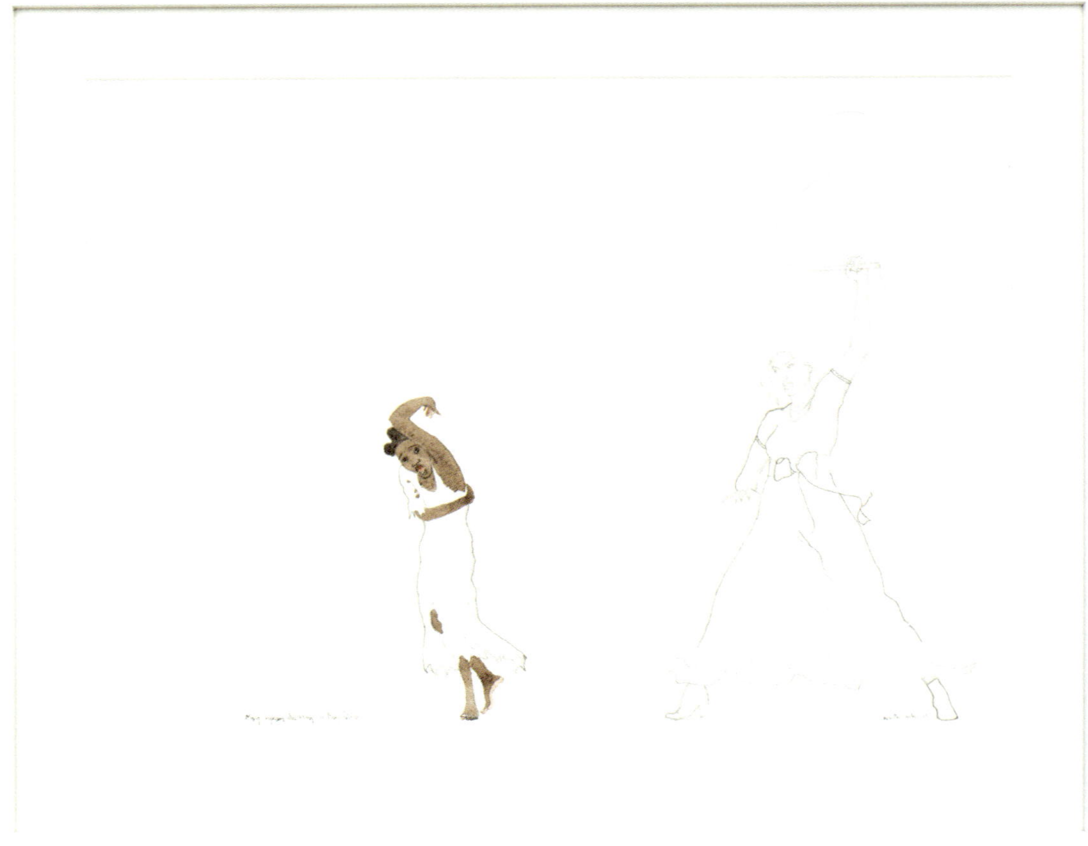

30

Kimathi Donkor (born 1965).
***The Life of Mary Prince (Mary
Ingham dictating to Mary
Prince)***, 2023.
Watercolour, ink and pencil on
paper, 39.5 × 49.5 cm (framed)
Courtesy of the Artist and Niru Ratnam,
London © The Artist. Left side of *Diptych
of the Life of Mary Prince*

Prince (Mary Prince dictating to Susanna Strickland) [31],
which together form a work titled *Diptych of the Life of Mary
Prince*, Donkor references the story of the escaped slave who
became an abolitionist. Prince was born in the late 1780s to
enslaved parents in Bermuda. Her last enslavers moved in 1828
from Antigua to London, where Prince was able to escape, and
was taken in by abolitionist Thomas Pringle, Secretary of the
Anti-Slavery Society. There, she related her story to his surrogate
daughter, author and abolitionist Susanna Strickland Moodie. In
February 1831, *The History of Mary Prince, A West Indian Slave,
Related by Herself* was published, which described the horrific
treatment Mary had suffered as a slave, as well as detailing the
system of slavery. The book was the first life of a Black woman
to be published in Britain, and was hugely important in the
campaign to abolish the institution of slavery, being reprinted
twice more during its year of publication alone [105]. *The History
of Mary Prince* remains to this day a powerful testament to
appalling abuse and determined survival. In these pendant
works, we see Prince's progress from terrified slave, cowering
at the cruelty of her enslaver, through to what she became:

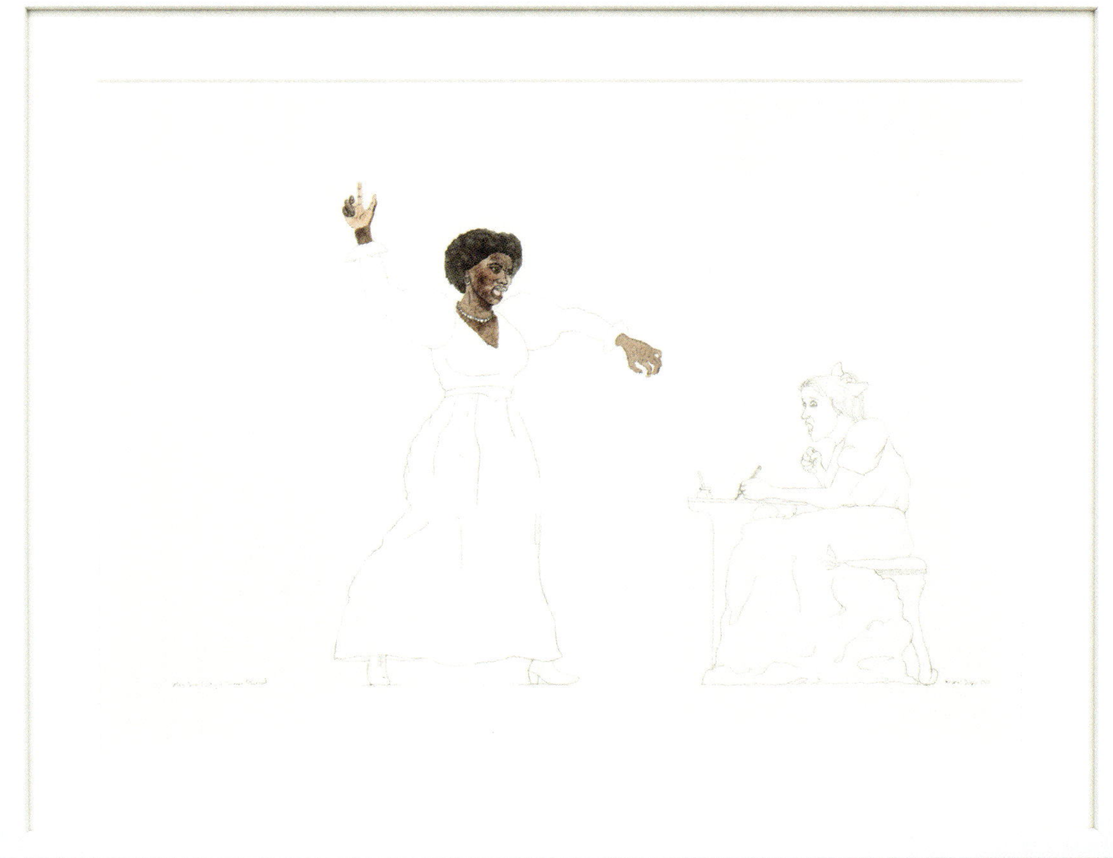

31

Kimathi Donkor (born 1965).
The Life of Mary Prince (Mary Prince dictating to Susanna Strickland), 2023.
Watercolour, ink and pencil on paper, 39.5 × 49.5 cm (framed)
Courtesy of the Artist and Niru Ratnam, London © The Artist. Right side of *Diptych of the Life of Mary Prince*

2. Mark Rappolt, 'Kimathi Donkor: History Painting Female', *Independent*, March 2023, https://www.independenthq.com/features/kimathi-donkor-history-painting-remade (accessed 23 July 2024).

a storyteller, an abolitionist and a rebel, gloriously in charge of her own narrative.

As Mark Rappolt has noted in his discussion of Donkor's work:

> In reality, history painting was more often than not exploited to tell a pack of lies, whether that lying occurred through omission, embellishment or plain making it up. Far from universal, they were white lies — bar the occasional 'noble savage' orbiting the white heroes, as in Benjamin West's *The Death of General Wolfe* of 1770.

Donkor's paintings address these lies and give agency back to figures who have been denied it for too long, 'insisting that we remember the histories Western societies have buried in their grand narratives of progress'.[2]

Forms of resistance

Enslaved people continually fought back and resisted in many different ways — both non-violent and violent. They feigned injury and illness, worked slowly, sold produce or pilfered goods illicitly, broke tools and damaged crops to sabotage productivity. They shared knowledge about medicine, community and spiritual care, and abortion.

Others escaped captivity, becoming 'runaways'. While some joined family members on other plantations or fled to relative anonymity in ports and on the seas, others formed self-sufficient communities of maroons that sought refuge on the margins of plantation tyranny.

Organised, large-scale, armed uprisings were a frequent reaction to the system's inhumanity. Men and women worked together in these armed struggles, with women acting as leaders, strategists, warriors, conduits of information and organisers of community provisioning.

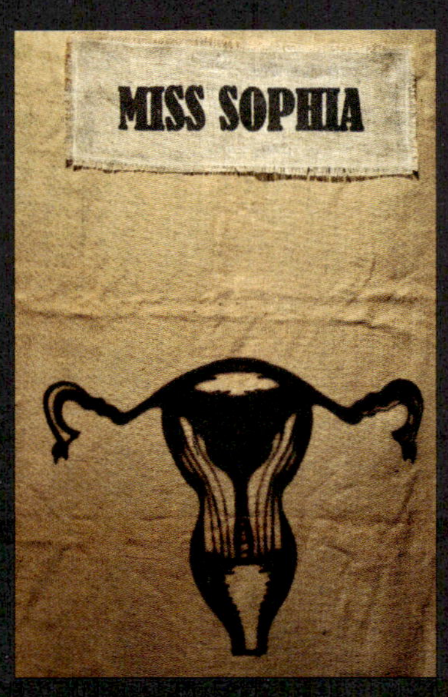

1

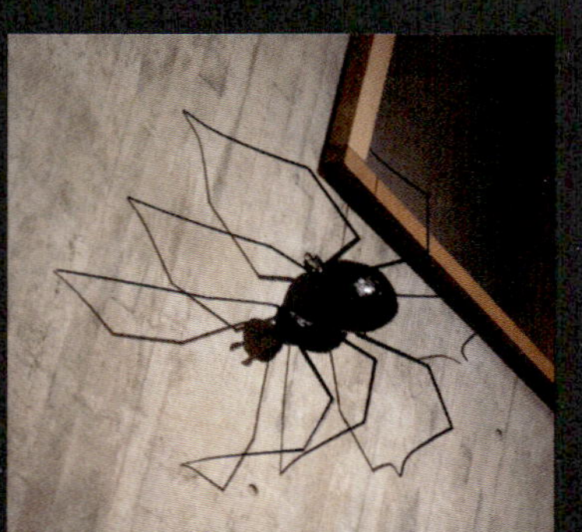

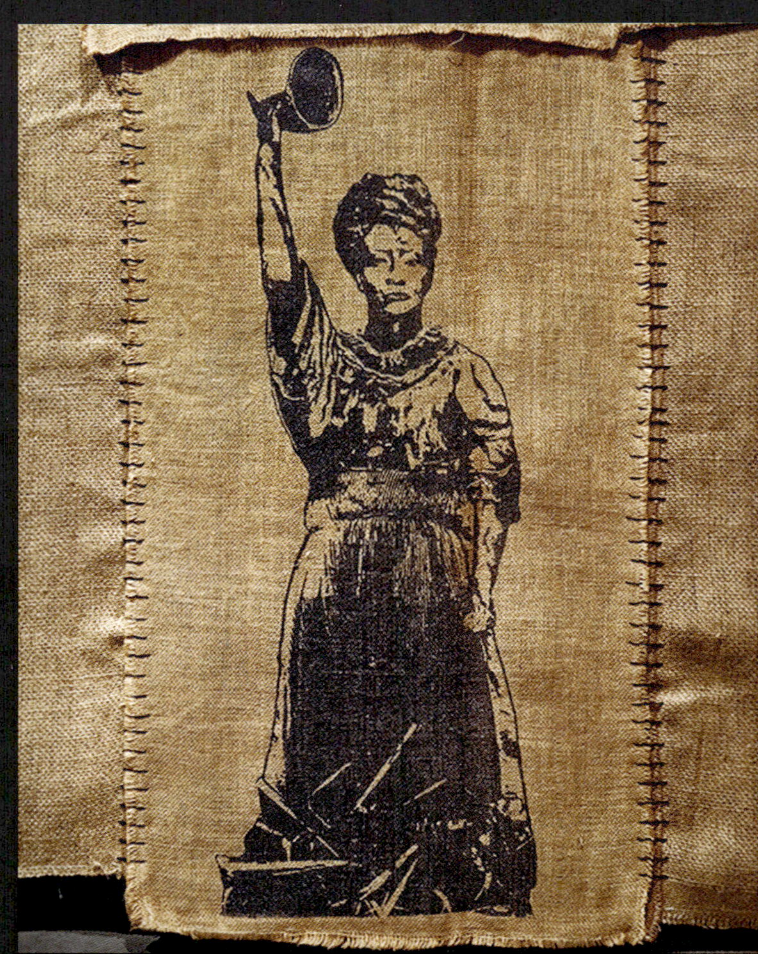

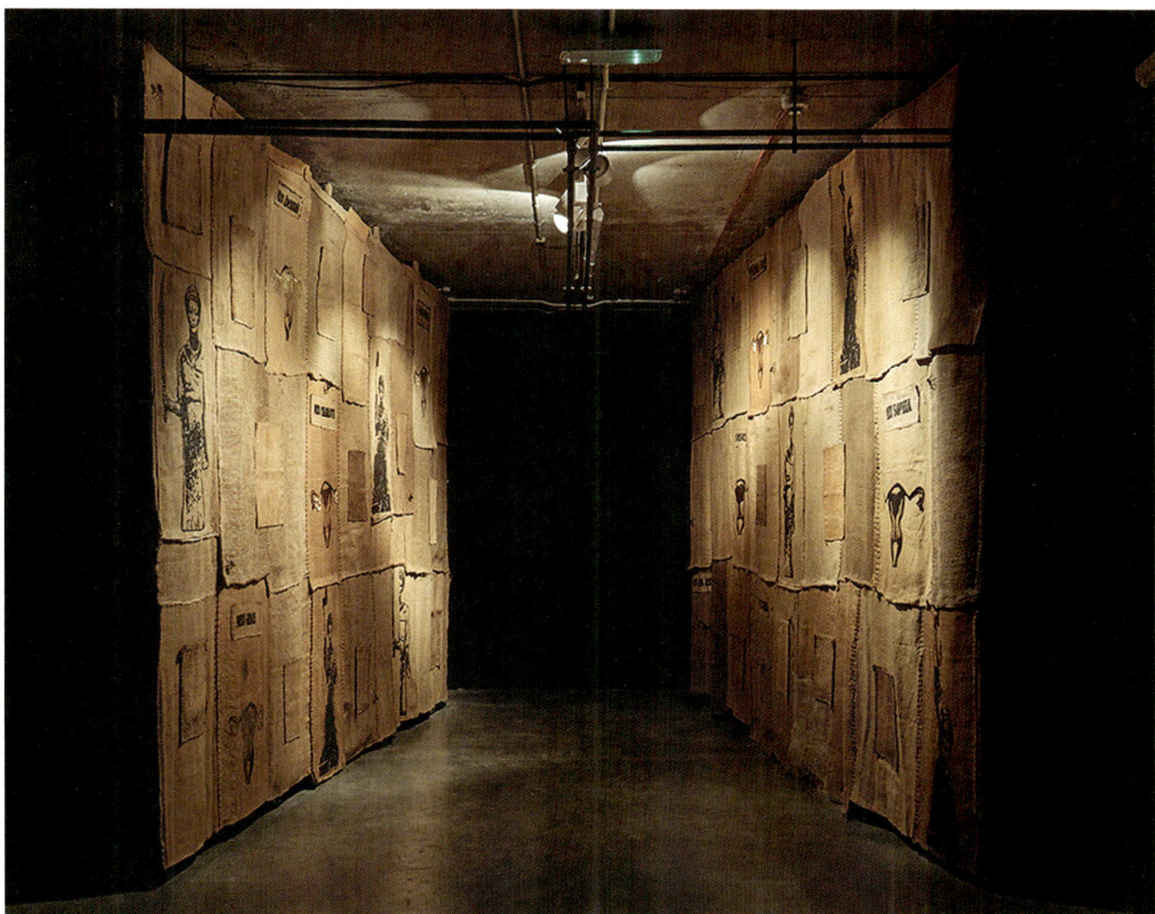

Karen McLean (born 1959). ***Ar'n't I a Woman! Woven Bodies 1**, 2021. Black and gold screen printing and branding on handmade hessian sacking made from recycled and new materials, dyed with tea and coffee, animal suture thread, 3D-printed plastic spiders, cowry shells, snap fasteners and Velcro tape, each panel: 5.28 × 3 m

Installation view above: *BLUE POWER / Ar'n't I A Woman!* (Block 336, London, 20 May—12 June 2021). Collection of the artist © Karen McLean

Details (left)
1. Miss Sophia's womb
2. Anansi, the oppressor-tricker
3. Queen Nanny, leader of the Jamaican Windward Maroons

Recalling Sojourner Truth's 'Ain't I a Woman?' speech of 1851, McLean's work subtly moves from a position of questioning to declaration about the multiple aspects that made up the lives of captive women. The enslaved woman's body was exploited and often violated, but she was also stoic and resistant, drawing on botanical knowledge to govern her womb, and finding fleeting moments of joy through dancing and celebration.

'Sophia' and the names of other enslaved women included in this work were found by McLean in an indenture for the Gale plantation in Jamaica, now in the Black Cultural Archives, Brixton. Enslaved women were not allowed to be given or use the title 'Miss', since this was reserved for white women. McLean deliberately ignores these historic racist hierarchies, honouring specific enslaved women, such as 'Miss Sophia', with this title. She portrays individuals via their reproductive organs rather than their faces to highlight enslaved women's resistance and defiance through the control they took over their wombs.

McLean also specifically portrays several crucial women freedom fighters who deserve better recognition, including Queen Nanny. Nanny was leader of the Windward Maroons, a community of formerly enslaved Africans who fought a guerilla war against the British authorities in eighteenth-century Jamaica. After suffering sustained losses, the British signed a treaty with Nanny and her maroon forces on 20 April 1740, granting them land, certain economic benefits and political autonomy.

The presence of Anansi, the multifaceted storytelling and trickster spider from Akan (present-day Ghana) folklore, reminds us of the importance of oral history, connecting the past to the present and preserving cultural traditions. Anansi stories gave enslaved people hope and represented resistance and survival as Anansi was always able to trick his oppressors.

Russell Newell (born 1965).
**Ten hair combs telling
the story of the Jamaican
Maroons**, 2013. Silver-plated
aluminium, 17.8 × 7.5 cm

Fitzwilliam Museum, Cambridge
(AF.5.2013—AF.14-2013). Given by the
artist, 2013 © Russell Newell. Commissioned
by the Fitzwilliam Museum for its exhibition
*Origins of the Afro Comb: 6,000 Years
of Culture, Politics and Identity*
(2 July—3 November 2013)

1. *At home in Africa*
2. *Capture!!*
3. *Arrival in a strange land*
4. *Escape!*
5. *To the Mountains*
6. *Unity of the Tribes*
7. *The fearless Captain Cudjoe*
8. *Ambush*
9. *The final victory over the English*
10. *The Peace Treaty*

Queen Nanny of the Eastern
(Windward) Maroons and Captain
Cudjoe of the Western (Leeward)
Maroons played key roles in colonial
resistance in Jamaica. During the First
Maroon War both groups resisted
eradication by British colonial forces
due to superior territorial knowledge
and advanced guerrilla warfare techniques. In 1739, Cudjoe signed a treaty
with British governor Edward Trelawny,
which granted the Leeward Maroons
1,500 acres of land. In return for
certain economic benefits and political
autonomy, the Leeward Maroons agreed
to provide military support to the British
in case of invasion or rebellion by the
enslaved Black workforce, and to return
'runaway slaves'. In 1740, similar treaties
were signed by the Windward Maroons.
Afro combs, rooted in African traditions
dating back thousands of years, have
become symbols of Black empowerment
and self-determination. The ten combs
here serve as a visual bridge between
the historical use of combs in African
societies and their role in modern
resistance movements.

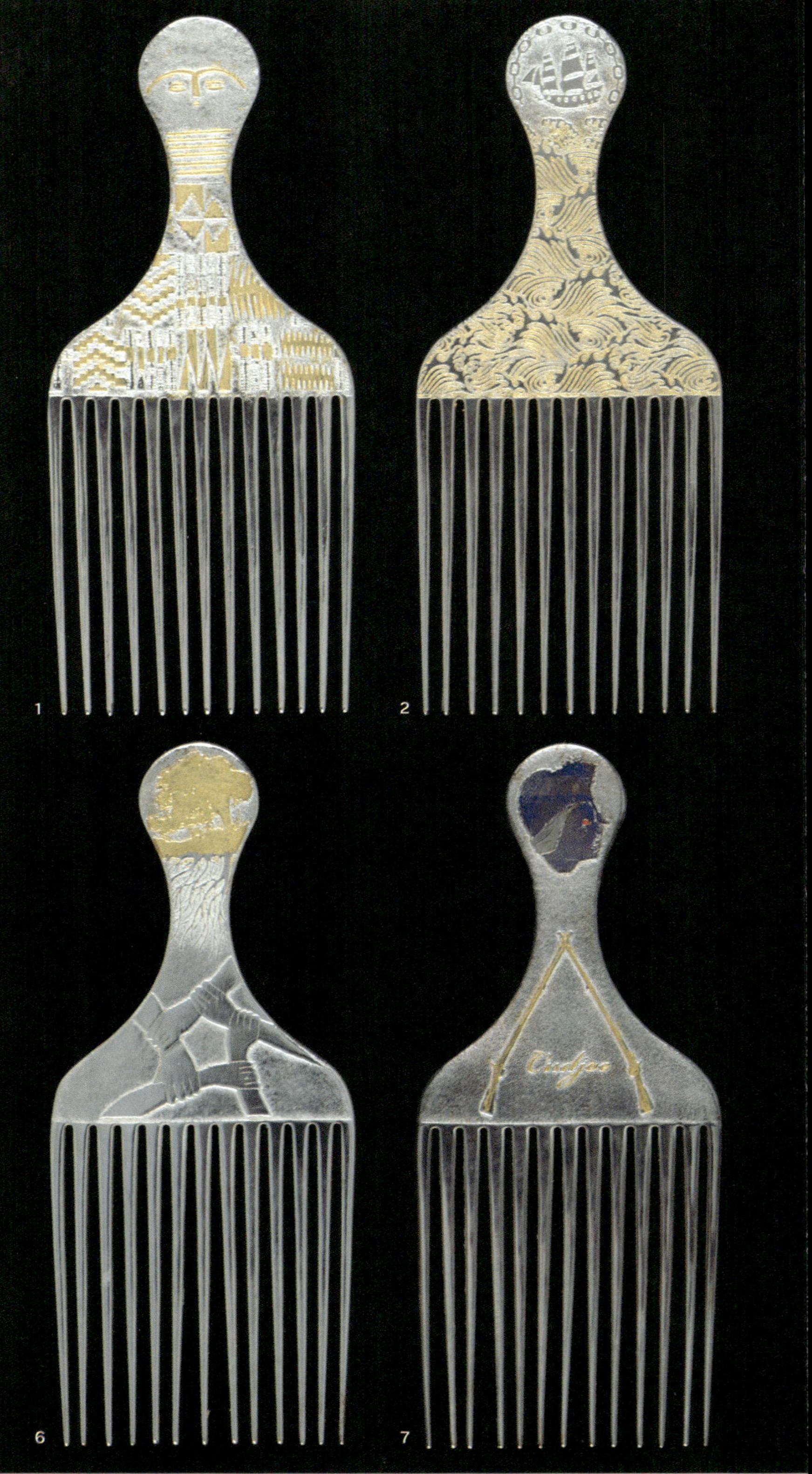

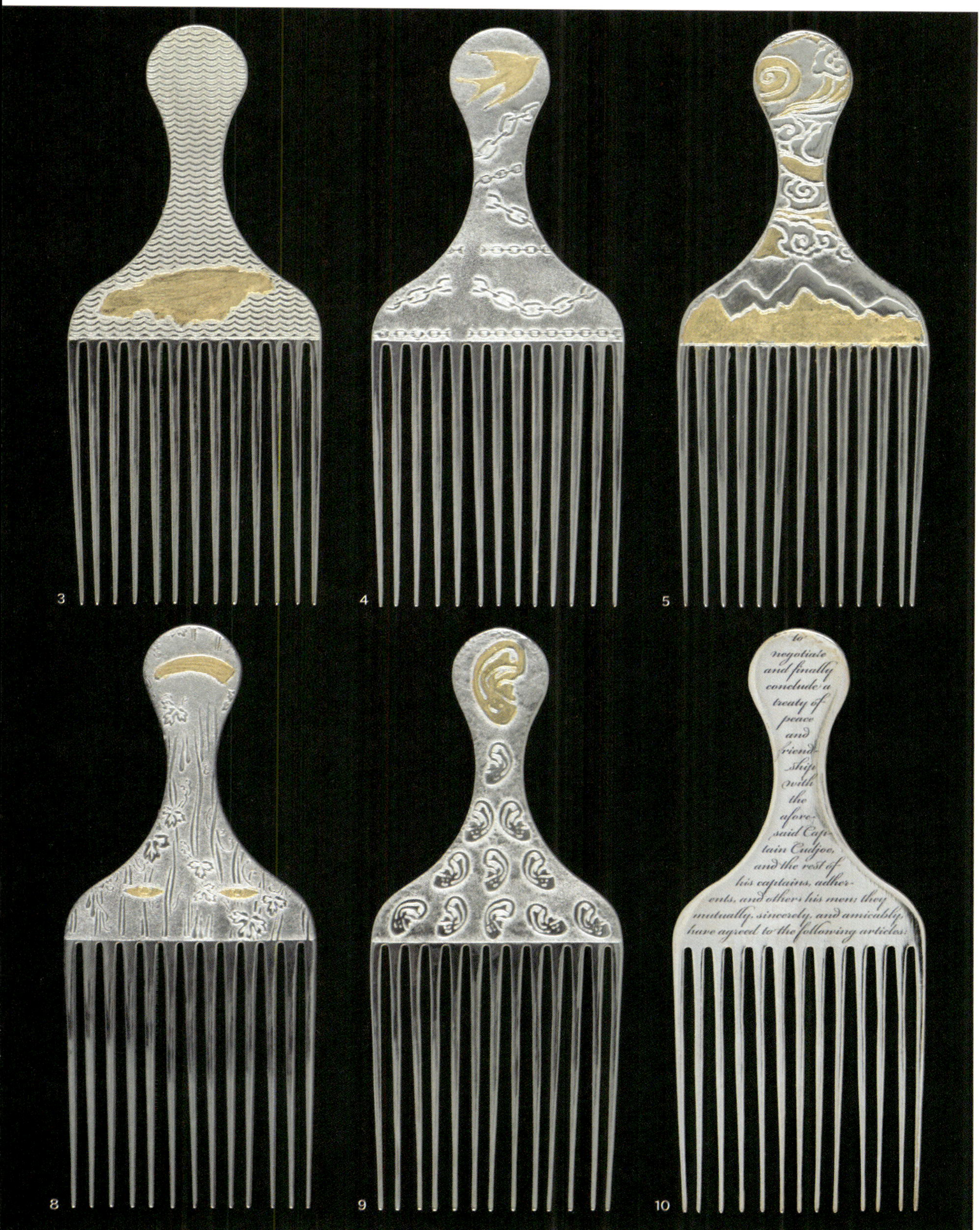

3
4
5
8
9
10
to negotiate and finally conclude a treaty of peace and friendship with the aforesaid Captain Cudjoe, and the rest of his captains, adherents, and other his men they mutually, sincerely, and amicably have agreed to the following articles:

Excavating *Uncomfortable Truths: Lost Vitrines and other vanished items*

Keith Piper

1. Press release for *Uncomfortable Truths*, V&A: 20 February—17 June 2007, https://media.vam.ac.uk/media/documents/legacy_documents/press_release/32156_press_release.pdf (accessed 23 July 2024).

In 2007, in an act that would, over subsequent years, form part of the 'blueprint of contrition' deployed by the great institutional holders of the nation's historical treasures, London's Victoria and Albert Museum staged an exhibition entitled *Uncomfortable Truths: The Shadow of Slave Trading on Contemporary Art and Design.*[1] A year rich with historical poignancy, 2007 marked the bicentennial of the passing of the Abolition of the Slave Trade Act of 1807, officially prohibiting the trading of slaves across the British Empire. Although the complex pathways leading to this historical landmark event, its direct aftermath, and the ways in which it formed a stepping stone towards the 1833 Slavery Abolition Act remain subjects of ongoing scholarship and reflection, the bicentennial remembrance of this Act allowed artists and researchers an opportunity to renew an examination of the terrible legacies of 'New World' slavery and the trade in captive Africans that fed it.

When invited by the V&A to propose a project, my response was to reflect upon the Museum as a holder of objects created when British society was awash with the material surpluses generated by slaveholding. The profits generated by unequal trade with West Africa, the expropriation of enslaved labour to work stolen land in the Americas, and the return of profitable goods to English ports, were extensive. This surplus created the resources necessary to fire industrialisation on the one hand and gave rise to the intricately fashioned desirable objects of the Georgian 'Enlightenment' found in the Eighteenth-Century Galleries of the V&A on the other. It was amongst these objects, contained as they were within vitrines and display cases located

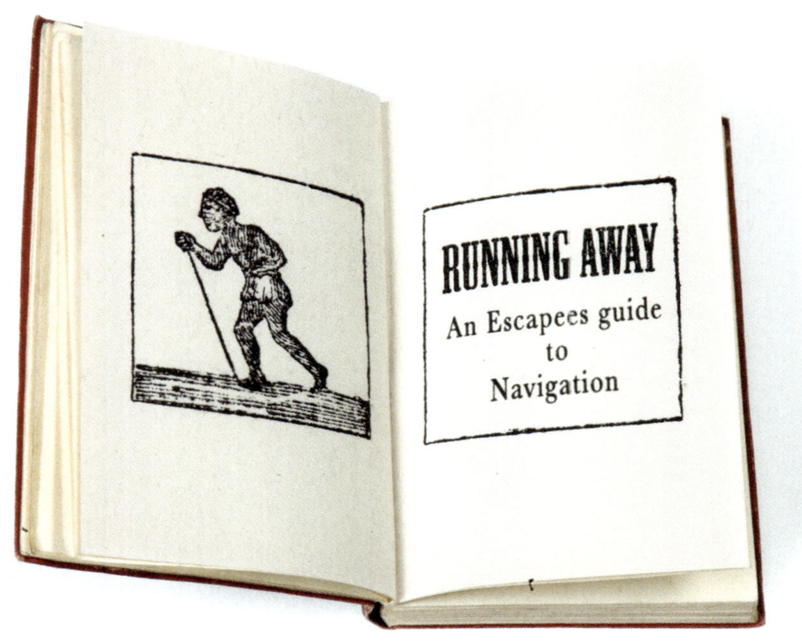

34
Keith Piper (born 1960). ***Running Away: An Escapees Guide to Navigation***, 2007. Digital print on paper, 16 × 11 × 2.3 cm

Collection of the Artist © Keith Piper. Made as part of Piper's *Lost Vitrines* site-specific project commissioned by the Victoria and Albert Museum, London, for its *Uncomfortable Truths* exhibition (Eighteenth-Century British Galleries, 20 February — 17 June 2007) in response to the bicentennial of the Abolition of the Slave Trade Act, 2007

Keith Piper
(born 1960).
Miss Mary's Micro-Resistance ToolKit,
2007. Wood, fabric,
glass and digital print on
paper, 45 × 29.2 × 34.5 cm

Collection of the Artist © Keith Piper. Made as part of Piper's *Lost Vitrines* site-specific project commissioned by the Victoria and Albert Museum, London, for its *Uncomfortable Truths* exhibition (Eighteenth-Century British Galleries, 20 February — 17 June 2007) in response to the bicentennial of the Abolition of the Slave Trade Act, 2007

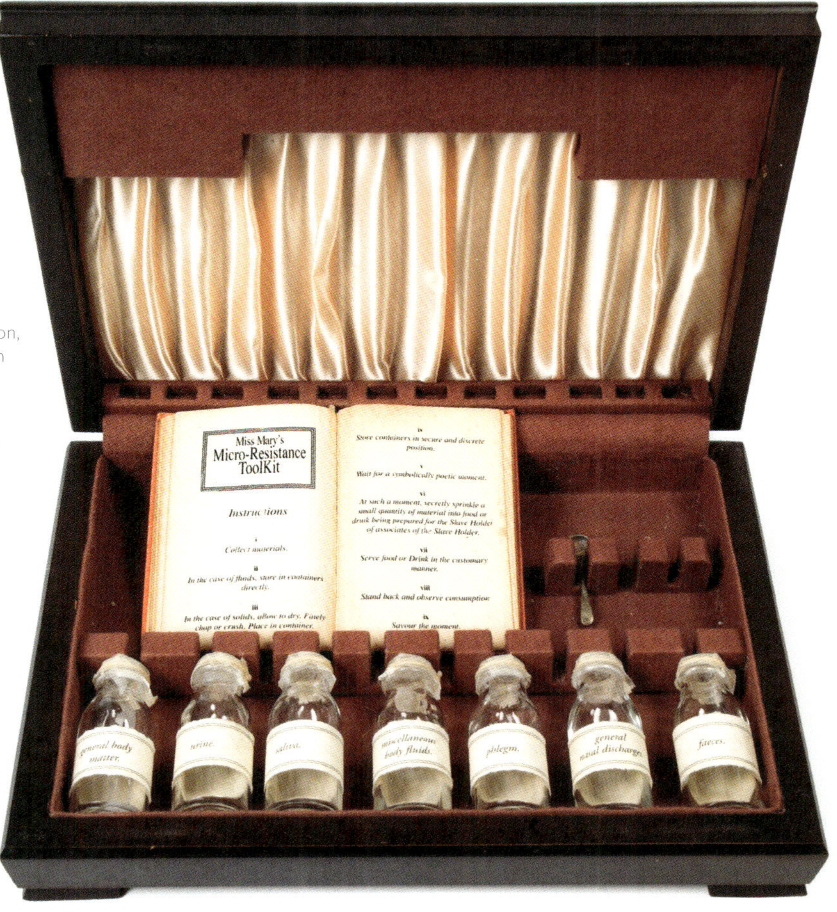

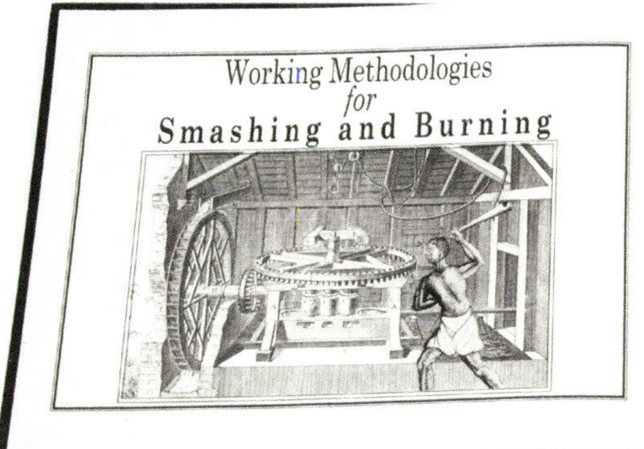

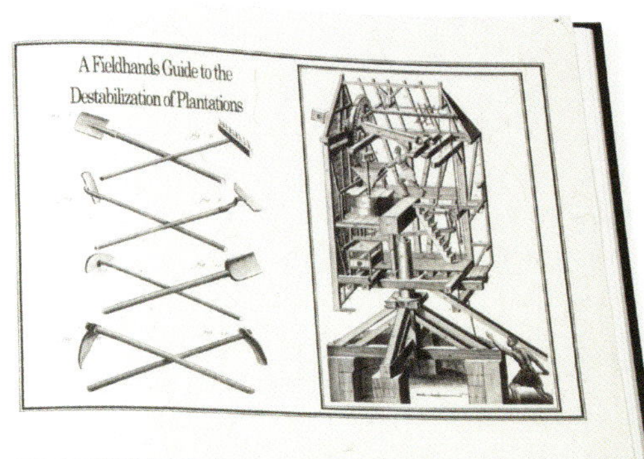

36

Keith Piper (born 1960).
Working Methodologies for Smashing and Burning, 2007.
Digital print on paper, 32 × 26 × 1.6 cm

Collection of the Artist © Keith Piper. Made as part of Piper's *Lost Vitrines* site-specific project commissioned by the Victoria and Albert Museum, London, for its *Uncomfortable Truths* exhibition (Eighteenth-Century British Galleries, 20 February — 17 June 2007) in response to the bicentennial of the Abolition of the Slave Trade Act, 2007 in the elegantly vaulted galleries of the V&A, that I planned an intervention for the *Uncomfortable Truths* exhibition.

The museum display case, or vitrine, has always fascinated me. Like a gallery plinth, it elevates the object it contains, enhancing its value by enclosing it in protective glass. This practice amplifies the perceived importance of the object and reinforces its significance to the nation's narrative and achievements. However, the visibility of the vitrine also highlights an absence: the objects excluded from the dominant narrative, left to decay because they tell a less palatable story of the era. My project, *Lost Vitrines* (2007), imagined these lost objects, fabricating them to mirror the period's aesthetics and reinserting them into the museum space. This act of imagining was a deliberate tricksterism, meant to jolt the viewer by covertly usurping the language of the vitrine.

Lost Vitrines imagined two distinct clusters of objects. Both are reflective of the ideas, politics and values found in populations of the period. One cluster imagines objects created by enslaved people who, by brutal design, were denied access to the tools and means of creating permanent objects. In this respect, these imagined objects are 'impossible', but reveal the strategic planning and subversive intent embodied within acts of rebellion, resistance and escape, that have been often misread as spontaneous and unplanned. Escape from the plantation is the subject of a published 'guidebook' entitled *Running Away: An Escapees Guide to Navigation* [34]. The targeting of plantation infrastructure during acts of insurrection is presented as a technical manual entitled *Working Methodologies for Smashing and Burning* [36]. The acts of revenge and resistance through which enslaved peoples sometimes covertly contaminated the food of plantation owners

Keith Piper (born 1960).
An Illustrated Guide to Ideal Plantation Dwellings, 2007. Digital print on paper with imaginary plans and elevations of two houses designed for enslaved African people on an English plantation in the Caribbean, 9 × 25 × 21.5 cm (on mount)

Fitzwilliam Museum, University of Cambridge (PB.10-2023). Bought with the Gow Fund, 2023 © Keith Piper. Made as part of Piper's *Lost Vitrines* site-specific project commissioned by the Victoria and Albert Museum, London, for its *Uncomfortable Truths* exhibition (Eighteenth-Century British Galleries, 20 February — 17 June 2007) in response to the bicentennial of the Abolition of the Slave Trade Act, 2007

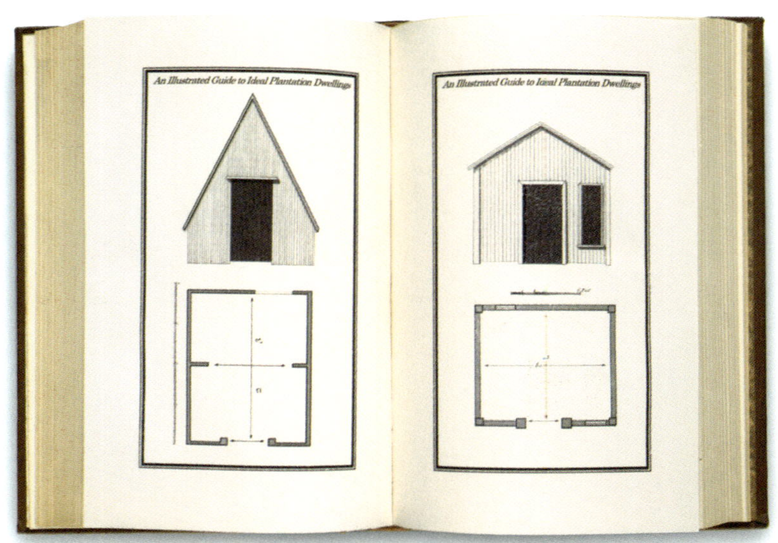

Keith Piper (born 1960).
***The Coloureds' Codex
(Enlightenment Edition)***,
2023. Mixed media including
wood, paper, pigment, textiles
and metals, 38 × 47 × 32 cm

Framed text: 'An Overseer's Guide to Comparative Complexion'. Fitzwilliam Museum, Cambridge (M.25-2023). Bought with the Gow Fund, 2023 © Keith Piper. Made for the Fitzwilliam Museum's *Black Atlantic: Power, People Resistance* exhibition (Founder's Galleries, 8 September 2023 — 7 January 2024) as a reworking of *The Coloureds' Codex: An Overseers' Guide to Comparative Complexion*, 2007, which was part of Piper's *Lost Vitrines* site-specific project commissioned by the Victoria and Albert Museum, London, for its *Uncomfortable Truths* exhibition (Eighteenth-Century British Galleries, 20 February — 17 June 2007), and purchased by the International Slavery Museum, Liverpool, 2018 (ISM.2018.11.1)

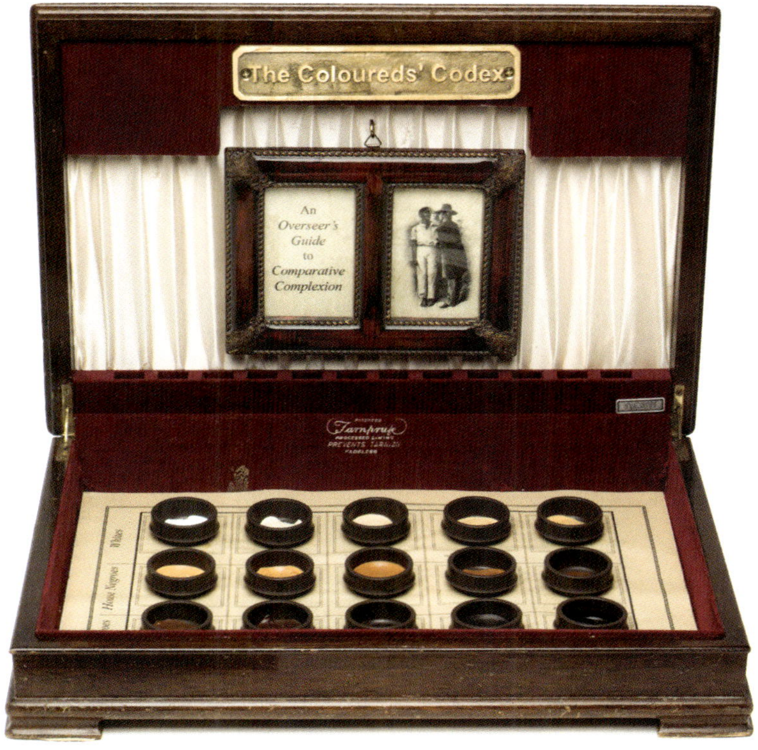

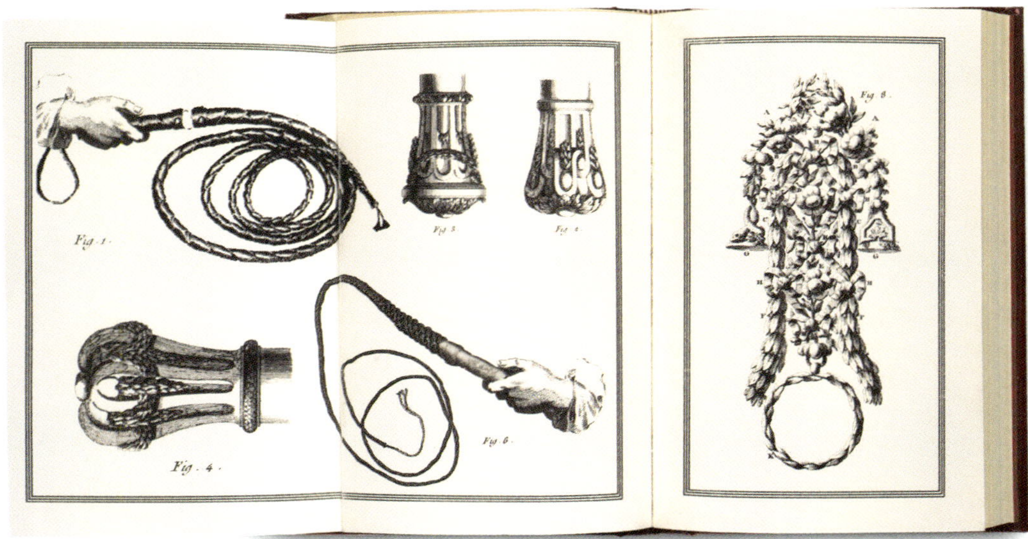

Keith Piper (born 1960). ***Catalogue***, 2007.
Digital print on paper with fold-out diagram of imaginary whip handle designs, 9.5 × 30 × 24 cm (on mount).

Fitzwilliam Museum, Cambridge (PB.9-2023). Bought with the Gow Fund, 2023 © Keith Piper. Made as part of Piper's *Lost Vitrines* site-specific project commissioned by the Victoria and Albert Museum, London, for its *Uncomfortable Truths* exhibition (Eighteenth-Century British Galleries, 20 February — 17 June 2007) in response to the bicentennial of the Abolition of the Slave Trade Act, 2007

with spit and other bodily fluids are elaborated through a gentile 'toolbox' entitled *Miss Mary's Micro-Resistance ToolKit* [35].

On the other side of this social equation sits another set of objects. In this case, emerging from the imagined needs of the empowered plantation owner. Visual tropes deployed in Georgian-era books illustrating elaborate designs for craft objects and architectural features are hijacked in a book illustrating decorative whip-handles entitled *Catalogue* [39]. The language representing the floor plans of grand buildings is used to represent tiny cabins used to house enslaved peoples in a book entitled *An Illustrated Guide to Ideal Plantation Dwellings* [37]. Finally, a work entitled *The Coloureds' Codex (Enlightenment Edition)* [38] echoes the imposed hierarchies of colourism, presenting a sliding scale of skin pigmentation with the white gentry at the top and the 'unseasoned' slave at the bottom. Fifteen pots of pigment arranged in three rows denoting 'Whites', 'House Negroes' and 'Field Negroes' reflect the twisted logic of a system that attempted to impose graduations on social status linked to skin pigmentation that reverberates into the present day.

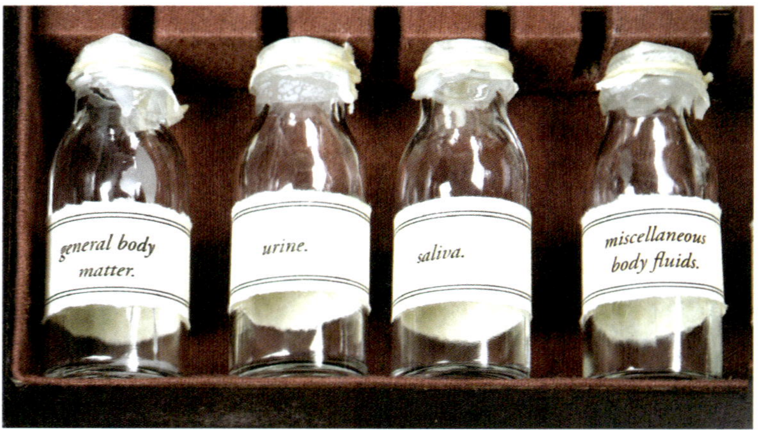

Detail of **35** (see page 65)

Nana

Jacqueline Bishop

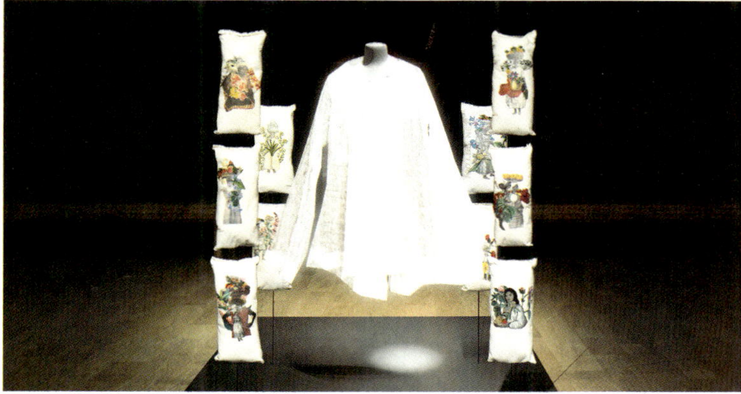

Jacqueline Bishop (born 1971). *Nana* (computer-generated version)

By Living Objects, 3D Designers for *Rise Up*, showing the proposed display in the exhibition

In 2023, I had the wonderful opportunity to visit Accra, Ghana. Although I had previously visited Africa, living in Morocco as a Fulbright Fellow, this was my first time in West Africa and a country where my ancestry DNA test indicated direct lineage. The weeks I spent in Ghana were powerful, starting with the drive from the airport where vendors moved through traffic selling goods, much like in my native Jamaica. The market women outside my hotel, effortlessly balancing baskets on their heads, reminded me of my great-grandmother and grandmother, both formidable market women.

At a slave site, I wrapped my arms around myself and thought of the nameless, faceless ancestor of mine, who had been at a place like this. I shivered as I thought of her in a horrendous ship's hold, then imagined as she stumbled out on the other side of the Atlantic balancing a basket on her head. When my market woman forebear arrived in Jamaica, she was allotted a small plot of land to grow food to feed herself and her progeny. In time, she exchanged or sold the excess food grown in weekend markets which led to the development of an internal, and subsequently an external, marketing system. The market woman is one of the most direct links to our West African forebears. She has become my muse.

It was slavery, sugar and sugarcane cultivation which brought the West African to the plantation societies of the Caribbean. In one part of the work that I am presenting here, I have embroidered and appliquéd images of Caribbean market women on West Indian sugar sacks [42]. In doing so, I hope to show that despite the inhumanity of the plantation system, these women maintained agency and autonomy, particularly as needleworkers and seamstresses, privileged positions within plantation society. Black needleworkers not only met the clothing needs of the enslaved but also earned extra income, empowering themselves.

On one of the sacks there is an exchange of knowledge and information between a West African market woman and an Indigenous woman. This work represents the intimate ties between the

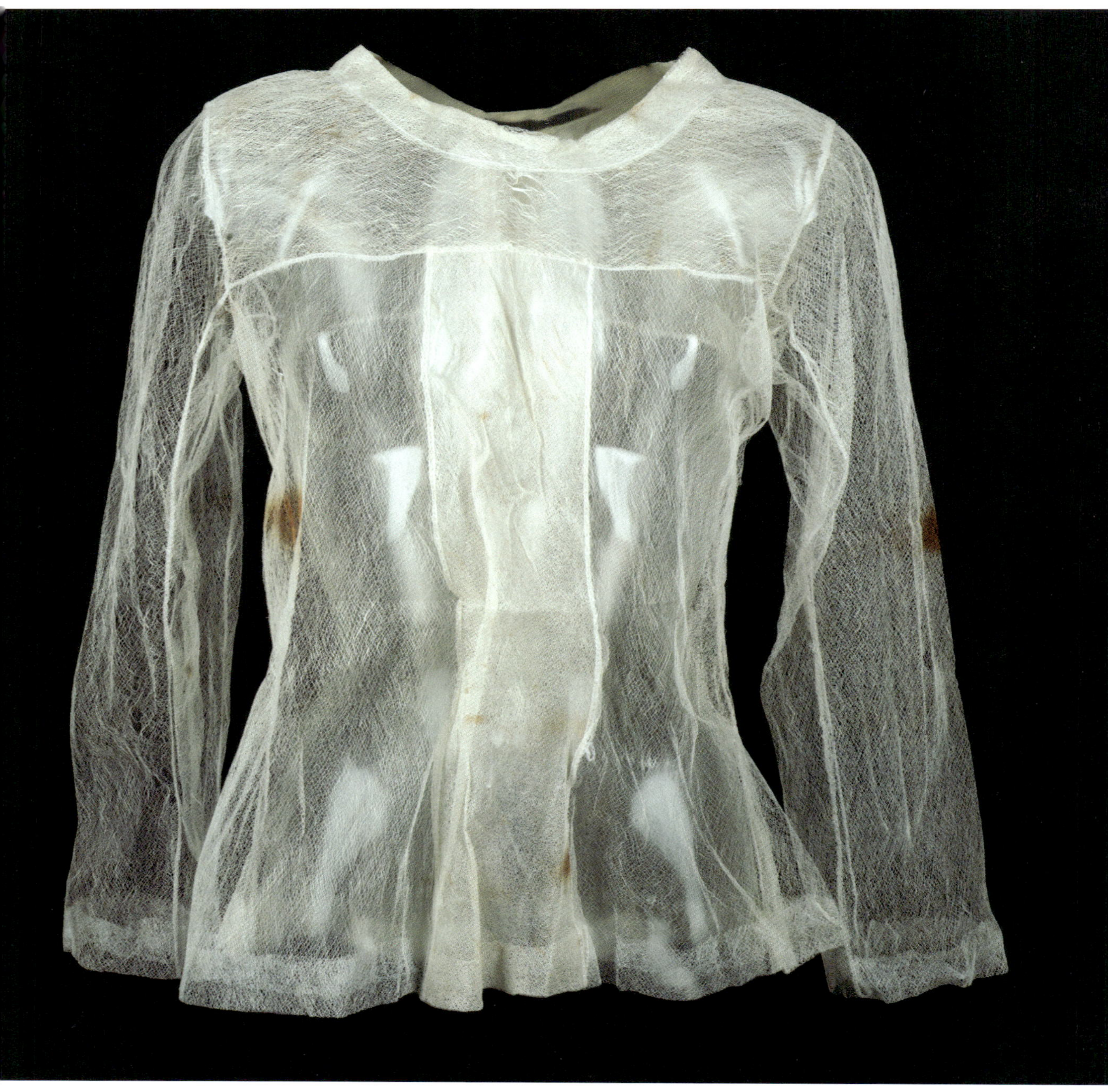

41

Jacqueline Bishop (born 1971). *Nana* (detail), 2024. Jamaican lacebark (chemise)

Fitzwilliam Museum, Cambridge (T.2-2024). Bought with the Cunliffe Fund, 2024. © Jacqueline Bishop.
Artwork made for *Rise Up: Resistance, Revolution, Abolition*

Indigenous and West African groups that met in Caribbean societies where both shared botanical and medical knowledge. The work *Nana* is meant to represent the meeting of indigeneity and West African knowledge systems on the island of Jamaica. To illustrate my point, I will tell a little story. One day I was talking to my uncle Moses about my great-grandmother Celeste, a market woman par excellence. This time, however, instead of talking about my great-grandmother's marketing skills, I was talking about her immense knowledge of Jamaican herbs and bushes. I mentioned to my uncle that I remembered hearing as a child that my great-grandmother delivered babies. My uncle corrected me and said it was Celeste's friend who delivered the babies, but my great-grandmother assisted because, as a market woman, she knew all the herbs and bushes to aid in the process.

I was intrigued.

'What about midwives?' I wanted to know.

'They did not exist,' my uncle answered. 'What you had instead were Nanas. And that isn't even an English word. That word sounds "African" to me.'

I was even more intrigued.

The area where my family hails from is home to a legendary freedom fighter and to date Jamaica's sole female National Heroine. Her name is Grandy Nanny. I began to see where her name came from. For you see Grandy Nanny too was a Nana, a herbalist, a botanist, a woman born in West Africa, transported to Jamaica who refused to submit to slavery and became a fighting Maroon and subsequently a mother of all Jamaica's children.

Inspired, I conceptualised a 'Nana blouse' to honour market women, Jamaica's botanical legacy, Grandy Nanny, my great-grandmother, and other influential women [41]. Using an enslaved chemise as a prototype, I incorporated lacebark, a material from the *Lagetta lagetto* tree, native to Jamaica, Cuba and Hispaniola. This fine netting was used in Victorian times to make various products. Embroidered onto the sugar sacks surrounding the chemise are herbs used by Nanas for birthing and fertility control during enslavement and afterwards. This patchwork marries Indigenous and West African botanical knowledge, reflecting the roots of Caribbean culture.

Through my work, I aim to show that despite the brutal realities of slavery, market women and needleworkers retained some control over their lives, contributing to the cultural and economic fabric of their societies. These women, both historically and in my family, exemplify resilience and agency, shaping the legacy of Caribbean and African heritage.

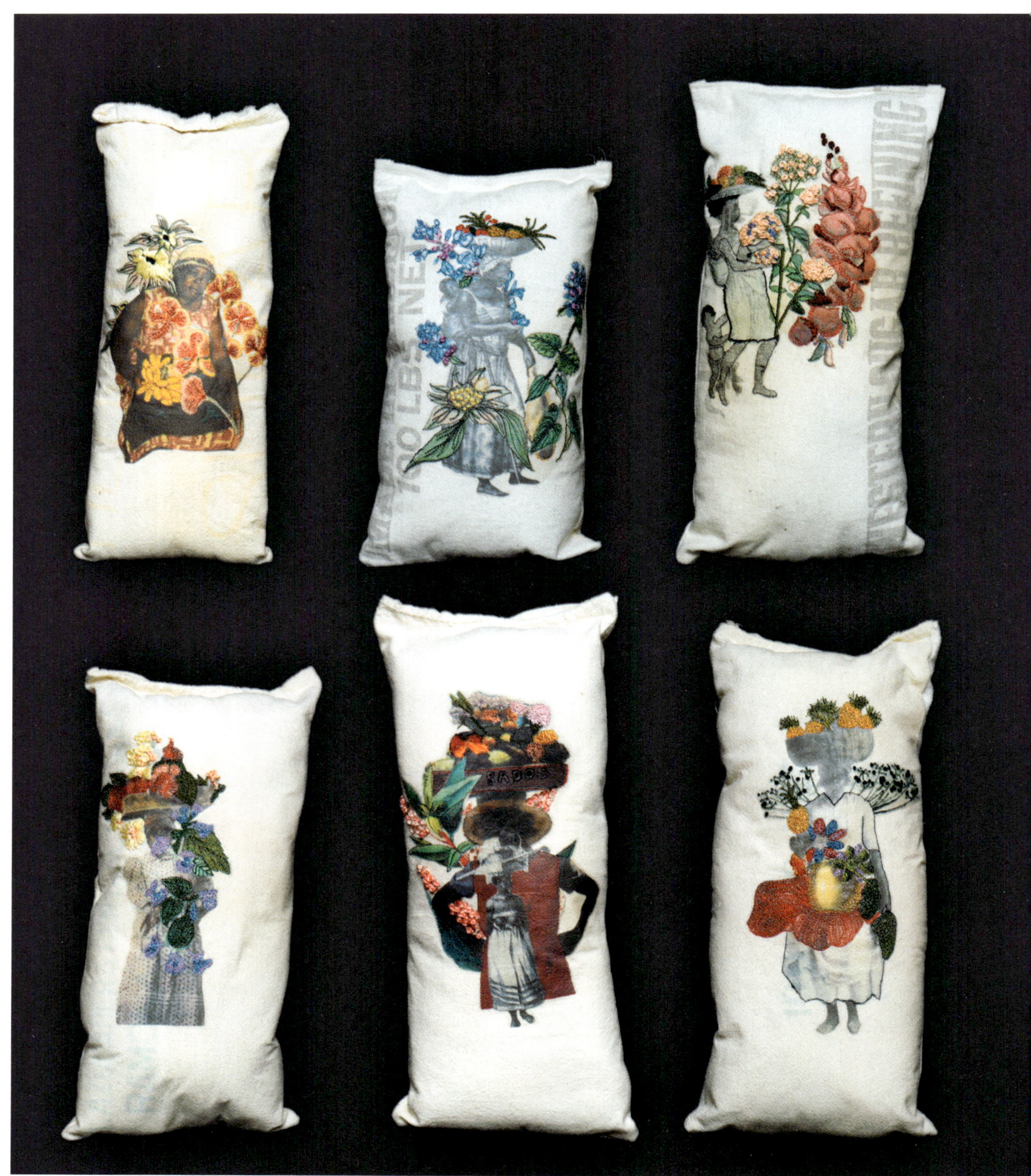

42

Jacqueline Bishop (born 1971). *Nana* (detail), 2024.
Hessian sugar sacks with appliqué and embroidery, each sack roughly 40 × 25 cm

Fitzwilliam Museum, Cambridge (T.2-2024). Bought with the Cunliffe Fund, 2024. © Jacqueline Bishop.
Artwork made for *Rise Up: Resistance, Revolution, Abolition*

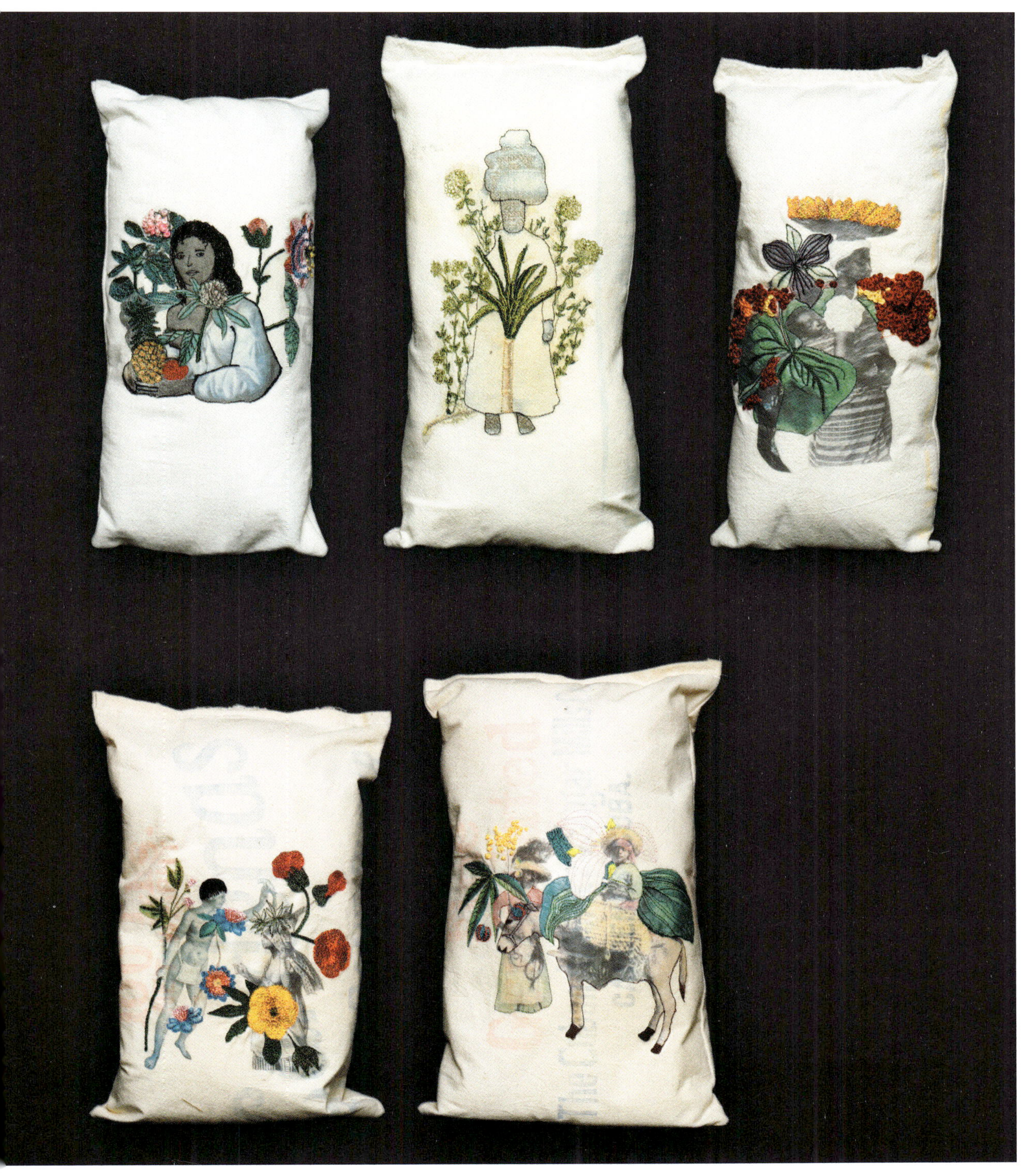

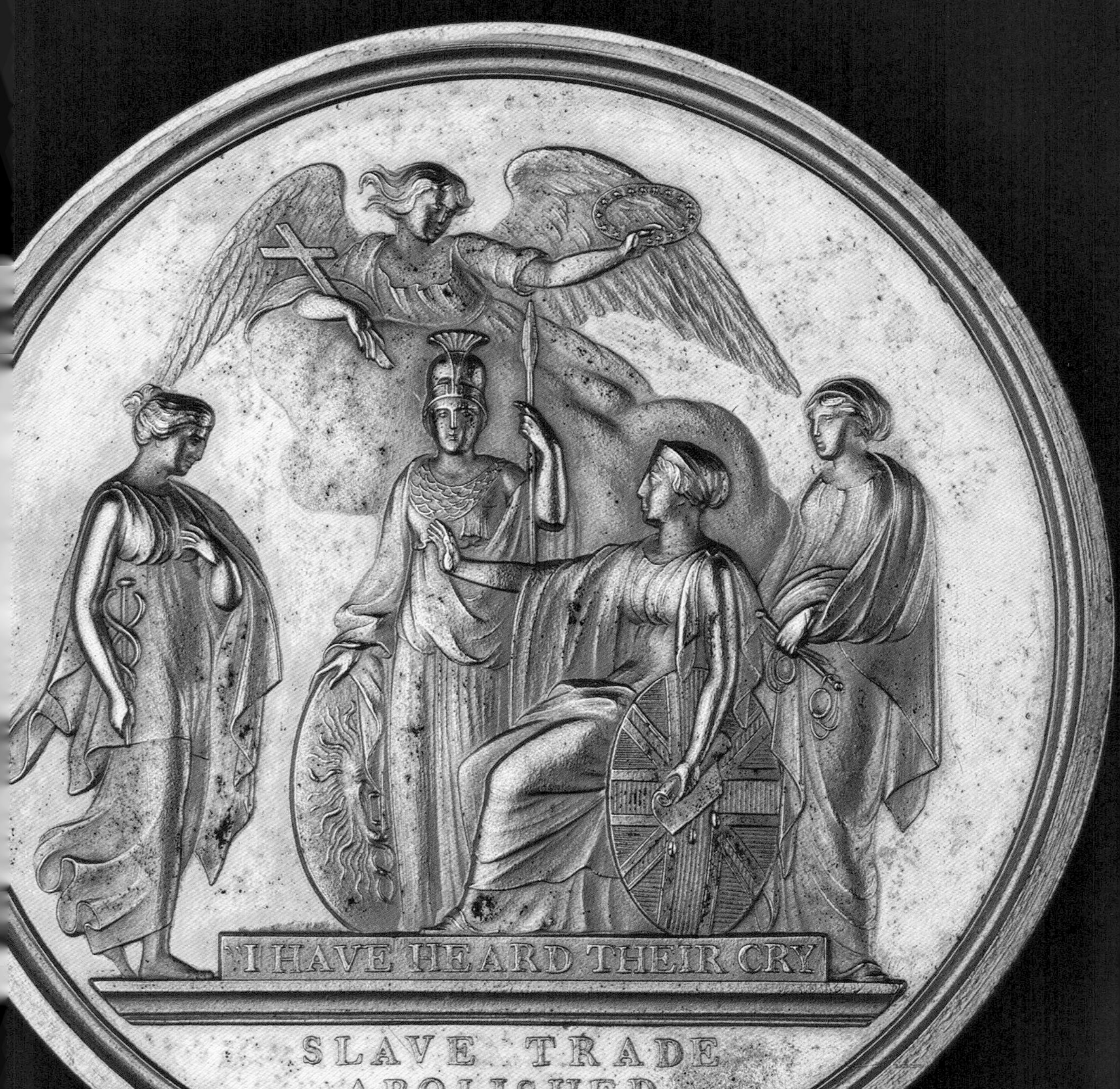

I HAVE HEARD THEIR CRY
SLAVE TRADE
ABOLISHED
MDCCCVII.

2

The British anti-slave trade campaign

Many factors combined to create momentum for abolishing the slave trade, including the continual resistance by enslaved people, the Haitian Revolution and other uprisings in British Caribbean colonies. Exposure of brutality on slaving ships and plantations, changing geopolitical realities and decreasing sugar profits also played their part.

Black abolitionists in Britain played crucial and effective roles in the anti-slave trade campaign alongside their more widely recognised and celebrated white counterparts. The Sons of Africa, a London-based Black abolitionist group, whose members included Olaudah Equiano and Ottobah Cugoano, petitioned establishment figures to end the slave trade and slavery itself. They worked in tandem with white abolitionist members of the Society of Friends (Quakers) and, from 1787, The Society for Effecting the Abolition of the Slave Trade (SEAST). William Wilberforce, a Cambridge graduate, represented SEAST in Parliament.

Detail of **68** (see page 108)

Breaking through: Black Georgian voices

From the 1770s onwards, British readers had access to literature about and by African activists that described the horrors of the slave trade, and their social and political aspirations. Books, newspaper articles, pamphlets and other texts spread the word of resistance and rebellions, and bore first-person testimony to the realities of enslavement.

The Sons of Africa demanded freedom, equality and justice. They effectively lobbied influential white political figures and galvanised support for abolition across British society.

Images were also made of Black Georgians. Some were disempowering, showing them as servants to their white masters. Others centred them as subjects in their own right, with autonomy, agency and authority.

43

Unrecorded Quaker copyist. **'To the truly Worthy Society of Gentlemen called Friends'**, copy of an address of thanks by Olaudah Equiano and the Sons of Africa to the Society of Friends (Quakers), 21 October 1785.

Britain Yearly Meeting of the Religious Society of Friends (Quakers) (LSF MS BOX W2_5_14). Part of the personal papers of feminist and abolitionist campaigner Anne Knight (1786—1862)

In his 1789 autobiography, Olaudah Equiano published this letter, explaining: 'In October 1785 I was accompanied by some of the Africans, and presented this address of thanks to the gentlemen called Friends or Quakers, in Gracechurch-Court, Lombard Street. These gentle-men received us very kindly, with a promise to exert themselves on behalf of the oppressed Africans, and we parted.' The Sons of Africa was a loosely constituted all-Black-male, London-based social justice group of formerly enslaved people whose members campaigned for abolition. This letter shows that Black and white anti-slavery groups supported each other before the creation of the Society for Effecting the Abolition of the Slave Trade (SEAST) in May 1787. Historian David Olusoga sees this letter as 'marking the effective start of Equiano's overt political life'.

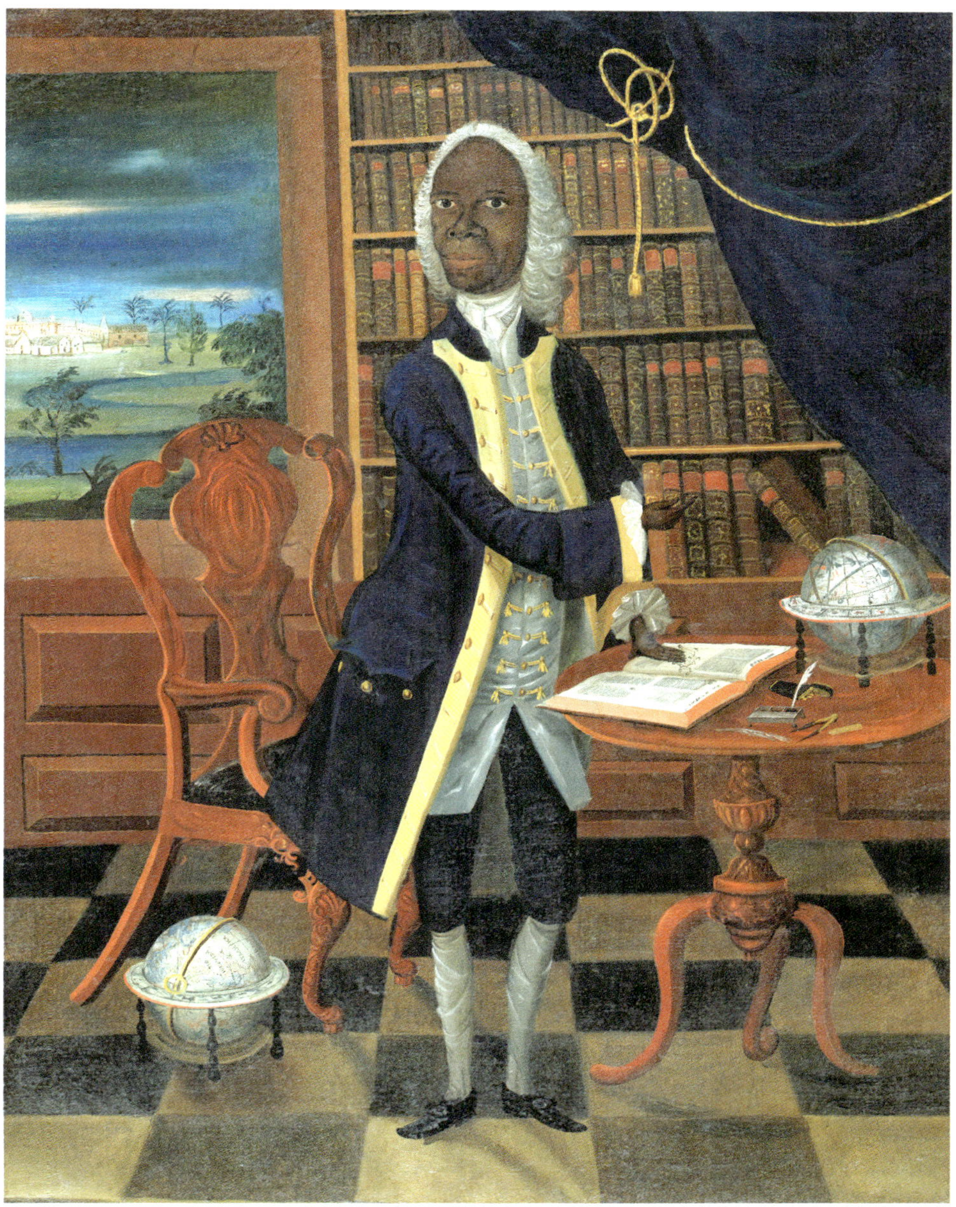

44

Unrecorded artist.
*Francis Williams, the Scholar
of Jamaica*, about 1760.
Oil on canvas, 66 × 50 cm

Victoria and Albert Museum, London
(P.83-1928). Given by Viscount Lord Bearsted
M.C. and Spink and Son Ltd through the
National Art Collections Fund, 1928. Bought
from Major H. Howard of Hampton Lodge, Seale,
Farnham, a direct descendant of historian and
enslaver Edward Long

In his 1774 *History of Jamaica*, Edward Long claimed that
Francis Williams — shown here as an elderly gentleman
scholar, surrounded by books and scientific instruments,
studying Newtonian astronomy — was sent to Cambridge
University by his wealthy Black parents to study science and
mathematics. Although this cannot be proved, Williams's
academic credentials and Cambridge connections are
not in doubt: on 25 October 1716, a group of Cambridge
scholars including mathematician Martin Folkes, Sir Isaac
Newton and Edmund Halley supported his election to
the Royal Society. Shockingly, the Royal Society turned
him down, seemingly due to his skin colour. Williams was
later admitted to Lincoln's Inn as a barrister. Inheriting his
father's plantations in mid-1723, he returned to Jamaica and
established a school for African and African-descended boys.

45

Thomas Gainsborough RA (1727–1788).
Ignatius Sancho, 29 November 1768.
Oil on canvas, 73.7 × 62.2 cm

National Gallery of Canada, Ottawa (58). Bought in 1907. Probably commissioned by George Brudenell-Montagu (1712–1790), Duke of Montagu and 4th Earl of Cardigan in 1768, and gifted to Sancho; inherited by Sancho's children, 1780; by whom gifted to William Stevenson (1741–1821), 1820

This striking image is the only known lifetime portrait of writer, businessman and London socialite Ignatius Sancho. According to family friend William Stevenson, it was painted by Gainsborough on 29 November 1768 in only a hundred minutes. It shows Sancho, brimming with self-confidence and at ease, aged thirty-nine, when he was the esteemed valet of George, 1st Duke of Montagu. According to contemporary comportment manuals, the hand-in-waistcoat pose denoted 'manly boldness tempered with modesty' appropriate for English gentlemen. Its adoption by the formerly enslaved Sancho when still employed as a servant shows his cultural assimilation and social aspirations. Likely commissioned by Montagu as a gift for Sancho, it remained one of his prized possessions, bequeathed to his children in 1780. Sancho's magnificent portrait remains, in the 2023 words of Anshuman Bhalla, 'an enduring symbol of Black presence and dignity during a time when these attributes were routinely denied to people of African descent'.

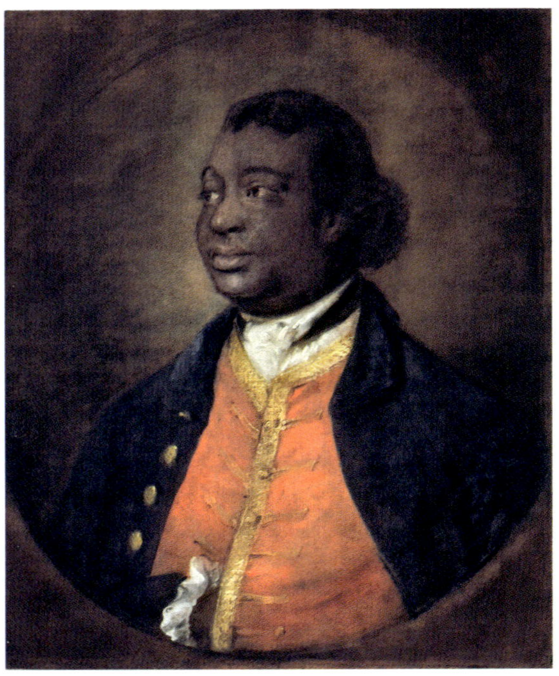

46

Ignatius Sancho
(*c.*1729–1780).
Letters of the Late Ignatius Sancho, an African. In Two Volumes. To which are prefixed, Memoirs of his Life,
vol. 1, London 1782

Cambridge University Library (Oates.483)

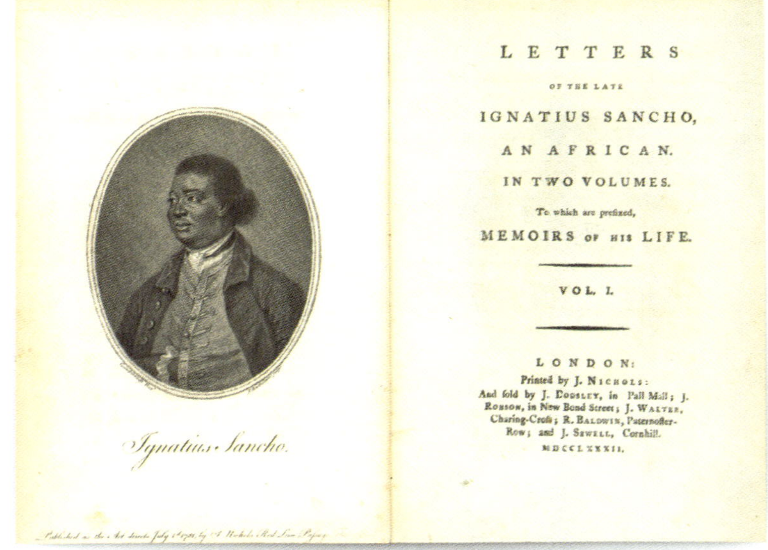

A man of letters, Sancho corresponded with many famous Georgians and was a respected member of London society. Two years after his death, part of his correspondence was published by his friend, political hostess Frances, Lady Crewe, to demonstrate that 'an untutored African may possess abilities equal to an European'. Sold by subscription to nearly 1,200 supporters, including the prime minister, Lord North, the letters covered London daily life and Sancho's anti-slavery views. Its frontispiece reproduces an engraved portrait by Francesco Bartolozzi after Gainsborough's original. It was probably commissioned by Sancho's widow, Ann, and their son, William, who were now running a book-printing and bookselling business. In 1803, William Sancho oversaw the fifth edition's printing, making this volume the first book to be both written and published by Black Britons.

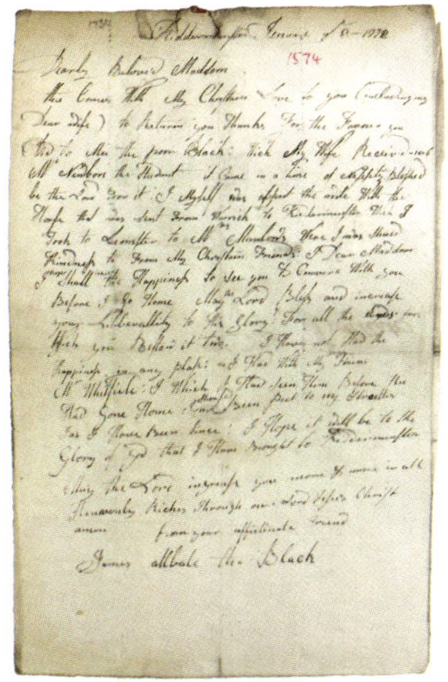

47

Ukawsaw Gronniosaw (James Albert) (*c.* 1705—1775). **Autograph letter to Selina Hastings, Countess of Huntingdon**, 3 January 1772

Cheshunt Foundation Archive, Westminster College, Cambridge Theological Federation affiliated to the University of Cambridge (F/1: 1574). Part of the personal papers of Countess of Huntingdon

Grandson of the king of Zaara in Bornu (north-eastern Nigeria), Ukawsaw Gronniosaw was enslaved aged fifteen. After gaining his freedom, he came to Britain, married, and had at least five children. This is the only known autograph letter by Gronniosaw, who signs off 'James allbate [Albert] the Black'. Written at the very start of 1772 to his new patron, the Countess of Huntingdon, Gronniosaw thanks her for an unspecified 'favour', which 'came in a time of Nesisity [sic]', explaining he had recently returned from Leominster, 'were I was shued Kindness to from my Christain friends [sic]'. At the time of writing, Gronniosaw was living in Kidderminster with his wife, Betty, and their three surviving infants, having been forced to relocate there from Norfolk following 'ill treatment' from local residents. Gronniosaw dedicated his narrative autobiography, published at the end of the same year, to the Countess.

48

Ukawsaw Gronniosaw (James Albert) (*c.* 1705—1775). *A Narrative of the Most Remarkable Particulars in the Life of James Albert Ukawsaw Gronniosaw ...*, Bath, December 1772

Cambridge University Library (6.77.16)

Ukawsaw Gronniosaw is the earliest known African-British author and his 1772 autobiography is the first 'slave narrative' published in Britain. It stands apart from later examples like those by Cugoano and Equiano in not directly criticising slavery as an institution. Gronniosaw dictated his life story to an unnamed female scribe in Leominster, possibly the 'Mrs Marlowe' mentioned in his letter to the Countess of Huntingdon. It narrates his abduction into slavery, his later conversion to Christianity, his time in the British Navy fighting against French forces during the Seven Years' War (1756—63) and his difficult life in Britain, where he faced daily discrimination and hardship. Gronniosaw's story gained wide readership and was republished in many editions.

49

John Russell (1745—1806).
The Right Honourable Selina, Countess of Huntingdon, Foundress and Benefactress,
about 1775—80. Oil on canvas, 93 × 78 cm

The Countess of Huntingdon is a paradoxical figure, like many of her contemporaries, as she was both an enslaver and an abolitionist. Her vast fortune derived partly from plantations in Georgia and South Carolina on which captive African people were forced to abour. She justified participating in slavery by using her wealth to support the work of Black evangelical Christians. She financially supported the publication of books by Phillis Wheatley [51], Ukawsaw Gronniosaw [48] and Olaudah Equiano [4]. The Countess of Huntingdon set up her own evangelical religious network ('Connexion') in opposition to the established Church of England, building chapels across Britain and sending Methodist missionaries to North America, including John Marrant to Nova Scotia [75].

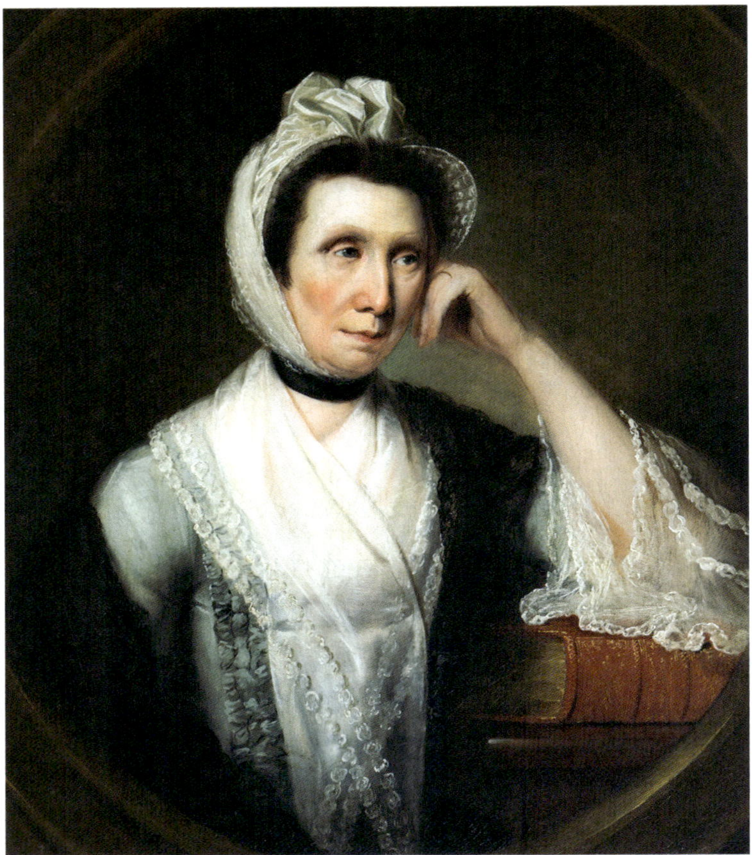

50

Phillis Wheatley (*c.*1753—1784).
Autograph letter to Selina Hastings, Countess of Huntingdon, 27 June 1773

This is one of only two dozen autograph letters by the Boston-based, enslaved, child prodigy Phillis Wheatley to survive from her extensive correspondence with political and religious leaders in America and England. Dated 27 June 1773, Wheatley informs her patron, the Countess of Huntingdon, of her safe arrival in London from Boston and her desire to meet. She talks of her forthcoming book of poems and thanks the Countess for the idea of including a portrait of herself as the frontispiece and for being willing to be its dedicatee.

Phillis Wheatley
(*c.*1753—1784).
Poems on Various Subjects, Religious and Moral, by Phillis Wheatley, Negro Servant to Mr. John Wheatley, of Boston, in New England
(frontispiece),
London 1773

Cheshunt Foundation Archive, Westminster College, Cambridge. Theological Federation affiliated to the University of Cambridge (136). Personal copy of Countess of Huntingdon, to whom Wheatley dedicated her book

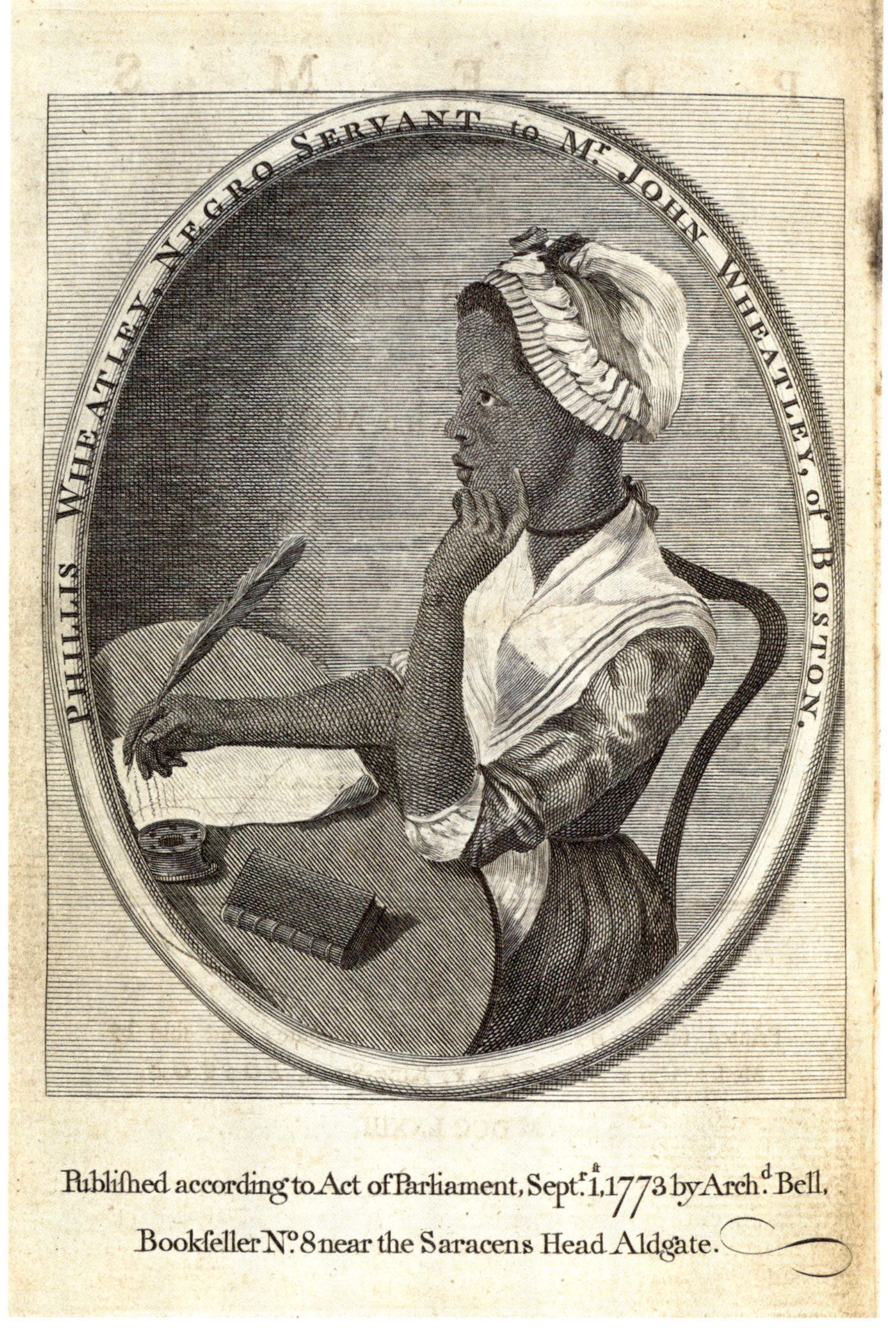

By February 1772, enslaved poet Phillis Wheatley had twenty-eight evangelical and abolitionist-themed poems to publish but was unable to find subscribers in Boston. Her Boston enslaver, Susannah Wheatley, enlisted the help of the Countess of Huntingdon, who catalysed the book's publication. In May 1773, Wheatley travelled to London, chaperoned by her enslaver's son, Nathaniel, to seek subscribers. She met several influential people including future Lord Mayor of London Sir Brook Watson and Benjamin Franklin (then on his second mission as colonial agent for the Pennsylvania Assembly). Unexpectedly recalled to Boston by Susannah Wheatley, now mortally ill, she missed out on meeting the Countess. Wheatley was finally legally freed in late 1773, after the publication of her book of poems, amid British outcry that she had been presented to London audiences as an African genius while still enslaved.

52

Attributed to Thomas Rowlandson (1757–1827).
Richard Cosway, Maria Cosway and Ottobah Cugoano in the garden of Schomberg House, Pall Mall, London, 1784.
Etching, 24.5 × 31.5 cm (sheet)

Proof, 1st state before the addition of an aquatint border. Royal Collection Trust (RCIN 653010). Bought by George IV, when Prince Regent, from Colnaghi and Co. for 5 shillings, 12 July 1813

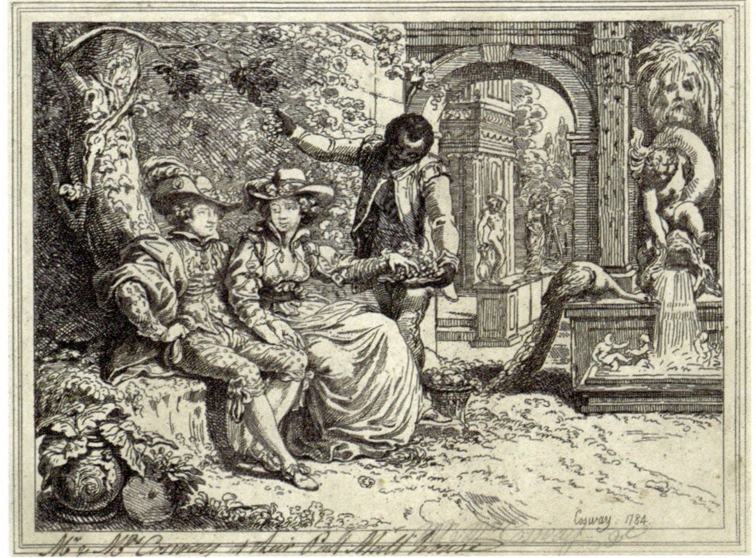

Kidnapped, aged thirteen, from his high-ranking Fante family in Ajumako, Gold Coast (present-day Ghana) and sold into slavery in Grenada, Cugoano laboured on a plantation in the Lesser Antilles until a Scottish plantation-owner purchased him. Brought to Britain in 1772, Cugoano secured his freedom following the Somerset Case ruling, and became a leading abolitionist. From 1784 to 1791, Cugoano was a servant to the society painters Richard and Maria Cosway. This contrived and visually witty engraving shows Cugoano attending to the Cosways in the garden of their new home, Schomberg House, but its composition deliberately imitates historic paintings of *The Rest on the Flight to Egypt*. Here, Cugoano takes over the role of the ministering angel or St Joseph offering dates to the Virgin Mary, and offers freshly plucked grapes to Maria Cosway. Schomberg House and its Italianate gardens became a fashionable meeting-place for London society, providing Cugoano with the chance to mix with the elite, including the future King George IV, Cosway's patron, who bought this print in 1813.

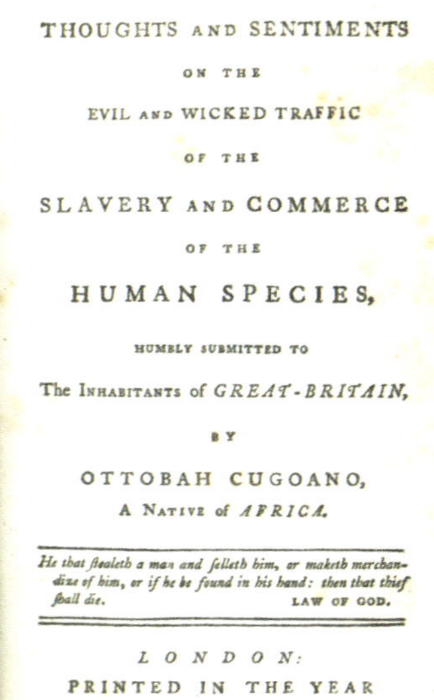

53

Ottobah Cugoano (*c*.1757–*c*.1791).
Thoughts and Sentiments ... by Ottobah Cugoano, A Native of Africa, London, 1787

Royal Collection Trust (RCIN 1125525). Acquired by George IV, when Prince of Wales, for his library at Carlton House, London; possibly the copy presented to him by Ottobah Cugoano, 1787

In 1787, formerly enslaved Ottobah Cugoano published his book of radical political philosophy, *Thoughts and Sentiments on the Evil and Wicked Traffic of the Slavery and Commerce of the Human Species*. It demanded immediate emancipation of all enslaved people on moral and economic grounds. Cugoano argued that it was the moral right and duty of enslaved people to fight slavery, if necessary with arms. He also argued that every white Briton was to some degree responsible for the institution of slavery and its perpetuation. Cugoano expressed support for the proposed establishment of a new free colony for the 'Poor Blacks' of London in Sierra Leone, and demanded schools be created in Britain for the education of African children. Reprinted at least three times in 1787, and translated into French in 1788, an abridged version was published in 1791, with many artists subscribing, including Joshua Reynolds. Cugoano sent one copy of his book to the Prince of Wales in 1787, and another to George III in 1788: this book is likely the former. Cugoano travelled to over fifty British towns to sell his book and promote the immediate and total abolition of slavery. In his last known letter of 1791, Cugoano records facing racism and finding 'complexion is a predominant prejudice'.

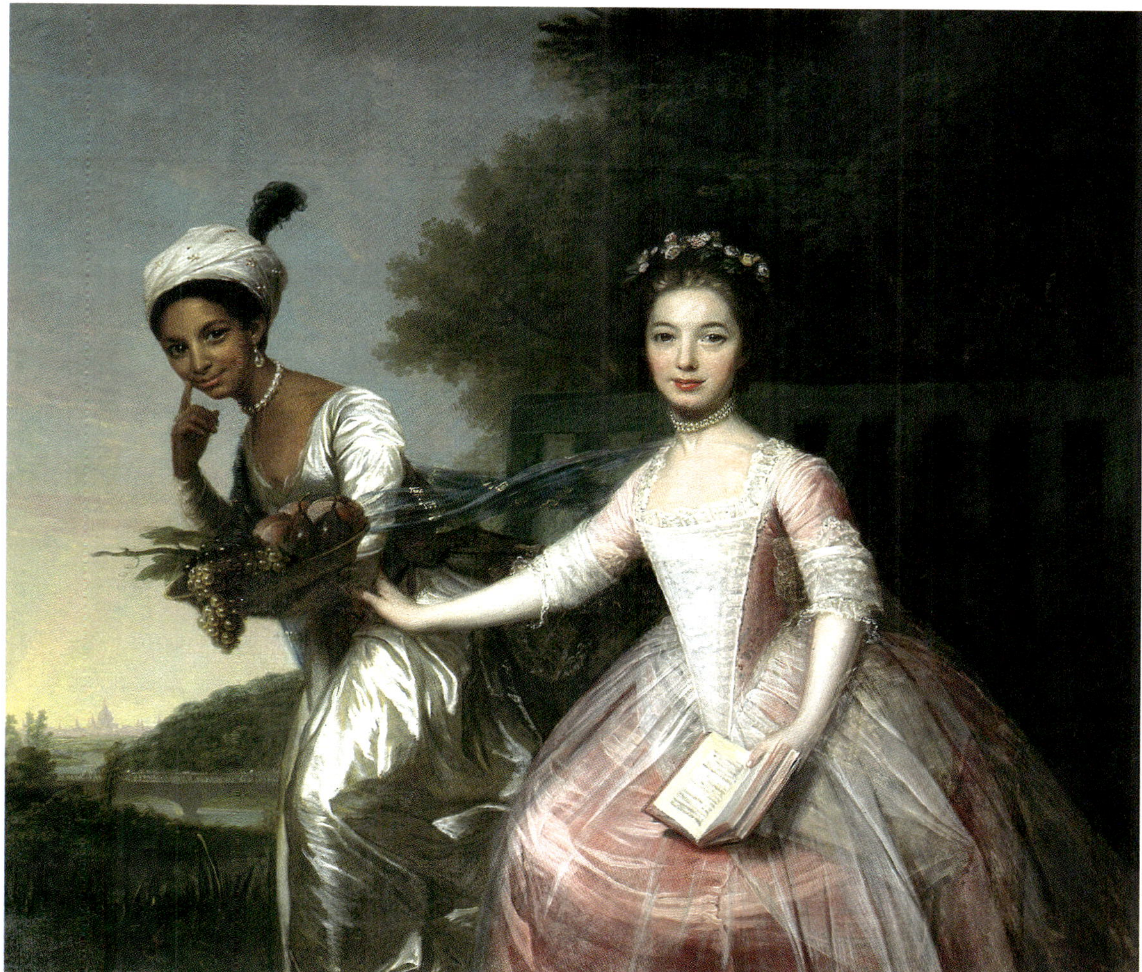

David Martin (1737—1797).
***Dido Elizabeth Belle and
Lady Elizabeth Murray
at Kenwood House***,
about 1776. Oil on canvas,
134 × 154 cm (framed)

Earl of Mansfield, Scone Palace,
Perth, Scotland (E327 E (018))

This remarkable portrait was traditionally believed to portray Lady Elizabeth Murray with an unidentified servant. Recent research, however, reveals the latter to be Dido Belle, the daughter of enslaved African woman Maria Belle and Royal Navy officer Sir John Lindsay, who was raised alongside Murray by their great-uncle Lord Mansfield. The two cousins were brought up almost as equals and Belle's accomplishments were used by moral philosophers and abolitionists to prove the intellectual parity of Africans to Europeans if given the same opportunities. Scrutiny of this complex double-image shows how Belle was racialised in comparison to her cousin: she is shown further back, wearing an 'exotic' turban and dazzling white dress designed to contrast with her brown skin, and holding a platter of tropical fruit. Why is she not wearing a rose garland in her hair or a pastel-coloured gown, or holding a book to show off her intellect like her cousin? These visual disparities partly explain why Belle's true identity was quickly forgotten and she was, until recently, misinterpreted as a servant.

Cambridge connections

Many people living in Cambridgeshire, or who lived elsewhere but sent their sons to the University of Cambridge, invested in the Atlantic slave trade and reaped financial rewards from it. But the town and county also emerged as an early centre of abolitionism, submitting three anti-slave trade petitions to Parliament in early 1788.

Inspired by Black writers such as Ignatius Sancho and Phillis Wheatley, Peter Peckard used his influence as Vice-Chancellor of Cambridge University to publicly decry the moral evils of slavery and argue for greater racial equality and alternative forms of trade with Africa. His radicalism attracted Cambridge graduates Thomas Clarkson and later William Wilberforce, both of whom became leading figures in the abolitionist movement.

Olaudah Equiano likely first visited Cambridge in 1789 at the start of a promotional tour for his autobiography, and met Peckard and other key Cambridge abolitionists then. In 1792, he married Susannah Cullen of Ely and settled in Soham, where he raised his family until 1796.

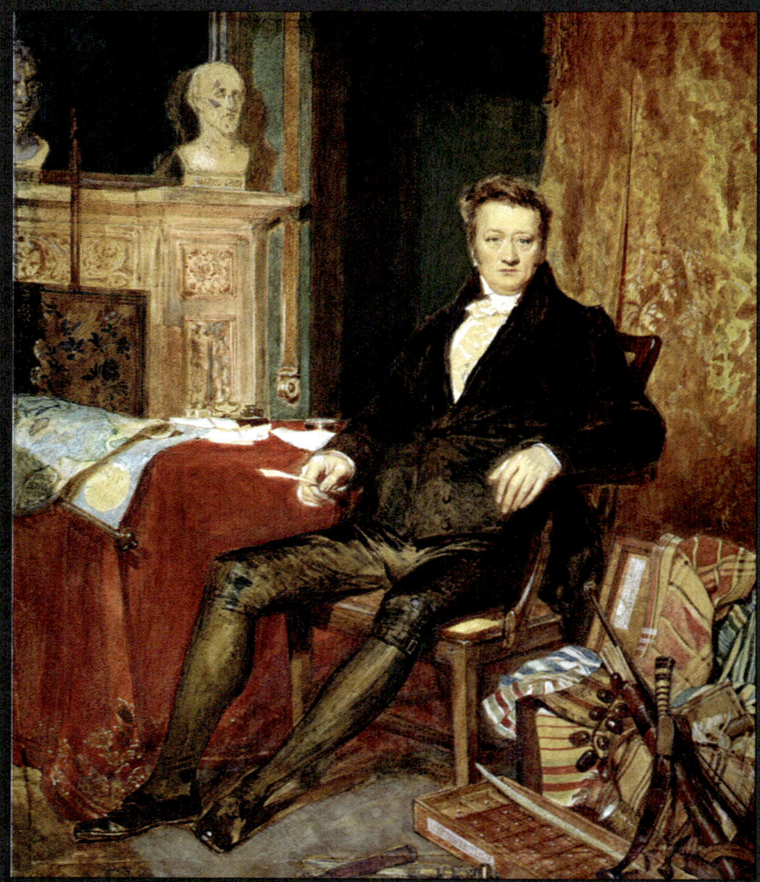

55

Alfred Edward Chalon RA (1780—1860).
Thomas Clarkson with his campaign chest, about 1824. Watercolour on paper, 44 × 35.2 cm (unframed)

84 × 75.5 cm (framed). Wilberforce House Museum, Hull Museums, Kingston-upon-Hull (KINCM:1980.840). Given by Mr J.A. Stephens, 1980, with earlier provenance linked to Clarkson's daughter-in-law. Exhibited: Royal Academy annual exhibition, 1824, no. 455

After graduating from Cambridge, Wisbech-born Clarkson devoted his life to abolitionism. A founder of SEAST, Clarkson supported Equiano, wrote abolitionist books and gave anti-slavery lectures across Britain. After the Abolition of the Slave Trade Act was passed in 1807, Clarkson worked towards the total abolition of slavery. Chalon's portrait shows Clarkson in his mid-sixties, when he was mobilising support for a bill to abolish slavery in the British Empire, finally enacted as the 1833 Slavery Abolition Act. In 1839, Clarkson founded the British and Foreign Anti-Slavery Society (now Anti-Slavery International), the world's first international human rights organisation, and in 1840 he was President of the first World Anti-Slavery Convention.

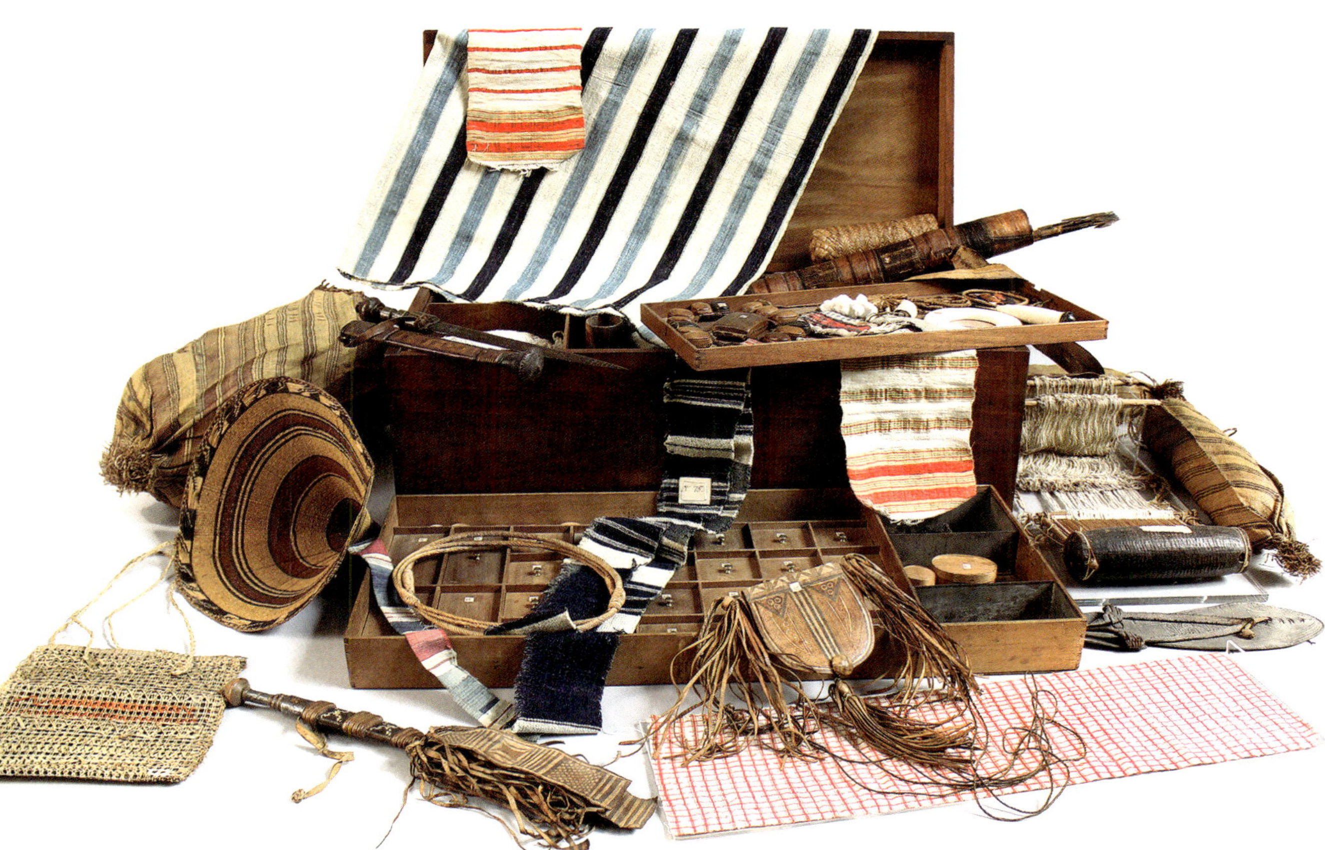

Thomas Clarkson
(1760—1846).
'Cabinet of Freedom',
Anti-slave trade campaign
chest, 1787—8. Portable
mahogany chest with four
internal 'divisions' filled with
natural resources and man-
made products from Africa
and objects of violence
associated with the slave
trade, 28.5 × 75.5 × 35.5 cm

Wisbech & Fenland Museum, Wisbech
(WISFM 1870.13). Kept by Clarkson at
his home Playford Hall, Ipswich; passed by
descent to his grandson, Thomas Clarkson III;
sold at auction (Broad, Pritchard & Wiltshire,
Contents of Playford Hall House Sale, 25 July
1867, lot 165); bought by Herman Biddell
(1832—1917) for 25 guineas, acting on behalf
of other Clarkson family members; given to
Wisbech & Fenland Museum by Mrs Mary
Dickinson (daughter of John Clarkson,
wife of Thomas Clarkson II, and mother of
Thomas Clarkson III), 28 November 1870

In 1787, Clarkson toured the docks of London, Liverpool and Bristol collecting
evidence on behalf of the Society for Effecting the Abolition of the Slave Trade to
present at the 1788—9 Privy Council inquiry into the slave trade. Wanting to shock
politicians into facing the unacceptable realities of slavery, Clarkson's chest included
a selection of violent objects used by Atlantic slave traders to restrain, torture and
punish African captives and, on occasion, the crews of slaving ships. These are no
longer present. He also gathered samples of 'African products' from merchants whose
ships traded on the African coast to convince Britain's policymakers that there was
a profitable alternative future Anglo–African trade relationship to be had without
enslavement. In terms of African artistry, Clarkson's chest included samples of
dyed and woven cotton cloths, some interwoven with European silk; rope from
aloes, grass and straw; fine string from tree roots; bags and hats woven from dried
and coloured grasses; etched and glazed clay pipes; leather goods including bags,
sandals and dagger-cases; iron knives and daggers; and intricate gold jewellery.
In terms of natural resources: hardwoods; ivory; peppers and spices; gums and
dyes; seeds, rice and beans; grasses and tobacco.

Clarkson's chest aimed to provide tangible evidence that African-derived
goods provided 'legitimate' (non-human) and, arguably, more lucrative cargoes
than enslaved African people. While effective, Clarkson's campaign chest and the
arguments it materialised and promoted are problematic. As historian James Walvin
put it, 'Freedom meant free trade, free labour, the free movement of capital, in effect
the freedom of an ascendant British economy to invest, exploit and control.' The
types of economic trade Clarkson advocated led to industrial-level exploitation of
Africa's natural resources for mainly European profit. The outcome was widespread
environmental degradation and destruction, with continued exploitation and forced
migration of African peoples, under a different guise.

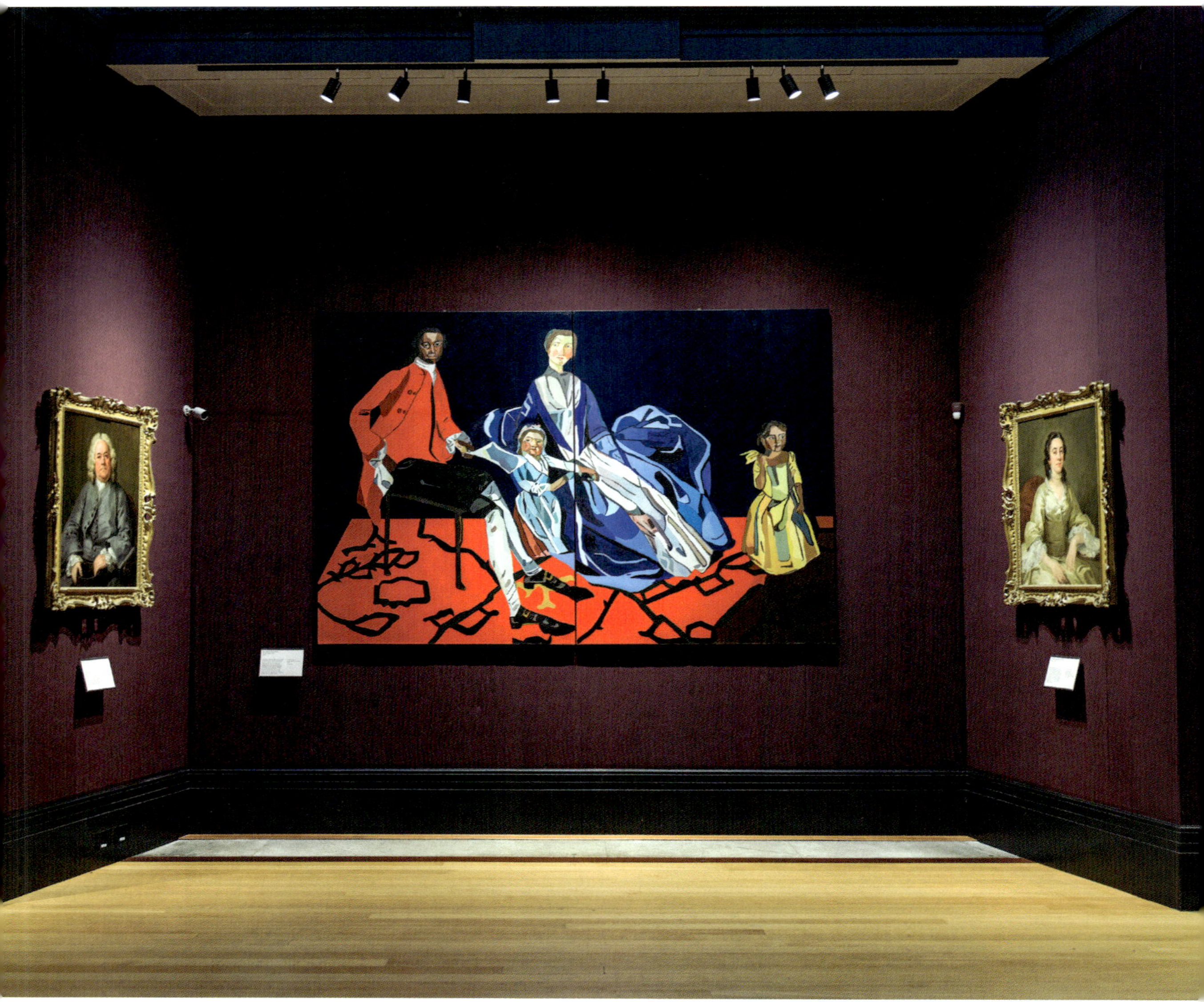

Founder's Galleries rehang, Fitzwilliam Museum, 2024. Featuring Joy Labinjo's *An Eighteenth-Century Family,* portraying Olaudah Equiano with his wife Susannah Cullen and their daughters Anna Maria (right) and Johanna (left)

Olaudah Equiano and Cambridge

Victoria Avery

Within his fifty-two-year lifespan, the time that Olaudah Equiano, also known as Gustavus Vassa, the African, spent in Cambridge might appear insignificant. His documented associations with the county of Cambridgeshire lasted less than seven years: from summer 1789 until spring 1796. That said, the people whom Equiano met there — and also elsewhere but who had connections to Cambridge — were to be significant to him and he to them. Indeed, the first letter of recommendation that Equiano published by way of preface to his autobiographical *Interesting Narrative* was from Peter Peckard, Master of Magdalene College, Cambridge [1].[1] Other early published letters of recommendations came about through the 'testimony' of both Peckard and Thomas Clarkson, a graduate of St John's College, Cambridge. Moreover, it was exclusively from his Cambridgeshire circle of friends that Equiano — one of the most widely travelled men of his time — selected both of his executors, John Audley and Edward Ind. It was a Cambridgeshire woman, Susannah Cullen, whom Equiano chose to marry; and Cambridgeshire was where he chose to settle down and raise his family. While much is known about Equiano's life, his East Anglian connections remain understudied. This essay explores more fully the 'interesting narrative' of Equiano and Cambridge, starting with some reflections on Cambridge as an early centre of abolitionism.[2]

Thomas Clarkson and SEAST

The man behind Equiano's visit to Cambridge in July 1789 was undoubtedly his friend, the heterodox Anglican abolitionist Thomas Clarkson.[3] They probably met through their mutual acquaintance Granville Sharp, whom Equiano had known since before 6 May 1780 and whom Clarkson first encountered in summer 1786.[4] Equiano and Clarkson were on cordial terms by 14 February 1789, when Equiano referred to Clarkson as 'a worthy friend of mine'.[5] Wisbech-born Clarkson had learned of the horrors of slavery as a student listening to anti-slavery sermons by Peter Peckard and researching his winning submission to the Vice-Chancellor's annual Senior Bachelor's Latin essay prize of 1785 on the topic of enslavement — *Anne liceat invitos in servitutem dare?* ('Is it right to make slaves of

1. Equiano, 3rd edn, p. vi; Peckard's letter reappeared in all subsequent lifetime editions. For Equiano's autobiography, see my 'Introducing Olaudah Equiano' essay in the present volume. For Peckard, see Venn Cambridge Alumni online database: unique identifier (hereafter Venn): PKRT753P. For Peckard's paradoxical status as abolitionist and slave trade beneficiary, see Sabine Cadeau's essay, 'Dark Finance' in the present volume.

2. For Equiano and Cambridge/shire, see 'Selected reading'. Also: James E. Bradley, 'Religion and Reform at the Polls: Nonconformity in Cambridge Politics, 1774—1784', *Journal of British Studies*, 23, no. 2 (Spring 1984), pp. 55—78; Ronald Hyam, 'Magdalene, Anti-Slavery and the Early Human Rights Movement from the 1780s to the 1830s', *Magdalene College Occasional Paper No 35* (2007); M.J. Murphy, 'Newspapers and Opinion in Cambridge, 1780—1850', *Transactions of the Cambridge Bibliographical Society*, 6, no. 1 (1972), pp. 35—55; Nicholas Roe, '"Mr. Frond's Company": Cambridge, Dissent, and Coleridge', in N. Roe, *Wordsworth and Coleridge. The Radical Years*, Oxford 1998, pp. 84—117; and M.J. Smith, 'Benjamin Flower and the "Cambridge Intelligencer", 1793—1803', *Transactions of the Cambridge Bibliographical Society*, 16, no. 3 (c), pp. 415—54.

3. Venn CLRK779T2. Anthony Page, 'Thomas Clarkson's Heterodox Anglican Christianity and Anti-Slavery', *Journal of Ecclesiastical History*, April 2024 (doi: 10.1017/S0022046924000010). For Clarkson and abolitionism, see also Sabine Cadeau's essay, 'Cambridge and Haiti' in the present volume.

4. For Equiano's first known letter to Sharp, dated 6 May 1780, see Karlee Anne Sapoznik (ed.), *The Letters and Other Writings of Gustavus Vassa (Olaudah Equiano, the African). Documenting Abolition of the Slave Trade*, Princeton, NJ 2013, pp. 20—2. For Clarkson's introduction to Sharp, via Phillips, shortly prior to June 1786, see note 6.

5. Vincent Carretta, *Equiano, the African. Biography of a Self-Made Man*, London 2005, p. 276.

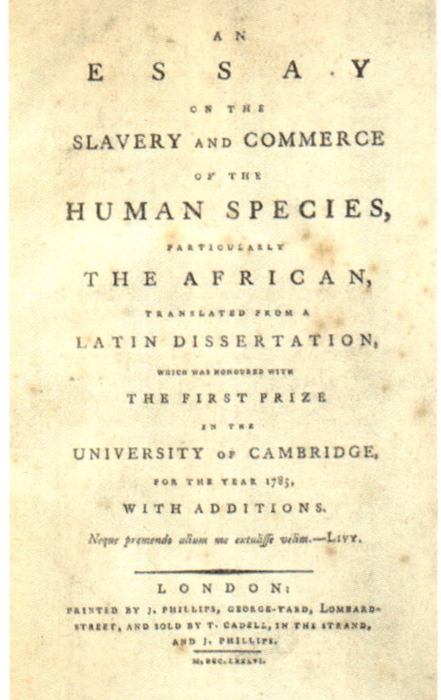

Thomas Clarkson
(1760—1846).
***An Essay on the Slavery
and Commerce of the Human
Species, Particularly the
African …***, London 1786

Cambridge University Library
(RCS.Case.c.252) [not in exhibition]

6. Thomas Clarkson, *The History of the
Rise, Progress, and Accomplishment of the
Abolition of the African Slave-Trade by the
British Parliament*, 2 vols, London 1808,
vol. 1, p. 210. This is part of Chapter VII
(pp. 203—17) that records the influence
of Peckard's anti-slave-trade sermon of
1784 (pp. 204—5); Peckard's setting the
anti-slavery essay in 1785 (p. 205); Clarkson's
researching the essay topic and winning
the prize for his submission in summer
1785 (pp. 205—9); the process of getting it
translated during winter 1785, and published
in expanded form in June 1786 (pp. 210—17);
and meeting Granville Sharp when the book
was 'in the press' (p. 216).
7. Venn WLBR776W. For Wilberforce
and abolitionism, see also Sabine Cadeau's
'Cambridge and Haiti' essay in the present
volume.
8. Venn PT773W. For Pitt and abolitionism,
see Sabine Cadeau's essay, 'Cambridge
and Haiti' in the present volume.
9. For the West India lobby's influence and
other pro-slavery phenomena at Cambridge,
see Nicolas Bell-Romero, *The University
of Cambridge in the Age of Slavery*
(forthcoming), and Sabine Cadeau's
'Dark Finance' in the present volume.

others against their will?'). Clarkson's findings were to change the course of his life. Originally destined for a standard Church of England career, Clarkson had a profound conversion in summer 1785:

> On returning however to London, the subject of [my Essay] almost wholly engrossed my thoughts. … I frequently tried to persuade myself in these intervals that the contents of my Essay could not be true. The more however I reflected upon them, or rather upon the authorities on which they were founded, the more I gave them credit. … a thought came into my mind, that if the contents of the Essay were true, it was time some person should see these calamities to their end.[6]

Clarkson felt divinely called to devote his life to abolishing the Atlantic slave trade and the institution of slavery itself. He went to London, translated his prize-winning essay into English, and had it published in June 1786 by Quaker abolitionist printer James Phillips [58].

The following year, he joined forces with Phillips, Sharp and a handful of other Quakers and Anglicans to establish the non-denominational Society for Effecting the Abolition of the Slave Trade (hereafter SEAST) with the London Committee first meeting on 22 May 1787. Making full use of his Cambridge networks, Clarkson quickly recruited William Wilberforce — with whom he had coincided at St John's — into the SEAST inner circle.[7] As Member of Parliament for Yorkshire from 1784 until 1812, Wilberforce enjoyed considerable political clout, and would soon lead the parliamentary campaign to end the British slave trade. Clarkson also recruited another sympathetic and even more powerful Cambridge alumnus: William Pitt the Younger, then the serving prime minister and one of two Members of Parliament for the University of Cambridge.[8] To help spread the word nationally, from summer 1787 Clarkson championed the establishment of local SEAST committees across Britain; the Cambridgeshire committee was led by Jonathan Peckover of Wisbech, an influential Quaker business-man and close friend of Clarkson. These county-based organisers were tasked with distributing news and pamphlets from the central London Committee to every subscriber in their locality as well as writing to prospective new supporters.

Cambridge University as an early centre for abolition and SEAST subscribers

Many merchants in the 'Africa Trade' and enslavers in the Caribbean sent their sons to Cambridge University, and there was an active pro-slavery lobby in both 'town and gown'.[9]

Cambridge was, however, also known as an early centre for abolition. From the minutes of SEAST meetings in 1787 and 1788, we know that several Cambridge University academics were early subscribers and correspondents, chief among whom was radical reformer William Frend, a fellow and tutor at Jesus College.[10] Having written to the London Committee on 3 December 1787 informing them that the University was to donate eighty guineas to SEAST,[11] Frend was invited to attend a meeting on 1 January 1788 to deliver this and report on its campaign work.[12] Another early SEAST subscriber and correspondent from Cambridge was eminent mathematician Thomas Jones, junior dean and tutor at Trinity College.[13] The minutes of SEAST's 29 January 1788 meeting record how: 'A Letter received from the Rev'd Thomas Jones dated Trinity College Cambridge the 26th Inst[ant] containing a Copy of a Petition to Parliament from that University was read'.[14] This referred to a pro-abolition petition that had been passed by the Senate three days earlier [60].

In addition, many other members of Cambridge University showed their abolitionist allegiances by donating to SEAST. Towards the end of 1788, SEAST published a full list of its subscribers to date. Significantly, there were so many from Cambridge University that it was accorded a section of its own, the only university to be singled out in this way.[15] Nine Cambridge colleges appear as institutional donors: Emmanuel, Jesus, Peterhouse, Sidney Sussex and St Catharine's (each giving two pounds and two shillings); Caius and Clare (five pounds, five shillings each); St John's (ten pounds, ten shillings); and Trinity (twenty-one pounds). Moreover, ten college masters subscribed, including the early anti-slavery advocate John Hinchliffe, Master of Trinity and Bishop of Peterborough.[16] Together with his college friend Richard Watson, Regius Professor of Divinity and Bishop of Llandaff, Hinchliffe had corresponded with Granville Sharp over abolition as early as 1781 and had invited him to Cambridge to discuss abolition.[17]

Also listed was Peter Peckard, Master of Magdalene [1], who as University Vice-Chancellor had set the Latin essay prize on slavery in 1785 that Clarkson had won. It was in great part due to Peckard that Cambridge University became such a hive of abolitionism in the late 1780s.[18] In addition to delivering several influential anti-slavery sermons in the University Church of Great St Mary's and his own college's chapel, he published anonymously a one-hundred-page anti-slavery tract, *Am I Not a Man? And a Brother? With All Humility Addressed to the British Legislature* (Cambridge 1788). Interestingly, Peckard not only used SEAST's motto in his title, but he also incorporated SEAST's logo into the title page, no doubt to promote the Society's work. Given that its design had only been approved on 16 October 1787, this must be one of the

10. Venn FRNT775W.
11. The 'Fair Minute Book of the Committee for the Abolition of the Slave Trade, Vol. I: 22 May 1787–26 Feb 1788', British Library: Add Ms 21254 (152 F.13); hereafter SEAST Minute Book. Quotation on fol. 22v.
12. SEAST Minute Book, fols 24v–25r. Frend is also recorded in SEAST meeting minutes on 9 February 1787 and 20 May 1788.
13. Venn JNS774T.
14. SEAST Minute Book, fol. 34r.
15. SEAST 1788 Subscription List, pp. 28–32. See Jirik 2020, pp. 756–7.
16. Venn HNCF750J.
17. Venn WT754R. Jirik 2020 pp. 751–2.
18. See especially Hyam 2007 and Jirik 2020.

earliest uses of the SEAST logo outside of that institution.[19] Peckard made an irrefutable case against slavery, tearing apart the pseudo-scientific ideas then in circulation which suggested that Europeans were intellectually superior to Africans, citing the letters of Ignatius Sancho [46] and the poems of Phillis Wheatley [51] as evidence of the equal mental capacities of Black and white people to disprove these racist theories.

The majority of the 1788 Cambridge University SEAST sub-scribers were fellows and tutors, with no fewer than sixty-two lower-ranking academics listed under their respective college. Amongst these was the evangelical Henry William Coulthurst of Sidney Sussex, another early SEAST correspondent.[20] Like many involved in abolitionism, Coulthurst was something of a paradox: born on Barbados into a slave-owning family he would, in 1792, inherit a part-share in the family plantation.[21] Even a handful of students subscribed, including James Scarlett of Trinity, who (like Coulthurst) was born in the Caribbean to enslavers.[22] All this to say that, according to Michael E. Jirik's calculations, Cambridge University donations comprised about 6% of SEAST's income in its inaugural year.[23]

Cambridge town SEAST subscribers

Support for abolition in Cambridge was not restricted to University circles. Many local residents were SEAST supporters, as the 1788 SEAST subscription list reveals. Four individuals were listed as living in Cambridge itself: 'Mr Charles Finch' who was surely Charles Finch, trustee of the politically active Stone-Yard Baptist Chapel (aka St Andrew's Street Baptist Church); 'Mr W. Fisher'; 'Mrs Essex'; and 'Mrs Peckard', namely Martha Ferrar, published poet and wife of Peter Peckard.[24] Several other subscribers were listed as Cambridgeshire residents: 'Mrs Woodham, Ely'; 'Lady Hatton of Lanstanton', likely Mary Hatton, eldest daughter of Sir Thomas Hatton and his wife Harriott Dingley.[25] and the aforementioned Jonathan Peckover in Wisbech.

Preparations for Cambridge

Given the large number of local SEAST supporters, it is hardly surprising that Equiano was keen to visit Cambridge shortly after his *Interesting Narrative* was published, to sell copies and secure subscribers for the second edition. Equiano would have been aware that, in addition to the anti-slavery petition sent from the Cambridge University Senate on 26 January 1788 [60] and presented before Parliament on 8 February 1788, two others from the locality had been sent at the same time: one from the mayor, bailiffs and burgesses of the borough (passed 21 January; presented 14 February), the other from

19. On 5 July 1787, it was 'Resolved, that a Seal be engraved for the use of this Society and that Joseph Woods, Dr Hooper, and Phillip Sansom, be requested to prepare a Design for the same, to be laid before the Committee' (SEAST Minute Book, fol. 7v [new p. 19]). On 16 October 1787, the design for the seal was approved: 'Joseph Woods on the Subcommittee appointed the 7th July last [sic] on the subject of a Seal for this Committee brought in a Specimen of a Design for the same, expressive of an African in Chains in a supplicating Posture, with this Motto "Am I not a Man & a Brother" which being approved the Subcommittee before appointed is desired to get it well engraved.' (SEAST Minute Book, fol. 16r—v [new pp. 29—30]).
20. Venn CLTT770WH.
21. See the entry for Coulthurst in the Centre for the Study of the Legacies of British Slavery database: https://www.ucl.ac.uk/lbs/person/view/2146634732 (accessed 17 August 2024).
22. Venn SCRT785J. For the 1788 SEAST Cambridge student subscribers, see Jirik 2020, pp. 756 and 768, note 35.
23. Jirik 2020, p. 757.
24. See 'Peckard [*née* Ferrar], Martha', *Oxford Dictionary of National Biography*, https://doi.org/10.1093/ref:odnb/74065 (accessed 17 August 2024).
25. See Sarah Murden, 'Art Detectives: Miss Mary Hatton by George Romney', *All Things Georgian*, 26 April 2018, https://georgianera.wordpress.com/tag/longstanton-hall/ (accessed 17 August 2024).

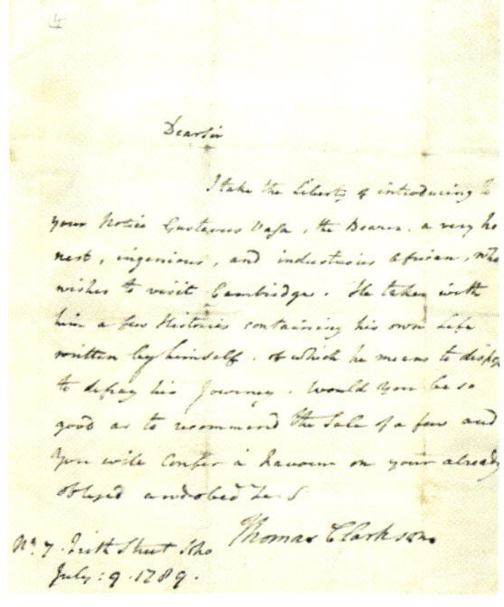

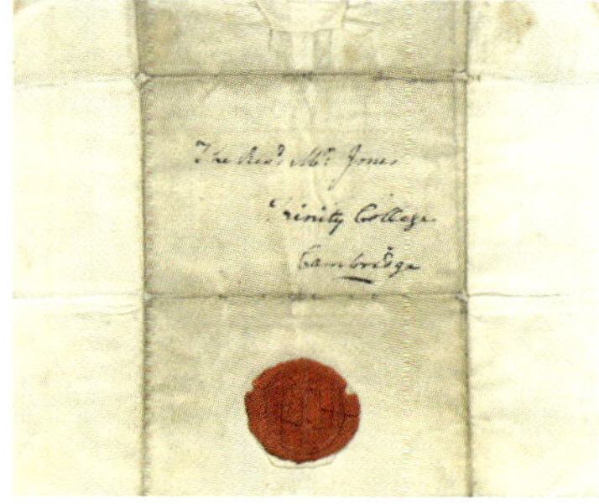

59

Thomas Clarkson
(1760—1846).
Autograph letter to Thomas Jones of Trinity College, Cambridge, 9 July 1789

St John's College, Cambridge
(GB 275 Clarkson/Folder 1-5/Doc. 4).
Part of Thomas Clarkson's personal papers

26. Abel 2022, pp. 50—1.
27. For example, Carretta 2005, p. 335; and Sapoznik 2013, p. 212.
28. *Jackson's Oxford Journal*, no. 1887 (Saturday 27 June 1789), p. 3. I am grateful to Dawna Ina Kreeger for drawing this notice to my attention.

the 'gentry, clergy, freeholders and others of the county of Cambridge' (passed 1 March; presented on 12 March).[26] Such vocal support from across Cambridge and Cambridgeshire society meant that Equiano could be guaranteed a warm reception.

It is often claimed that Equiano's visit to Cambridge, which is documented as having taken place in July 1789, was the preliminary stop on this first of many book-promotion tours.[27] However, this can now be disproved, thanks to an overlooked notice published in the *Oxford Journal* on 27 June 1789, which clearly states that Equiano was 'now in Town' to sell first edition copies of his autobiography.[28] What distinguishes Equiano's visit to Cambridge is the lack of any such announcement in the local papers. This presupposes that none was needed because Equiano knew that he could count on assistance from the many people in Cambridge — both townspeople and University academics — who had been actively lobbying for abolition since the mid-1780s.

That said, to ease Equiano's passage, Thomas Clarkson appears to have written letters of introduction to key abolitionists resident in Cambridge. One such letter survives in the St John's College archives. Written from Frith Street, Soho, on 9 July 1789, it is addressed to the aforementioned Thomas Jones of Trinity [59]. Clarkson alerts Jones to Equiano's imminent arrival in town and asks him to enjoin others to buy copies of the *Interesting Narrative*:

> I take the Liberty of introducing to your Notice Gustavus Vasa [sic], the Bearer, a very honest, ingenious, and industrious African, who wishes to visit Cambridge. He takes with him a few Histories containing his own Life written by himself of which he means to dispose to defray his Journey. Would you be so good as to recommend the Sale of a few and you will confer a favour on your already obliged and obed[ient] Serv[an]t

The letter's reverse is revealing. It has a wax seal impressed with SEAST's logo but no postmark, which indicates two things. First, Clarkson wrote the letter on behalf of SEAST (had it been in a personal capacity, he would have used his own seal), which means that Equiano's visit to Cambridge had SEAST approval. Secondly, Clarkson cannot have posted his letter direct to Jones (or it would bear a postmark), which means he likely gave it to Equiano to hand-deliver as 'the bearer' to Jones. This makes 9 July 1789 the earliest possible day that Equiano could have left London for Cambridge, meaning his tour of Cambridge probably started on or soon after 10 July; in other words, straight after his visit to Oxford with only a brief turnaround in London.

**Unrecorded University clerk.
'To the Honourable the
Commons of Great Britain
in Parliament assembled'.**
Fair copy of the petition from
'The Chancellor, Masters &
Scholars of the University of
Cambridge' in support of the
'Suppression of the Slave Trade
Bill', University of Cambridge
Grace Book, 26 January 1788

Cambridge University Library
(*Liber Gratiarum Lamda*), fols 207—8

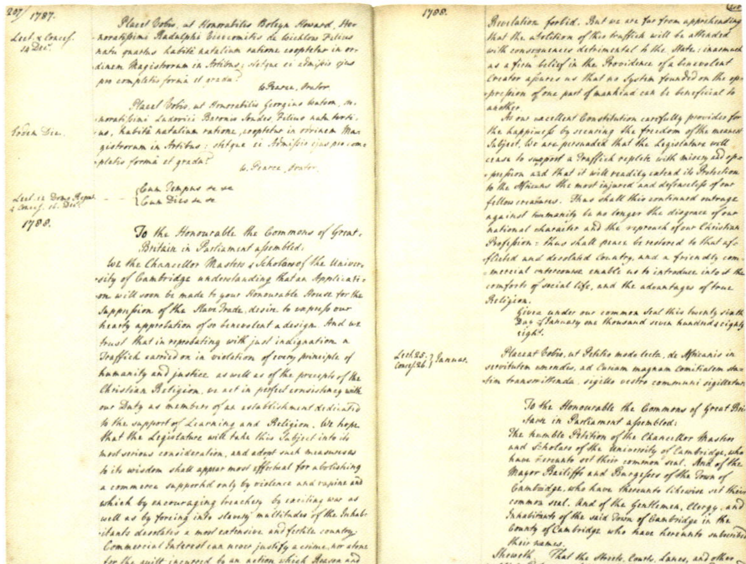

July 1789: Equiano's first documented Cambridge visit

Equiano must have set off for Cambridge confident of a warm
welcome and good sales, and he was not to be disappointed.
There is no evidence as to where Equiano stayed, which book-
sellers agreed to sell his books, whether he gave any public
lectures, nor whom he met. However, Equiano surely went to
Trinity College to meet Thomas Jones armed with his letter
from Clarkson. And we can equally assume that he would have
sought to meet those Cambridge residents who had subscribed
to the first edition. Prime among these — assuming he is the
'Mr Robinson' listed — was Robert Robinson, the passionate
radical abolitionist minister of St Andrew's Street Baptist church,
and author of the March 1788 Cambridgeshire parliamentary
petition.[29] By the late 1780s, Robinson was well established,
having been Baptist minister since 1759. A brilliant preacher,
Robinson had grown his congregation to 120 members by 1775,
with regular attendances of between 600 and 800 people. He
also organised lectures in private houses and country barns
in over a dozen villages within a ten-mile radius of Cambridge,
with around 2,300 attendees.[30] Robinson used his pulpit to
preach abolitionism: in February 1788, for example, he delivered
a sermon on the inconsistency of slavery with Christianity.[31]
He was also a popular hymn-writer. Equiano liked his words
for 'Come Thou Fount of Every Blessing' enough to include
a couplet from it in his autobiography: 'O! to grace how
great a debtor / Daily I'm constrain'd to be!'[32]

Equiano may have also targeted Cambridge SEAST supporters
who had not subscribed to his first edition, reckoning that these

29. Abel 2022.
30. Bradley 1984, pp. 59—60.
31. Abel 2022, p. 50.
32. Equiano 1789, vol. II, p. 132. I am grateful
to Dawnanna Kreeger for this observation.

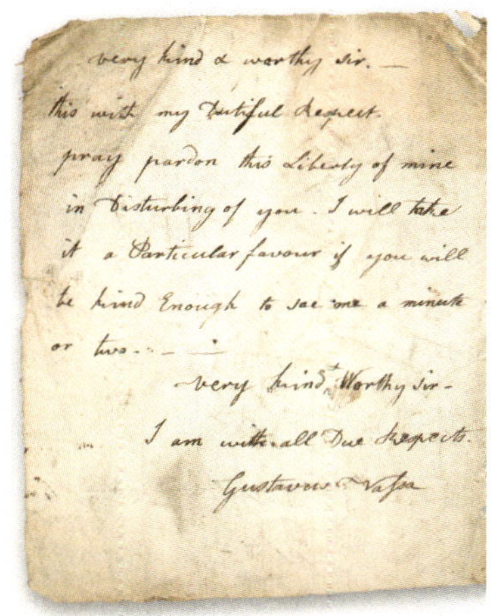

61

Olaudah Equiano
(*c.*1745—1797).
Autograph letter to Peter Peckard, Master of Magdalene College, Cambridge, undated but probably mid-to-late July 1789

Magdalene College, Cambridge (Ferrar Papers: F/FP/2273). Part of Peter Peckard's personal papers

33. Venn JWT769J.
34. My thanks to Eleanor Stephenson and Dawnanna Kreeger for assistance with analysis of subscribers.
35. Thomas Mott (ed.), *The Posthumous Poetical Works of the Late Edward Ind, Esq. of Cambridge; With a Biographical Sketch of his Life*, Cambridge 1822; and Abel 2022.

could be persuaded to sign up to the second. One such was Clarkson's mentor, Peter Peckard, with whom we know Equiano attempted to connect thanks to an undated autograph note still in Cambridge [61]. Herein, Equiano requested a meeting with Peckard:

> Very kind & worthy sir,
> This with my Dutiful Respect, pray pardon this liberty of mine in disturbing of you. I will take it a particular favour if you will be kind enough to see me a minute or two.
> Very kind & worthy sir, I am with all Due Respects,
> Gustavus Vassa

The reverse of Equiano's note bears no postmark or postal address, merely the recipient's name, which suggests that he wrote it when already in Cambridge. That this rather scrappy note was deemed worthy of retention by Peckard (now in his family papers in Magdalene College archives) surely indicates the esteem in which he held Equiano. There is no record that the meeting took place, but the fact that Peckard subscribed to the second edition suggests that it did. Similarly, Equiano seems to have approached Joseph Jowett, Fellow and Tutor of Trinity Hall and Regius Professor of Civil Law, who was a 1788 SEAST subscriber and part of a Cambridge evangelical group comprising men like the outspoken social reformer Charles Simeon, vicar of Holy Trinity, Cambridge.[33] While Jowett had not subscribed to Equiano's first edition, he did sign up to the second, most likely because he met Equiano in Cambridge in July 1789.

A logical third target group for Equiano were those Cambridge residents who had subscribed neither to the first edition of his autobiography nor to SEAST, but whose religious and/or political leanings made them sympathetic to the abolitionist cause. Scrutiny of Equiano's second edition subscribers reveal several new Cambridge-based people not amongst the first edition subscribers who may have met Equiano or heard him speak in July 1789.[34] Particularly significant amongst this group are Edward Ind and John Audley, his future executors. Born in St Ives, Ind was a wealthy businessman-brewer, Alderman of Cambridge (elected 1782) and poet, about whom much is known thanks to the 'biographical sketch' included in a posthumous anthology of his poems, published in 1822 [66], and from recent research by Matthew Abel.[35] Through political alliances with John Mortlock (Alderman, Banker to Cambridge University, MP for Cambridge, and thirteen times Mayor of Cambridge) and his brewing properties and profits, Ind was an influential voice in non-academic circles. As a committed evangelical Anglican, Ind worshipped at Holy Trinity, Cambridge, where he also attended vestry meetings and was elected churchwarden on numerous occasions. His parish priest was the above-mentioned evangelical, abolitionist and Claphamite Charles Simeon, who knew Granville Sharp and William Wilberforce through the Clapham Sect. This was a group of mainly Church of England philanthropists, civic-political and socio-economic rights activists and abolitionists associated with the church of Holy Trinity, Clapham, which coalesced around its influential evangelical minister, Cambridge alumnus Henry Venn.[36] Indeed, it was Ind who had led the committee responsible for drafting the Cambridge Borough's petition to Parliament in late January 1788.[37] Audley, mean-while, was an influential and wealthy Cambridge wool-stapler and an active dissenting Christian, who was a lay preacher in the Independent Church circuit around Cambridge, and who also attended Holy Trinity vestry meetings with Ind. Both Audley and Ind were friendly with Baptist minister Robert Robinson, through whom they may have first met Equiano and been persuaded to subscribe to the second edition of his autobiography. They clearly became firm allies, both sub-scribing to all subsequent editions. Several Cambridge-based key abolitionists and reformers, drawn mainly from St Andrew's Street Baptist Church and Holy Trinity, met regularly in a politically orientated book club, informally known as Alderman Ind's Club, because Ind was the Treasurer.[38] It is feasible that Equiano may have attended a meeting during his first sojourn in Cambridge, and indeed joined other meetings after his marriage to Susannah Cullen, when he was present in the locality.

From an effusive letter of thanks sent to Francis Hodson, printer of the *Cambridge Chronicle*, dated 30 July 1789, we know that Equiano deemed his Cambridge visit a success [62]. Although he only refers generically to 'particular marks of kindness' and 'favours' received from 'the Gentlemen of the University, and the inhabitants of this town', from later amend-ed versions of this same letter we know that this meant book purchases and new subscriptions.[39] But Equiano received more than just book sales in Cambridge. His letter proves that he received a truly warm welcome. Grateful for 'acts of kindness and hospitality', he reports being 'more particularly delighted with that universal fellow-feeling they have discovered for my very poor and much oppressed countrymen', having experienced 'true civility without respect to colour or complexion'. Equiano also quipped: 'Nor have even the amiable fair-sex refused to countenance the sooty African', which suggests he had received the attentions of one or more local women. Significantly, although Equiano would publish similar versions in local papers after visits elsewhere, he never again reprinted this line. This has led to the suggestion that it was during this visit of July 1789 that Equiano first met his future wife, Susannah Cullen.[40] While this may be so, Susannah did not subscribe until the third edition (London, 30 October 1790), which raises the possibility that they instead

36. Venn VN742H. Having studied at Cambridge in the mid-1740s, Venn became a fellow at Queens' College (1749—57) and held several posts within the Dioceses of Ely and Huntingdon. In 1754, he had become curate of Holy Trinity, Clapham.
37. Abel 2022, pp. 51 and 59, note 62.
38. Abel 2022, pp. 53 and 60, notes 77—8.
39. Sapoznik 2013, pp. 129—33.
40. For example, Carretta 2005, p. 347; John Bugg, 'The Other Interesting Narrative: Olaudah Equiano's Public Book Tour', *Publications of the Modern Language Association of America*, 121, no. 5 (2006), pp. 1424—42 (p. 1436); and Sapoznik 2013, p. 212.

62

Olaudah Equiano
(*c.* 1745—1797).
**Vote of thanks addressed
to Francis Hodson, proprietor,
printer and publisher of
the *Cambridge Chronicle*,**
30 July 1789

Published in the *Cambridge Chronicle and Journal*, 1 August 1789. Cambridge University Library, Cambridge
[not in exhibition]

To the Printer of the CAMBRIDGE CHRONICLE.

SIR,

HAVING received particular marks of kindness from the Gentlemen of the University, and the inhabitants of this town, I beg you to suffer me thus publicly to express my most grateful acknowledgements to them for their favours. I have been more particularly delighted with that universal fellow-feeling they have discovered for my very poor and much oppressed countrymen. Here I experience true civility without respect to colour or complexion. Nor have even the amiable fair-sex refused to countenance the sooty African. These acts of kindness and hospitality have filled my grateful heart with longing desires to see these worthy friends on my own estate, where the richest produce of Africa should be devoted to their entertainment: they should there partake of the luxuriant Pine-apple, and the well-savoured virgin-palm-wine. And to heighten the bliss, I would burn a certain kind of tree that would afford us a light, as clear and brilliant as the virtues of my guests. Such shall be our joy, if it please God I am ever restored to my lost estate, and meet these my friends in my native country.

I am Sir,
Your humble servant
GUSTAVUS VASSA,
The African.

CAMBRIDGE, *July* 30*th*, 1789.

met between the publication of the second and third editions: after early January 1790 and before late October 1790. If so, then they most likely met during Equiano's second visit to Cambridge.

May 1790: Equiano's second Cambridge visit

Looking at surviving evidence, a case can be made for Equiano returning to Cambridge in late May 1790. Two documents exist that, when read together, appear to support this hypothesis. First, there is the warm letter of support that Peckard wrote for Equiano on 26 May 1790. Although the original is lost, we know of it from Equiano's third edition:

> To the Chairmen of the Committees for the Abolition of the Slave Trade.
>
> Magdalen College, Cambridge, May, 26, 1790.
>
> Gentlemen,
>
> I take the liberty, as being joined with you in the same laudable endeavours to support the cause of humanity in the abolition of the Slave Trade, to recommend to your protection the bearer of this note, Gustavus Vassa, an African; and to beg the favour of your assistance to him in the sale of his book.[41]

41. Equiano 1790 (3rd edn), p. vi; Sapoznik 2013, p. 59.

Secondly, an advert in *Aris's Birmingham Gazette* on 14 June 1790 announces that copies of the second edition were available for purchase in several locations including being '*Sold by the Author*, at Mr [William] Bliss's, Grocer, Aston-street [my emphasis]'.[42] Although Peckard's letter does not in itself prove that Equiano was present in Cambridge on 26 May 1790 as Sapoznik supposed (the letter could have been mailed to him), it is more likely than not to have been written in Equiano's presence in order that he could take it directly with him to Birmingham (as argued above in the case of Clarkson's letter to Jones).[43] Moreover, Cambridge would have been a logical layover for Equiano travelling from London to Birmingham.

Susannah Cullen

Thanks to recent archival research undertaken primarily by Dawnanna Kreeger, we know that Susannah Cullen was born in Ely and baptised on 24 May 1762 in her family's parish church of Holy Trinity, which at the time occupied the Lady Chapel of Ely Cathedral.[44] She was the fifth of nine surviving children (the second of six daughters) of James Cullen and Ann Jones, who had married in 1753. While her mother was from Shropshire farming stock, her father was from Cambridgeshire. An ironmonger by trade, he ran a profitable business from Fore Hill in central Ely, which also served as the family home. After his death, in August 1781, Susannah's mother and oldest brother took over the business, and ran it jointly until February 1788, when the partnership was dissolved. At some point after this, Susannah's mother moved to Soham, settling in the parish of St Andrew's. It seems that Susannah and her other unmarried siblings went too: certainly, Susannah's oldest sister Anne was married in St Andrew's, Soham, in October 1790; and her younger brother Thomas was buried there in April 1798. It was also in St Andrew's that Susannah married Equiano in April 1792, where their two daughters were baptised — Anna Maria (January 1794) and Johanna (April 1795) — and where she was buried in February 1796. Given their strong faith, it seems probable that Equiano and Susannah met through the ecclesiastical networks that linked Cambridge to Ely and the wider diocese: perhaps through Susannah's parish priest in Soham, who undoubtedly knew the local Anglican clergy given that his living came via Pembroke College, or via the Baptist circuit, through Cambridge-based Robert Robinson and his Soham counterpart, Francis Bland. Certainly, Bland became friendly enough with the couple to be a witness at their wedding.

Equiano's views on intermarriage

From various discussions of the legitimacy of mutually respectful and equal love between Africans and Europeans included in the first edition of his *Interesting Narrative*

42. Sapoznik 2013, p. 111.
43. Sapoznik 2013, p. 15.
44. Holy Trinity, Ely, 'A Register of the Parish of Ely Trinity', 1753—80, n.p., 'Christenings 1762', under date: Cambridgeshire Record Office, Ely: P/67/1/5.

onwards, it is evident that Equiano's passionate belief in intermarriage as an expression of racial equality predated his meeting Susannah Cullen — and so it was not a result of this but rather a catalyst for it. Equiano was keen, for example, to highlight the dire consequences that could occur when intermarriage was forbidden, when he recalled the tragic tale of an enslaved Black man who committed suicide after his enslaver had forcibly prevented him from marrying his white love.[45] Equiano was undoubtedly aware that the subject of intermarriages in late eighteenth-century Britain was increasingly a cause for anxiety and consternation in certain circles.

The clearest and most forceful case that Equiano made for intermarriage was not in the first edition of his autobiography but rather over a year earlier, in a review of 28 January 1788.[46] It formed part of his blistering attack on two racist and offensive pamphlets by leading pro-slavery activist James Tobin, *Cursory Remarks* (London 1785) and its sequel, *Short Rejoinder* (London 1787).[47] A former member of His Majesty's Council in Nevis, and a member of the Bristol West India Association, Tobin wanted to counter the abolitionist arguments of James Ramsay and others and undermine claims for equality for Black people (whether free or enslaved). Following racial purity arguments, Tobin railed against intermarriage as degenerate, unchristian and against the natural order of things, vilified the union of Black men and white women, and argued that intermarriage should be banned by law.[48] Equiano launched a powerful counterattack, destroying Tobin's arguments. His review ended with a rigorous defence of intermarriage, citing biblical justification, and arguing that it would strengthen the British nation:

> If the mind of a black man conceives the passion of love for a fair female, he is to pine, languish, and even die, sooner than an intermarriage be allowed, merely because the complexion of the offspring should not be tawney — A more foolish prejudice than this never warped a cultivated mind … God looks with equal good-will on all his creatures, whether black or white — let neither, therefore, arrogantly condemn the other. … why not establish intermarriages at home, and in our Colonies? and encourage open, free, and generous love … subservient only to moral rectitude, without distinction of colour of a skin? … Away then with your narrow impolitic notion of preventing by law what will be a national honour, national strength, and productive of national virtue — Intermarriages![49]

Betrothal and marriage

Whether Equiano first met Susannah in July 1789 or May 1790, they appear not to have been formally betrothed until

45. Equiano 1789 (1st edn), pp. 122—3.
46. *The Public Advertiser*, no. 16754 (28 January 1788), pp. 1—2; Sapoznik 2013, pp. 94—8.
47. See 'Tobin, James', *Oxford Dictionary of National Biography*, https://doi.org/10.1093/ref:odnb/53030 (accessed 17 August 2024).
48. James Tobin, *Cursory Remarks*, London 1785, p. 113.
49. Sapoznik 2013, pp. 96—7.

after the publication of his autobiography's fourth edition (May 1791). This is because up to and including this edition, Equiano included a brief note to the effect that he was an eligible bachelor looking for a suitable wife: 'My hand is ever free, if any female Debonair wishes to obtain it'.[50] Equiano expunged this line, however, from the fifth edition (June 1792) because he had married Susannah two months earlier.[51] Presumably, Equiano would not have retained this line about his eligibility in the third and fourth editions had he and Susannah already been engaged. If my interpretation is correct, then Equiano and Susannah were betrothed at some point after 20 May 1791. Given Equiano's punishing book-tour schedule it seems that they cannot have seen much of each other from when they first met to their betrothal, and nor from their betrothal to their marriage in April 1792, and so it is tempting to think that their relationship deepened through correspondence — assuming that Susannah was literate, which is implied in her subscribing to the third and fourth editions of Equiano's book.

That Equiano had no intention of abating his abolitionist activities after marriage is evident from a letter to his Nottingham-based friend, mathematician, theologian, Royal Society Fellow and radical dissenter, George Walker, written on 27 February 1792, just before he tied the knot.[52] Equiano tells Walker about his forthcoming marriage and invites him to his wedding, but this important news is lost amongst all the details of his recent successful book tour in Ireland, his recognition by leading white abolitionists, and his plans to go to Scotland immediately after his wedding to publish and sell his fifth edition:

> Sir, I went to Ireland & was there 8½ months, & sold 1900 Copies of my narrative. I Came here on the 10th Inst [February 1792] — & I now mean as it seem Pleasing to my Good God! — to Leave London in about 8 — or, 10 Days more, & take me a Wife — (one Miss Cullen —) of Soham in Cambridge shire — & when I have given her about 8 or 10 Days Comfort, I mean Directly to go to Scotland, & sell my 5th Editions — I Trust that my going about has been of much use to the cause of the abolition of the accu[r]sed Slave Trade — a Gentleman of the Committee [SEAST], The Rev'd Dr. Baker has said that I am of more use to the Cause than half of the People in this Country — I wish to God I Could be so. ... I will be Glad to see you at my Wed[din]g.[53]

It is interesting that Equiano says so little of his bride-to-be, except giving her family name and informing Walker that she lives in Soham. That Equiano intended to stay on in London until the second week of March, rather than returning to Soham to see Susannah is telling, as is the fact that Equiano had already decided to leave his new wife in Soham so soon

50. Equiano 1789 (1st edn), pp. 237—8; Equiano 1789 (2nd edn), p. 240; Equiano 1790 (3rd edn), p. 341 (where the venue is corrected to 'Whitehart-Court, Lombard-Street'); Equiano 1791 (4th edn), p. 341.
51. Equiano 1792 (5th edn), p. 342.
52. See 'Walker, George', *Oxford Dictionary of National Biography*, https://doi.org/10.1093/ref:odnb/28481 (accessed 17 August 2024).
53. Sapoznik 2013, pp. 32—4.

after their wedding for his tour of Scotland. Marriage was clearly not going to interrupt his work schedule. However, close reading of a short text that Equiano inserted into the fifth edition of his autobiography (likely written in Edinburgh after his marriage in later April or May 1792) shows that he changed his plans after writing to Walker, once again in favour of work. Equiano did not, in fact, leave London for Soham as planned on 6 March 1792, but rather stayed in the capital conducting business until 3 April 1792:

> Soon after I returned [from Belfast] to London [10 February 1792], where I found persons of note from Holland and Germany, who requested of me to go there; and I was glad to hear that an edition of my Narrative had been printed in both places. I remained in London till I heard the debate in the House of Commons on the Slave Trade, April the 2d and 3d. I then went to Soham in Cambridgeshire, and was married on the 7th of April to Miss Cullen, daughter of James and Ann Cullen, late of Ely.[54]

The debate that Equiano was keen to hear was Wilberforce's latest bill to abolish the slave trade, his first bill having been defeated in 1791. This time the House voted in favour of abolition (230 for and 85 against) but with the frustrating amendment by Henry Dundas, MP for Midlothian, that abolition should be gradual not immediate. Equiano must have had to hurry back to Soham to be in time for his wedding on 7 April 1792. The ceremony at St Andrew's — conducted under a marriage licence that Equiano had obtained in London on 28 March 1792 — was witnessed by Susannah's younger brother, Thomas, and Soham Baptist minister Francis Bland, as their marriage certificate attests [63].[55]

Equiano's marriage to Susannah was reported in several papers. The *Cambridge Chronicle* recorded how, 'On Monday fortnight [sic] Gustavus Vassa the African, well known in most parts of this kingdom as a preacher, was married at Soham, to Miss Cullen, daughter of the Late Mr. James Cullen of Ely.'[56] The *General Evening Post* gave further details:

> Gustavus Vassa (Equiano Olaudah), the African, well known in England as the champion and advocate for procuring a suppression of the Slave Trade, was married at Soham, in Cambridgeshire to Miss Cullen, daughter of Mr. Cullen of Ely, in the same County, in the presence of a vast number of people assembled on the occasion.[57]

It is likely that many of the wedding guests were abolitionists, and amongst those on whom the West India Committee and pro-slavery lobby were keeping tabs. As Adam Hochschild explains, having budgeted £1,600 for articles to be published

54. Equiano 1792 (5th edn), p. 359.
55. Equiano's marriage bond and marriage allegation are held at Lambeth Palace Library archives: FM II/183, under 28 March 1792.
56. *Cambridge Chronicle and Journal*, 21 April 1792 p. 3.
57. *General Evening Post*, 19—21 April edition.

**Marriage certificate
of Olaudah Equiano and
Susannah Cullen**, St Andrew's
Parish Church, Soham,
Cambridgeshire, 7 April 1792

Soham Register for Marriages MDCCLXXVII,
fol. 74, no. 220, Cambridgeshire Archives,
Ely (P142/1/11)

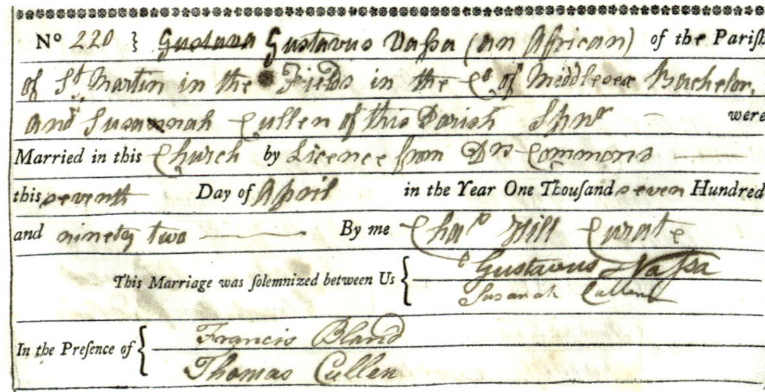

'in the Newspapers and otherwise', the West India Committee
had established a subcommittee by March 1792 to scour the
press daily and to reply 'to what may be therein inserted by
the Favourers of the Abolition', and acquired copies of a pro-
slavery book for distribution 'in the Country, *particularly
at Cambridge* [my emphasis]'.[58] Clearly, the Cambridge
abolitionist support-base was recognised as a real threat
by planters and enslavers.

Despite racial prejudice and societal norms dictating otherwise, Equiano's successful intermarriage was an achievement
of which he was immensely proud and one he attributed
directly to God's mercy and providence. It is therefore hardly
surprising that he wanted to celebrate his marriage publicly
and quickly by inserting a few lines about it in the fifth edition
(quoted above), which went to press shortly afterwards
(Edinburgh, June 1792). He also added a footnote with no fewer
than four references to national and local papers in which the
wedding had been reported.[59] Significantly, this is the final
piece of biographical information that Equiano included in
his autobiography; and he obviously considered it to be highly
important because he retained it in all subsequent editions.

April 1792 – February 1796: Equiano's family life in Soham

Following his marriage, Equiano made Soham his family
home until Susannah died in February 1796. How much time
Equiano spent in Soham and Cambridge from April 1792 until
his wife's untimely death is open to conjecture, but it was
certainly curtailed by his punishing book-tour schedule. From
surviving letters and newspaper advertisements, we know
that he was constantly on the road earning a living through
his book sales and other business dealings. Even as a new
husband, Equiano put his abolitionist agenda before his wife:
immediately after their wedding, Equiano went to Scotland
to sell his fifth edition. Although Susannah accompanied him
to Edinburgh, she appears to have returned home to Soham

58. Adam Hochschild, *Bury the Chains:
The British Struggle to Abolish Slavery*,
London 2005, pp. 229–39; Abel 2022,
pp. 52–3.
59. Equiano 1792 (5th edn), p. 359.

shortly afterwards. Certainly, when Equiano wrote to his close friend Thomas Hardy (radical founder of the working-class London Corresponding Society [LCS], which demanded constitutional reform and universal male suffrage) from Edinburgh on 28 May 1792, he made almost no mention of his new wife. Instead, Equiano wrote about his book sales in Glasgow and Paisley, his plans to visit Dundee, Perth and Aberdeen, his attendance at the General Assembly of the Church of Scotland when it agreed to send an anti-Slave Trade petition to the House of Lords, and his approbation of Hardy's LCS. Indeed, he only mentioned his new status as a married man at the very end of his letter, when he lamented to Hardy how:

> & now I am again obliged to slave on more than before if possible — as I have a Wife. May God ever keep you & me from a tachement [sic] to this evil World, & the things of it — I think I shall be happy when time is no more with me, as I am Resolved ever to Look to Jesus Christ — & submit to his Preordinations.[60]

Hardly the comments one might expect from a newlywed! That said, Equiano did add a postscript: 'pray get me the Gentlemens Magazine for April 1792 & take Care of it for me', which shows his keenness to obtain a copy of that issue with its announcement of his marriage. Equiano remained in the north for several months, only returning south via Hull in November 1792. Equiano must have been back in Soham by early to mid-January 1793, as this is when his first daughter, Anna Maria, was conceived (assuming the pregnancy went full-term) but he was absent for much of Susannah's pregnancy and may still have been travelling when Anna Maria was born on 16 October 1793 because, most unusually, her baptism was delayed until 30 January 1794.

Speaking publicly in favour of political reform of any kind, including abolition, became increasingly risky following the execution of the French King, Louis XVI, in January 1793. This sent shock waves across the British establishment and led Britain to declare war on France and institute a national crackdown on all types of reform, now regarded as synonymous with enemy doctrines of republicanism. The potential danger in which Equiano was placing himself and his family by his high-profile abolitionism was brought home by the experiences of his friend Thomas Hardy, with whom Equiano had corresponded and stayed on several occasions. Hardy was arrested in May 1794 on the charge of high treason and suffered a violent attack on his house by a 'church and king' mob during which Hardy's heavily pregnant wife, Lydia, was injured. Significantly, Equiano's above-mentioned letter of 28 May 1792 was found amongst Hardy's papers at the time of his

60. For Equiano's letter of 28 May 1792 to Thomas Hardy, see Sapoznik 2013, pp. 35—40, with quotation on p. 40. The original is in the National Archives, TS 24/12/2.

arrest. Although Hardy was acquitted in November 1794, Lydia had died in childbirth, and her death was commonly blamed on the mob attack. This truly tragic turn of events would no doubt have been felt keenly by Equiano and Susannah.[61]

However, aware that the fight for abolition had stalled, Equiano disregarded fears for his own safety to push sales of his eighth edition and to seek subscribers for the ninth, as two pieces of surviving correspondence from the second half of 1794 make clear: first, a well-known letter of 20 June 1794 from Equiano (then in Colchester) to Mr and Mrs Liversege of Ipswich; and second, a virtually unknown letter of 30 September 1794 from Equiano (then in London) to Belfast-based abolitionist Thomas Attwood Digges [64]. When read together, these letters allow us to trace Equiano's activities in summer 1794 and show that the only compromise Equiano made towards his family was that this final bookselling tour focused on East Anglia, presumably so that he could occasionally get home. Equiano's letter to the Liverseges provides insights into his recent hectic schedule (London: early June; Sudbury: 19 June) and his upcoming plans (Colchester: 19–24 June; Kelvedon: around 26 June; Chelmsford: afterwards), and the danger many believed him to be in:

> I make no doubt but you have heard of the false report which the Sons of Belial have raised of Late in saying that the Kings messengers were in quest of me, & my friends here persuaded me to go to London. — so I did & inquired of Gentlemen in Power — my friends — & they went to the Privy Council & were told that there was not any messengers after me. So I went to Soham to see my family which is well. I left them ten days past — & are again selling the Last 110 Copies of my narrative — which I hope to sell against I go from Chelmsford.[62]

It also shows that Equiano had managed a brief visit home to Soham in early June 1794 to see Susannah and eight-month-old Anna Maria. It was likely during this visit that Equiano and Susannah conceived Johanna (assuming the pregnancy went full term), given that she was born on 11 April 1795.

Meanwhile, Equiano's letter to Digges three months later confirms that he had kept to this planned itinerary and schedule, leaving pregnant Susannah at home with Anna Maria. It also gives important new insights into the publication of the ninth and final edition of his *Interesting Narrative*. Equiano recounts to Digges how, having sold all copies of his eighth edition, he had returned to London on 11 September 1794 to prepare the ninth edition, which had gone to press on 27 September, in a small run of 500 copies. He was now planning a bookselling trip to various places in Essex, Suffolk,

61. Carretta 2005, p. 362; Chris Day, 'The 1794 Trial of Thomas Hardy: 'New-Fangled Treasons', *The National Archives*, 21 March 2023, https://blog.national archives.gov.uk/the-1794-trial-of-thomas-hardy-new-fangled-treasons (accessed 2 August 2024).
62. Wellcome Library, London: MS 7151/10; Sapoznik 2013, pp. 43–5.

64

Olaudah Equiano (*c*.1745—1797).
Autograph letter to
Belfast-based abolitionist
Thomas Attwood Digges,
30 September 1794.

The Moorland Spingarn Research Center
Collection, Howard University Library,
Washington DC (General Museum
Collection) [not in exhibition]

Norfolk and Cambridgeshire, including Bocking, Manningtree, Chelmsford, Bury St Edmunds, Kings Lynn and Wisbech:

London Sep[tembe]r 30th, 1794

My Very D[ea]r & Worthy friends &c

This with my best respect to you & family — hope you are all well as I am & mine with many thanks to our almighty God for his every favours.

D[ea]r Sir not having any of my narrative left to take to any of the places that you were please to give me recommendations to, I Came here on the 11th, Inst[ant], & have finished on Saturday last another small edition Viz. 500 Copies of my Life — with which I mean next week to go to Bocking, & Manningtree, Thro, Chelmsford — & visit Bury & then to Lynn & Wisbech — & afterwards use your very kind Letters — This edition is 5 s[hillings] a Copy, & has some additions, printed on 20 s[hillings] a ream paper which is about the Quality of the paper that you have.

I hope you got the Letter I sent to you in May, if so, I am sorry in not hearing from you.

I beg you will be kind enough to make my best respect to Mr. & Mrs. Printice, & the friendly Rev'd Mr. Read, & all others of my Worthy acquantences [sic].

D[ear] Sir if you think it Convenient, I will be very much obliged to you for a few lines to the good Lady &c. that you were pleased to mention to me — about Newington — or Else where.

I hope one time or another to have the Heart felt satisfaction to see you again — I have indulged my self to insert your name in the List of Subscribers — in my book out of great respects — & also the Rev'd Dr Temple.

D[ea]r Friends, I am with Christian Love & Gratitude &

many prayers for your soul, & bodily well fare — to the God who ever regards the prayers of faith — may he give you & y[ou]rs both the upper & the neither spring Blessings — Adieu &c

Gustavus Vassa
The African

At Mr. Hamiltons No 30 Eagle Street, Holborn, London.[63]

This autograph letter shows, yet again, that Equiano was ever on the move, soliciting subscriptions, working on new editions, keeping supporters updated through letters and visits, and generally trying to earn a living to support his young family. Preoccupied with work, all Equiano could say about his family was that they were all well.

It was only following the publication of the ninth edition in late September 1794, and sufficient sales of it that Equiano seems finally to have ended his book tours and allowed himself to enjoy family life in Soham. The following spring, on 11 April 1795, Susannah gave birth to their second child, Johanna. No evidence has yet emerged as to how 'Mr and Mrs Vassa' and family spent the following year. Sadly, Equiano's domestic bliss — represented so evocatively in Joy Labinjo's imaginary Vassa-Cullen family portrait [8] — cannot have lasted much beyond the birth of Johanna given that Susannah was mortally ill by late autumn 1795. On 12 December 1795, Susannah wrote her will leaving all her property to Equiano (with no mention of her children or bequests to anyone else) and gave him full discretion over where she was to be buried. She died two months later, on 16 February 1796, aged just thirty-four years old, bringing a tragic and abrupt end to their marriage.[64] On 20 February 1796, the *Cambridge Chronicle* announced the death of 'Susannah the wife of Gustavus Vassa of Soham in the County of Cambridge, Gentleman ... after a long illness, which she supported with true Christian fortitude'. Equiano poignantly chose St Andrew's, Soham, as Susannah's final resting place, where they had been married only four years earlier: the burial register of St Andrew's, Soham, records 'Susanna, wife of Gustavus Vassa the African, late Cullen, aged 34. Buried Feb. 21 1796'.[65]

Equiano's removal from Cambridge, his death and his Cambridge executors

Susannah's untimely death left Equiano, now in his early fifties, a widower and single father of two girls under the age of two and a half. He must have felt that Soham was no place for him without Susannah, and that he was personally unable to care for Anna Maria and Johanna in an appropriate way because by late May 1796, he had moved permanently back

63. The Moorland Spingarn Research Center Collection, Howard University Library, Washington DC (General Museum Collection). An image of this letter was published in Thomas C. Battle and Donna M. Wells (eds), *Legacy: Treasures of Black History*, Washington DC 2006, p. 42, but without transcription or analysis.
64. 'Will of Susanna, wife of Vassa, of Soham (nee Cullen). 12 December 1795', Cambridgeshire Record Office, Ely: 132/B4.
65. St Andrew's Church, Soham, 'Register of Burials 1795 &c', fol. 25, entry no. 54: Cambridgeshire Record Office, Ely: P/142/1/11.

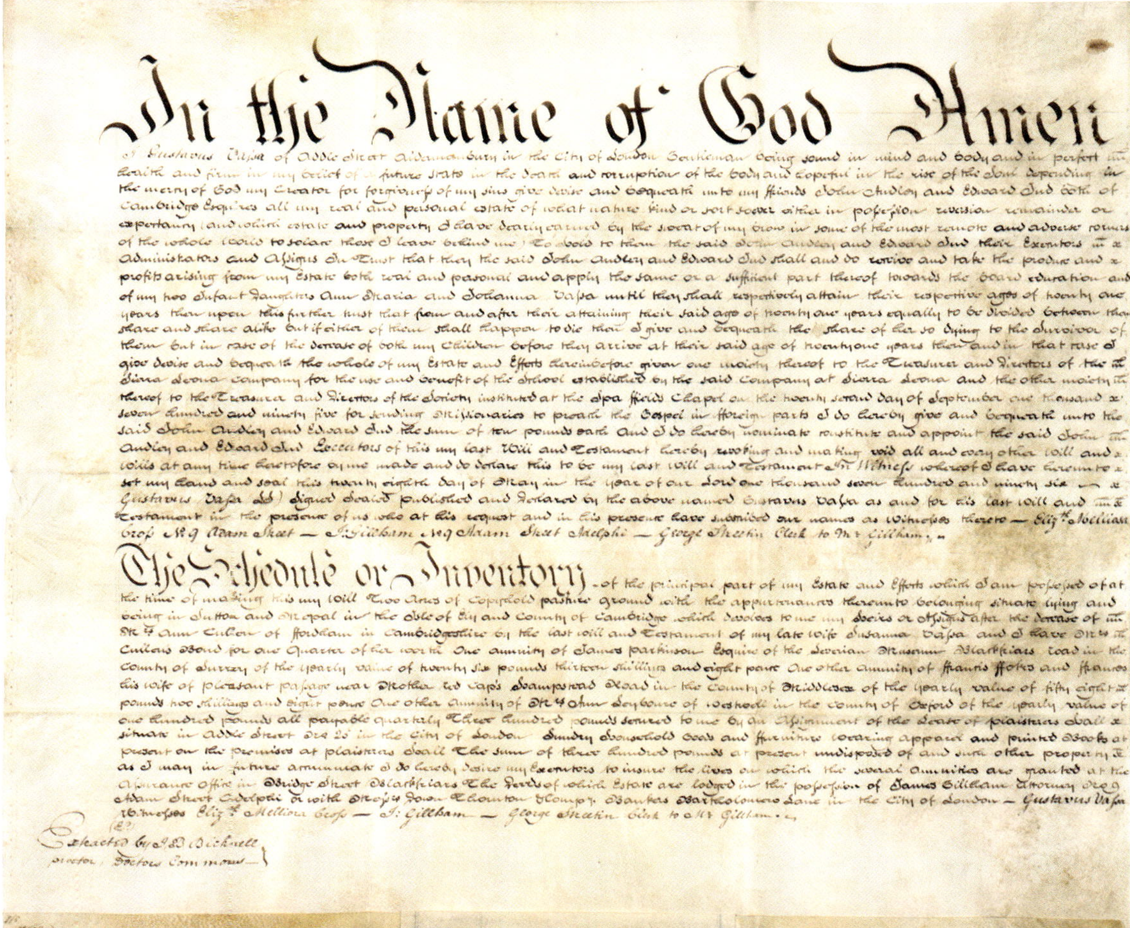

65

**Will and inventory
of Olaudah Equiano**,
28 May 1796
Cambridgeshire Archives, Ely (K132/B/10)

66. 'Extract from the Prerogative Court
of Canterbury of the will of Vassa, with
schedule of property', Cambridgeshire
Record Office, Ely: 132/B11.

to London, seemingly without his daughters. This is deduced
from Equiano's will and inventory that he drew up on 28 May
1796 [65], when he gives his address as in London and he lists
'Sundry Household Goods and Furniture, wearing Apparel
and printed Books *at present on the Premises at Plaisterers
Hall* [my emphasis]'.[66] This proves that Equiano must have left
Soham very soon after Susannah's death. It is unclear to whom
Equiano entrusted his daughters' care. Perhaps, in the first
instance, it was their aunt Anne and her farmer-blacksmith
husband, who lived in Fordham. Or perhaps, instead, their
grandmother Ann, who by the time of Equiano's will was
also living there.

Equiano left his entire estate — 'dearly earned by the Sweat
of my Brow in some of the most remote and adverse Corners of
the whole world' — for 'the Board Maintenance and Education
of my two infant Daughters Ann Maria and Johanna Vassa until
they shall respectively attain their respective Ages of Twenty

one years.' Should one sister die before reaching this age, the other was to inherit his entire estate. Should neither girl reach twenty-one, then his estate was to be split equally between 'the Treasurer and Directors of the Sierra Leona Company for the Use and Benefit of the School established by the said Company at Sierra Leona' and 'the Treasurer and Directors of the Society instituted at the Spa Fields Chapel ... for sending Missionaries to preach the Gospel in Foreign Parts' (the future London Missionary Society). The only other gifts that Equiano made was 'the Sum of ten Pounds Each' to his two co-executors, John Audley and Edward Ind. Describing them as 'my friends ... both of Cambridge Esquires', Equiano entrusted his entire estate to them in trust for Anna Maria and Johanna until they came of age. Equiano clearly held Audley and Ind in close affection and high esteem, trusting in their business sense, Christian piety, moral probity and scrupulousness.

Edward Ind's epitaph to Anna Maria Vassa and her father

Tragically, Equiano was not destined to outlive Susannah for very long: he died just over a year later (31 March 1797). As a result, Audley and Ind had to take on their executorial roles far sooner than they might have envisaged or wished. They must have placed the orphaned Vassa girls in the care of someone living in the parish of St Andrew's Chesterton, as this is where Anna Maria, who died less than four months after her father, was buried. The most likely foster family was that of Thomas Ind, Edward's younger brother, and his wife Mary, who were parishioners of St Andrew's Chesterton, and whose two sons were the same age as Anna Maria and Johanna.[67]

Significantly, Ind, who was an amateur poet, composed a poignant and lengthy epitaph for Anna Maria [66], which was inscribed, probably at his insistence, onto a large stone plaque. It is entitled: 'Near this Place lies Interred ANNA MARIA VASSA, Daughter of GUSTAVUS VASSA The AFRICAN. She died July 21 1797. Aged 4 Years' [67].[68] This extraordinary memorial stone was affixed onto the exterior north wall of St Andrew's at an unknown date but presumably shortly after Anna Maria's death. It would have been an expensive undertaking and a lavish gesture for anyone to make, let alone for a not-quite-four-year-old dual heritage girl. But, of course, while ostensibly dedicated to Anna Maria, Ind's moving encomium — replete with abolitionist subtexts and praise for her parents' bravery in defying racism and societal norms through their 'divinely ordained' intermarriage — was as much a permanent celebration and commemoration of the achievements of his Cambridge friend, Olaudah Equiano, or Gustavus Vassa, the African.

67. For further discussion, see Dawnanna Kreeger's and my forthcoming article on 'Equiano's Women'. This possibility was first raised by Nick Moir in his online blog about Anna Maria Vassa, published in *Chesterton Chimes*, issue 11 (July 2021), p. 4: https://www.standrews-chesterton.org/wp-content/uploads/2021/06/July-Chimes-2021-Final.pdf (accessed 2 August 2024).

68. The epitaph was first published posthumously by the *Scots Magazine* in 1809, and then re-published in 1822 in an anthology of Ind's poetry: Mott 1822 (see note 35 and [66]). It was Nick Moir who first correctly identified Edward Ind as author of this poem in his July 2021 blog (see note 67).

LINES

Inscribed on a Tablet placed in Chesterton Church Yard, to the Memory of ANNA MARIA VASSA, *Daughter of* GUSTAVUS VASSA, *the African. July 1797.*

———

SHOULD simple village rhymes attract thine eye,
Stranger, as thoughtfully thou passest by,
Know that there lies beside this humble stone,
A child of *colour* haply not thine own.
Her father born of Afric's Sun-burnt race,
Torn from his native fields, Ah, foul disgrace!
Through various toils at length to BRITAIN came,
Espous'd, so Heaven ordain'd, an English dame,
And follow'd CHRIST: their hope two infants dear,
But one a hapless Orphan, slumbers here.
To bury her the village children came,
And dropp'd choice flowers, and lisp'd her early fame:
And some that lov'd her most, as if unblest,
Bedew'd with tears the white wreath on their breast:
But she is gone and dwells in that abode,
Where some of every clime shall joy in GOD.

E

66

Edward Ind (1751—1808). **'Lines: Inscribed on a Tablet placed in Chesterton Church Yard, to the Memory of Anna Maria Vassa, Daughter of Gustavus Vassa, the African, July 1797'** in Thomas Mott (ed.), *The Posthumous Poetical Works of the late Edward Ind Esq. of Cambridge*, Cambridge 1822, p. 49

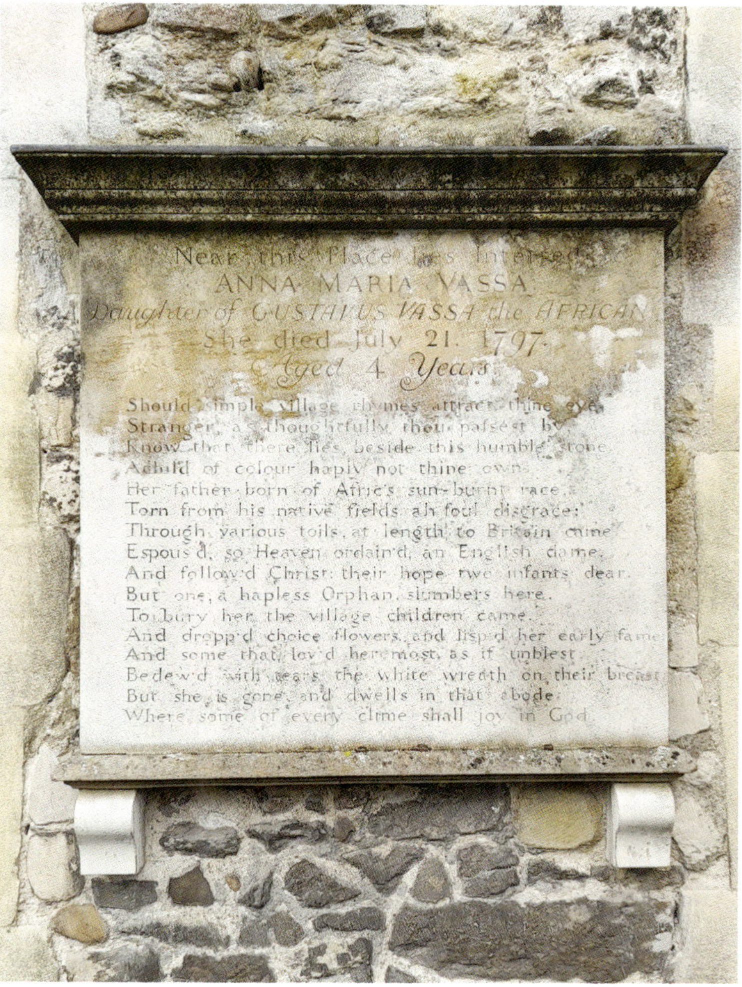

67

Epitaph to Anna Maria Vassa, with words composed by Edward Ind in late July 1797, and installed on the north wall of St Andrew's church, Chesterton

Photograph by Revd Philip Lockley [not in exhibition]

My sincere thanks to Matthew Abel, Vincent Caretta, Emma Jones, Dawnanna Kreeger, Nick Moir and Paul Lovejoy for insightful feedback on earlier drafts. Much of the archival research for this essay was undertaken at my instigation by independent archival researcher Dawnanna Kreeger. For an in-depth discussion of Olaudah Equiano, Susannah Cullen and their family, see our forthcoming article, 'Equiano's Women'.

Selected reading

• Olaudah Equiano (Gustavus Vassa), *The Interesting Narrative of The Life of Olaudah Equiano, or Gustavus Vassa, The African. Written by Himself*, 1st edn, London, 26 March 1789; and subsequent lifetime editions: 2nd edn, London, 24 December 1789; 3rd edn, London, 30 October 1790; 4th edn, Dublin, 20 May 1791; 5th edn, Edinburgh, June 1792; 6th edn, London, 30 December 1792; 7th edn, London, August 1793; 8th edn, Norwich, March 1794; and 9th edn, London, 27 September 1794
• Matthew Abel, 'Edward Ind (1751—1808): Brewer, Poet, Abolitionist', *Brewery History*, 190 (2022), pp. 44—61
• Michael E. Jirik, 'Beyond Clarkson: Cambridge, Black Abolitionists, and the British Anti-Slave Trade Campaign', *Slavery & Abolition*, 41, no. 4 (2020), pp. 748—71

Ongoing abolition campaigning

By the late eighteenth century, the Atlantic slave trade was under increasing public scrutiny. The tide was turning, but the pro-slavery lobby, headed by the West India Committee in London, fought back hard, using the considerable resources and political power at its disposal. Propaganda was widely circulated, and anti-slavery legislation was repeatedly blocked in Parliament.

Any change would be hard won. Anti-slavery activists from diverse backgrounds mobilised and kept up the pressure. Though not an activist, Queen Charlotte was among those who began to boycott commodities produced by enslaved labour, such as sugar. Their numbers and influence grew as a new century dawned.

When the Abolition of the Slave Trade Act was passed in 1807, it marked a significant step towards curtailing transatlantic enslavement, but the battle to end slavery was far from won.

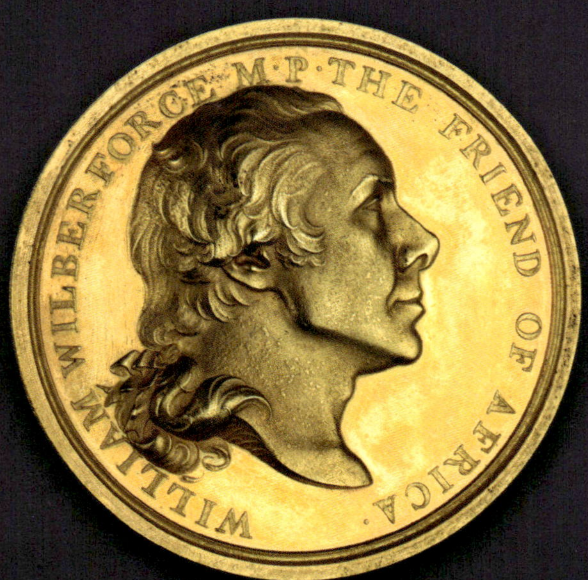
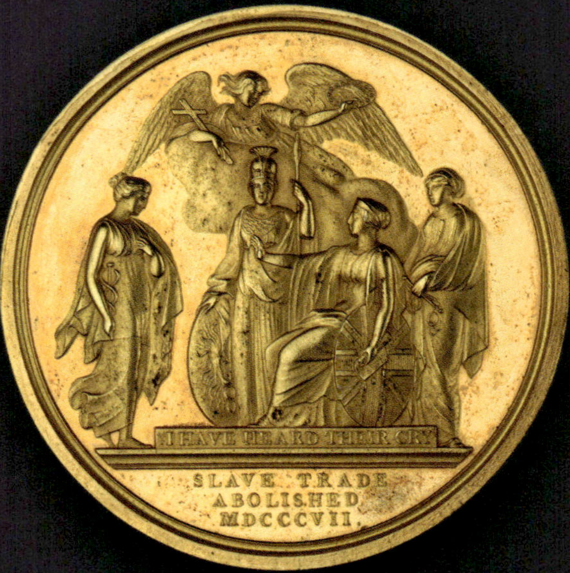

68

Thomas Webb (active *c*.1804–29).
Medal celebrating William Wilberforce and the Abolition of the Slave Trade Act, 1807.
Inscribed: (obverse) 'WILLIAM WILBERFORCE M · P · THE FRIEND OF AFRICA ·' (reverse) 'SLAVE TRADE ABOLISHED MDCCCVII.' and (on Britannia's throne-dias) 'I HAVE HEARD THEIR CRY'. Gilt-bronze, diam. 5.4 cm

Fitzwilliam Museum, Cambridge (CM.284-1989). Given anonymously, 1989

Many objects and artworks were made to celebrate the 1807 Abolition of the Slave Trade Act, including this triumphalist medal. Its obverse features 'William Wilberforce, The Friend of Africa' and its reverse, a personification of Britannia, enthroned and pronouncing, 'I have heard their cry'. Medals like this one — adopting the individualist conventions of the medium — ensured that abolitionist success was associated for decades to follow with a single white man. This has contributed to the neglect of countless other stories of resistance by millions of enslaved African and African-descended people, many of whom died fighting for their freedom. Artworks like this continue to impact how the national history of abolition is told, who is remembered, and who is not.

John Raphael Smith
(1752—1812).
Slave Trade, 1814.
Mezzotint, printed in colour,
58 × 76 cm

After a painting by George Morland
(1763—1804), *Slave Trade (Execrable
Human Traffick, or The Affectionate
Slaves)*, 1788. National Maritime Museum,
Greenwich, London (ZBA2507). Part of
the Michael Graham-Stewart Slavery
Collection bought with assistance of the
Heritage Lottery Fund, 2002. Smith made
an earlier version of this print, dedicated
to the Prince of Wales, and with an
explanatory poem, in 1791

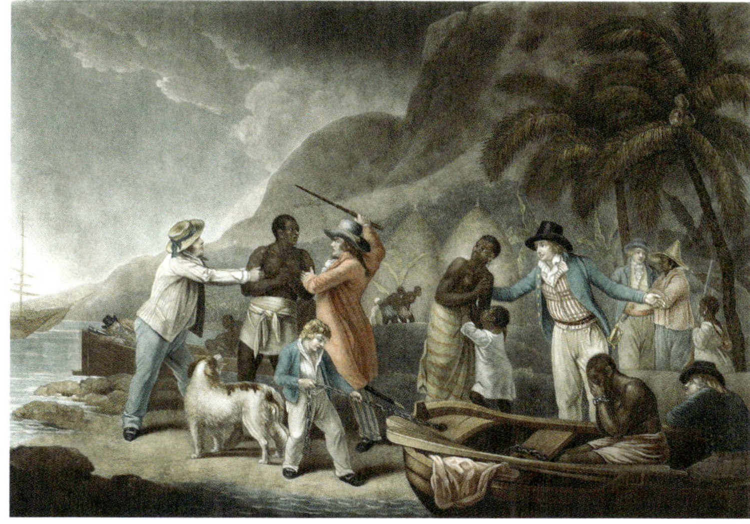

Pro-slavery and anti-slavery groups waged a massive propaganda war from the mid-1780s. The anti-slavery campaign circulated images designed to arouse maximum sympathy for the enslaved, mainly through graphic portrayals of violence enacted by white (and occasionally Black) enslavers and plantation owners on captive African men, women and children, and depictions of the anguish of family separation. This print, based on a 1788 oil painting by George Morland, combines all of these elements into a single image, and even unusually shows a Black trader in enslaved people bargaining with a white counterpart. When first published in 1791, the print had the following explanatory caption: 'Lo! the poor Captive with distraction wild, Views his dear Partner torn from his embrace! A diff'rent Captain buys his Wife and Child. What time can from his Soul such ills erase?'

Grada Kilomba (born 1968).
***Untitled Poem (one sorrow,
one revolution)***, 2022.
Charcoaled wood, engraved
poem, hand painted with
gold leaf, 24 × 86 × 24 cm

Artist's proof of edition 1 + 1A? Fitzwilliam
Museum, Cambridge (M.23-2023) © Grada
Kilomba. Given by the Contemporary Art
Society through the Collections Fund at
Frieze, 2023/24. This is *Verse 15* from
Kilomba's *18 Verses* with 8-channel sound
installation, 2022

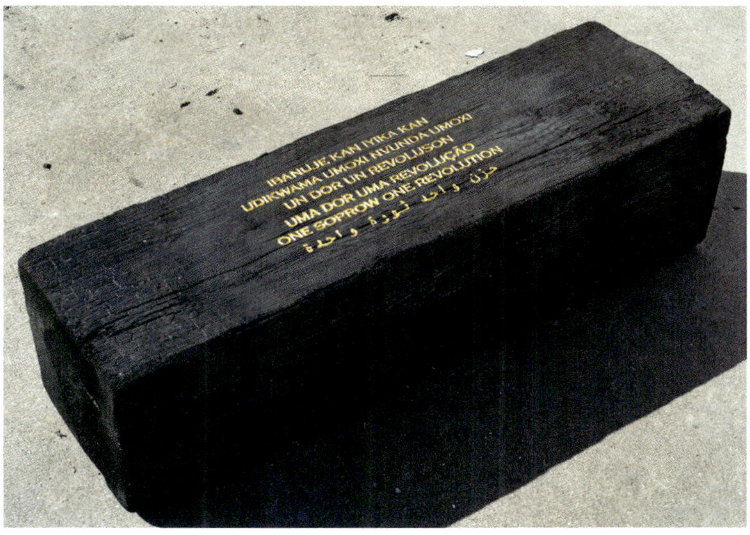

The cyclical process of burning and cleansing the pine wood allows for its fine texture on the surface to remain with a skin-like quality. A verse taken from a poem, which was written by the artist, is engraved and hand painted with gold leaf in Kimbundu, Yoruba and Creole from Cabo Verde, alongside Portuguese, English and Arabic. The metaphorical tomb stands in the absence of the millions of Africans that were trafficked across the 'Middle Passage' as well as those migrants and refugees who risk their lives crossing the Mediterranean today.

James Wright of Haverhill (1739–1811).
Broadside advertising Wright's refusal to sell
West Indian sugar made by enslaved labour,

Bury St Edmunds, about 1791

Britain Yearly Meeting of the Religious Society of Friends (Quakers)
(LSF Box L 176_36)

From the early 1790s, anti-slavery campaigners actively promoted 'ethical consumerism'. They encouraged shoppers to make informed choices and to abstain from buying products made by 'slave' labour as a means of undermining the economic foundations of slavery. The first campaign to boycott West Indian 'slave-produced' sugar took place between 1791 and 1792. This early 'Fair Trade' movement was also endorsed by some shopkeepers, including Quaker abolitionist James Wright of Haverhill, Essex. This is a copy of the broadside Wright had printed around 1791 telling his customers that he now refused to sell West Indian sugar because of the appalling conditions under which it was produced. Wright is believed to be the first British shopkeeper to boycott a product on moral grounds.

JAMES WRIGHT,
OF HAVERHILL,

BEING impreſſed with a Senſe of the unparalleled SUFFERINGS of our FELLOW-CREATURES, the AFRICAN SLAVES in the WEST-INDIA ISLANDS, and alſo with the abominable Means practiſed in procuring them, and towards them after they are procured; the Accounts of the Robberies, Murders, burning of Towns, ſtirring up and exciting the Natives to make War and Depredations on each other, in Order to obtain Captives to ſell to European Traders in the Human Species; and alſo the extreme Cruelties and unchriſtian Treatment that is exerciſed towards them after captivated, and on Board the Slave Ships, with the Brandings, Whippings, and cruel Torturings that are inflicted after their Arrival at the Place of Deſtination, the mere Recital of which is ſhocking to Humanity; which Accounts appear ſo indiſputably authenticated, that even thoſe Men concerned in this unrighteous Traffic have not diſproved:—Therefore being impreſſed (as I have ſaid) with the Sufferings and Wrongs of that deeply injured People, and alſo with an Apprehenſion, that while I am a Dealer in that Article, which appears to be a principal Support of the Slave-Trade, I am encouraging Slavery; I take this Method of informing my Cuſtomers, that I mean to diſcontinue ſelling the Article of SUGAR, (when I have diſpoſed of the Stock I have on Hand) 'till I can procure it through Channels leſs contaminated, more unconnected with Slavery, and leſs polluted with Human Blood.—My Motive for publiſhing the above was, leaſt ſome of my Cuſtomers, whoſe Favours I have experienced many Years (and yet earneſtly ſolicit a Continuance of, for ſuch Articles that I am free to deal in) ſhould be at a Loſs to account for my Conduct in this Matter.

About the Year 1791

BURY: PRINTED BY P. GEDGE, AGENT TO THE SUN FIRE OFFICE.

I Iſaac Wright, then an Apprentice with my above ſaid Couſin & in about 2 years afterwards was taken into partnerſhip & the Slave Trade being declared by act of Parliament unlawful, reſumed the ſale of Weſt India Sugar, witneſs my hand. J. Wright 1840

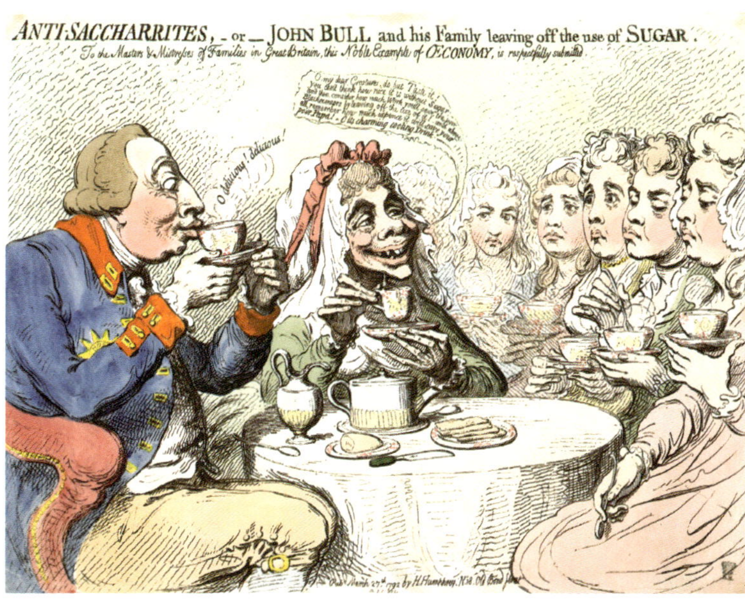

James Gillray (1756–1815). *Anti-saccharrites,*
— or — John Bull and his Family leaving off the use of Sugar,

27 March 1792, Hand-coloured etching, 31.3 × 39.7 cm

Published by Hannah Humphrey (c.1745–1818). British Museum, London (1851,0901.592).
Given by print dealer and collector William Smith (1808–1876), 1851

This print shows King George III and his wife, Queen Charlotte, taking tea without West Indian sugar and using various economic and moral arguments to persuade their unenthusiastic daughters to follow suit. It was made after the 1791 bill for the Abolition of the Slave Trade was defeated in Parliament and the launch of a nationwide campaign to boycott sugar produced by enslaved labour. Several pamphlets making the case circulated, including William Fox's *An Address to the People of Great Britain on the Propriety of Abstaining from West India Sugar & Rum* of 1791, which saw twenty-five editions in only a few months. Fox argued that British consumers were partly responsible for the persistence of the slave trade and the atrocities it entailed. According to Thomas Clarkson in January 1792, Fox's pamphlet had helped the abolitionist cause and changed the buying habits of many: '25,000 Persons have left off Sugar & Rum … Sugar Revenue by Report has fallen off £200,000 this Quarter'. In fact, according to The Abolition Project, the number was more like 400,000 British boycotters, many of whom were women.

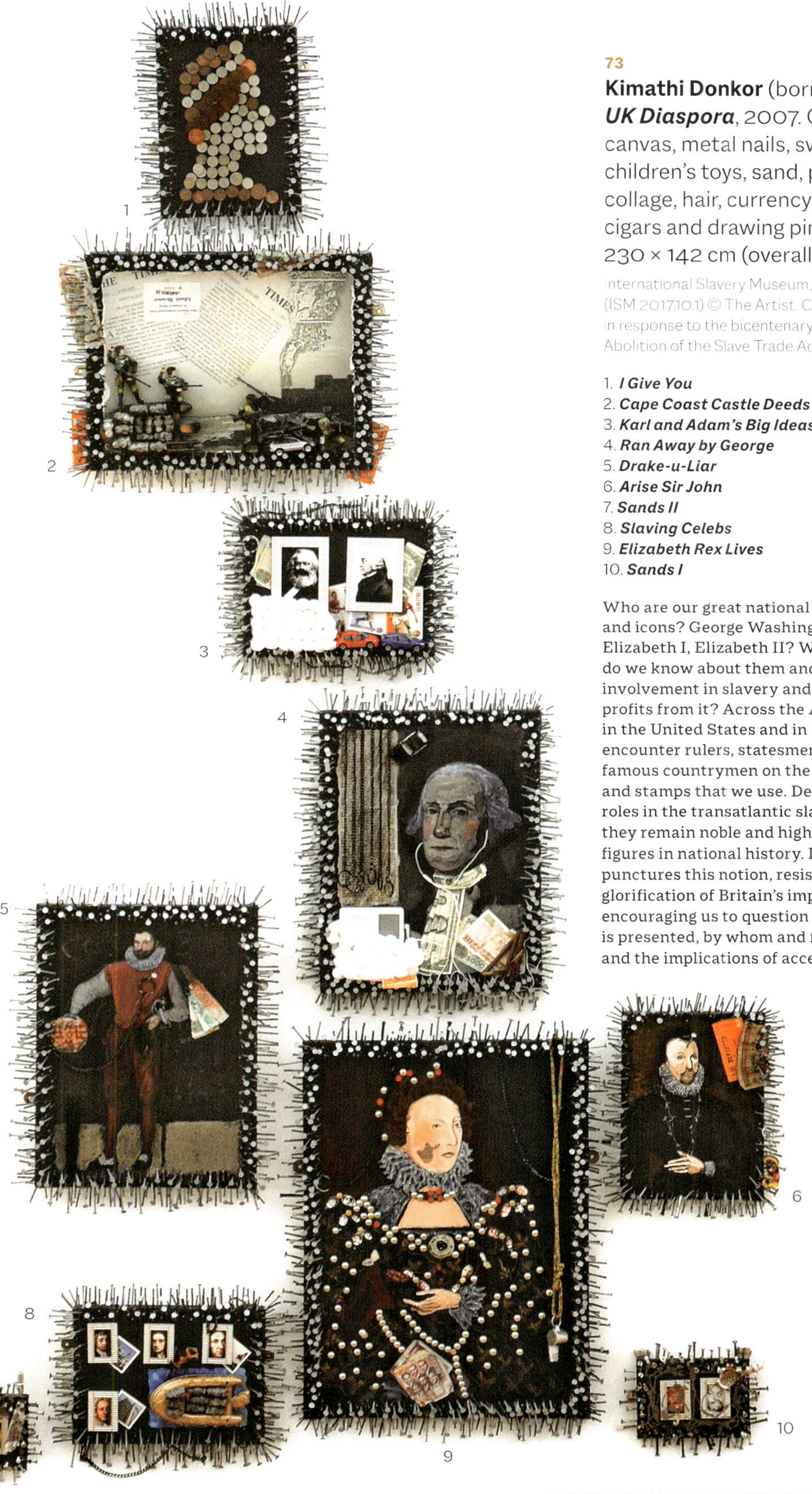

Kimathi Donkor (born 1965). *UK Diaspora*, 2007. Oil paints, canvas, metal nails, sweets, children's toys, sand, paper collage, hair, currency, iPod, cigars and drawing pins, 230 × 142 cm (overall)

International Slavery Museum, Liverpool (ISM.2017.10.1) © The Artist. Created in response to the bicentenary of the Abolition of the Slave Trade Act, 1807

1. *I Give You*
2. *Cape Coast Castle Deeds*
3. *Karl and Adam's Big Ideas*
4. *Ran Away by George*
5. *Drake-u-Liar*
6. *Arise Sir John*
7. *Sands II*
8. *Slaving Celebs*
9. *Elizabeth Rex Lives*
10. *Sands I*

Who are our great national heroes and icons? George Washington, Elizabeth I, Elizabeth II? What do we know about them and their involvement in slavery and their profits from it? Across the Atlantic in the United States and in Britain, we encounter rulers, statesmen and other famous countrymen on the currency and stamps that we use. Despite their roles in the transatlantic slave trade, they remain noble and highly revered figures in national history. Donkor punctures this notion, resisting the glorification of Britain's imperial past, encouraging us to question how history is presented, by whom and for whom, and the implications of acceptance.

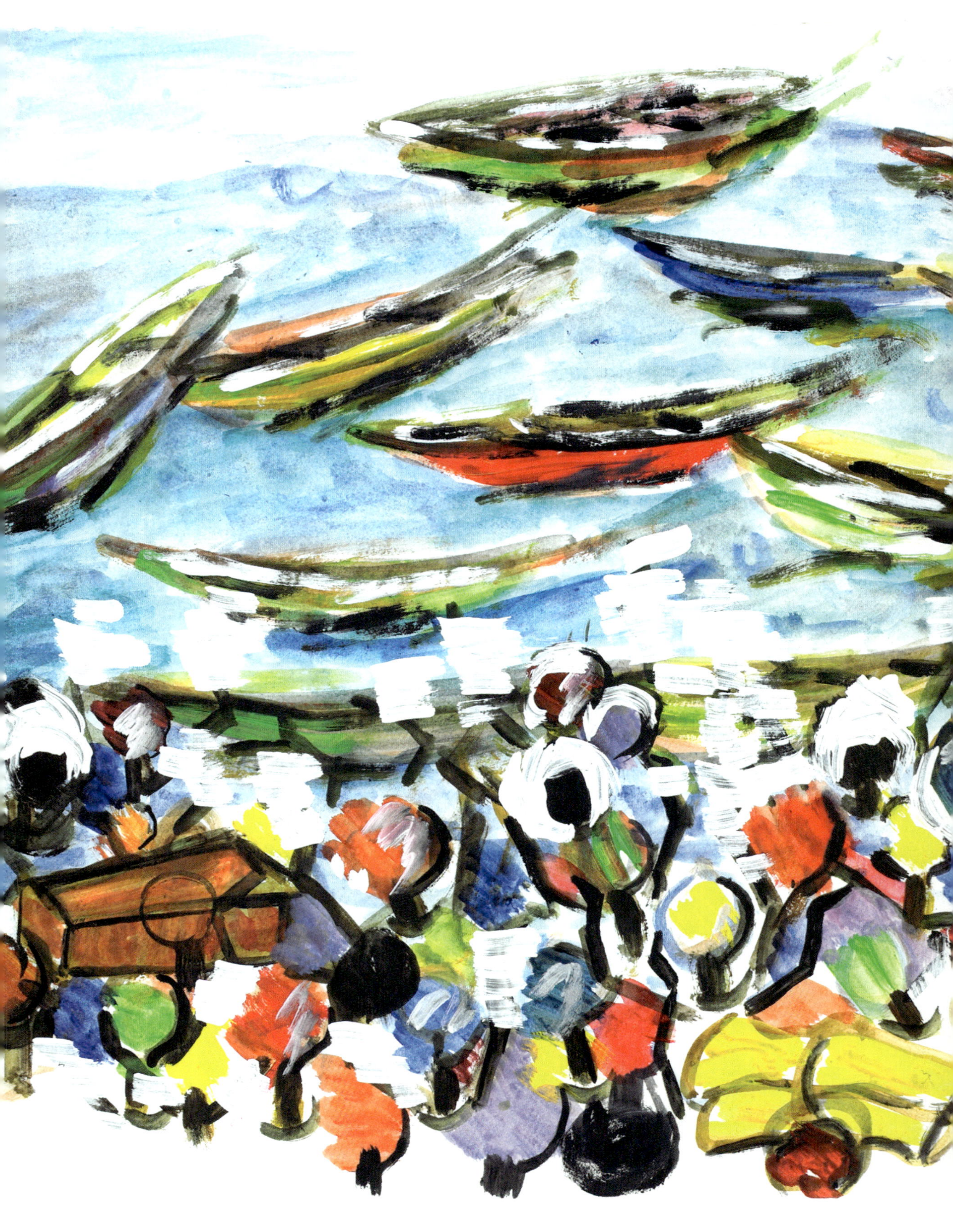

Britain's colonies in Nova Scotia and Sierra Leone

Following the tumultuous events of the War of American Independence, about 3,000 Black Loyalists and their families who had supported Britain were offered passage from New York to Nova Scotia, Canada, in 1783. Promised equal status, rations and land as white settlers, they faced much harsher realities.

Meanwhile, back in Britain, in 1787, the recently formed Committee for the Relief of the Black Poor coerced around 400 Black Londoners of limited means, defined as the Black Poor, into volunteering for 'resettlement' in West Africa. Sierra Leone became the first British colony in Africa, and was endorsed by both white and Black abolitionists, including Thomas Clarkson and Olaudah Equiano, though Equiano later became a vocal critic after witnessing the committee's mismanagement and exploitation of vulnerable people. Many of those transported from Britain were former soldiers and sailors who had served in the British army and navy. They agreed to leave on condition that they would remain British subjects and live free under the protection of the British Crown and the Royal Navy.

In 1792, many disillusioned Black settlers opted to leave Nova Scotia, taking up the offer of passage to the new colony in Sierra Leone. Would they finally find a welcoming home there?

Detail of **82** (see page 121)

Nova Scotia: northern exposure

In 1783, the British Empire received a major blow: it lost the War of American Independence. Now Britain had to fulfil earlier promises made by Lord Dunmore and General Sir Henry Clinton to free all enslaved Africans who had agreed to fight on the British side.

As a 'reward' for their loyalty, around 3,000 newly emancipated Black Loyalists, and other free people of colour and their families, were offered land in Nova Scotia, a remote British colonial province on the eastern coast of Canada. There, they experienced harsh frontier conditions, bitter winters and discrimination. They were targeted in race riots initiated by other Loyalist settlers, many of them enslavers.

In 1792, nearly 1,200 disillusioned Black settlers chose to leave Nova Scotia, following promises made about a better life across the Atlantic in the British colony of Sierra Leone.

Vessels Names and their Commanders	Where Bound	Negroes Names	Age	Description	Claimants		Names of the Persons in Whose Possessions they were &c
					Names	Residence	
29th July 1783							
Sally Wm Bell	River St Johns	John Primus	22	Stout fellow			William Bell
		James	26	Stout fellow			William Bell
Nancy Robt Bruce	Halifax	Versula Fortune	24	Stout Wench			Capt Fraser Quarter Mr of Pioneers
		Simon	12	Fine Boy			Ditto
		Jeff	9	Ditto	John Fox	Halifax	John Fox
		Andrew Moore	23	Stout Man			Ditto
		William Allen	23	Ditto			Robert Bruce
Spencer Robt Valentine	River St Johns	Lucinda	25	Stout Molatto Wench	Manuel Housterman	River St Johns	Manuel Housterman
Hesperus Saml Clarke	Ditto	Tom	23	Stout Man			Samuel Clarke
		Tom	14	Stout Boy	Saml Clarke of ye Hesperus		Samuel Clarke
		Sally	23	Stout Wench			Ditto
Fishburn Joseph Gill	Ditto	James Langford	21	Stout fellow			William Kneuttor
		Gabyel Philcox	22	Ditto			Henry Ellis
		Stach	17	Stout Wench	Gabriel Fowler	River St Johns	Gabriel Fowler
		Joe	9 months	likely Child	Ditto	Ditto	Ditto
		Fortune	12	likely Boy			William Gray
		Richard Fowler	25	Stout fellow			Gabriel Fowler
Mary Thomas Rowbottam	River St Johns						
Brig Kingston John Atkman	Port Rozeway	George Peters	23	Ditto			James Duncan
		Thomas Channell	24	Ditto			Duncan Cameron
		Benjamin Dunn	24	ditto frost bit in the feet			Alexr Munns
		Jack Sweley	12	Stout Boy			Robert Lavender
		Clarissa Channell	20	Stout Wench			Duncan Cameron
			30	ditto			William Morris

Samuel Birch (1735—1811). **Register of 3,000 formerly enslaved Africans**, registered by the British Commissioners and embarked from New York to Nova Scotia between 23 April and 31 July 1783 ('The Book of Negroes').

The National Archives, Kew (PRO 30/55/100). From papers of Sir Guy Carleton, 1st Baron Dorchester (1724—1808); given by Maurice Morgann (Carleton's Secretary) to John Symmons; given by him to the Royal Institution of Great Britain, 1804; acquired by Dr A.S.W. Rosenbach, 1929; sold by him to John D. Rockefeller Jr, 1930; presented by him to Colonial Williamsburg, Williamsburg, VA, 1935; gifted by this museum to HM Queen Elizabeth II, 1957, and given to the Public Record Office in the same year.

This document gives vital glimpses into the identities and lives of around 3,000 African American men, women and children who were relocated as Black Loyalist refugees to Nova Scotia, following the American War of Independence. Their names, ages, brief descriptions and remarks were registered as they boarded British ships that would transport them from New York to different ports in Nova Scotia in 1783. Also listed are the names of their enslavers, the name of the ship embarked on and its destination. Compiled by General Samuel Birch, after whom Birchtown, Nova Scotia is named, this list was an 'IOU' for loss of 'property' to the United States.

---

(67)

Remarks

Says he was born free and produces a Certificate dated 29th July from Robt. Ballingall commissioner of claims at Charlestown, he is hired as a Sailor on Board —

Formerly the Property of Mr. Smith of Savannah, Georgia left him three years agoe — he is hired as a Sailor

Says She was born free, Served her time with Mr. Benjamin Hubbert nigh Fredericksburgh Virginia

Formerly Slave to Syrus Griffin Esqr. Virginia left him in the Year 1780

Property of John Fox, purchased by his Brother who gave him to him

Formerly Slave to James Pray nigh Augusta Georgia, left him four years agoe

Says he was born free at St. Kitts, Cook of the Nancy

She is Wife to Manuel Housterman

Formerly the property of Carey Kelly, of New York who died about 12 years agoe, he says he gave him his freedom

Property of Samuel Clarke as pr. Bill of Sale produced

Formerly the property of Captain Phillips who brought her from Guinea to Savannah where he died and left her free

Formerly the property of Capt. Langford of Dord County Maryland, left him two years agoe. G. B. C

Formerly the property of Frances Melden Cecil County Maryland left him five years agoe G. B. C

His property by Bill of Sale produced

Son to Stack

The Boy says he was taken from Wm. Churchills House of Virginia by a Capt. Dempsey who commanded a Privateer three years agoe

Formerly the property of Benjn. Conway Eastern Shore Virginia, he was taken by a Privateer four years agoe & brought into New York G. B. C

No Negroes or property of any kind belonging to the United States

Formerly Slave to Christian Jenkins of Indianland South Carolina, who died before the War left the Estate five years agoe

Formerly the Property of Dr. John Channell, Savannah, Georgia left him five years agoe

Formerly the Property of Mr. Hoyt, Charlestown So. Carolina, left him four years agoe

Born free in the Island of Jamaica, apprentice to Robert Lavender

Formerly the Property of Mrs. Delahaut of Charlestown South Carolina left her Seven years agoe

Formerly the Property of Thomas Porter of Boston left him in 1776

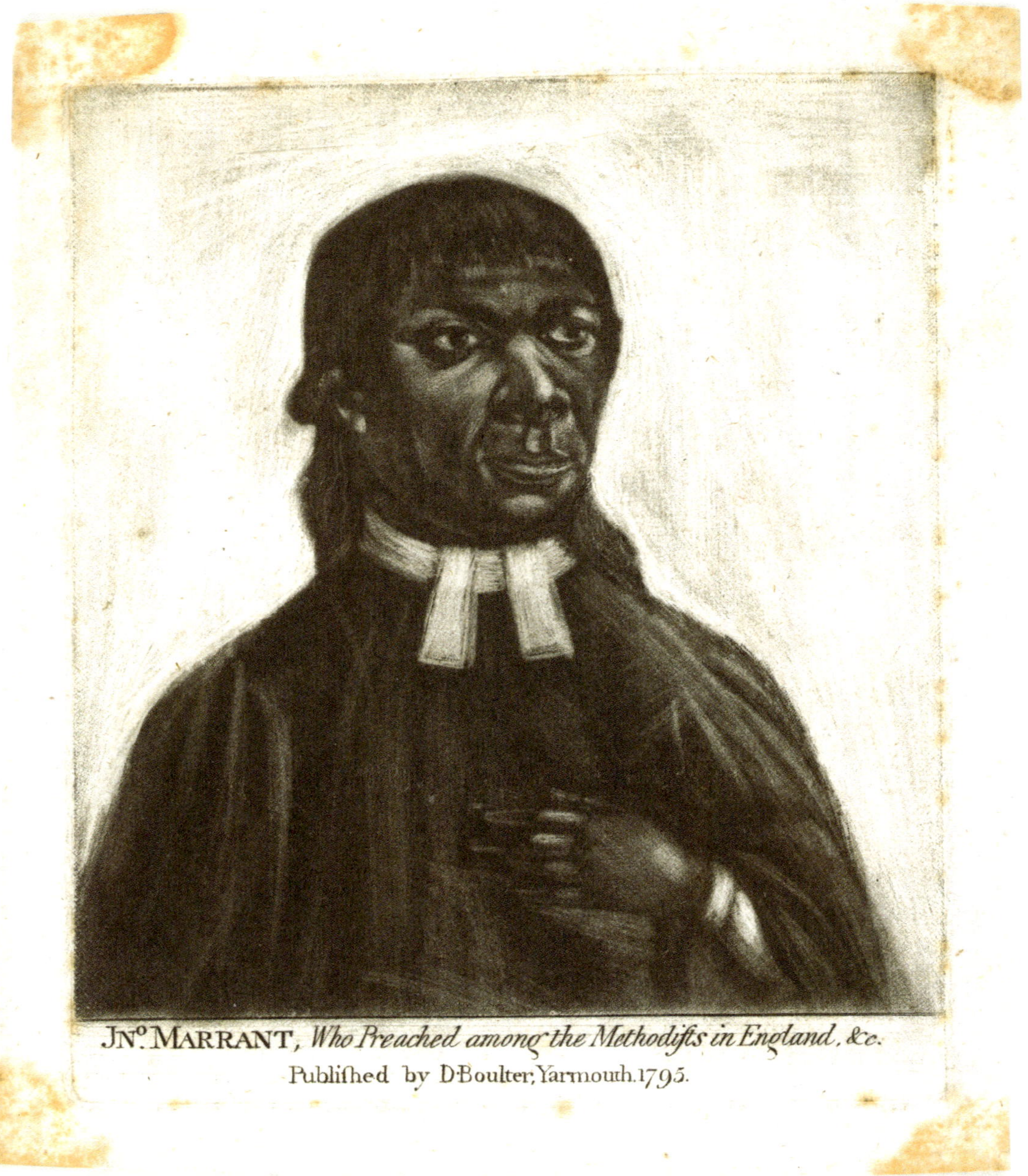

75

Unrecorded artist.
John Marrant, 1795.
Mezzotint, 15 × 13 cm

Published by Daniel Boulter
(1740—1802). Inscribed (below):
'J[OH]N MARRANT, Who Preached
among the Methodists in England,
&c.'. Fitzwilliam Museum, Cambridge
(P.346-1947). Bought from the
Charles E. Russell collection with
the Perceval Fund and a donation
from Louis C.G. Clarke, 1947

This posthumous portrait commemorates Marrant the Methodist preacher, its
caption reinforced through his vestments and hand-on-chest speaking gesture.
John Marrant's ordination as a Methodist minister (Bath, May 1785) was prompted
by a letter from his Black Loyalist brother in Nova Scotia, outlining the community's
desire for Christian instruction. Sponsored by the Countess of Huntingdon, Marrant
arrived in Halifax, Nova Scotia, in early December 1785. After opposition from other
non-conformist missionaries, he established a religious community of forty Black
settler families in Birchtown, where he preached four times a week to over one
hundred pupils in Birchtown school. He also ministered to the Indigenous Micmac
community, other Black Nova Scotian settlements nearby and a handful of white
settlers. Marrant ordained two Black ministers, Cato Perkins and William Ash, to
carry on the Huntingdonian ministry after his return to England in 1789, when he
subscribed to the second edition of Equiano's autobiography.

American-born freeman, musician
and Methodist preacher John Marrant
recorded his remarkable life in his
spiritual autobiography, published
with support from the Countess of
Huntingdon. He describes his early
conversion to Christianity, time
among Indigenous American
Cherokee communities in South
Carolina, and surviving several naval
battles after being press-ganged by the
Royal Navy. Marrant's popular book ran
to at least twenty-one printings, and a
Welsh translation, with later editions
expanded to include his Methodist
ministry amongst the Black Loyalists
of Nova Scotia. It established his
spiritual credentials in the white-
dominated Methodist world.

A

NARRATIVE

OF THE

LORD's wonderful DEALINGS

WITH

JOHN MARRANT,

A BLACK,

(Now going to Preach the GOSPEL in NOVA-SCOTIA)

Born in NEW-YORK, in NORTH-AMERICA.

Taken down from his own Relation,

ARRANGED, CORRECTED, and PUBLISHED

By the Rev. Mr. *ALDRIDGE.*

THE FOURTH EDITION,

Enlarged by Mr. MARRANT, and Printed (with Permiſſion)
for his Sole Benefit, WITH NOTES EXPLANATORY.

THY PEOPLE SHALL BE WILLING IN THE DAY OF THY
POWER, Pſalm cx. 3.

DECLARE HIS WONDERS AMONG ALL PEOPLE.
Pſalm xcvi. 3.

LONDON:

PRINTED FOR THE AUTHOR,

By R. HAWES, No. 40, Dorſet Street Spitalfields.

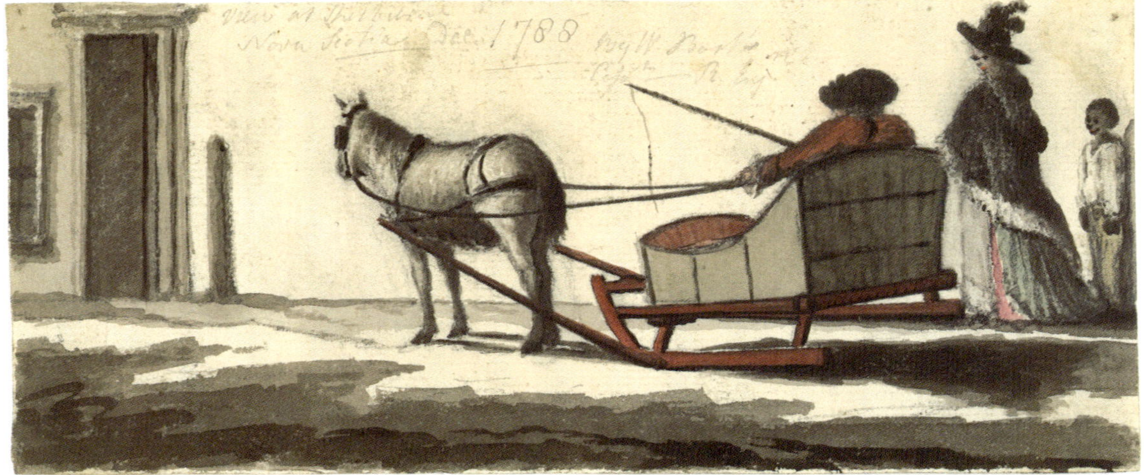

77

William Booth (active 1778—1822).
Figure on a horsedrawn sled in Nova Scotia,
December 1788. Graphite, pen and ink with
watercolour on laid paper, 8 × 18.5 cm

Inscribed: 'View of Shelburne / Nova Scotia, Dec[ember] 1788 /
by W[illiam] Booth / Capt[ai]n — R[oyal] Eng[inee]rs'. Fitzwilliam
Museum, Cambridge (PD.525-R). Bequeathed by English amateur
antiquary, geologist and benefactor to Cambridge University,
Spencer George Perceval (1838—1922), 1922

These sketches by Captain William Booth, Corps of
Engineers, give unique insights into life in colonial Nova
Scotia in the late eighteenth century. Booth's watercolours
include the earliest known representations of Black Nova
Scotians and visual records of daily working life in frontier
townships such as Birchtown, where John Marrant based his
ministry, and nearby Shelburne (originally, Port Roseway),
the entry point for most Black Loyalists. Settlers worked
primarily in the fishing industry but also as land-clearers,
farmers and wood-cutters.

78

William Booth
(active 1778—1822).
***Winter view of Water Street,
Shelburne, Nova Scotia***, 1789.
Graphite, pen and ink with
watercolour on laid paper,
15.5 × 23 cm

Inscribed (recto): 'Winter. View in
Shelburne in Nova Scotia by William Booth';
(verso): 'View in Water Street / Shelburne
N[ova] Scotia / 1789 / W[illiam] B[ooth]'.
Fitzwilliam Museum, Cambridge (PD.524-R).
Bequeathed by English amateur antiquary,
geologist and benefactor to Cambridge
University, Spencer George Perceval
(1838—1922), 1922

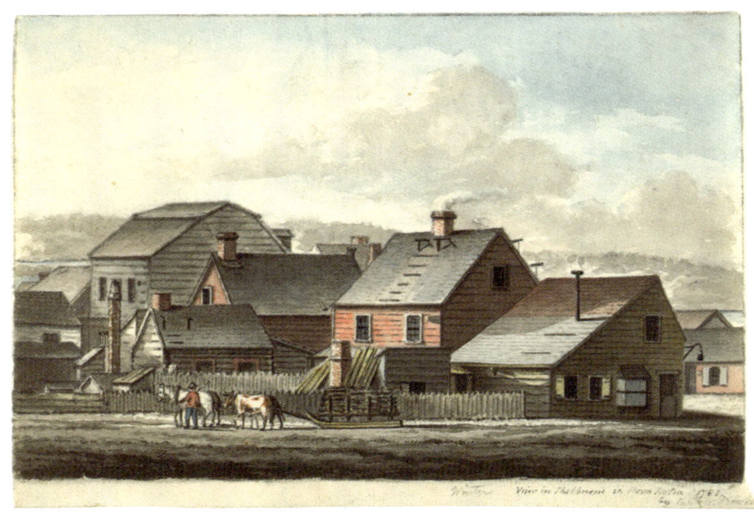

Booth spent four years posted as a military engineer in Nova Scotia, suffering illness
and the loss of his wife to tuberculosis. His journal and watercolour sketches record
a bleak, hardscrabble frontier landscape, where townships such as Shelburne are
framed against a backdrop of unforgiving wilderness. A 1784 census records 8,000
residents in Shelburne but just three years later, in 1787, when Booth's journal began,
360 houses had been deserted. The mass exodus continued: only 2,623 residents are
recorded in Shelburne's 1827 census.

Leone:
ovince
dom'?

Abolitionists, including Granville Sharp, Thomas Clarkson, and Olaudah Equiano, believed that people of African descent could be settled successfully in Sierra Leone. Equiano changed his mind when the corruption of the project's management became clear, and the colony failed to deliver on its intended goals.

The project, which ultimately sought to bolster British imperial strength and displace pre-existing African political claims to the region, was a failure. After a harrowing voyage, 'repatriated Africans' faced challenging conditions upon arrival in 1787, including the threats of hunger, disease and capture by local slave-traders. The first colony failed in less than three years.

Remaining settlers established Freetown, boosted by newly arrived Black Loyalists from Nova Scotia in 1792. The colony grew with subsequent waves of settlers, including the Trelawny Maroons of Jamaica. Following the 1807 Abolition of the Slave Trade Act, more than 85,000 African 'recaptives' were forcibly relocated to Freetown by Royal Navy anti-slave trade patrols.

stool (1762–1844).
 New Settlement
t Sierra Leona,
t and etching
ouring, 55 × 68 cm
m left): 'C.3.W.
. drew it') and (bottom
ostool exec[uvi]t'
executed it'). British
aps K.Top 117.100).
George II

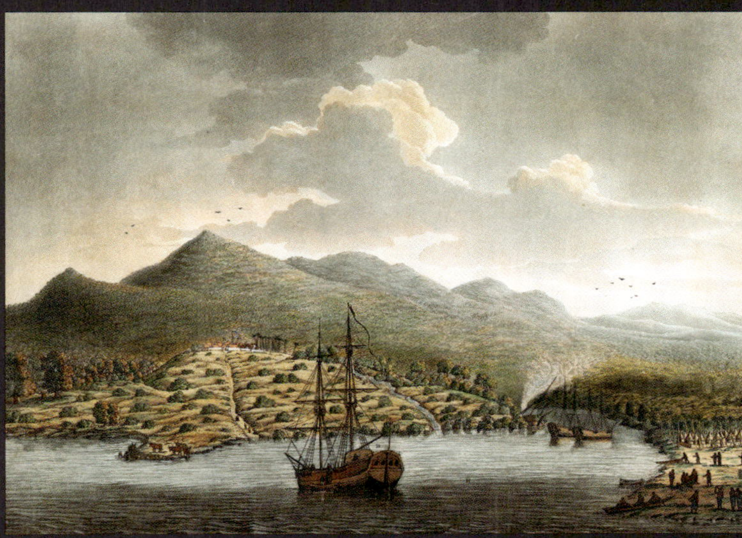

This aquatint offers a glimpse of the emergent British colony in Sierra Leone, West Africa, before 1,200 Black Nova Scotians resettled there in 1792. It depicts the fledgling settlement of King Tom's Town, named after the Temne ruler of the land that had been carved out as a British protectorate and part-designated as the Province of Freedom. A slaving ship on the river is a reminder that the risk of abduction was still ever-present for emancipated early settlers.

Susannah Edwards (life dates unrecorded, active 1830s). **Needlework sampler**, Sierra Leone, finished December 1833. Sampler canvas (linen or cotton), coloured silk or cotton thread, 34 × 21.5 cm

Stitched inscriptions: 'Susannah Edwards Liberated African Sierra Leone Dec[embe]r 1833'; 1-line biblical verse: 'Create in me a clean heart Psa[lm] LI'; 4-line devotional verse: 'Dear Jesus let an Infant claim / The favour to address thy name / Thou wast so meek that babes might be / Encourag'd to draw near to thee'; alphabet and numerals. Fitzwilliam Museum, Cambridge (T.1-2024). Given by the Friends of the Fitzwilliam Museum, 2024. Bought at auction (Cheffins, Cambridge, *The Fine Sale*, 21 March 2024, lot 406). From a private collection, Cambridge

This signed and dated sampler is the only known evidence we have about Susannah Edwards, an enslaved African girl, 'rescued' by the British Navy's West Africa Squadron from an illegal slaving ship, probably in the late 1820s or early 1830s. Resettled in Sierra Leone, Susannah was sent to be educated in one of the colony's Church Missionary Society (CMS) girls' schools. Given this sampler's similarity to one stitched by another 'Liberated African', 'Elizabeth Ba[xx]get' in 1829 in the CMS school in the mountain village of Bathurst, it is probable that Susannah was also a pupil there. If so, Susannah would have been taught needlework for at least two hours a day, five days a week, producing mainly clothes for herself and for 'Liberated African' boys. The term 'Liberated African' was used deliberately by the CMS for fundraising purposes and to obscure the contained forced indenture of those removed from slaving ships. Samplers with this wording were sent back to UK-based sponsors, which presumably explains why this sampler ended up in England rather than remaining in Sierra Leone.

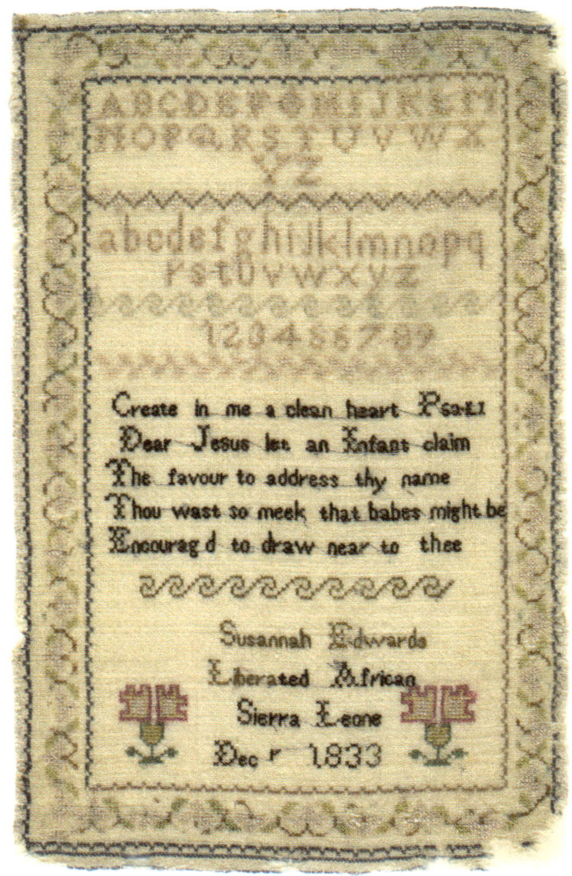

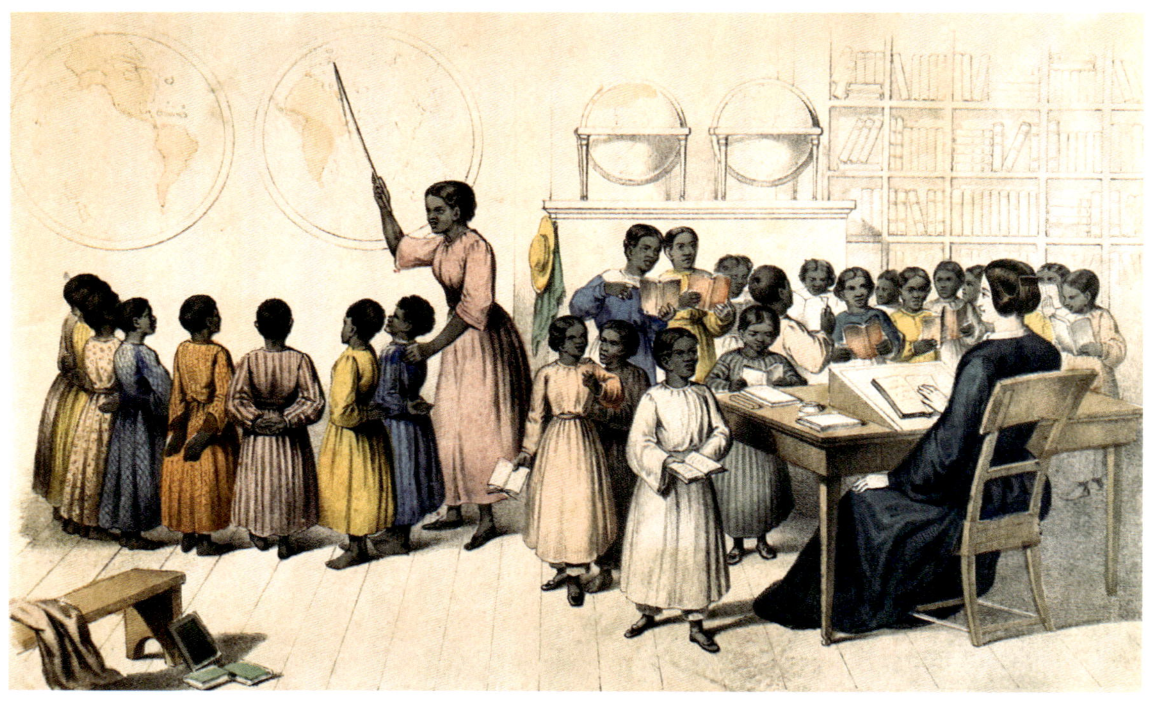

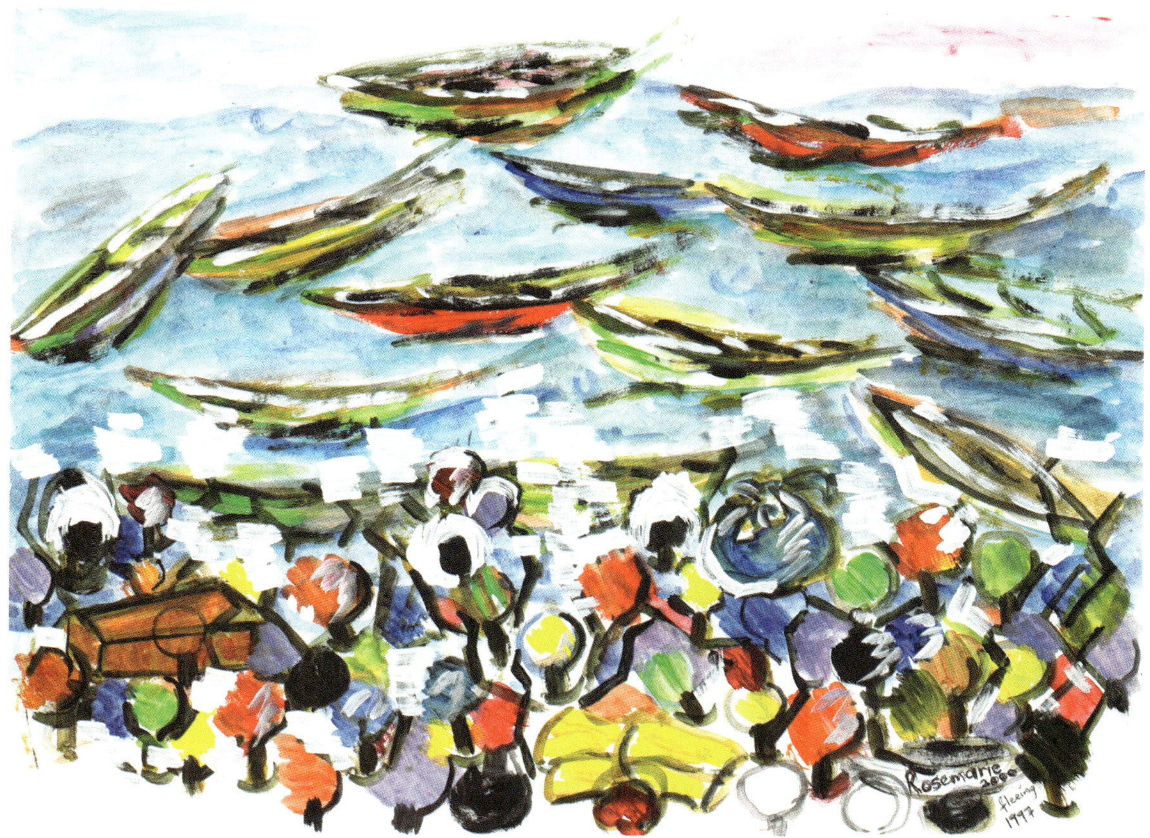

81 left

Unrecorded artist and engraver.
Interior of a Girls' School, Sierra Leone,
about 1850—60. Hand-coloured lithograph,
19 × 31 cm

The Card-Feynolds Collection, London. Bought from Sanders
of Oxford, 2015. This is no. 2 of a series of four lithographs issued
by the Anglican Church Missionary Society (CMS). It depicts the
Female Institution, Freetown, Sierra Leone, founded by the CMS
as the first secondary school for African girls in Sierra Leone, 1849

One of a series of lithographs promoting the educational
and spiritual outreach work of Church Missionary Society
schools in Sierra Leone, this demonstrates the paternalistic
role of the Church of England in Britain's colonies. It shows
The Female Institution in Freetown with a white Anglican
missionary teaching older African girls (wearing shoes) to
read, while a Black assistant is teaching younger (unshod)
pupils geography from a white colonial perspective. It is often
said that the pupil dressed in white and closest to the front is
the Yoruba girl Omoba Aina renamed Sarah Forbes Bonetta
upon Christian baptism in 1850. As a protégée of Queen
Victoria, she was sent to be educated in the CMS Freetown
school from 1851 until 1855.

82 above

Rosemarie Marke (still active).
Which One, No Choice — Fleeing,
2000. Oil on canvas, 35.6 × 50.8 cm

Rosemarie Marke (Artist and Owner) © Rosemarie Marke

In 1997, in the midst of the Sierra Leone Civil War, Rosemarie
Marke was forced to flee Freetown. A crowd had gathered on
the beach, attempting to board a few wooden canoes that had
been carved from hollowed-out trees. The fear of the unknown
was worsened by the fact that she couldn't swim. A kind
neighbour, a tall Lebanese man, carried her on his shoulders
whilst also fleeing with his family. The painting captures this
moment of escape, loss and the collective anticipation of an
uncertain future.

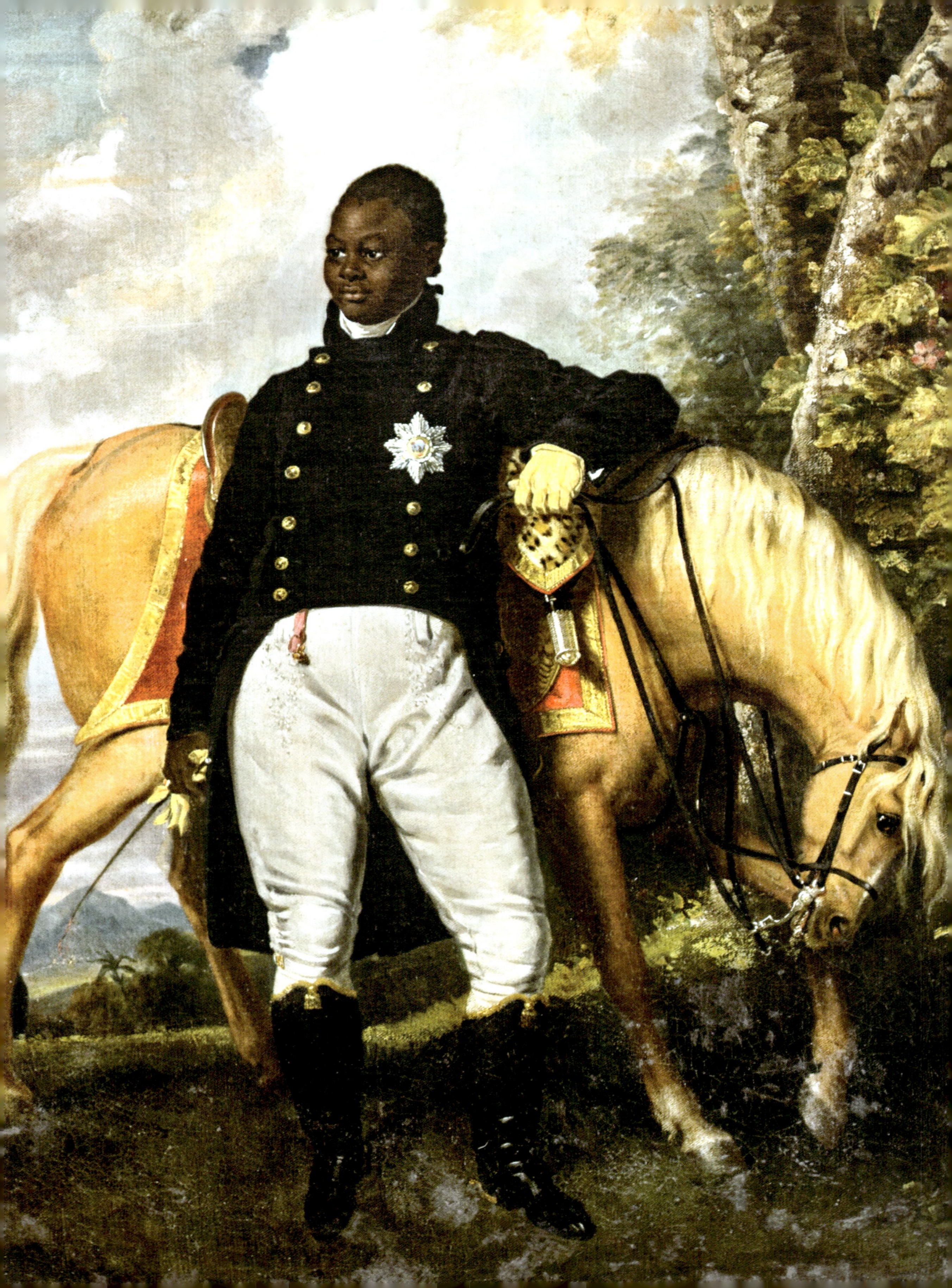

4

Revolutions in the Caribbean

News of the 1807 Abolition of the Slave Trade Act sent shockwaves across the Atlantic, which was still reeling from the downfall of the French monarchy during the French Revolution (1789—99).

The rising heat of resistance fanned the flames of revolution. Organised uprisings had long been a response to brutal conditions on plantations, and an expression of enslaved African people's political visions and determination to gain their freedom.

On the Caribbean island of Saint-Domingue, after over a decade of dogged fighting, self-liberated people helmed by military leaders including Toussaint L'Ouverture and Jean-Jacques Dessalines overthrew French rule in 1804. The revolutionaries declared a new independent republic — Haiti. In 1811, Henry Christophe created a separate kingdom in the north and proclaimed himself Henry I, King of Haiti.

This transformational moment shook European notions of empire, racial hierarchy and world order to their foundations.

Now, further rebellions grew in number, scale and power. Across the Caribbean, thousands of enslaved and freed African men and women took renewed action and pushed for freedom. Although none of these uprisings achieved lasting success, and many involved died or suffered punishment, they helped drive forward the 1833 Slavery Abolition Act.

Detail of **94** (see page 143).

Creation of Haiti: republic and kingdom

It was a seismic moment when the republic of Haiti was founded in 1804 — the first independent Caribbean state led by former captives.

Henry Christophe, one of the revolutionary leaders, subsequently established a separate kingdom in northern Haiti, over which he ruled as King Henry I, creating a lavish royal court that rivalled any monarchy in Europe.

Royal palaces and grand châteaux were built to reinforce his power. The new kingdom grew rich through trade agreements with Britain, but Christophe's rule did not last. His slide into despotism ended in suicide in 1820, and his son and heir, Prince Jacques-Victor Henry, was assassinated. With British help, his wife, former Queen Marie-Louise, and their daughters escaped to exile, first in Britain (including a short stay with Thomas Clarkson and his family) and then Italy.

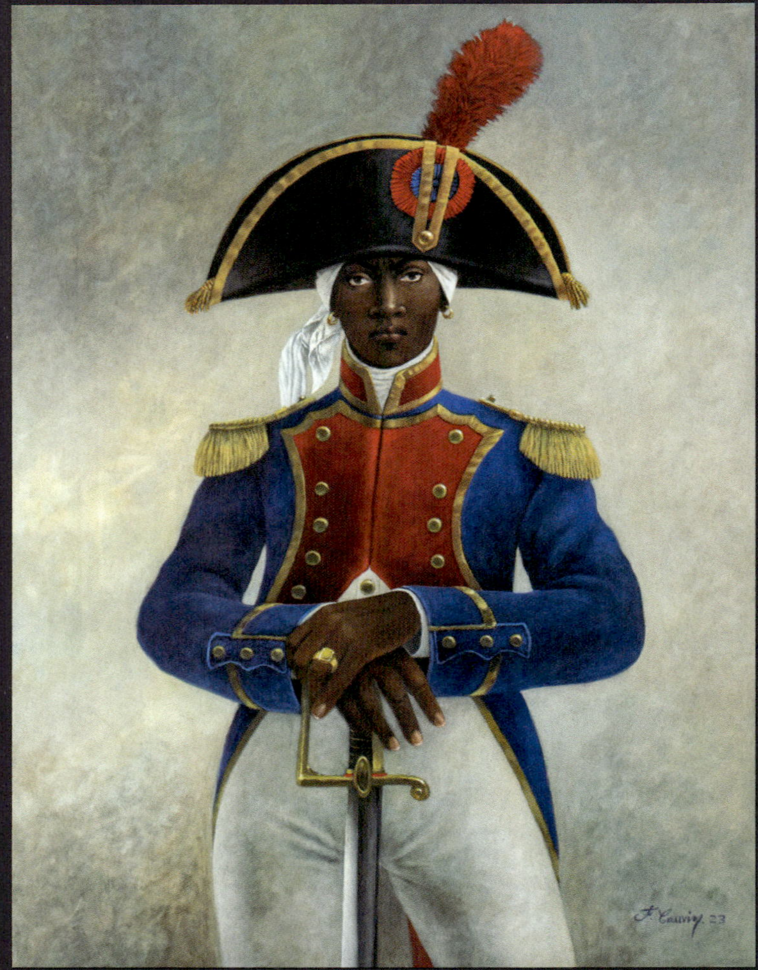

83

François Cauvin (born 1956). *Sanité Bélair*, 2023.
Acrylic on canvas, 182.9 × 142.2 cm (framed)

François Cauvin (Artist and Owner)
© François Cauvin

Acclaimed Haitian-born artist François Cauvin's family story intersects with Haitian history and sites of memory, including several main revolution battlefields. Cauvin has created a number of imagined portraits of key Haitian revolutionaries, including this one of Sanité Bélair, to give them greater visual presence and authenticity. Denounced by Haitian revolutionary leader Jean-Jacques Dessalines in her lifetime as a 'ferocious woman', Bélair was described by Haitian historian Thomas Madiou in 1847 as a 'Black woman of great beauty'. Bélair's story calls attention to the fact that countless other female Haitian revolutionaries remain unknown and unnamed in the archives. As with most major figures of the Haitian Revolution, especially key women, there is no historical portrait of Bélair, so she has been reimagined here by Cauvin in her lieutenant's uniform: the personification of resilience and resistance. This and other recent portraits by Cauvin, Kimathi Donkor, Joy Labinjo and other contemporary artists prove the power of images to resuscitate the memory of historic individuals written out of modern narratives.

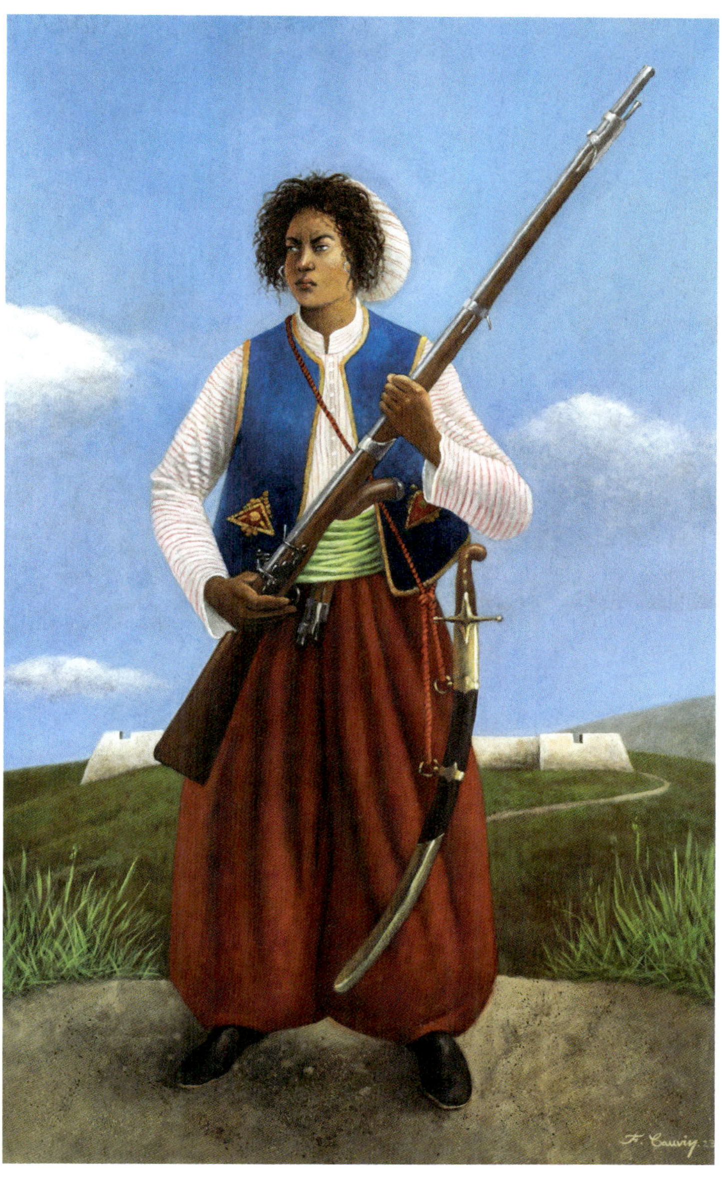

84

François Cauvin (born 1956). ***Marie Jeanne Lamartinière***, 2023. Acrylic on canvas, 147.3 × 94 cm (framed)

Probably born into slavery on a Leogane plantation near Port-au-Prince, the daughter of an enslaved African woman and a white French enslaver, Marie-Jeanne Lamartinière is another historically documented female Haitian revolutionary, soldier and nurse. In 1954, she featured on a Republic of Haiti fifty-cent stamp issued to commemorate the 150th anniversary of Haitian independence, fighting valiantly alongside her army-officer husband, Louis Daure Lamartinière, in the Battle of Crête-à-Pierrot against the French (4–24 March 1802). Historic accounts record her dressed as a Mamluk in battle wearing a waistcoat with wide pantaloons and a cutlass attached to her belt, some elements of which are picked up in Cauvin's imagined portrait. Haitian songs record Lamartinière as having become a *manbo* (*Vodou* priestess) possessed by *Ogoua* (spirit of courage); today, Haitians often refer to her as their Joan of Arc.

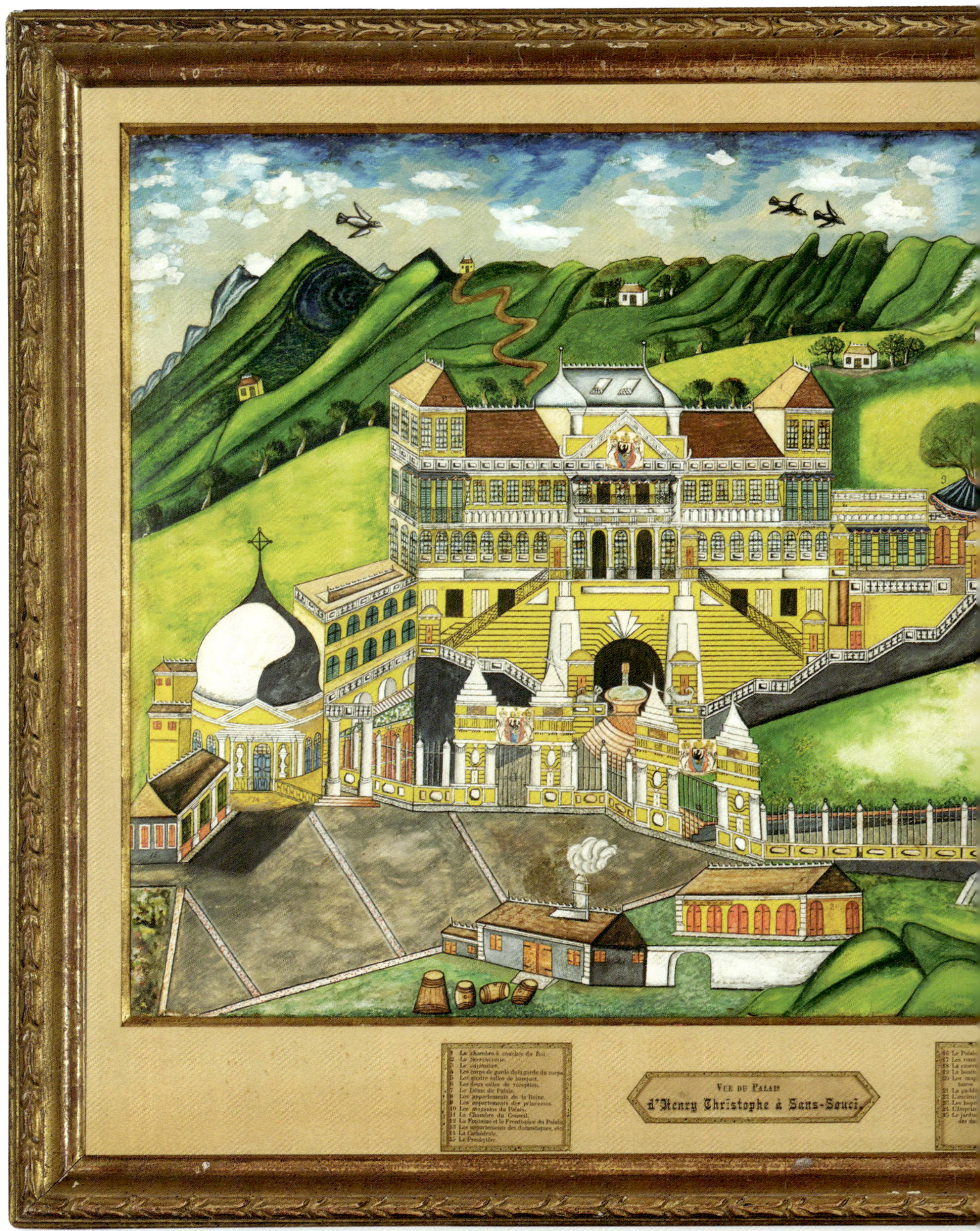

Vue du Palais
d'Henry Christophe à Sans-Souci.

1 La chambre à coucher du Roi.
2 La [illegible]
3 Le [illegible]
4 Les corps de garde de la garde du corps
5 Les quatre salles de banquet.
6 Les deux salles de réception.
7 Le Dôme du Palais.
8 Les appartements de la Reine.
9 Les appartements des princesses.
10 Les magasins du Palais.
11 La Chambre du Conseil.
12 La Fontaine et le Frontispice du Palais
13 Les appartements des domestiques, etc.
14 La Cathédrale.
15 Le Presbytère.

16 Le Palais
17 Les [illegible]
18 La caser[ne]
19 La bout[illegible]
20 Les [illegible]
    taires
21 La guild[illegible]
22 L'ancien[illegible]
23 Les hôpit[illegible]
24 L'Impér[illegible]
25 Le jardin
    des [illegible]

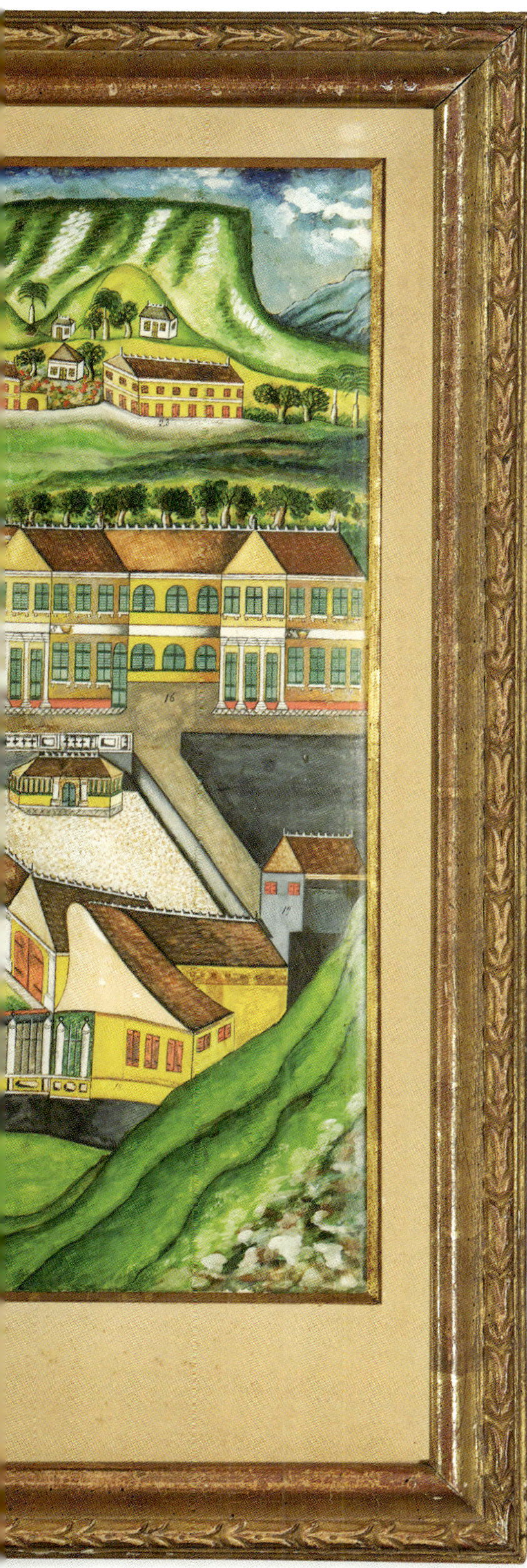

85

Numa Desroches (1802–1880).
***View of Henry Christophe's Palace at
Sans-Souci***, about 1817–before October 1820.
(*Vue du Palais d'Henry Christophe à Sans-Souci*).
Watercolour, pen and ink on paper,
83.2 × 100.3 cm (framed)

Signed 'N. Desroches' with the original typed key to buildings below.
Collection of Josh Feldstein, USA. Bought by Harry Bull, New York,
from a private collection, Haiti, 1936; sold to André Wauters Gallery,
New York, 1978; sold to private collection, 1986; sold by auction
(Sotheby's, New York, *The Vanguard Spirit: Modern and Surrealist
Masterworks from an Important Estate*, 19 January 2024, lot 58)
to present owner

Numa Desroches was a Haitian-born painter, raised under the
care of Henry Christophe from 1807 (when his officer-father
was executed for dereliction of duty). While largely self-taught,
Desroches may have received some training in the kingdom of
Haiti's art academy from Richard Evans, when King's Painter
from September 1816 until 1817, or his successor, documented
only as Revinchal (indicating his formerly enslaved status).

Sans-Souci was built incredibly quickly with forced labour,
and also income from forced labour under the *corvée* system,
where people worked without pay instead of paying taxes.
It was designed to rival the palace complexes of African and
European kings in scale and grandeur. Desroches's cityscape
is the most detailed contemporary visual record to survive
of Henry I's palace complex, now a ruin following civil
insurrection and earthquakes. Its key identifies the main
buildings within the grandiose grounds, including the four
banqueting halls (no. 5), the queen's apartments (no. 8), the
cathedral (no. 14), the palace of the prince royal (no. 16), the
king's goldsmith's shop (no. 19), the arsenal of the king's guard
(no. 20), the hospitals of the king's guard (no. 23) and the king's
printing house (no. 24).

Unrecorded artist. 'General Armorial of the Kingdom of Haiti' ('Armorial général du Royaume d'Hayti'), pl. 1: The arms of the King. Kingdom of Haiti (probably Cap-Henry, now Cap-Haïtien), about 1811—14. Watercolour on paper with iron gall ink captions, 26.9 × 19.2 × 3.1 cm

By permission of the Kings, Heralds and Pursuivants of Arms (College of Arms Ms JP177 ID3318). Acquired by the Kings, Heralds and Pursuivants of Arms as part of the legacy of James Pulman FSA, Clarenceux King of Arms (1783—1859)

One of the first acts of the newly crowned King Henry I of Haiti was to create a grandiose court, with a new social class of titled nobility based on the Napoleonic French system of nobility. Henry elevated his key supporters to the rank of chevalier, baron, count, duke or prince, and granted newly invented coats of arms to every title-holder. This official armorial book was made to record in colour the arms of the king, queen and prince royal as well as the capital city of Cap-Henry (now Cap-Haïtien) and the eighty-seven men awarded titles of nobility between 1811 and 1814. The heraldry is based on European equivalents but has been inventively adapted and developed, incorporating everyday items as well as African and Caribbean flora and fauna.

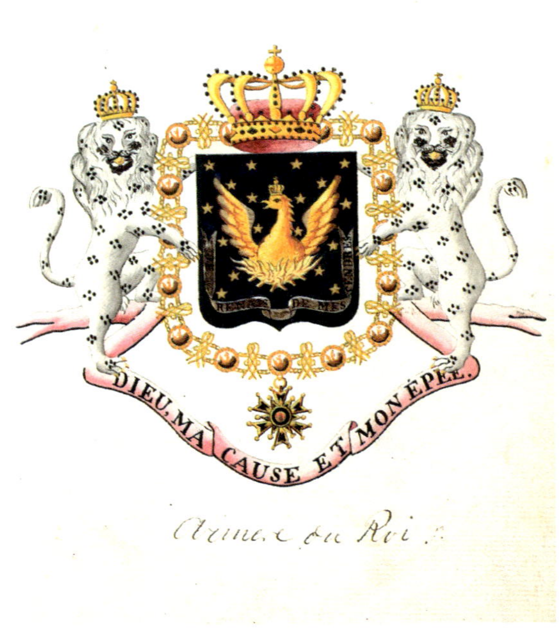

87

Spode Ceramic Works, Stoke-on-Trent. **Dinner plate with lobed edge and royal arms of King Henry I of Haiti**, 1811—20. Bone china, painted with enamels and gilded, diam. 27.8 cm

Inscribed (reverse): 'Christophe, King of Hayte'. Victoria and Albert Museum, London (2619-1901). Transferred from the Museum of Practical Geology, Jermyn Street, 1901

King Henry I of Haiti wanted his pleasure palace to live up to its name Sans-Souci, meaning 'free of care'. He spent vast sums of money, derived from coffee and sugar exports, high taxes and bound plantation labour one step removed from slavery, to pay for all manner of objects, from carriages to clothing, the majority imported from high-end British retailers. Henry I hosted lavish banquets served on exquisite tableware, all decorated with his royal coat of arms incorporating the mythical phoenix rising from the ashes, often with his personal motto '*Je renais de mes cendres*' ('I am reborn from my ashes'). This bone china plate is one of very few that survive from his English dinner service ordered from the prestigious Spode Ceramic works.

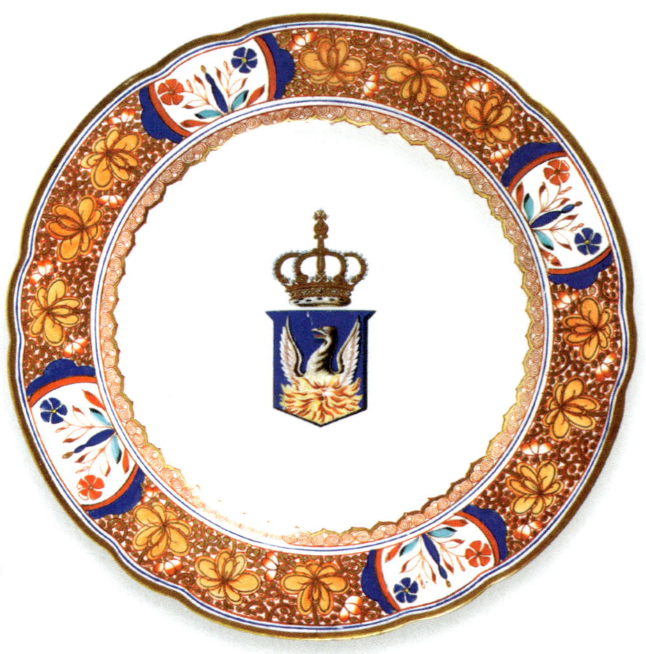

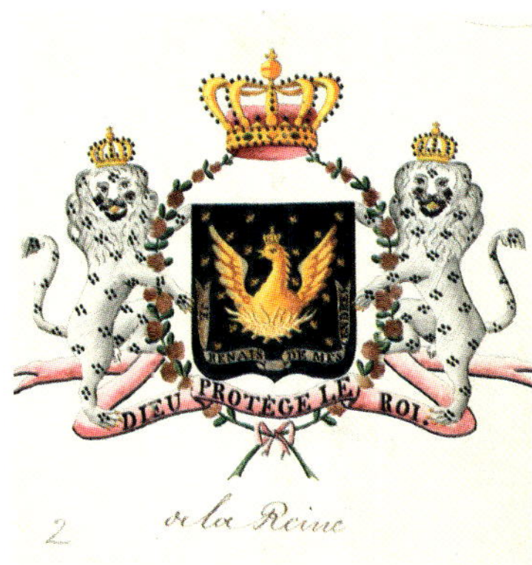

The arms of the Queen

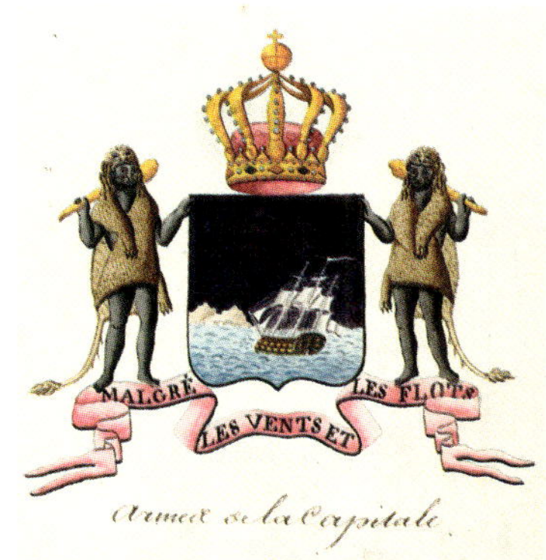

The arms of the Capital

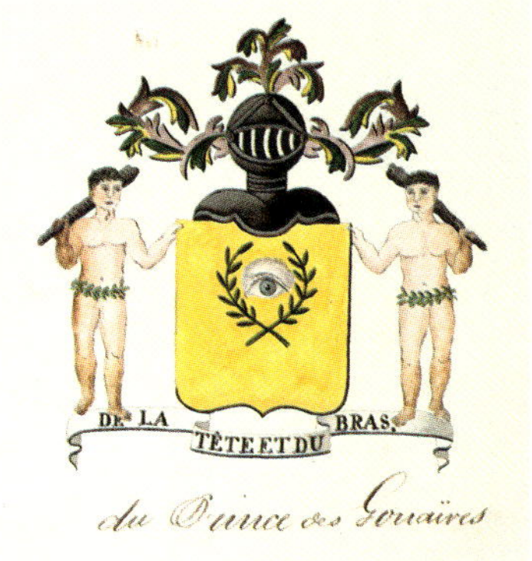

The arms of the Prince des Gonaïves

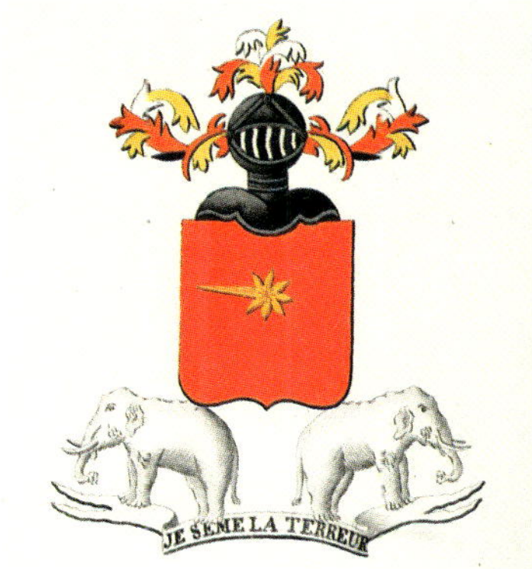

The arms of the Prince de Saint-Marc

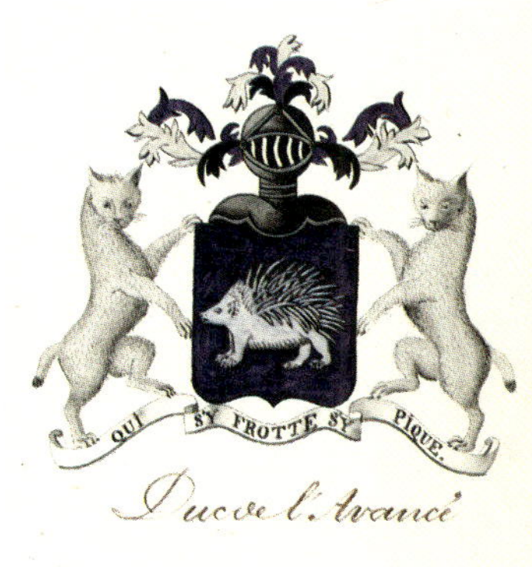

The arms of the Duc de l'Avancé

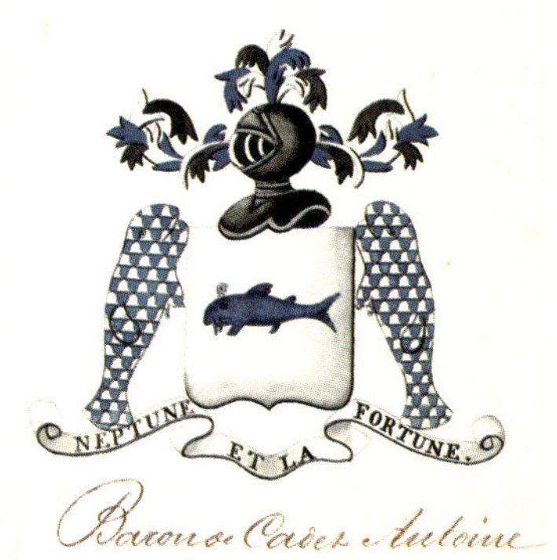

The arms of Baron Cadet Antoine

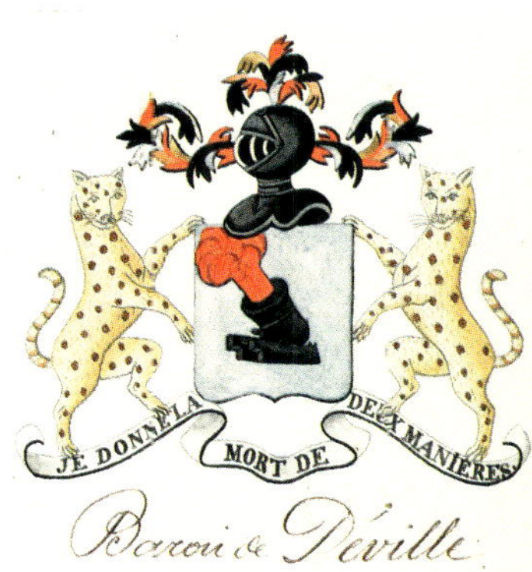

The arms of Baron Déville

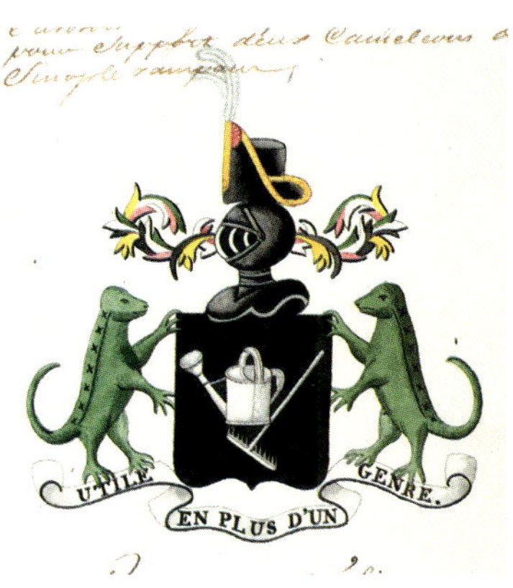

The arms of Baron Béliard

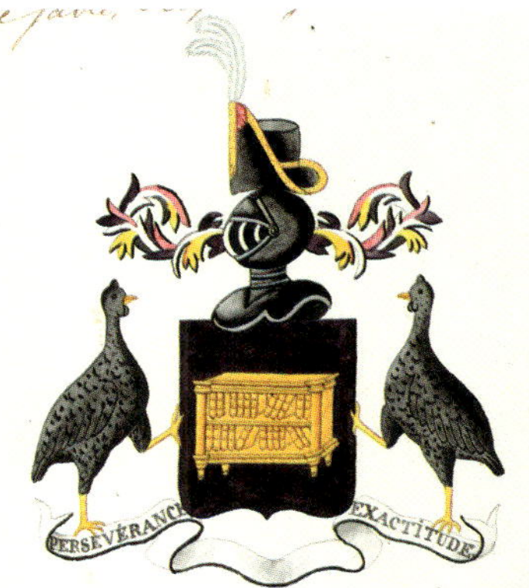

The arms of Baron Sévelinge

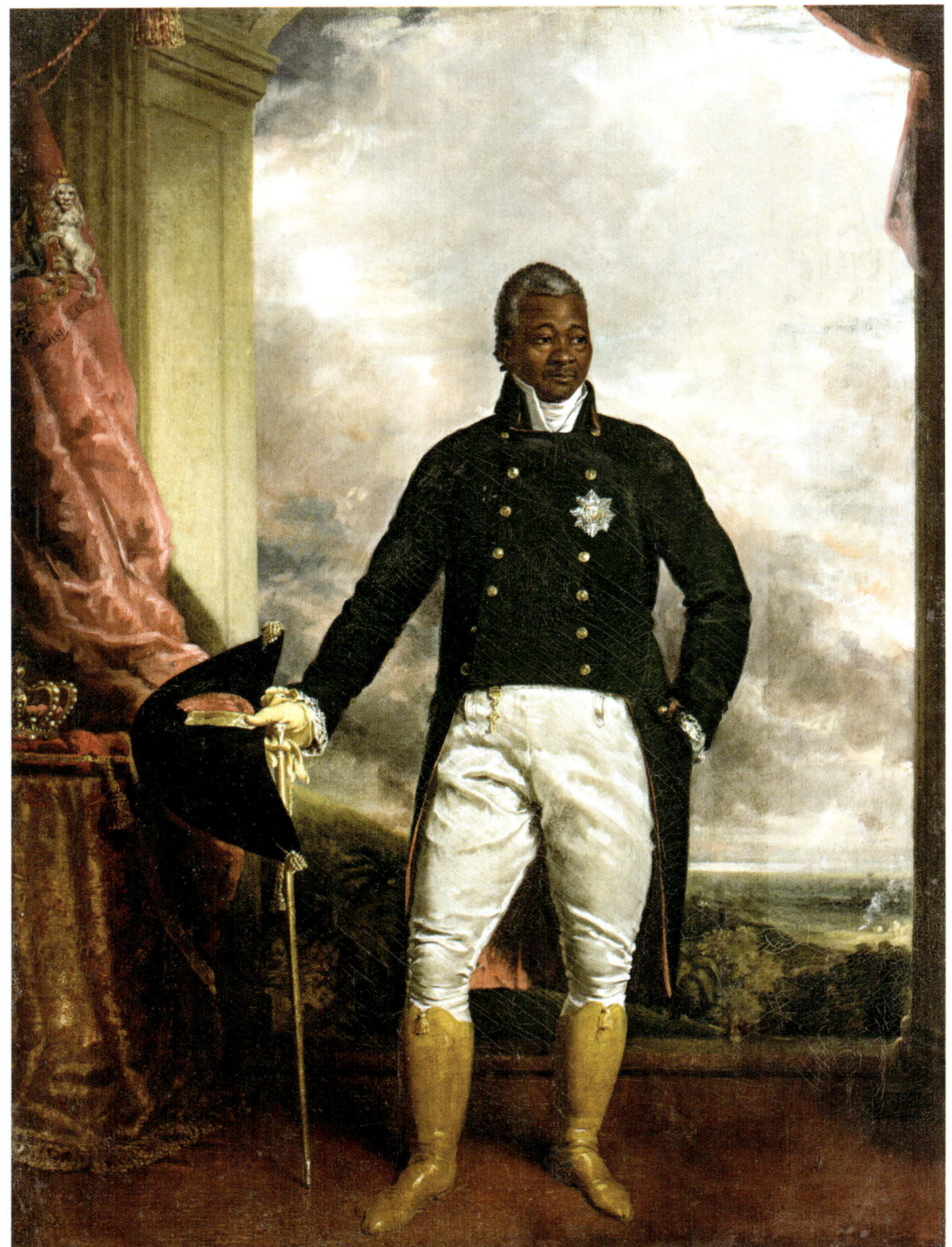

88

Richard Evans (1784—1871). *Henry Christophe, King of Haiti*, about 1816.
Oil on canvas, 111 × 87.5 cm (framed)

Cambridge and Haiti: slavery, the Haitian Revolution and British abolitionism

Sabine F. Cadeau

Resistance and rebellion were intrinsic to the history of Atlantic slavery. Slave uprisings, escapes and maroon settlements were the chronic concerns of colonial slave-owners, and slave ships were frequent sites of mutiny.[1] Many major slave rebellions and countless minor ones took place throughout the Americas over the centuries. The earliest occurred in 1521 in the Spanish colony of Santo Domingo on the Caribbean island of Hispaniola. However, the August 1791 uprising in the French colony of Saint-Domingue was distinct in that it gave rise to a new nation-state led by former slaves who had freed themselves. The former slave Jean-Jacques Dessalines founded the independent nation of Haiti on 1 January 1804. When Dessalines was assassinated in 1806, Haiti was divided into two rival states. Henry Christophe, previously Dessalines's top general, took power in northern Haiti where he crowned himself king and ruled until 1820 [88]. He became a close political associate of British abolitionists and Cambridge graduates William Wilberforce and Thomas Clarkson. The growth of scholarship on the Haitian Revolution helps to elucidate the far-reaching effects of this event, which has a significant but largely unknown place in British history and in the history of the University of Cambridge. In 1793, Prime Minister William Pitt the Younger, another Cambridge graduate, launched Britain's invasion of Saint-Domingue with the goal of conquering the island for Britain and restoring slavery.[2]

The violent end of slavery in Haiti and the advent of the independent Black nation-state gave rise to a complex relationship with Britain and its abolitionists. Historian Craig Wilder argues that universities 'stood beside church and state as the third pillar of a civilization built on bondage'.[3] Universities not only thrived on the basis of colonial wealth, as Cambridge certainly did, but they also produced alumni who contributed to the expansion of slavery and empire across centuries. Major University of Cambridge figures played important roles in the

1. Maroons were runaways who formed autonomous enclaves in the geographical margins of 'New World' colonies. Some of these communities survived for centuries and still exist.
2. David Patrick Geggus, *Slavery, War, and Revolution: The British Occupation of Saint Domingue, 1793–1798*, Oxford 1982. For William Wilberforce (1759–1833): see Venn Cambridge Alumni online database unique identifier (hereafter Venn) WLBR776W.
3. Craig Steven Wilder, *Ebony & Ivy: Race, Slavery, and the Troubled History of America's Universities*, New York 2013, p. 11.

history of colonial slavery, and of the Haitian Revolution, in ways that the historiography of British universities has yet to acknowledge. Haiti is a site that enables historians to observe the influence that some of the University of Cambridge's most famous graduates, both statesmen and thinkers, had in both defending and challenging Atlantic slavery. As one of England's premier intellectual forums for the production and refinement of colonial and imperial ideology, the University of Cambridge had multiple connections to colonial Saint-Domingue and, later, the independent state of Haiti.

The island of Hispaniola is today divided between the Dominican Republic and Haiti. Spain claimed the entire island as a colony from 1492 until 1697, when it ceded the western third to France. The French named their new colony Saint-Domingue. By the late eighteenth century, Saint-Domingue had become the world's largest importer of slaves and the largest exporter of sugar and coffee. On the eve of the Haitian Revolution, Saint-Domingue was the most profitable colony in the world. Historian David Geggus calculates that France's Caribbean colonies 'produced about half the Western world's sugar and coffee, and three-quarters of this produce was re-exported from France, earning vital foreign exchange.'[4] The capital-intensive agriculture of the eighteenth-century Caribbean colonies came at the cost of enslaved Africans who had the shortest life spans and lowest birth rates in the Americas. The hard currency and proliferation of credit that this system generated famously led the sadistic colonists to work newly arrived African slaves to death and rapidly replace them as a kind of large-scale human 'grist' for their sugar mills.

In August 1791, an enslaved man, Boukman Dutty, led a mass insurrection in the main sugar region of northern Saint-Domingue, outside the colonial port of Cap-Français. This event marked the outbreak of the Haitian Revolution, an especially violent and complex event that culminated in the creation of the independent state of Haiti in 1804. The 1791 insurrection began an unstoppable process of Black self-emancipation. Haiti's *Vodou* religion was central to the organisation and planning of this revolt. *Vodou* iconography appears in the coins minted subsequently by the Republic of Haiti. Surviving documents record that the rebels first gathered at a *Vodou* ceremony at Bois Caïman, near Cap-Français, where they swore to rise in unison against their captors.[5] Thousands of slaves took up arms to kill their masters, and they destroyed the sugar plantations, and everything associated with them. Within weeks the rebel ranks numbered tens of thousands. By obtaining Spanish arms and military commissions from neighbouring Santo Domingo, the rebel leaders, including the country's future governor-general, Toussaint L'Ouverture, began transforming their ranks into formal military units.

4. David Geggus, 'Racial Equality, Slavery, and Colonial Secession during the Constituent Assembly', *American Historical Review*, 94 (December 1989), pp. 1209–308 (p. 1291).
5. For details about sources on 1791, see John D. Garrigus, *A Secret Among the Blacks: Slave Resistance Before the Haitian Revolution*, Cambridge, MA 2023.

These irreversible acts of self-emancipation had a complex, evolving relationship with the revolution then unfolding in France. In 1793, in order to preserve Saint-Domingue as a colony for France, desperate French Republican authorities were forced to declare general emancipation there in order to enlist the support of armed rebels. In February 1794, during the radical Jacobin phase of the French Revolution, the National Convention in Paris ratified the achievements of the Caribbean insurgents by universally emancipating all slaves in France's colonies, making self-emancipated Black fighters equal citizens of the French Republic. This policy convinced L'Ouverture and his closest followers to rally behind the French Republican tricolour. Meanwhile, France's chief rival, Great Britain, had plotted to invade Saint-Domingue with the support of French royalist planters based in Saint-Domingue and restore slavery under British rule. The British occupation of Saint-Domingue began in 1793 and lasted until 1798.[6]

Britain's history of involvement with Hispaniola did not, however, begin in 1793, but rather over two centuries earlier, in 1586, when Francis Drake captured and pillaged Santo Domingo, the capital city of Hispaniola. Moreover, in 1655, during the Commonwealth, Oliver Cromwell devised his 'Western Design' to capture Santo Domingo from the Spanish and turn it into an English colony. When his forces were repulsed, they set their sights instead on capturing Jamaica. In the early eighteenth century, several monied Irish families invested in Saint-Domingue's booming sugar economy. While Master of Trinity Hall, Cambridge, the English jurist Nathaniel Lloyd represented the Irish O'Kelly family in a 1712 legal dispute with the French government over plantations in Saint-Domingue.[7]

Britain's own Caribbean colonies also took in French plantation owners who fled Saint-Domingue during the Haitian Revolution. More than a dozen individuals involved in the 1834 British slavery compensation scheme in Jamaica were from exiled Saint-Domingue slave-owning families.[8] Charles D'Aquin Senior and Charles D'Aquin Junior, for example, were plantation owners in Jamaica who had fled from Haiti when the Revolution began in August 1791. The revolutionaries had managed to kill one of the family's sons on the beach while the rest hastily clambered aboard a boat bound for Jamaica.[9] The Verleys were another family of French exiles from Saint-Domingue who sought refuge in Jamaica. Their descendants would later study at the University of Cambridge. Vincent Everard Louis Verley of Jamaica, for example, listed as a 'planter', entered Trinity College in 1890 as a pensioner, while Bertie Louis Verley, probably Vincent's cousin, entered Cavendish Hall in the same year.[10] Cambridge University educated not only the heirs of British planters from Barbados, Jamaica and other British colonies long after slavery had ended,

6. For a detailed history of the British occupation of Saint Domingue, see Geggus 1982.
7. Nathaniel Lloyd (1670–1741): Venn LLT710N. For further discussion of the 1712 dispute, see Nicolas Bell-Romero's forthcoming book, *The University of Cambridge in the Age of Slavery*.
8. For the comparative history of Haiti and Jamaica, see Matthew J. Smith, *Liberty, Fraternity, Exile: Haiti and Jamaica after Emancipation*, Chapel Hill, NC 2014.
9. 'Charles D'Aquin (1771–1834)', *University College London, Centre for the Study of the Legacies of British Slavery Database* (hereafter UCL LBS database), https://www.ucl.ac.uk/lbs/person/view/2146636457 (accessed 18 August 2024).
10. See 'Lewis Francis Verley', UCL LBS database: https://www.ucl.ac.uk/lbs/person/view/17447 (accessed 18 August 2024); Bertie Lewis Verley (1873–1907): Venn VRLY390BL; Vincent Lewis Everard Verley (1871–1930): Venn VRLY890VE; Marcia Thomas, 'Kingston's Millionaires' Corner — Intersection of Trafalgar, Hope and Water oo Roads', *The Jamaica Gleaner*, 9 April 2023.

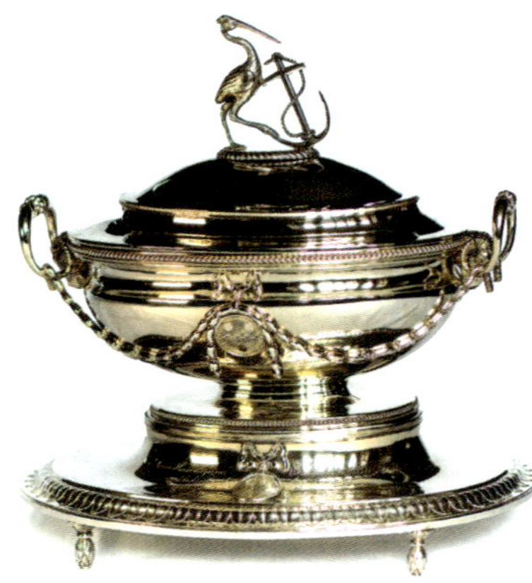

John Wakelin and William Taylor (active 1776—92). **Lidded tureen on stand given by William Pitt to Pembroke College in 1784**. London 1778. Silver

Pembroke College, Cambridge
[not in exhibition]

11. For William Pitt (1759—1857), see Venn PT773W.
12. For more on the British occupation of Haiti, see Geggus 1982.
13. H. Whitridge Millicent and Lonsdale Accounts 1740—56, Pembroke College Archive.
14. For further discussion of Peckard and South Sea Company assets, see my essay 'Dark Finance: The Intertwined History of Slavery and Abolition at the University of Cambridge' in the present volume.

but also the heirs of French planters from Saint-Domingue a century after their ancestors had fled the Haitian Revolution and re-established themselves as enslavers in Jamaica.

Britain's most significant involvements in Haiti, however, occurred during the Haitian Revolution and the early decades of Haitian independence. Cambridge-educated Prime Minister Pitt urged Parliament to abolish the slave trade in 1792.[11] Nevertheless, as head of state, Pitt's legacy is marked by slavery. As mentioned above, at the request of royalist French colonial planters, such as Baron de Malouët and Vicomte de Charmilly, Pitt's government launched a costly five-year military invasion of Saint-Domingue in 1793, with the primary goal of suppressing the revolution and restoring slavery under British rule.[12] Pitt also helped to facilitate a major bequest from his friend Sarah Lonsdale to Pembroke College. Lonsdale's fortune was largely derived from South Sea Company annuities inherited from her father. She used the money to buy an estate at Barham, Linton, which she later bequeathed to Pembroke.[13] Indeed, Pitt is one of many Cambridge University alumni who had a major involvement in Atlantic slavery and was later memorialised with professorships, buildings and statues: the Pitt Professorship, the Pitt Building, the Pitt statue and the Pitt silver at Pembroke College [89] are among the most prominent and visible of Pitt's material legacies at Cambridge. Pitt's story, like that of Peter Peckard of Magdalene College, Cambridge, demonstrates that the contradictory inter-twinement of abolitionism and slavery existed at multiple levels from individuals to institutions to the country at large.[14]

The Haitian Revolution successfully defeated multiple competing European colonial powers and gave rise to a new Black nation-state led by self-emancipated former slaves. On 1 January 1804, having ousted the French colonials, the revolutionaries renamed Saint-Domingue Haiti, a name derived from *Ayiti*, an indigenous name for the mountainous western part of the island. The revolution still figures prominently in Haitian art, as seen, for example, in the painting of Dessalines leading Haitian forces against the French by Haitian painter Pierre Sylvain Augustin, alias 'Payas' [90]. The painting is an homage to an earlier historical theme by Ulrick Jean-Pierre but, unlike the original, Payas depicts an unknown female insurgent at the centre of the battle scene to commemorate the vital — but all too often forgotten — role of women freedom-fighters such as Sanité Bélair and Marie-Jeanne Lamartinière.

Jean-Jacques Dessalines, the founding ruler, proclaimed Haiti an independent state and, in his 1805 constitution, declared himself emperor. Dessalines was assassinated in 1806, and the subsequent internal power struggle led to Haiti being split into two. Southern Haiti became the Republic of Haiti, with

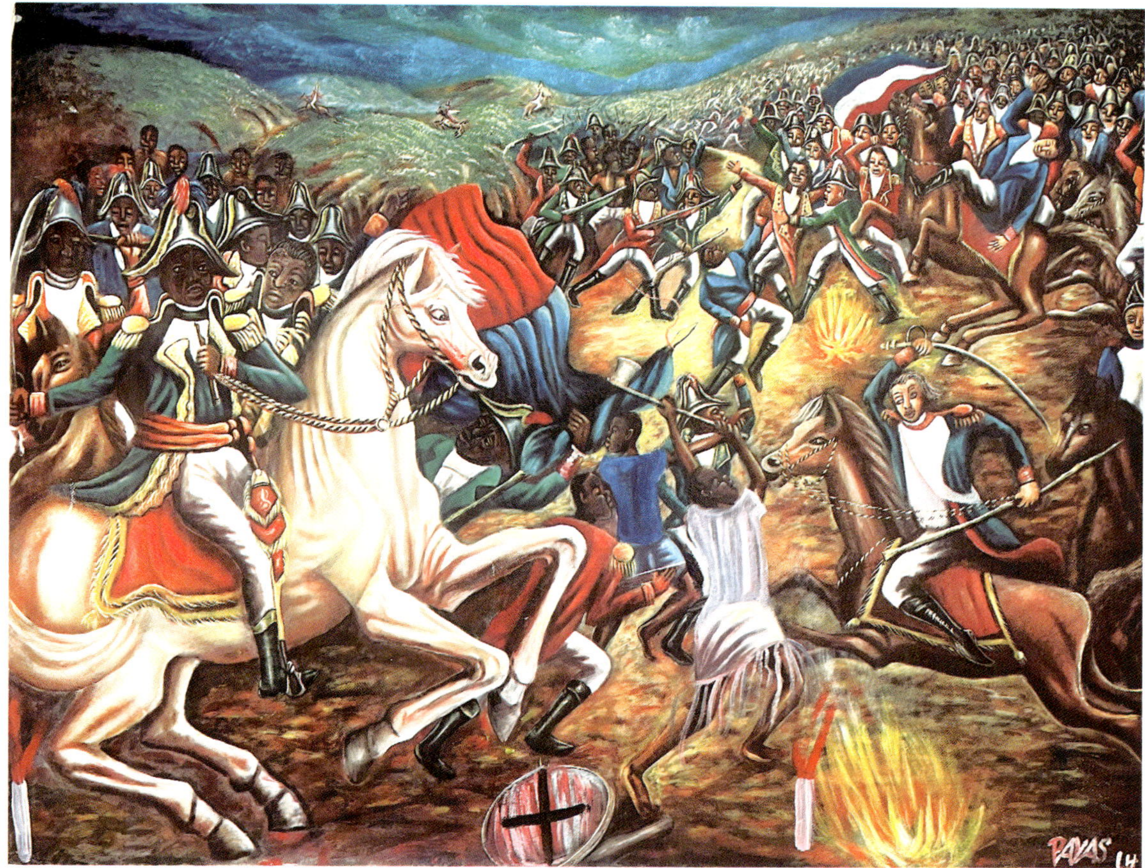

90

Pierre Sylvain Augustin, alias Payas (born 1941). ***Jean-Jacques Dessalines leading Haitian forces against the French***, Port-au-Prince, 2014. Acrylic on canvas, 91.4 × 121.9 cm

Collection of Sabine F. Cadeau, Canada
© Pierre Sylvain Augustin [not in exhibition]

15. See Anne Eller, *We Dream Together: Dominican Independence, Haiti, and the Fight for Caribbean Freedom*, Durham, NC 2016; and Graham Nessler, *An Island-Wide Struggle for Freedom: Revolution, Emancipation, and Reenslavement in Hispaniola, 1789—1809*, Chapel Hill, NC 2017.

Port-au-Prince as its capital. Alexandre Pétion served as first president of the Republic of Haiti until his death in 1818, when he was succeeded by Jean-Pierre Boyer. Northern Haiti became the Kingdom of Haiti and was ruled by Henry Christophe as King Henry I from 1811 until 1820. After the British withdrew from Saint-Domingue in 1798, following their five-year occupation, they became the key de facto military allies of L'Ouverture and Dessalines against the French. But it was Christophe who most embraced British influence, modelling his monarchy and hereditary nobility partly on the British system but melding it with West African influences. After the Kingdom of Haiti collapsed and Christophe committed suicide in 1820, Boyer succeeded in first reunifying northern and southern Haiti into a single republic and then, in 1822, uniting the entire island under his rule, and abolishing slavery.[15]

Haitians paid — and are still paying — a terrible price for taking freedom into their own hands and defeating the white colonialist powers. The French clamoured for revenge and plotted new invasions of Haiti. Anticipating this, both Dessalines and Christophe had built massive fortresses to preserve Haitian

16. Alex Dupuy, *Rethinking the Haitian Revolution: Slavery, Independence, and the Struggle for Recognition*, Lanham, MD, 2019.
17. See Matt Apuzzo, 'The Ransom: Haiti's Reparations to France', *New York Times*, 27 May 2022, https://www.nytimes.com/live/2022/05/23/world/haiti-france-ransom (accessed 18 August 2024).
18. The 1831 Baptist War, also known as the Christmas revolt, pushed the passage of the Slavery Abolition Act of 1833, by which a period of 'apprenticeship' began in 1834 and lasted until 1838. The apprenticeship system was designed by the Colonial Office to train slaves (and their former masters) in preparation for the freedom that would eventually come. In order to do this, former slaves were required to work for their master without pay; thereafter they were able to sell their labour for a wage.
19. For more on this emancipation process, see Thomas Holt's important book, *The Problem of Freedom: Race, Labor, and Politics in Jamaica and Britain, 1832—1938*, Baltimore 1992, pp. 56—7.
20. Rayford Whittingham Logan, *The Diplomatic Relations of the United States with Haiti, 1776—1891*, Chapel Hill, NC 1941, p. 302.
21. See 'Compensation paid out to slave owners recorded in database', *Société de plantation, histoire & mémoires de l'esclavage à la Réunion*, https://www.portail-esclavage-reunion.fr/en/compensation-paid-out-to-slave-owners-recorded-in-a-database/ (accessed 19 August 2024). Slavery researchers from the French colony of Réunion estimate that these 127 million francs, allocated in 1849, represented 1.3% of the country's national income at the time and correspond to a contemporary estimation of €27 billion, comparable in magnitude to estimates surrounding the Haiti indemnity.
22. For a consideration of the financial dimensions of 'neocolonialism' in the Caribbean, see Peter Hudson, *Bankers and Empire: How Wall Street Colonized the Caribbean*, Chicago 2017.
23. Much of what we know about L'Ouverture's early life comes from a memoir by his son: Isaac L'Ouverture, 'Mémoires d'Isaac L'Ouverture', in Antoine Métral, *Histoire de l'expédition des Français à Saint-Domingue*, 1825; reprint, Paris 1985.

independence. In 1825, a flotilla of French ships arrived at Port-au-Prince and aimed their cannons at the Presidential Palace. President Boyer felt compelled to sign a highly punitive indemnity of 150 million francs to pay former colonial planters for the loss of their lands and human property. This indemnity also granted tax breaks to French merchants trading with Haiti. No other nation in history has had to pay reparations for a war it actually won. But Haiti did in fact pay reparations to France until 1947.[16] In 2003, Haitian president Jean-Bertrand Aristide called for restitution and demanded that France pay back the money, estimated at that point to be a staggering $21 billion. The 2022 *New York Times* series on Haiti's history of slavery debt proposed that Haiti's losses from the debt imposed by France amounted to 'as much as $115 billion in losses for Haiti over time — many times the size of its entire economy today'.[17] The 1825 indemnity has had a profoundly negative impact, seriously limiting economic growth in Haiti and undermining its capacity to develop its own institutions.

The hostility that the newly created Black Republic faced from the US and European slave-holding empires meant that Haiti did not receive immediate diplomatic recognition. Indeed, Britain and the US only recognised Haitian sovereignty once they had initiated their own emancipation policies. In the aftermath of the 1831 slave rebellion in Jamaica, known as the Baptist War, Britain passed the Slavery Abolition Act in 1833 and began implementing the 'apprenticeship' system in 1834.[18] After this 'half-way covenant', as historian Thomas Holt describes it, Britain proclaimed complete emancipation in 1838.[19] It was only after this that Britain concluded its first treaty with Haiti in 1839. The United States formally recognised Haiti only in 1862 as it grappled with wartime emancipation policy.[20] Meanwhile the French model of paying reparations to former Saint-Domingue slave-owners to compensate them for loss of human property was adopted in many countries, including France itself. In a different but related way, Britain followed France by paying £20 million to compensate former enslavers throughout its Caribbean colonies. Similar compensation schemes also occurred in South American countries. In 1848, when France abolished slavery for the second time, it paid former slave-owners compensation amounting to 126 million francs.[21] The 1825 French indemnity set a precedent not only in compensating former enslavers, but also in establishing neo-colonial relations through financial control, asymmetrical trade policies and gunboat diplomacy.[22]

Leaders of the Haitian Revolution: Toussaint L'Ouverture and Jean-Jacques Dessalines

It is difficult to reconstruct the early life of Toussaint L'Ouverture [92].[23] Born a slave on the Bréda plantation outside Cap-Français (Le Cap), L'Ouverture was the son of an enslaved African prince who had been taken to Saint-Domingue from the region of Benin. He rose to the rank of coachman before being freed by his master sometime in the 1770s. L'Ouverture spoke the Arada language of his parents and was educated by his godfather, Pierre Baptiste, a free Black man from Le Cap who taught him to read. A small planter before the revolution, L'Ouverture owned and leased a small number of slaves. Although he was not the initial leader of the 1791 uprising, he emerged within months as one of the most important leaders of the Haitian Revolution. He first fought under Jean François and Georges Biassou in alliance with the Spanish. L'Ouverture — the opening — was not his original name. His *nom de guerre* reflected his political and military acumen. He trained one of the most successful military forces of the early modern era. In August 1793, L'Ouverture declared his policy of general liberty to the Black rebels at Camp Turel. After conquering the Spanish colony of Santo Domingo, he promulgated the 1801 Saint-Domingue constitution, which abolished slavery on the entire island of Hispaniola.[24] The visionary Toussaint L'Ouverture was by far one of the most brilliant political leaders within a revolutionary period that produced many extraordinary figures. Highlighting L'Ouverture's early struggles to establish a Caribbean nation-state against the opposition of mighty empires, historian C.L.R. James celebrated L'Ouverture as the 'first and greatest of West-Indians' and compared him to Fidel Castro.[25]

By defeating and coming to terms with the British in 1798 and subsequently winning an internal civil war, L'Ouverture was able to consolidate his position as Haiti's foremost military leader. While he nominally ruled in the name of the French Republic, he ruled de facto as an independent head of state based on his 1801 constitution, which designated him governor-general for life. L'Ouverture presided over the first of many troubled transitions from slavery to freedom in the Americas. The Haitian generals' vision of a profitable plantation system was largely incompatible with the masses' yearning for land and freedom. Like his successors Dessalines, Christophe, Pétion and Boyer, L'Ouverture attempted to reconcile emancipation with rebuilding the plantation economy using forced labour, which led to a number of more radical rebellions from below.[26] In 1802, unwilling to accept his rise to power, Napoleon Bonaparte, then First Consul of the French Republic, sent a massive expeditionary force to disarm and reconquer Saint-Domingue for France and re-establish slavery. Despite L'Ouverture's brilliant military leadership, he was caught and deported to France, where he died in prison in 1803.

Following L'Ouverture's death, his lieutenant Jean-Jacques Dessalines led the Haitian Revolution against Napoleon's troops.

24. Laurent Dubois, *Avengers of the New World: The Story of the Haitian Revolution*, Cambridge, MA 2004, pp. 171—2.
25. C.L.R. James, *The Black Jacobins: Toussaint L'Ouverture and the San Domingo Revolution*, London 1938, p. 418.
26. For a rethinking of the postcolonial tragedies, L'Ouverture and Haiti's postcolonial predicament, see David Scott, *Conscripts of Modernity: The Tragedy of Colonial Enlightenment*, Durham, NC 2004.

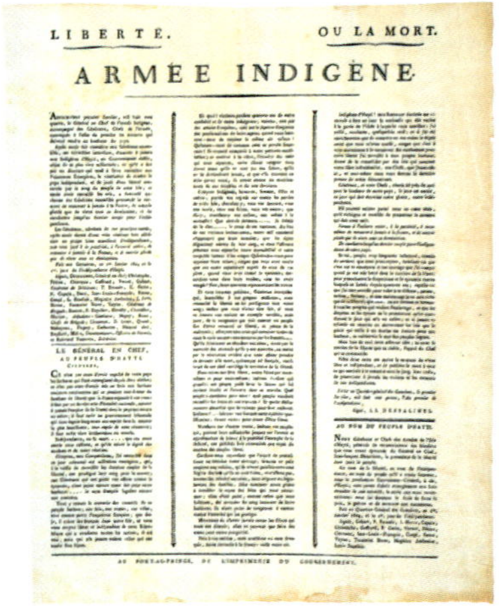

91

**Haitian Declaration
of Independence**, 1 January 1804

The National Archives, Kew (CO 137/111/1)
[not in exhibition]

Faced with an uncontrollable insurgency, France attempted to subdue Saint-Domingue using the most brutal measures. French generals Leclerc and Rochambeau determined that, to reverse universal emancipation, they would have to kill off the entire Black population over the age of twelve and rebuild the plantation system by importing new slaves from Africa. Napoleon's forces were ultimately defeated, and Dessalines declared Haitian independence on 1 January 1804. This made Haiti the first modern Black nation-state and the second independent nation-state in the Western hemisphere after the United States.[27] Haitian American anthropologist Michel-Rolph Trouillot observed that these 'unthinkable' events challenged 'the ontological order of the West and the global order of colonialism.'[28] As the first country to emancipate all slaves and break free from colonialism to become an independent Black state, Haiti produced political documents of enormous importance to the history of democracy and human rights, including L'Ouverture's 1801 constitution, Dessalines's 1804 Declaration of Haitian Independence [91] and his 1805 constitution.

Ideals of racial equality, anti-slavery, anticolonialism and Black self-determination had their earliest and most forceful expressions in early Haitian political thought. Indeed, Trouillot described Haiti's as the 'most radical revolution of that age'.[29] The independence struggles in South and North America preserved and further entrenched slavery respectively. While Napoleon reversed the 1794 emancipation decree and violently restored slavery in France's colonies from 1802, Haiti's revolutionaries maintained an unwavering vision of Black freedom and sovereignty.[30]

Henry Christophe

Second only to L'Ouverture, Haitian revolutionary Henry Christophe [88] figures prominently in British history, especially because of his political relationship with Cambridge alumni and abolitionists William Wilberforce and Thomas Clarkson. Christophe was most likely born in Grenada and may have come to Saint-Domingue sometime around 1779. As a youth he was among the volunteer troops from Saint-Domingue who participated in the American Revolution and fought against the British at the Siege of Savannah in 1779. Before the revolution he had lived as a free Black man in the northern port of Cap-Français. Like L'Ouverture, Christophe joined the Haitian Revolution soon after it broke out. He fought alongside Dessalines, first under the Spanish and later the French. He was Dessalines's leading general after independence, and when Dessalines was assassinated in 1806, Christophe consolidated power in northern Haiti, where he crowned himself monarch of the new Kingdom

27 For an overall history of these events, see James 1938; Carolyn Fick, *The Making of Haiti: The Saint-Domingue Revolution from Below*, Knoxville, TN 1990; and Dubois 2004.
28 Michel-Rolph Trouillot, *Silencing the Past: Power and the Production of History*, Boston 2015.
29 Trouillot 2015, p. 47. Trouillot criticises Hobsbawm for largely ignoring Haiti in his book, *The Age of Revolutions*.
30 For more on the reversal of slave emancipation in France's colonies, see Laurent Dubois, *A Colony of Citizens: Revolution and Slave Emancipation in the French Caribbean, 1787–1804*, Chapel Hill, NC 2012.

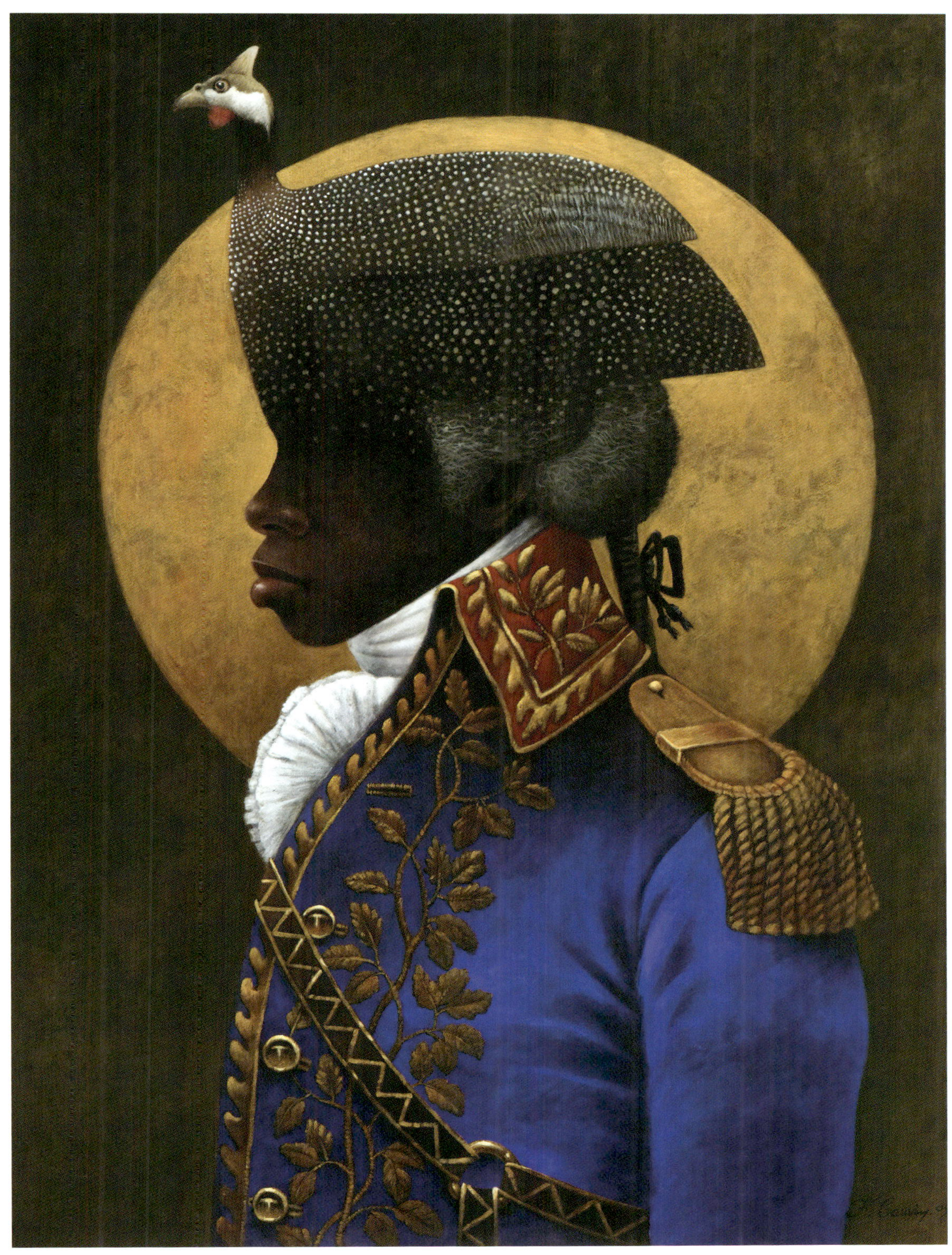

92

François Cauvin (born 1956). ***Toussaint L'Ouverture***, 2009. Acrylic on canvas, 129.5 × 106.7 cm (framed)

François Cauvin (Artist and Owner) © François Cauvin

of Haiti. To deter the French from future invasions, he
constructed massive fortresses, the largest of which was
the Citadelle Laferrière outside the rechristened Cap-Henry,
formerly Cap-Français and today Cap-Haïtien. Alongside
that fortress he built his majestic palace complex Sans-Souci,
whose magnificence was recorded by Haitian painter Numa
Desroches [85].[31] Christophe's regime championed the cause of
Black freedom but depended on forced labour for its militarised
agrarian economy and massive fortress projects. Desroches's
colourful painting of Sans-Souci ignores the system of forced
labour that Christophe relied on to build it.[32] Christophe's
kingdom hardly championed radical ideals of social equality.
Instead, in an effort to consolidate his regime, he instituted
a British-inspired system of hereditary landed nobility. The
original copy of Christophe's armorial [86] is kept at the
College of Arms in London.

While British abolitionists ignored Haiti during its revolutionary
years, in 1813, almost ten years after Haiti had won independence,
Wilberforce [93] and Clarkson [55] began a vigorous and lengthy
correspondence with Christophe.[33] Clarkson hoped to glean
information on Haiti in order to rebut pro-slavery ideologues.[34]
King Henry, in turn, wanted to prove that Haiti could succeed
as an independent Black kingdom. He fostered relations with
Clarkson and Wilberforce with the goal of securing diplomatic
recognition from Britain, which would guarantee Haiti from
being re-invaded by European colonial powers. Theirs was
a mutually beneficial political relationship, with both sides
hoping that the other could help them advance their goals.

Clarkson also corresponded with Haitian author Baron
de Vastey, Christophe's principal scribe and ideologue.[35]
Wilberforce also read de Vastey's works and expressed
concern over whether the baron would survive the violent
fall of Christophe's kingdom in 1820. From Christophe's Sans-
Souci palace, de Vastey selectively raged against the atrocities
committed by the French slaveowners while praising the
British abolitionists and their Sierra Leone colonisation project.
Following the military and financial failure of Pitt's invasion
of Saint-Domingue in the 1790s, Haitian regimes had come
to rely on de facto trade and strategic relations with Britain,
which they obtained in exchange for guarantees not to
interfere with Britain's surrounding plantation colonies.
While Britain became the key strategic guarantor of Haiti's
independence from its chief rival, France, it still refused to
formally recognise Haiti.

Clarkson was not only a publicist and interlocutor for
Christophe but a formal diplomatic agent for the Kingdom of
Haiti. Christophe sent money to Clarkson in the hope that he
would help Haiti secure diplomatic recognition from Britain

31. For a recent biography on King Henry,
see Paul Clammer, *Black Crown: Henry
Christophe, the Haitian Revolution and the
Caribbean's Forgotten Kingdom*, London
2023. Christophe has featured heavily in
the Caribbean literary imagination. See Aimé
Césaire, *The Tragedy of King Christophe:
A Play*, trans. P. Breslin and R. Ney, Evanston,
IL 2015; Derek Walcott, *The Haitian Trilogy*,
New York 2002; and Alejo Carpentier, *The
Kingdom of This World*, trans. P. Medina,
New York 2017.
32. For more on forced labour in early
nineteenth-century Haiti, see Johnhenry
Gonzalez, *Maroon Nation: A History of
Revolutionary Haiti*, New Haven, CT 2019.
33. For Henry Christophe I, King of Haiti,
and Thomas Clarkson, see Earl Leslie
Griggs and Clifford Holmes Prator (eds),
*Henry Christophe, Thomas Clarkson.
A Correspondence*, Berkeley 1952.
34. Seymour Drescher, *The Mighty
Experiment: Free Labor Versus Slavery in
British Emancipation*, Oxford 2002; David
Geggus (ed.), *The Impact of the Haitian
Revolution in the Atlantic World*, Columbia
2020; Jack Webb, *Haiti in the British
Imagination: Imperial Worlds, 1847–1915*,
Liverpool 2020; and Clammer 2023.
35. For more on the Baron de Vastey,
see Pompée-Valentin Vastey, *The Colonial
System Unveiled*, trans. C. Bongie, Liverpool
2014; and Marlene Daut, *Baron de Vastey
and the Origins of Black Atlantic Humanism*,
New York 2017.

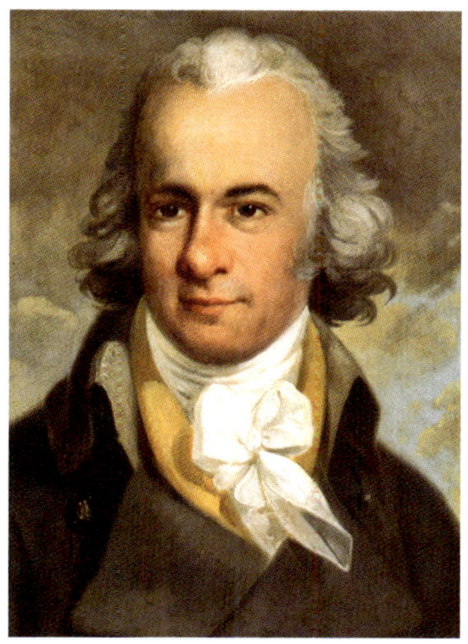

93

Karl Anton Hickel (1745—1798). ***William Wilberforce***, 1793. Oil on canvas, 59 × 49 cm (detail)

and other European states. The Haitian revolutionaries had only succeeded by dextrously playing empires against each other. Spain, France, Britain and even the newly established United States were all potential sources of arms and support for one Haitian faction or another. Christophe's goal was to use his diplomatic ties with Britain to end Haiti's economic and political ostracism and the continual threat of another French invasion. Christophe also hoped that Clarkson, Wilberforce and other British abolitionists would help him establish formal primary education in Haiti. Historian Julia Gaffield points out that one of Christophe's most important surviving texts is his 1816 letter to Clarkson, in which he describes his efforts to bring professors to Haiti to teach in the 'institutions of public instruction', which he envisaged would enable Haitians to overcome the 'shameful prejudice' heaped upon them by slave-holding nations and to 'astonish the world by their knowledge'.[36]

Clarkson and Wilberforce advised Christophe on various aspects of his new court, including establishing an academy of painting and drawing along the lines of the Royal Academy in London. Christophe hired Royal Academician Richard Evans to serve as its first director, and by late 1816, Evans had painted pendant portraits of both the king and his son, Royal Prince Jacques-Victor Henry Christophe [88 and 94]. Christophe gifted these (or copies) to Wilberforce to thank him for a portrait of Wilberforce that Wilberforce had sent to him. This exchange of images demonstrates the respect and cordial friendship that existed between the two of them.[37] Indeed, these portraits of the Haitian royal dynasty remained with the Wilberforce family until 1912. Clarkson was similarly friendly with Christophe. Following Christophe's suicide in 1820, his widow, former Queen Marie-Louise, fled with her daughters to England. They were given refuge by Clarkson and his family in their home at Playford Hall, Suffolk. They stayed there for several months, passing the winter with the Clarksons before settling into rented accommodations in Blackheath, Kent. Interestingly, despite their close interest in Christophe's kingdom, Clarkson and Wilberforce never visited Haiti. However, another Cantabrigian abolitionist and Wesleyan missionary, William Woodis Harvey of Queens' College, did make the voyage in 1818 and stayed there until 1824.[38]

Impact of the Haitian Revolution

The Haitian Revolution had an enormous impact on European intellectuals. French author Victor Hugo used the Haitian Revolution as inspiration for some of his earliest fiction.[39] Philosopher and intellectual historian Susan Buck-Morss has argued compellingly that German philosopher Georg Wilhelm Friedrich Hegel conceived his master-slave dialectic during a period when he religiously read the German newspaper

36. Julia Gaffield, 'King Christophe and the English Abolitionists', in Laurent Dubois et al. (eds) *The Haiti Reader: History, Culture, Politics*, Durham, NC 2020, pp. 41—4.
37. For a letter from Christophe to Wilberforce dated 18 November 1816, see Robert Isaac Wilberforce and Samuel Wilberforce (eds), *The Correspondence of William Wilberforce*, London 1840, vol. 1, p. 362.
38. William Woodis Harvey (1798—1864): Venn HRVY824WW; William Woodis Harvey, *Sketches of Hayti from the Expulsion of the French to the Death of Christophe*, London 1971; first published 1827.
39. Chris Bongie, 'Victor Hugo and the Melancholy Novel: Reading the Haitian Revolution in *Bug-Jargal*', *French Studies: A Quarterly Review*, 72, no. 2 (2018), pp. 176—93.

Minerva, which was replete with news on the Haitian Revolution.[40] Information on Haiti spread far and wide across Atlantic shipping lanes, in print media and through military and civilian communication networks. Britain, like France, was a major centre of writing on Haiti in the early nineteenth century. British army captain Marcus Rainsford met Toussaint L'Ouverture in Saint-Domingue in 1799, and upon his return to Britain he published two books on Haiti. Scottish diplomat Charles Mackenzie was a Caribbean plantation heir and veteran of Fedon's Rebellion, the Haitian-influenced revolutionary war in Grenada. He was appointed British consul to Haiti in 1825 and published a book in England based on his fact-finding mission to Haiti.[41]

Not surprisingly, Haiti and its fight for independence drew the attention of Britain's intelligentsia at Cambridge and elsewhere. In 1802, as L'Ouverture languished in a French prison, Cambridge alumnus and poet William Wordsworth wrote a sonnet dedicated to him that was published in the *Morning Post* in 1803.[42] Wordsworth's 'To Toussaint L'Ouverture' was a reflection on the former general's time in 'the deep dungeon's earless den'. The sonnet, in which Wordsworth called L'Ouverture 'the man of Men' and an exemplar of 'man's unconquerable mind', shows that the Haitian Revolution planted a seed for the possibility of transforming the racial ideology of the period. Wordsworth clearly recognised that Black colonial subjects were struggling against nearly impossible odds to assert their intelligence, honour and independence. Wordsworth's sonnet celebrated the idea that ephemeral and perhaps romantically transcendent forces were on the side of the oppressed.

Wordsworth studied at St John's College, Cambridge, from 1787 to 1791, well after Clarkson and Wilberforce, although he became friends with them later and wrote poems dedicated to Clarkson. His younger brother, Christopher Wordsworth, served as Master of Trinity College from 1820 until 1841. Like other major figures of the era, William Wordsworth's biography reflected the wider importance of Atlantic slavery in British economic life. His father, John Wordsworth, was a lawyer for James Lowther, 1st Earl of Lonsdale, who had been educated at Peterhouse and whose legendary family fortune included a major Barbados plantation that had 222 slaves in 1834.[43] Wordsworth undoubtedly contributed to the lionisation of L'Ouverture in Europe. Wordsworth contemplated L'Ouverture's importance for posterity, writing that:

> There's not a breathing of the common wind
> That will forget thee.

Wordsworth's notion that the world was replete with natural allies of L'Ouverture was both politically and poetically

40. Susan Buck-Morss, 'Hegel and Haiti', *Critical Inquiry*, 26 (summer 2000), pp. 821—65; and Susan Buck-Morss, *Hegel, Haiti and Universal History*, Pittsburgh 2009. For more on Atlantic slavery and Western philosophy, see David Brion Davis, 'Toussaint L'Ouverture and the Phenomenology of Mind', *The Problem of Slavery in the Age of Revolution, 1770—1823*, New York 1999, epilogue: pp. 557—64.
41. See Marcus Rainsford, *A Memoir of Transactions that Took Place in St. Domingo in the Spring of 1799*, London 1802; Marcus Rainsford, *An Historical Account of the Black Empire of Hayti*, London 1805; and Charles Mackenzie, *Notes on Haiti, Made During a Residence in That Republic*, London 1971. For Fedor's Rebellion, see David Barry Gaspar and David Patrick Geggus (eds), *A Turbulent Time: The French Revolution and the Greater Caribbean*, Bloomington, IN 1997; and Tessa Murphy, 'A Reassertion of Rights: Fedon's Rebellion, Grenada, 1795—96', *La Révolution Française*, 14 (2018), https://doi.org/10.4000/lrf.2017 (accessed 19 August 2024).
42. William Wordsworth, Sonnet No. 111: 'To Toussaint L'Ouverture', *Morning Post*, 2 February 1803. Historian Julius Scott echoes Wordsworth's historic lines in the title of his influential book, *The Common Wind: Afro-American Currents in the Age of the Haitian Revolution*, London 2020.
43. 'James Lowther 1st Earl of Lonsdale', *Centre for the Study of the Legacies of British Slavery*, https://www.ucl.ac.uk/lbs/person/view/2146645255 (accessed 19 August 2024).

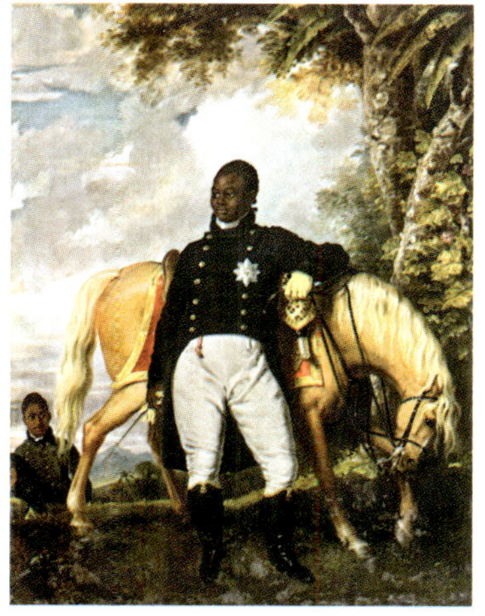

94

Richard Evans (1784—1871).
Prince Royal Jacques-Victor Henri Christophe, about 1816.
Oil on canvas, 111 × 87.5 cm (framed)

Alfred Nemours Collection, Library System, University of Puerto Rico, Río Piedras Campus, San Juan, Puerto Rico (no accession number assigned). Gifted by King Henry I to William Wilberforce in 1816. Remained in Wilberforce family's possession, by descent; sold to Dr Nemours Auguste (1850—1915; Haitian diplomat and *chargé d'affaires* to Jacques Nicolas Leger, Secretary of State), London, 1912; inherited by his son, Alfred Auguste Nemours (1883—1955; Haitian military officer, diplomat and military historian) in 1915; sold by his widow to the University of Puerto Rico, 1962

romantic. It did not foresee the rising tide of scientific racism in the nineteenth century. Haiti's leaders had few allies apart from British abolitionists Clarkson and Wilberforce, and they only engaged with Haiti well after the Haitian Revolution had ended.

During the waves of revolution and resistance to slavery that rolled incessantly across the Atlantic during the turbulent 1790s, Britain was the main enemy for the thousands of Black insurgents in the Caribbean who rallied behind the French tricolour following France's abolition of slavery in 1794. The Haitians drove the British out of Saint-Domingue, and French Republicans operating out of Guadeloupe seeded major rebellions against the British at Grenada, Dominica, Saint Lucia and Saint Vincent. While only Haiti remained in the hands of Black insurgents, who managed to establish their own independent state, slave rebellions helped push along the abolition of the Atlantic slave trade and the eventual emancipation of slaves in British colonies. This occurred following further mass uprisings in Barbados in 1816, in Guyana in 1823, and in Jamaica from 1831 to 1832. Black resistance against slavery put Britain and other empires into what writer Olaudah Equiano observed to be a constant 'state of war'.[44] As evidenced in the interactions between Haitian revolutionaries and Clarkson and Wilberforce, former slaves corresponded, negotiated and debated with elite abolitionists in ways that contributed to the end of the slave trade and slavery. The history of these transformative interactions offers lessons on how vastly unequal and historically opposed parties might manage to cultivate modes of exchange and work collectively to address today's pernicious and ongoing legacies of colonialism and enslavement.

44. Olaudah Equiano, *The Interesting Narrative of the Life of Olaudah Equiano, or Gustavus Vassa, The African. Written by Himself,* London 1789 (2nd edn), p. 225.

Tipping points: Barbados, Guyana and Jamaica

After the Haitian Revolution, other major uprisings of enslaved people followed. In Barbados, an enslaved African man named Bussa led some 400 enslaved men and women in an uprising in 1816. The colonial militia killed Bussa in battle, but his supporters fought on until their rival's greater resources won out.

In Demerara (then a province of British Guiana), an uprising spread quickly in 1823. Around 13,000 enslaved people rose up on sixty plantations, including some with connections to the University of Cambridge. They demanded emancipation and recognition of their rights but did not seek to eliminate the white population or plantation agriculture. British forces repressed them with extreme violence.

In Jamaica, a Black Baptist deacon named Samuel Sharpe led an initially peaceful general strike over Christmas 1831. More than 60,000 enslaved people united to demand greater freedom and wages for their labour. The rebels, including Kitty Scarlett from the Cambridge plantation, St James, caused extensive property damage. Violent reprisals by the colonial Jamaican government killed over 200 protestors. But this could not extinguish their demands for freedom and justice.

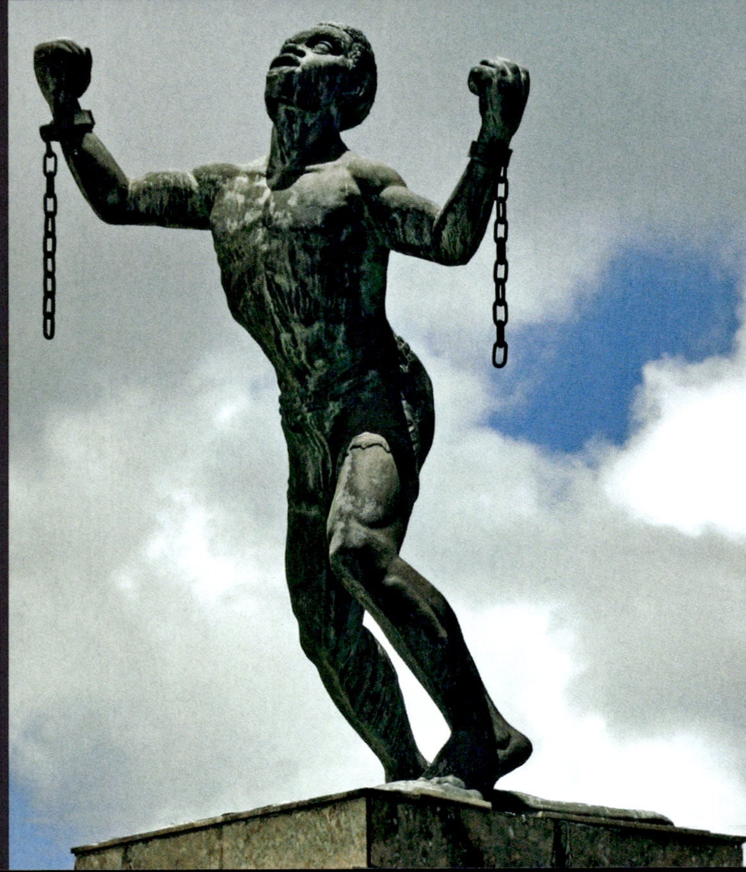

95
Karl Broodhagen (1909—2002). *Emancipation Statue: Slave in Revolt*, also known as *Bussa*, 1985. Bronze, over lifesize. J.T.C. Ramsay roundabout, east of Bridgetown, Barbados

Photograph by Daniel L. Berek
[not in exhibition]

Barbados: Bussa's Rebellion

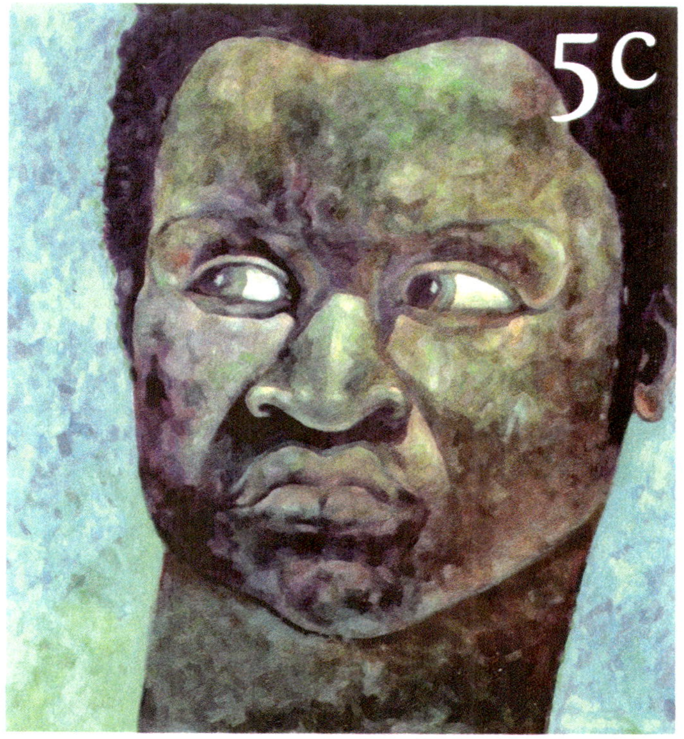

96

Five-cent stamp featuring Bussa issued by the Barbados Post Office as part of its 'Builders of Barbados' series, 2016.

The portrait of Bussa (acrylics on canvas, 196 x 172 cm) was made by Akyem-i Ramsay (born 1953) in 1998. It was commissioned by the Barbados National Heroes Committee, National Collection, Barbados [not in exhibition]

Few historical records exist to tell us about Bussa's life before his leadership of the largest uprising of enslaved people against racism and white planter-oppression in Barbados' history. So key was Bussa in this uprising, which took place between 14 and 16 April 1816, that it is named after him. Believed to have been enslaved as a child in Igboland and transported to Barbados, Bussa was forced to work as a Ranger (plantation manager) on Bayley's plantation, St Philip. Having to maintain plantation boundaries and fences gave Bussa greater freedom of movement than most enslaved people and opportunities to connect with enslaved people on neighbouring plantations.

When Governor Leith returned to Barbados from Guadeloupe in 1816, the enslaved population mistakenly believed that he brought with him a 'free paper' to liberate them. When this did not happen, Bussa commanded about 400 men and women against the colonial forces, mainly militia troops of the West India Regiments (an all-Black branch of the British Army with an estimated 13,400 enslaved men purchased as recruits between 1795 and 1807). Bussa was killed in battle, but his freedom fighters fought on until they were defeated by superior firepower. While only one white civilian and one Black British soldier were killed, fifty enslaved people died in battle, seventy were executed in the field, 144 were captured, tried, sentenced to death and executed, and 132 were captured, tried and sentenced to deportation and hard labour on other British colonies in the Caribbean.

In 1998, the Government of Barbados recognised 'The Right Excellent Bussa' as one of just ten National Heroes. Having already featured on the one-cent stamp issued by the Barbados postal service in 2007 to commemorate the Bicentenary of the Abolition of the Slave Trade Act, Bussa appeared again on the new five-cent stamp, issued in January 2016, as part of a new series entitled 'The Builders of Barbados'.

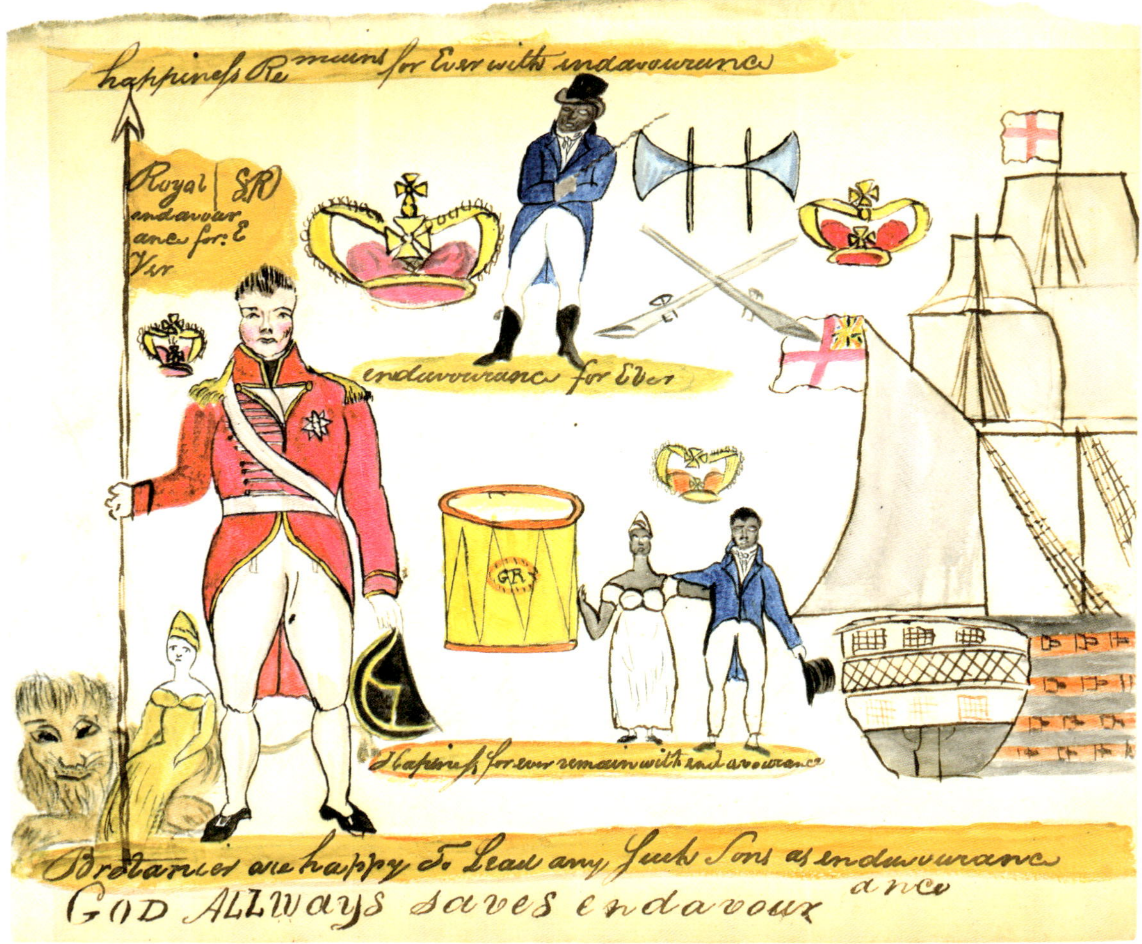

97

Unrecorded artist. Sketch of a martial flag seized from enslaved insurgents during Bussa's Rebellion, Barbados, April 1816.
Watercolour and ink on paper, 19 × 23 cm

Inscribed (top banner): 'happiness Remains for Ever with endeavourance'; (flag): 'Royal GR endeavourance for Ever'; (central logo): 'endeavour for Ever'; (logo under drum): 'Hapiness for ever remain with endavourance'; (bottom banner): 'Britanier are happy to lead any such Sons as endeavourance GOD Always saves endeavourance'. The National Archives, Kew (MFQ 1/112 [1]). This sketch and another similar one were originally enclosed in a dispatch of 30 April 1816 from Admiral John Harvey (1772—1837). Commander-in-Chief Barbadoes and Leeward Islands at the Royal Navy station at the English Harbour, Antigua, 1816—18 (ADM 1/337)

Battle flags have been used throughout history to project a group identity embodying military might. Enslaved people who engaged in violent resistance against their enslavers often created flags as acts of defiance. They often modified or subverted imagery taken from their oppressors' flags, assigning new meanings and asserting autonomy in the face of European subjugation. Historic records about Bussa's Rebellion reveal that the enslaved freedom fighters went from plantation to plantation seizing arms and setting over seventy plantations on fire. They were led by a standard-bearer called Johnny, who like Bussa was from Bayley's plantation; several other fighters also carried flags. Contemporary accounts describe white cotton flags with simply drawn figures and mottoes, several of which were captured and recorded in watercolour sketches. Three survive: two in the National Archives (both included in Admiral John Harvey's 30 April 1816 despatch) and one in the New York Public Library (sent by 'Mr Holden' to the 'Colonial Club' on 16 June 1816).

Unrecorded artist. Sketch of a martial flag seized from enslaved insurgents during Bussa's Rebellion, Barbados, April 1816.
Watercolour and ink on paper, 19 × 25.4 cm

Inscribed (top banner): 'happiness ever, remain with endeavor'; (flag): 'Royal G.R Endeavour for once'; (central logo): 'Endeavour for once'; (bottom banner): 'Br tannier are always happy to assist all such Sons as endeavour'; (variously located colour indicators): 'blue', 'red' and 'yellow'; (caption underneath image): 'Communicated to the "Colonial Club" by Mr Holden June 18th. 1816'. New York Public Library, Manuscripts and Archives Division (MssCol 2483). From the Gordon Lester Ford Collection, Gift of Worthington Chauncey Ford and Paul Leicester Ford, 1899. This sketch forms the preface to the manuscript, 'An account of the late Negro insurrection which took place in the island of Barbados on Easter Sunday, April 14, 1816', bound after John Poyer's 1808 publication, *The History of Barbados, from the First Discovery of the Island, in the Year 1605, till the Accession of Lord Seaforth, 1801*, London 1808, into a single volume

This sketch of a captured insurgent flag is bound into a historic collection of written material about Bussa's Rebellion from Barbados newspapers, private letters, accounts of plantation damage and losses, and Sir James Leith's proclamation clarifying that no order had been sent to free emancipated people in the Caribbean (as widely understood within enslaved communities to have been the case). The imagery includes traditional symbols of British dominion, such as Britannia seated on the British Lion, ships flying the Royal Navy's White Ensign and 'Royal GR' alluding to the Royal Cypher *Georgius Rex* ('King George [III]'). But, radically, it also has signifiers of African power, including an enthroned Black king and queen on either side of a Black insurgent armed with a plantation machete. This combination of iconographic motifs shows the insurgents' desire to claim the protection of Britain's monarch while simultaneously conveying their desire for liberty and autonomy.

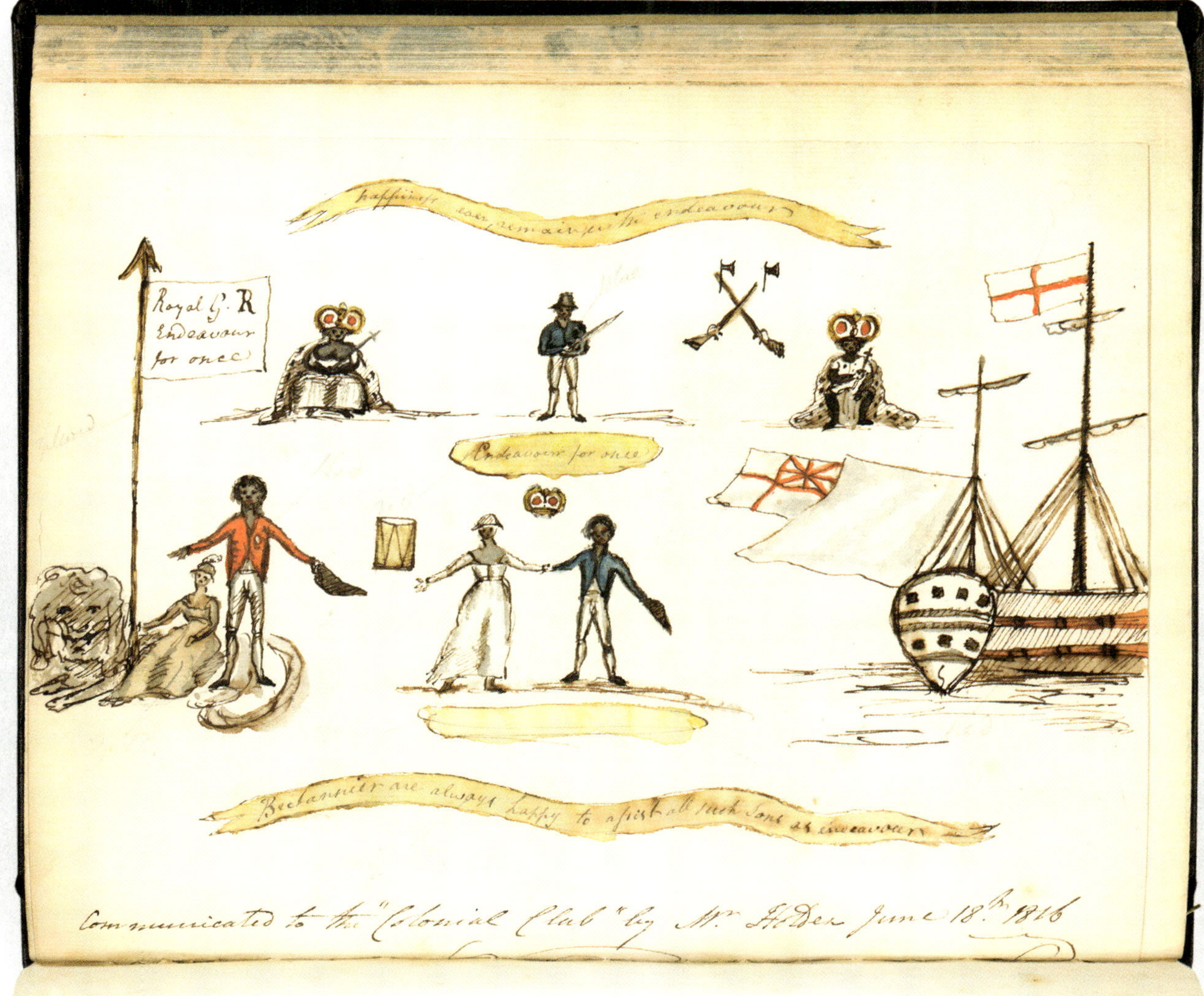

Communicated to the "Colonial Club" by Mr Holden June 18th 1816

Guyana: the Demerara Uprising

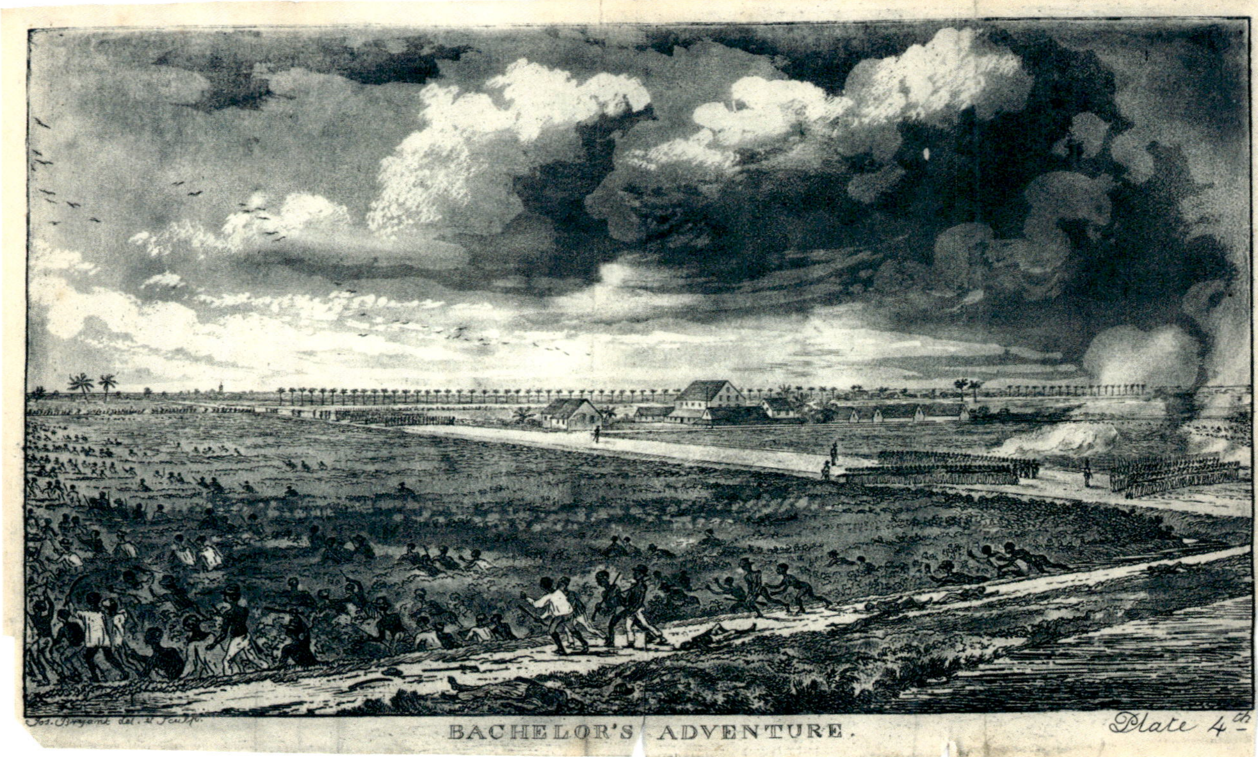

99

Joshua Bryant (active 1798—1831).
Bachelor's Adventure, 1824. Etching, 20 × 33 cm

Plate 4 in Joshua Bryant, *Account of an Insurrection of the Negro Slaves in the Colony of Demerara, which broke out on the 18th of August, 1823*, Georgetown, Demerara 1824. Inscribed (bottom left): 'Jos[hua] Bryant del[ineavit] et sculp[sit]' ('Joshua Bryant drew it and engraved it'); and (bottom right): 'Plate 4th'. John Carter Brown Library, Providence, Rhode Island: D824 B915. [Version in exhibition: British Library, London (8157.bb.9 (1.))]

This is one of thirteen plates that British artist and fifteen-year Demerara resident Joshua Bryant included in his 'eye-witness' *Account* of the 1823 Demerara Uprising. Although Bryant's stated aim was 'the communication of truth', he worked for Demerara's white slaveholding elite, and so his visual narratives replicate their perspectives and his text is critical of the uprising.

This illustration shows enslaved insurgents on Bachelor's Adventure, a large cotton plantation at the heart of the revolt, which at the time was jointly owned by Benjamin Hopkinson (born in Tobago in November 1785) and his younger first cousin Thomas Hopkinson (born in Demerara in about 1800), both sons of white Yorkshire brothers and free women of colour from Demerara. Both Hopkinson cousins had been sent to Trinity College, Cambridge, to complete their education: Benjamin matriculated in 1804 but there is no record of his graduation; Thomas matriculated in 1819 and graduated in 1824, making him one of the first students of colour to complete a degree at the University of Cambridge. Having worked as a merchant in London, Benjamin returned to Demerara in 1821 to manage several family-owned plantations, including Bachelor's Adventure. Benjamin experienced the Demerara Uprising firsthand through his capture and placement in stocks by his enslaved labourers. Thomas did not because he was studying in Cambridge at the time, accompanied by his enslaved servant, Cesar.

Errol Ross Brewster (born 1953).
Jack Gladstone, 2021. Pen and ink on paper,
27.9 × 21.6 cm

National Portrait Gallery, London (NPG D49536) © Errol Ross
Brewster. Purchased from Brewster by the National Portrait Gallery's
Board of Trustees, 2023, for permanent display in its 'Radicals,
Resistance and Reform' gallery. Originally created by Brewster
in response to a call for artwork for Thomas Harding's 2022 book,
White Debt: The Demerara Uprising and Britain's Legacy of Slavery

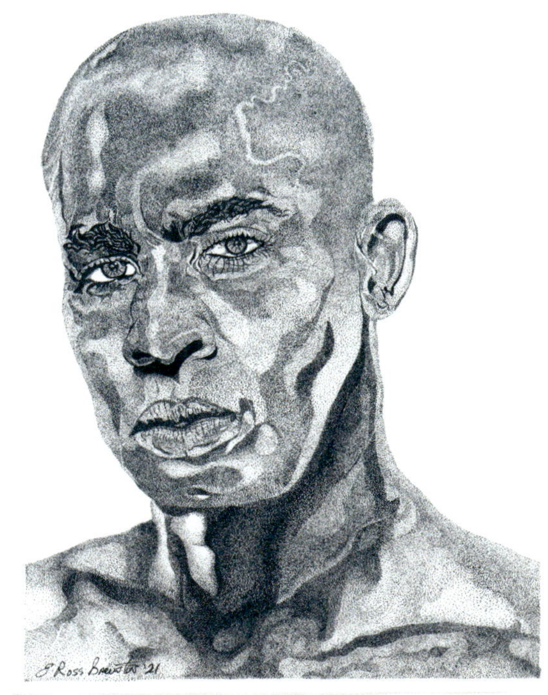

Errol Ross Brewster based this imagined portrait of
Jack Gladstone, enslaved leader of the Demerara Uprising,
on a 'Wanted' advertisement published in an 1823 Demerara
paper. Offering 1,000 Guilders for his capture alive, the
advertisement described Gladstone as 'twenty-five years
of age; handsome, well made; rather a European nose; good
white teeth; 6 feet 2 inches tall'. In this speculative portrait,
Brewster recalls wanting to show Jack's 'tremendous presence,
and engaging aura' and to reflect his documented 'strength
of character, bold decisiveness, daring, intensity, questioning
concentration', which is why he gave Gladstone 'a furrowed
brow, square set jaw line, determined chin (dimpled for good
measure), a penetrating gaze from out sensitive eyes, and
lips, fulsome with probing questions.'

Errol Ross Brewster (born 1953).
Amba Gladstone, 2021. Pen and ink on paper,
27.9 × 21.6 cm

National Portrait Gallery, London (NPG D49537) © Errol Ross
Brewster. Gifted by an anonymous donor to the National Portrait
Gallery Trustees, 2023, for permanent display in its 'Radicals,
Resistance and Reform' gallery. Originally created by Brewster
in response to a call for artwork for Thomas Harding's 2022 book,
White Debt: The Demerara Uprising and Britain's Legacy of Slavery

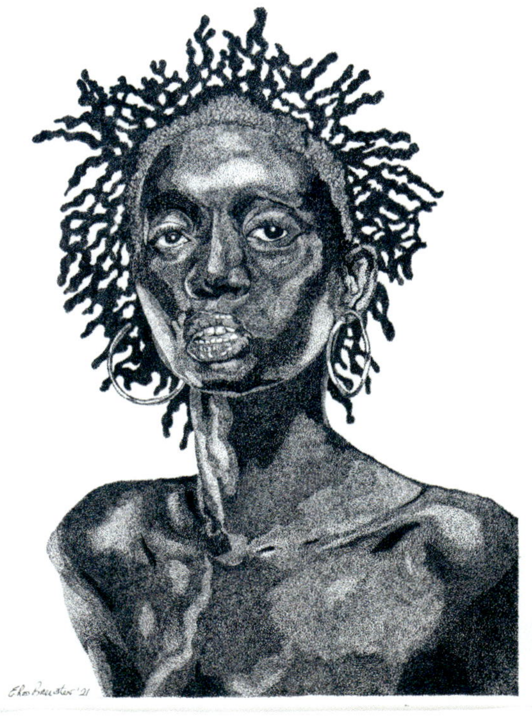

Amba Gladstone was an enslaved labourer on the
Success sugar plantation (owned by the father of future
Prime Minister William Gladstone) and a key leader in the
1823 Demerara Uprising. Recorded in her post-insurrection
trial as tall, wiry and with narrow shoulders, Brewster chose
to imagine her, 'like a broomstick, but strong. The force of her
command came from her determination'. Brewster was keen to
show Amba's courage, single-mindedness and non-conformity,
having learnt from the court transcripts that it was Amba
who had ordered her less brave male counterparts to drag
the overseer to the plantation stocks. So Amba has uncovered
locs standing 'prominently on her head, seeming to mirror
the fighting men' and 'a steely, laser-focused determination',
in the 'sure knowing of [her] purpose'.

Jamaica: the Emancipation War

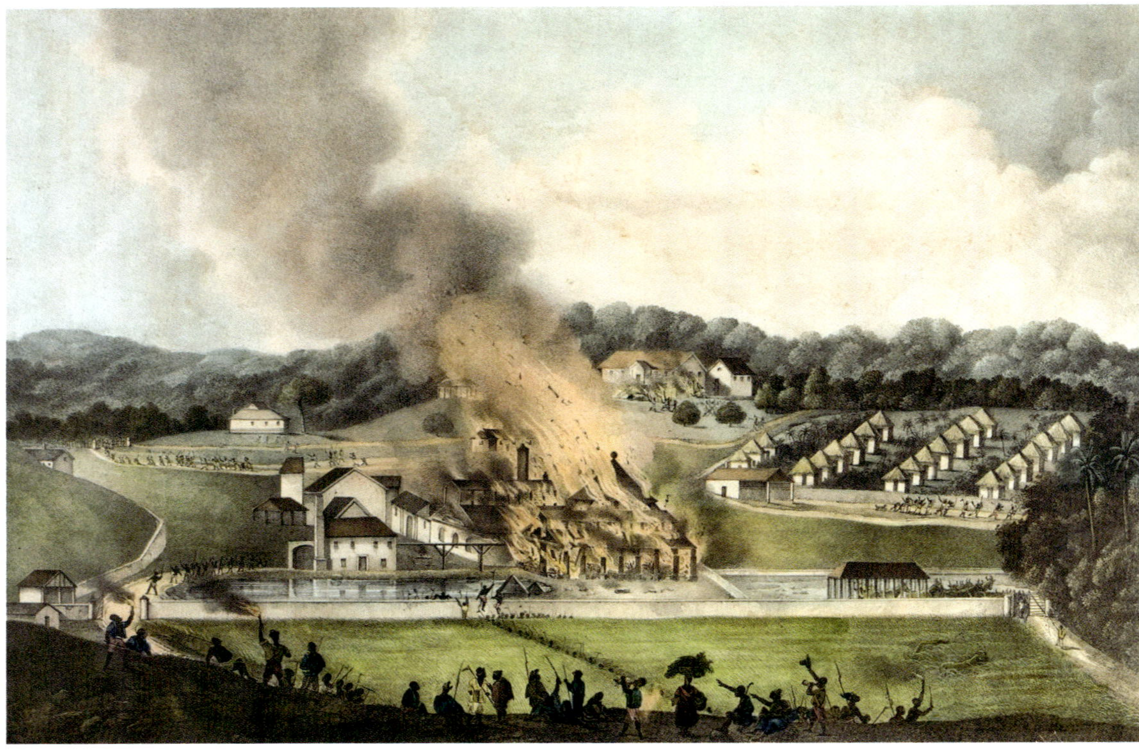

102

Adolphe Duperly (1801—1865).
***Roehampton Estate Destroyed by Insurgent
Negroes in Jamaica in Jan[uar]y 1832***,
Jamaica 1833. Hand-coloured lithograph,
29.2 × 41.3 cm

Proof before title added, with handwritten title and printed signature,
'A. Duperly Lith[ographer] Jamaica 1833'. Maggs Bros Ltd, Rare
Books and Manuscripts, London. Bought at auction (Christie's,
South Kensington, *Live Auction 4826*, 25 April 2012, lot 282).
This print was subsequently produced with the printed title, *The
Destruction of Roehamton* [sic] *Estate in the Parish of Saint James'
in January 1832, the Property of J.Baillie, Esq.*

Based in Kingston, Jamaica, French artist Adolphe
Duperly produced a number of lithographs in 1833, which
superimpose scenes from the 1831 Emancipation War onto
the fictionalised images of plantation life created for Jamaica's
white plantation owners by English artist James Hakewell.
Duperly based this *Roehampton Estate* image on an earlier
one by Hakewell, which had employed the artistic conventions
of the pastoral idyll to normalise plantation life and render it
tranquil, harmonious and natural. Duperly has here rejected
Hakewell's timeless and static landscape and transformed
it into one of contemporary specificity and violent action,
thereby commemorating the courageous resistance of the
enslaved insurgents.

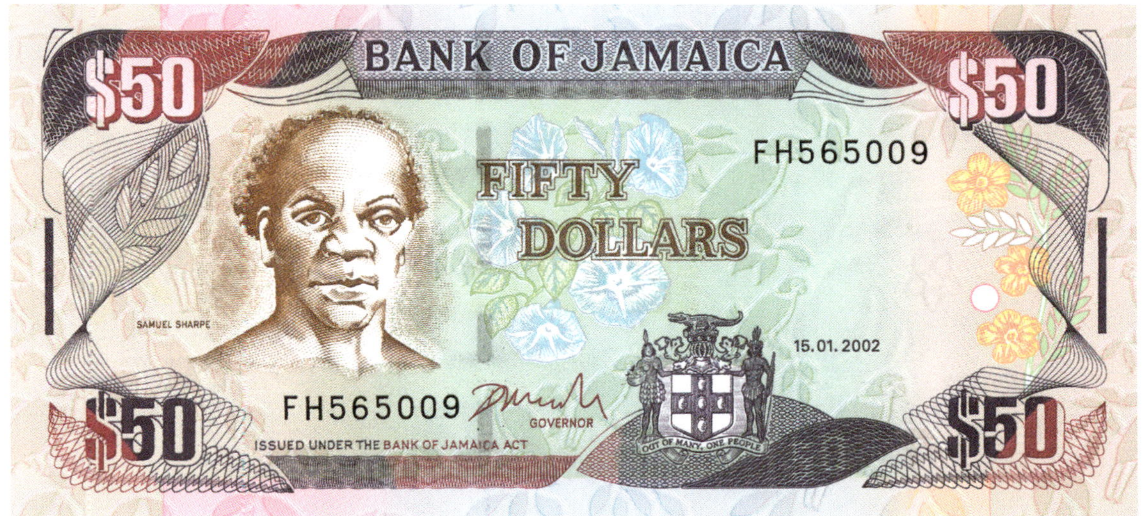

103 above

Bank of Jamaica. Contemporary uncirculated $50 banknote featuring imagined portrait of Samuel Sharpe, issued 1 August 1988. Plastic polymer, 6.8 × 14.5 cm

Designed and printed by De La Rue. Fitzwilliam Museum, Cambridge (CM.7-2024) © Bank of Jamaica. Given by Dr Victoria Avery, August 2024. Purchased from internet seller

Although the 1831 Emancipation War was ultimately suppressed, it is acknowledged as a decisive factor in persuading a still-reluctant British government to enact the 1833 Slavery Abolition Act. Samuel Sharpe, a well-respected, enslaved deacon of the Baptist Church in Montego Bay, has been recognised by post-independence Jamaica for the leading role he played. In 1975, the government of Jamaica proclaimed him a National Hero. In August 1988, the Bank of Jamaica introduced a $50 bill and featured his imagined portrait on the front.

104 below

Bank of Jamaica. Contemporary uncirculated $500 Polymer New Design UNC banknote featuring imagined portraits of Nanny of the Maroons and Samuel Sharpe, issued June 2023. Plastic polymer, 6.8 × 14.5 cm

Designed and printed by De La Rue. Fitzwilliam Museum, Cambridge (CM.8-2024) © Bank of Jamaica. Given by Dr Victoria Avery, August 2024. Purchased from internet seller

On 31 March 1982, Nanny of the Maroons and Samuel Sharpe were named National Heroes by the Jamaican government. They are still celebrated as National Freedom Fighters: in June 2023, the Bank of Jamaica's new polymer banknotes entered circulation with Nanny and Samuel both featured on the $500 bill. According to the Bank of Jamaica, 'the spirit of Nanny of the Maroons remains today as a symbol of that indomitable desire that will never yield to captivity'.

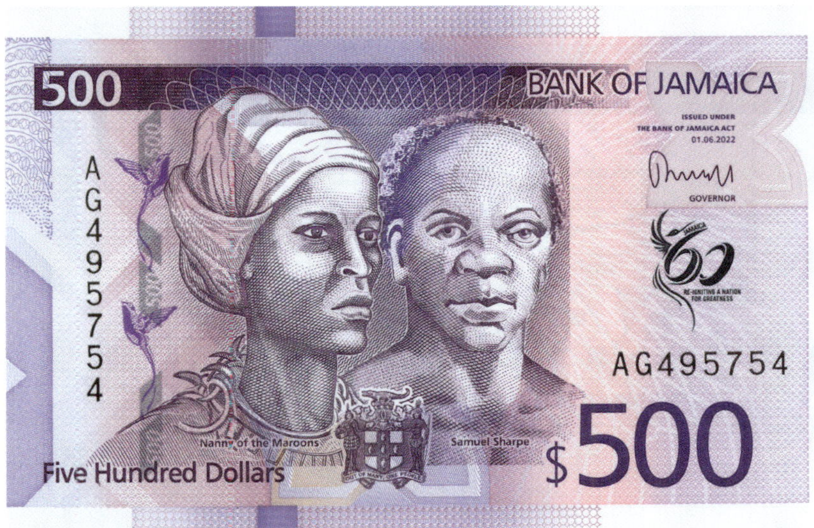

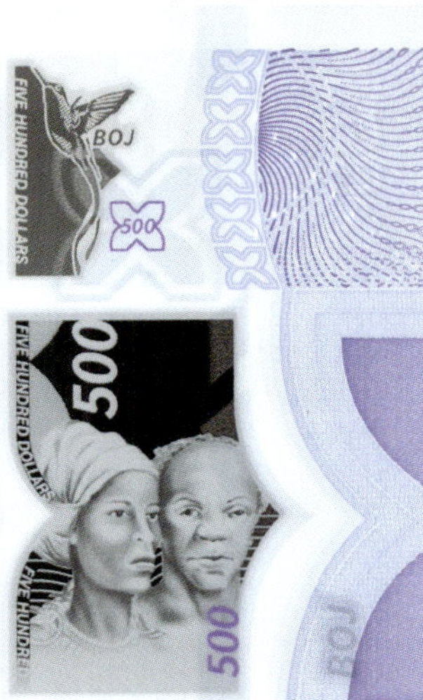

THEATRE ROYAL,
CAMBRIDGE.

By Permission of the Right Worshipful the Vice-Chancellor, and the Worshipful the Mayor.

Under the Management of Mr. HOOPER.

THIS EVENING,
For the BENEFIT of

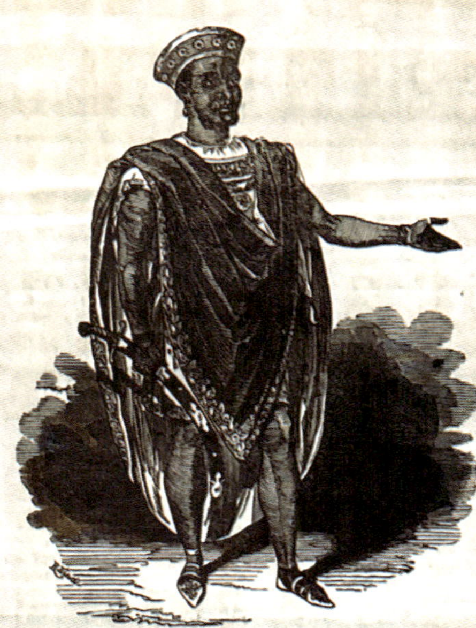

THE AFRICAN ROSCIUS

And his last Appearance.

On FRIDAY, September the 13th, 1850,
Will be Presented the Classical Tragedy of

REVENGE
Or, the CAPTIVE MOOR,

Written by the Rev. Dr. Young, Dean of Lichfield, author of "Night Thoughts."

Zanga (the Captive Moor) - - Mr. IRA ALDRIDGE.

Don Alonzo, Mr. L. MELVILLE—Don Carlos, Mr. VANDENHOFF—Don Alvarez, Mr. ERSER JONES
Don Manuel, Mr. BRISK.—Fernando, Mr. WILSON—Gomez, Mr. FITZGERALD.
Donna Leonora, Miss CHALMERS————Isabella, (her Attendant), Miss BYRNE.
Attendants, Guards, &c., &c.

Duett, "I know a bank" by the Misses WARD.

"I'm Unhappy" by Mr. SUTER.

In the course of the Evening the AFRICAN ROSCIUS will deliver a

Farewell Address.

After which, the COMEDIETTA of

WHY DON'T SHE MARRY,
Or, the SWISS COTTAGE

5

Ending British slavery

The 1807 Abolition of the Slave Trade Act made it illegal for British people and ships to trade in enslaved people anywhere in the empire. While this decision reshaped the system and experience of the Atlantic slave trade, it was only a first step towards eradicating enslavement.

Ironically, the situation for enslaved people actually worsened in many ways due to various factors, including intensification of commodity production to offset general soil depletion and decreased profits, and increased illegal slave-trading activities. More than 800,000 African, African-descended and Indigenous people in the Caribbean were still rendered as property, held captive in lives of abuse and exploitation. The pro-slavery lobby in Westminster continued to resist further reform, and the British government was complicit in delays to enacting the Slavery Abolition Act.

Abolitionists knew the fight would only be won with dogged determination and targeted action to change the British Empire's legal and economic infrastructure. Words and images were employed as effective propaganda by both abolitionists and their opponents. It was not until 1833 that the Slavery Abolition Act was finally passed, only to be replaced by other pernicious systems of exploitation.

Detail of **127** (page 169)

Women's activism

White British women supported and benefited from slavery directly and indirectly for far longer than they worked against it. Many did not oppose slavery because they were investors in it and owned plantations and enslaved people.

However, a new generation of radical female campaigners and activists emerged, including the enslaved Bermudian Mary Prince, who was the first known Black woman to have her life story published, and Quaker Elizabeth Heyrick, who published a book demanding immediate not gradual abolition. They fought for emancipation as well as rights for women.

Abolitionist women found many ways to promote their cause, such as using print media and messaging on everyday items such as teapots. They encouraged the public to boycott plantation goods such as sugar produced by enslaved labour — an early form of ethical consumerism.

105

Mary Prince (1788—after 1833). ***The History of Mary Prince, A West Indian Slave, Related by Herself* ...**, 2nd edn, London and Edinburgh 1831

Cambridge University Library (RCS.Case.c.25)

In mid-1828, Mary Prince was forcibly brought from Antigua to London by her enslaver, without her free Black husband Daniel James whom she had married in December 1826. There she met abolitionist Thomas Pringle, Secretary of the Anti-Slavery Society, who helped her escape and took her into his home as a paid domestic servant. While living in the Pringle household, Prince narrated her story to Thomas's surrogate daughter, author and abolitionist Susanna Strickland Moodie. Pringle edited the text and financed its publication in February 1831. Prince's narrative autobiography was the first life of a Black woman ever published in Britain, and it was an immediate bestseller with no fewer than three editions published in 1831 alone. Prince's voice became a call to action at a time when the anti-slavery movement was fast gaining momentum, leading ultimately to the Slavery Abolition Act of 1833. The Act's third section freed all enslaved people who prior to its passing had been brought to any part of Britain with their enslaver's consent. On 28 August 1833, when the Act received Royal Assent, Mary Prince would have been at liberty to plan her return to Antigua and her husband, although her eventual destiny remains a mystery.

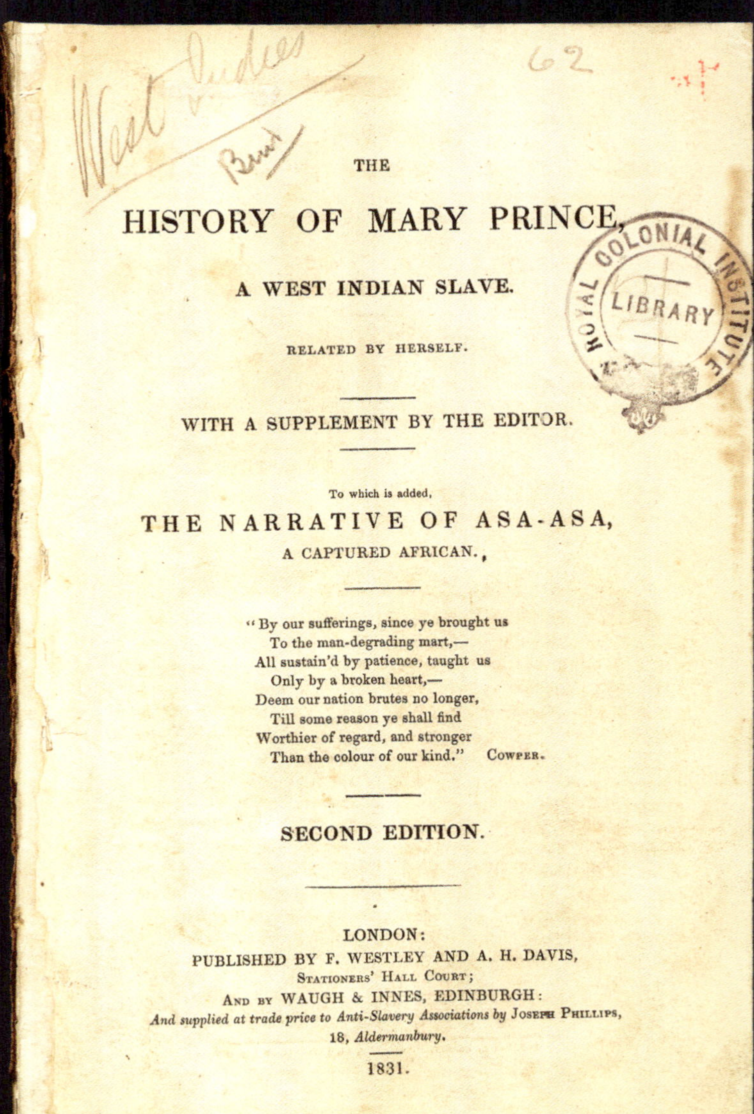

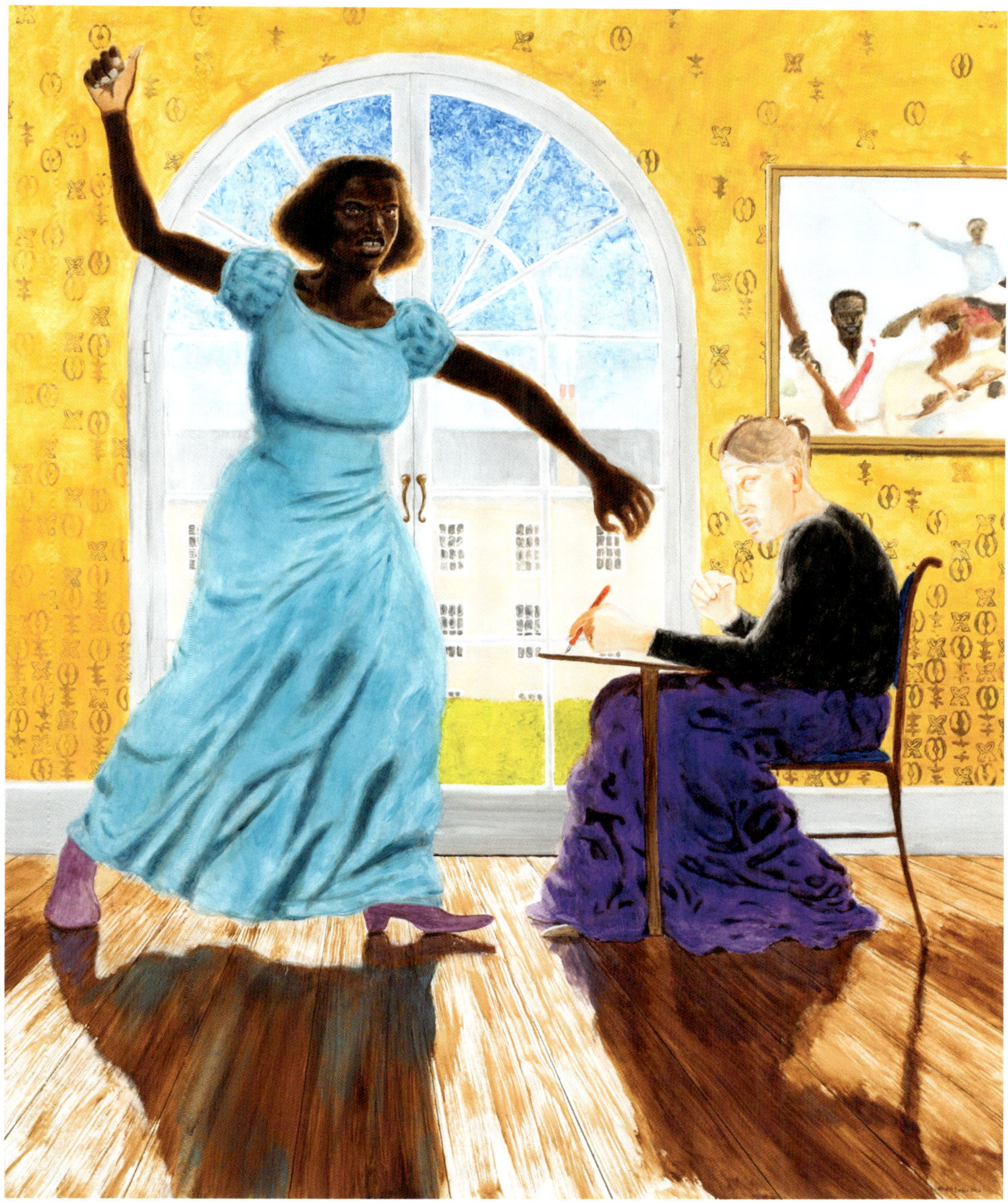

Kimathi Donkor (born 1965).
***Mary Prince dictating to
Susanna Strickland***, 2023.
Acrylic on linen, 200 × 160 cm

Courtesy of the Artist and Niru Ratnam,
London © The Artist

Donkor's painting is an imagined scene of Mary Prince dictating her life story to her white friend and ally Susanna Strickland Moodie. Prince appears to be re-enacting how Mary Ingham, a particularly cruel former enslaver, would flog her 'as an ordinary punishment for even a slight offence'. It illustrates the emotional depth of Prince's narrative, focusing on her struggle for autonomy. The wallpaper features *adinkra* symbols from the Gyaman people of Ghana and Côte d'Ivoire, symbolising hope, bravery and self-determination. Donkor also includes part of his earlier painting of Haitian leader Toussaint L'Ouverture, creating a powerful interplay of visual symbols and historical figures. Together, they emphasise the significance of personal and collective stories of emancipation.

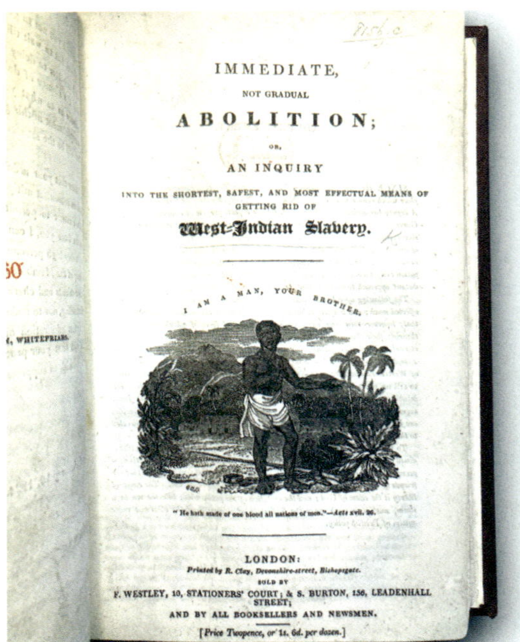

107

Elizabeth Heyrick (1769—1831).
Immediate, not Gradual Abolition …,
London 1824.

British Library, London (8156.c.71.(7)). [Version in exhibition: Cambridge University Library (Ddd.18.7. UkCU, item 2)]

In 1824, angry at the lack of progress by 'gradual abolitionists' in getting slavery outlawed, Elizabeth Heyrick published her radical tract arguing for the immediate and total outlawing of colonial slavery: 'The perpetuation of slavery in our West India colonies, is not an abstract question, to be settled between the Government and the Planters, it is a question in which we are all implicated; we are all guilty.' Heyrick's pamphlet was also radical in its reimagining of SEAST's racist logo, with the enslaved African man now shown as emancipated, free of shackles, standing upright and stating, 'I AM A MAN, YOUR BROTHER'. Denouncing Wilberforce and Clarkson for being too 'polite' and 'accommodating' of enslavers', Heyrick became a thorn in the Anti-Slavery Society's side. Wilberforce and others, who felt a gradual phasing out to be more prudent, tried to suppress this pamphlet and ordered withdrawal of support for all women's anti-slavery societies that espoused Heyrick's ideas. But many people supported Heyrick and followed her lead in boycotting West Indian sugar made by enslaved people.

108

Unidentified English ceramic factory,
possibly William Hackwood, Stoke-on-Trent.
Abolitionist teapot shaped as a tea kettle
with pseudo-Copeland & Garrett Italian design, 1827—early 1830s. Earthenware, blue transfer-printed, 27 × 29 × 28 cm

Inscriptions: rhyming couplet (exterior, twice-repeated): 'Ladies I hope you will make free and tell me how you like your tea'; rhyming couplet (interior, bottom): 'Health to the Sick, Honour to the Brave, Success to the Lover, and Freedom to the Slave'; (underside of lid): 'WH' mark, probably initials of manufacturer William Hackwood (1774—1849), Hanley. Fitzwilliam Museum, Cambridge (C.15 & A-2022). Given by the Friends of the Fitzwilliam Museum, 2022. Bought at auction (Lawrences Auctioneers of Crewkerne, Somerset, *Pictures, 19th/20th Century Design & Ceramics*, 12 October 2022, lot 797) by E. & H. Manners for the Fitzwilliam Museum

At the height of the second sugar boycott in the later 1820s, approximately 400,000 Britons gave up West Indian sugar. Many were women who, keen to advertise their abolitionist sentiments, bought 'free labour' sugar bowls and other domestic wares decorated with anti-slavery slogans. This teapot reveals a more subtle approach to promoting the abolitionist cause, using the traditional form of rhyming couplets. While the second couplet, 'tell me how you like your tea' appears straightforward in terms of ascertaining whether the tea-drinker would like milk, lemon or sugar added to their brew, the first couplet, 'Ladies, I hope you will make free', could be taken to mean not so much the freeing of the tea-consumer's tongue as the freeing of enslaved people. This messaging is repeated inside, across the bottom, but while the couplet's last line, 'Freedom to the Slave', is a clear message supporting abolition, its surreptitious placement means that it could only have been seen when the pot was empty.

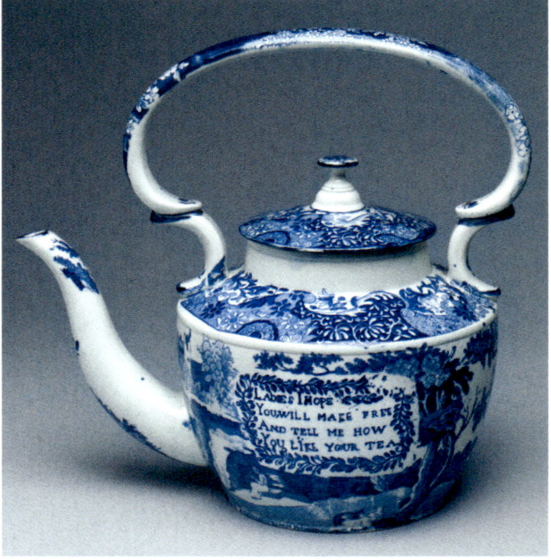

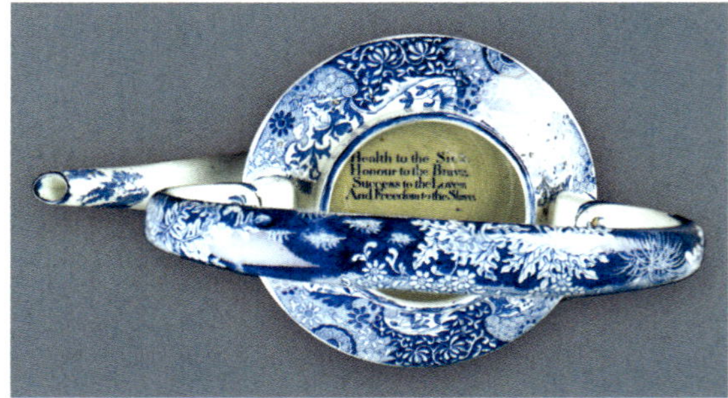

The Ladies' Society for the Relief of Negro Slaves.

Abolitionist promotional prints associated with the bags [110 and 111], about 1828 to 1833.

Fitzwilliam Museum, Cambridge (PM.1-2022 to PM.18-2022). Given by the Friends of the Fitzwilliam Museum, 2022. Bought at auction (Historical & Collectable online auction, 18 October 2022, lot 77)

Here are a few of the abolitionist texts and images that were placed inside work bags and albums made by the Ladies' Society for the Relief of Negro Slaves, and also printed onto their outsides [110 and 111]. According to the Society's 1825 Annual Report, these were intended to 'waken attention, circulate information, and introduce to the notice of the affluent and influential classes … the real state of suffering and humiliation under which British Slaves yet groan.' Donations from sales were sent to support the work of anti-slavery groups in Britain or overseas. As with earlier abolitionist texts and images, while well-intentioned and highly effective as a means to elicit sympathy, raise awareness and gain supporters, they are now regarded by many as problematic and demeaning in stereotyping captive African people as passive victims in need of white saviours, and as ignoring the fact that millions of enslaved African people spent their lives resisting captivity, and many successfully self-emancipated.

Ladies' Society,

FOR

THE RELIEF OF NEGRO SLAVES.

CARD EXPLANATORY OF THE CONTENTS OF THE SOCIETY'S

WORK BAGS AND ALBUMS.

EXTRACTS from the Jamaica Gazettes are placed in the Work-Bags and Albums of this Society, to show from the Planters' own statements, *in their own authentic records*, the sufferings which our present system of Colonial Slavery must produce. For instance, if we see whole columns filled with advertisements of runaway Slaves in one week's Jamaica Gazette, and many of them described by their brand-marks, and wounds, and mutilations, and the indelible marks of the lacerations of the cart-whip, we must be sure that great cruelty exists, although we ourselves may not have met with those who have witnessed it. If we see a Negro *boy*, named DUKE, put up for sale by himself, and other Slaves to be sold " in families, or so much, and such *part* or *parts* thereof, as shall be sufficient," &c. we must perceive that the tenderest ties of nature are still wrenched asunder, and the feelings of the wretched sufferers no more regarded than those of the beasts of the stall.

Clarkson's " Argument" is founded on similar facts, from a former Jamaica Gazette. His reasonings are, for the most part, closely applicable to any Gazette of a subsequent date issuing from the same quarter.

The account of a " Shooting Excursion," also taken from the Planters' own Gazettes, proves that the Negro can be as industrious as the European, when *free*, and when labour is not a badge of Slavery. It proves likewise the *demoralizing influence* of the *system* now existing, as it affects the white population, and that Mr. Canning had good reason to admonish us, " Trust not the Masters of Slaves in what concerns legislation for Slavery."

As soon as it can be procured, the picture of a Slave Ship will be added to the contents of the Work-bags and Albums. It is hoped that it may realize to many, some of the cruel sufferings inflicted on the African race so long, and still so " re-

'Ladies' Society for the Relief of Negro Slaves …', late 1820s. Letterpress with handwritten additions in pen and ink, 26 × 21 cm (PM.1-2022)

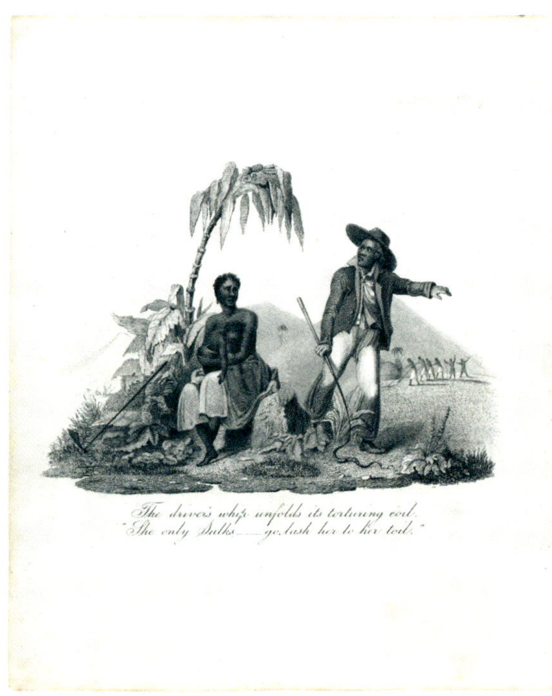

Samuel Lines (1778—1863; designer). **'The driver's whip unfolds its torturing coil. She only sulks — go lash her to her toil'**, about 1828. Etching with engraved lettering, 25.6 × 20.6 cm (PM.6-2022)

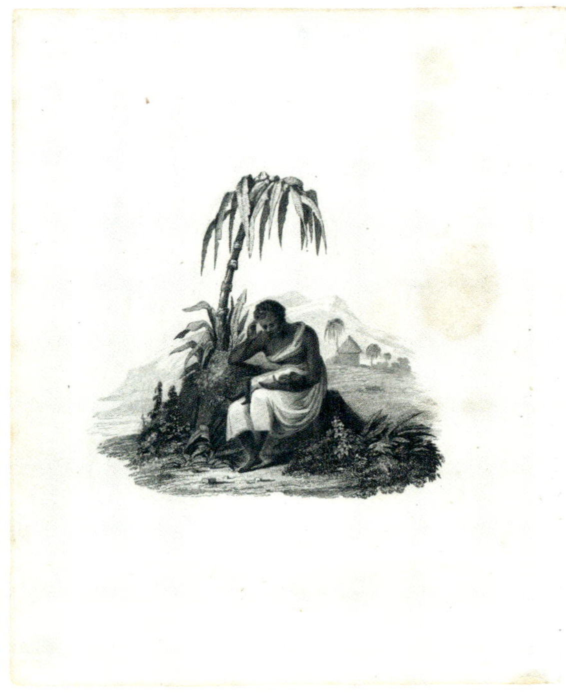

Samuel Lines (1778—1863; designer). **Enslaved African woman and sick child**, about 1828. Etching, 25.8 × 21 cm (PM.7-2022)

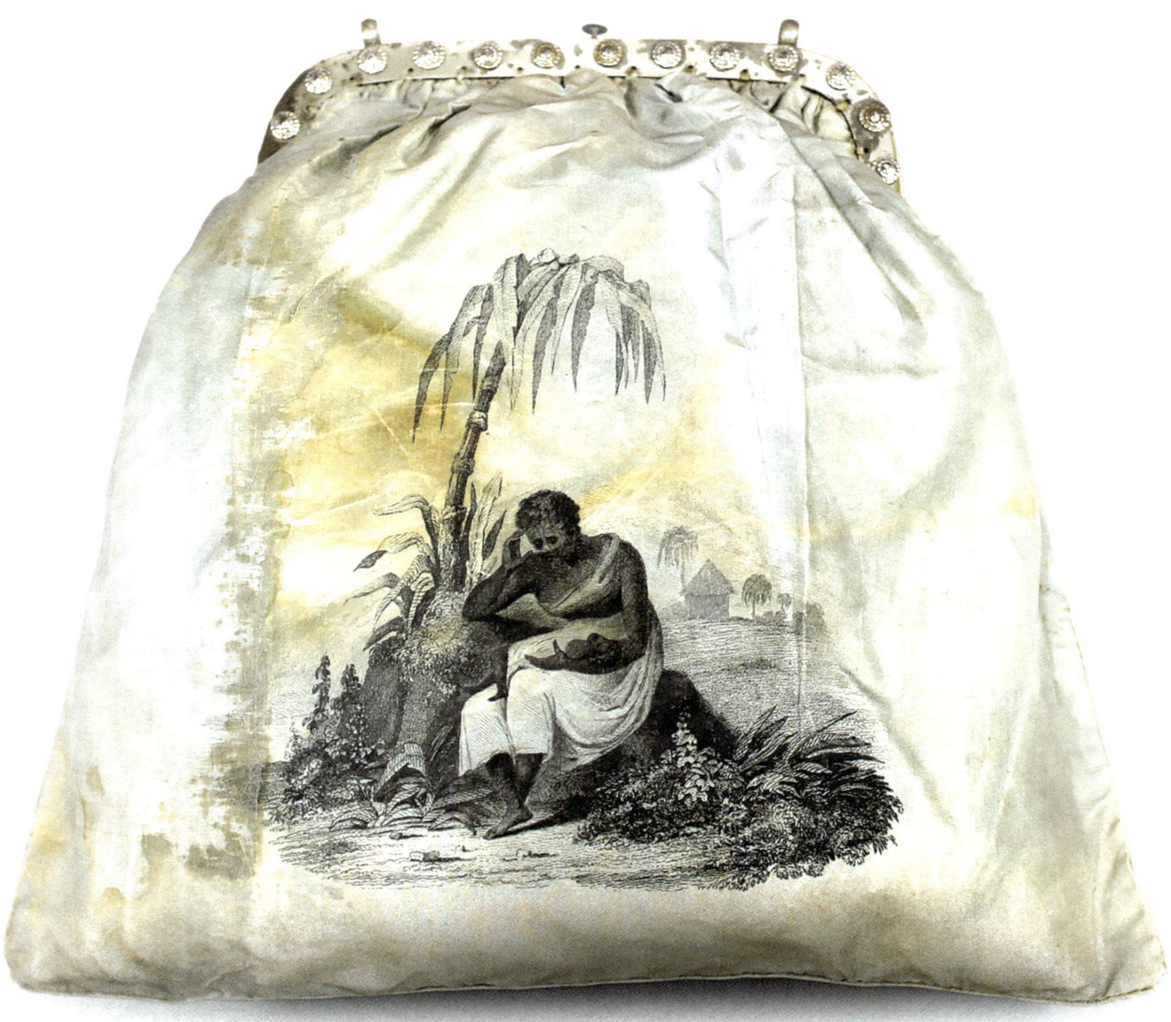

110

Unrecorded maker and
Samuel Lines (1778—1863).
Abolitionist blue silk reticule (small handbag)
with silver clasp, about 1828—33. Silk, silver foil,
metal, glass, ink, 21.5 × 23.3 × 5 cm

Produced by the Ladies' Society for the Relief of Negro Slaves (renamed, around 1830, the Female Society for Birmingham). Front: screen-printed with an untitled image, created by Samuel Lines in 1828, of an enslaved African mother with a sick baby on her lap. Back: screen-printed with lines: 'Negro Woman who sittest pining in captivity and weepest over thy sick child though no one seeth thee. God seeth thee, though no one pitieth thee. God pitieth thee; raise thy voice forlorn and abandoned one; call upon him from amidst thy bonds for assuredly He will hear thee.' Extracted from verse 7 of Hymn VIII, published in Anna Letitia Barbauld, *Hymns in Prose for Children*, London 1781, pp. 60—1. Britain Yearly Meeting of the Religious Society of Friends (Quakers) (LSF MO 421). Given by Elizabeth Fox Howard, 1915. Originally belonged to the donor's grandmother, Rebecca Fox of Tottenham

Many white British women became active abolitionists from the late 1780s (despite often simultaneously benefiting from the profits of slavery) and gave financial support first to SEAST and then to its successor, the Anti-Slavery Society. However, women remained excluded from leadership roles and many became frustrated by the cauticus 'gradualist' approach to abolition. In 1825, a group of female activists in West Bromwich, including Elizabeth Heyrick, founded the Ladies' Society for the Relief of Negro Slaves (renamed the Female Society for Birmingham, around 1830). Its aim was the immediate and total abolition of slavery in the colonies, focusing on enslaved women and children. Similar societies were formed across Britain in the later 1820s. To promote and fundraise, members made objects decorated with abolitionist images and texts, such as this fashionable reticule, which would have contained printed promotional material [109].

Unrecorded maker and
Samuel Lines (1778—1863).
Abolitionist work bag with drawstring,
about 1828—33. Cotton and black ink, 27 × 22 cm
Produced by the Ladies' Society for the Relief of Negro Slaves
(renamed, around 1830, the Female Society for Birmingham). Front:
screen-printed with an untitled image, created by Samuel Lines in
1828, of an enslaved African mother with a sick baby on her lap being
forced to return to work in the sugar-cane field by a threatening
African slave-driver. Back: screen-printed with the same extracted
verse lines as on silk reticule. Fitzwilliam Museum, Cambridge
(T.1-2022). Given by the Friends of the Fitzwilliam Museum, 2022.
Bought at auction (Historical & Collectable online auction,
18 October 2022, lot 76), 2022

From 1828 onwards, the Ladies' Society for the Relief of
Negro Slaves and other women's anti-slavery groups made
promotional bags for sale or gifting to raise awareness of
their cause. This is one of the cheapest kinds: a simple cotton
work bag for storing sewing and darning tools and materials
at home. More expensive bags were made from dyed silk,
to be carried in public to show allegiance [110]. Four or five
narrative images for printing onto the front of these bags
were commissioned from Samuel Lines in 1828, focusing on
African mothers (and, in one case, a father) with their children
[109]. These images aimed to elicit sympathy and compassion
by speaking directly to issues of captive women's suffering,
maternal care and domesticity. Lines's images were also
sold as stand-alone engravings. A handwritten note on an
engraving of the present image, now in the British Museum,
London, records, 'This is Laura who complained … that when
she used to creep from her work to feed her sick baby, the
manager flogged her.'

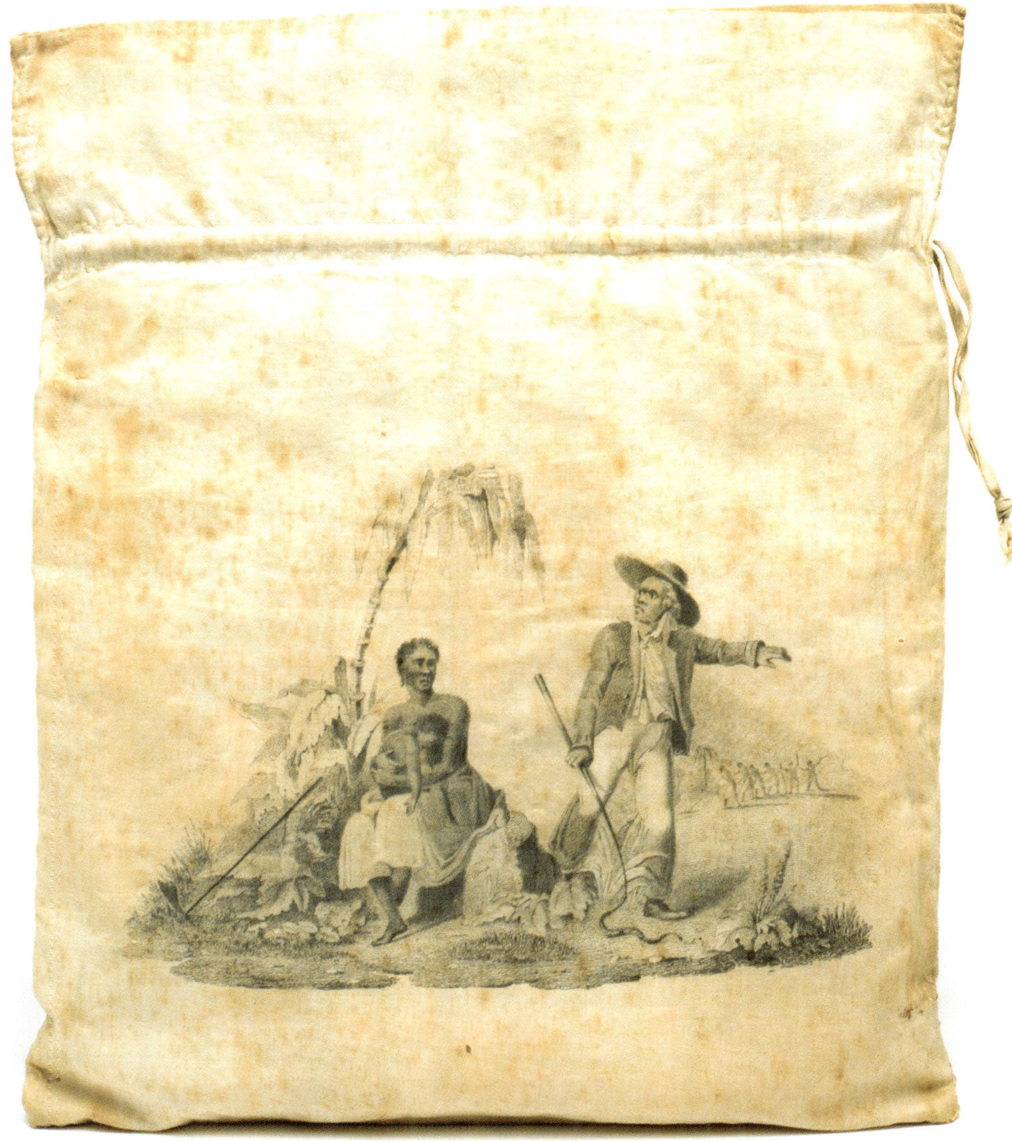

112

Isaac Robert Cruikshank
(1789—1856).
***JOHN BULL taking a Clear
View of the Negro Slavery
Question!!***, London, July 1826.
Print and paint on paper,
26 × 39.4 cm (framed)

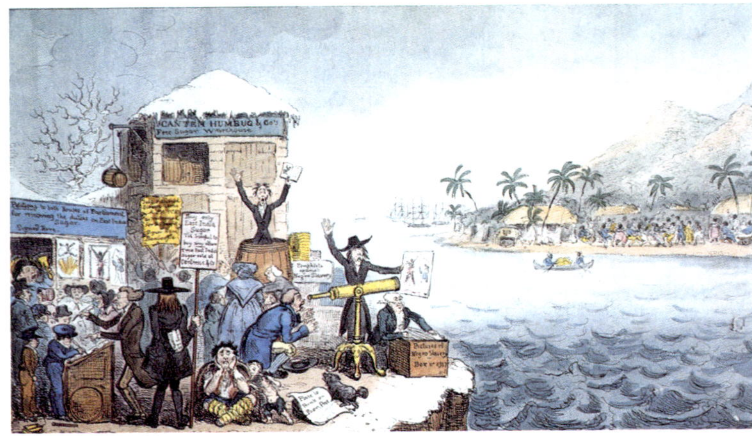

This hand-coloured engraving is an example of the visual propaganda distributed
by pro-slavery campaigners in the 1820s. It sought through visual irony to undermine
abolitionists by making them look like wild-eyed extremists who exaggerated the
awful extent of the living conditions of enslaved people in the Caribbean. Pro-slavery
Cruikshank shows a Quaker abolitionist distorting the view of John Bull (the 'every-
man' embodiment of white England) who is looking through a telescope to 'take a
clear view of the slavery question'. To stop him from seeing a beautiful Caribbean
island shoreline with happy dancing enslaved people, the abolitionist holds up to
the telescope lens an image of an enslaved person being whipped by a white planter.
This engraving also criticises abolitionists for focusing so intently on Black people
living in far-flung lands that they fail to see the plight of the white industrial poor
living in their midst.

113

Unidentified British ceramic factory,
possibly Staffordshire. **Emancipation jug**.
Pearlware, transfer-printed on glaze in black,
13 × 15.5 × 12.2 cm

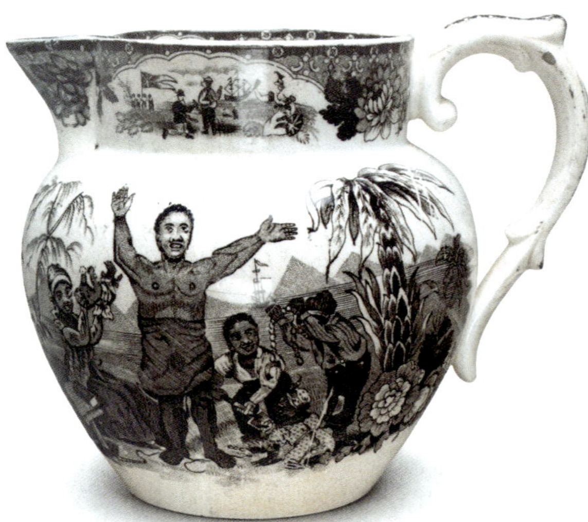

On 28 August 1833, Parliament passed the Slavery Abolition
Act abolishing slavery within all of the British Empire outside
of Asian territories controlled by the East India Company,
and emancipating more than 800,000 enslaved women,
men and children. Although it received Royal Assent on
28 August 1833, it only came into effect eleven months
later, on 1 August 1834. This key legal milestone was widely
celebrated, with British ceramic manufacturers keen to cash
in: this jug is one example of the many different types of
domestic ware produced to commemorate the empire's newly
legislated benevolence. It shows a rejoicing family of formerly
enslaved people holding broken shackles and trampling an
enslaver's whip with an 'Emancipation Notice' tacked onto
a palm tree. The image is a rather crude rendering of David
Lucas's popular print, *To the Friends of Negro Emancipation,
this Print is Inscribed*, itself based on a painting by Alexander
Rippingille. Lucas's print was published in London on 1 August
1838 with the nationalistic under-title caption: 'A glorious and
happy era on the first of August, bursts upon the Western
World; England strikes the manacle from the slave, and bids
the bond go free.' While some emancipation ceramics were
expensive, this jug with its transfer-printed design was
aimed at less well-off buyers.

Freedom at last?

In 1833, the Slavery Abolition Act was finally passed by Parliament, making slavery illegal in almost all of the British Empire. But what did this new freedom actually mean for emancipated African and African-descended people living in the Caribbean?

The Act only immediately freed children under six. Formerly enslaved adults endured a gradual abolition process. They were forced to become 'apprentices' and still lived and worked as indentured servants under conditions similar to those of slavery. Those who were liberated often faced financial hardship and discrimination. Options were limited and choices were few.

In order to get the 1833 Slavery Abolition Act passed, Parliament enacted an astonishing £20-million compensation scheme (about £17 billion today), paying off 4,000 former enslavers for their loss of 'property', making many people wealthy overnight. Not a penny in compensation was given to those they had enslaved. The tide of compensation wealth, funded by taxpayers' money, would have far-reaching effects on society; the government debt was finally 'paid off' in 2015.

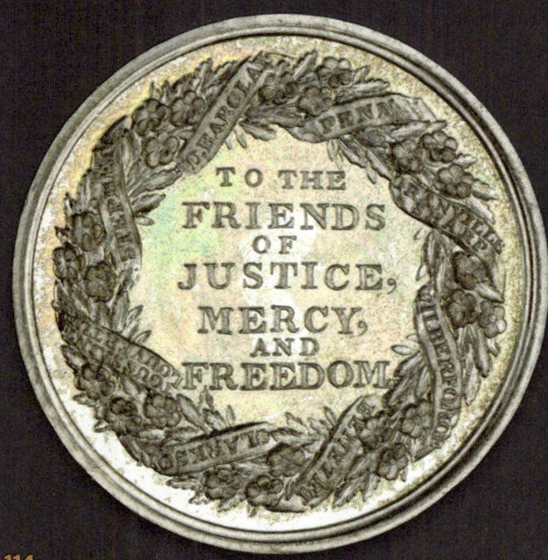
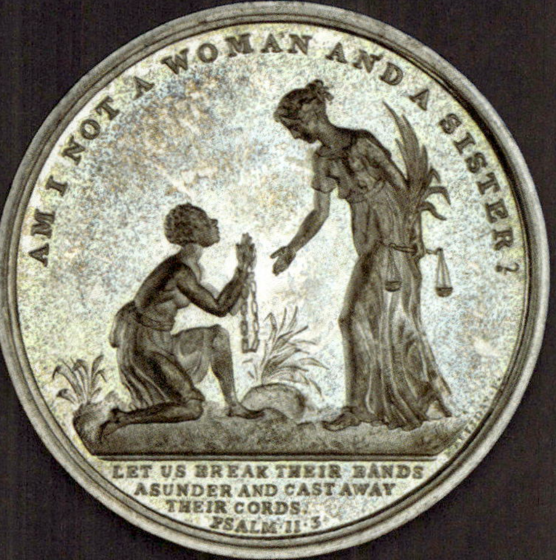

114

Thomas Halliday (*c.* 1780—*c.* 1854; designer).
Medal commemorating the abolition of slavery in the British colonies, 1834. White metal alloy, diam. 4.1 cm

Inscribed (obverse): 'AM I NOT A WOMAN AND A SISTER?' and 'LET US BREAK THEIR BANDS ASUNDER AND CAST AWAY THEIR CORDS. PSALM II.3'; (reverse): 'TO THE FRIENDS OF JUSTICE, MERCY AND FREEDOM' surrounded by a flowering wreath with ribbon inscribed with the following abolitionist names: 'CLARKSON', 'TOUSSAINT LOUVERTURE', 'STEPHEN', 'D. BARCLAY', 'PENN', 'GRANVILLE SHARP', 'WILBERFORCE', 'BENEZET'. Trinity College, Cambridge, on loan since 1937 to the Fitzwilliam Museum, Cambridge (CM.TR.2598-R)

In the 1820s, white feminist abolitionists reimagined the 1787 SEAST logo. Their version featured an enslaved African woman pleading: 'AM I NOT A WOMAN AND A SISTER?' Here a white woman, personifying the abstract qualities of justice, mercy and freedom (symbolised by the scales, outheld hand and victor's palm), is also included shown coming to the aid of the helpless Black woman. By retaining the standard pose of petition, it reinforced stereotypes, enshrined power relationships, and rendered resistance by enslaved women as passive — a comforting fiction perhaps for white abolitionists. It 'whitewashes' the effective resistance enacted by millions of enslaved women across British colonies whose autonomy was often self-achieved.

INTER-COLONIAL APPORTIONMENT.

COLONY	Average Value of a Slave from 1822 to 1830			Number of Slaves by the last Registration in this Country	Relative Value of the Slaves			Proportion of the £20,000,000 to which the Colony is entitled		
	£	s.	d.		£	s.	d.	£	s.	d.
Bermuda	27	4	11¾	4,203	114,527	7	5¼	50,584	7	0½ .43
Bahamas	29	18	9¾	9,705	290,573	15	3¾	128,340	7	5¾ .47
Jamaica	44	15	2¼	311,692	13,951,139	2	3	6,161,927	5	10¾ .38
Honduras..........	120	4	7½	1,920	230,844	0	0	101,958	19	7½ .48
Virgin Islands..... .	31	16	1¾	5,192	165,143	9	2	72,940	8	5¼ .76
Antigua	32	12	10½	29,537	964,198	8	10½	425,866	7	0¼ .13
Montserrat	36	17	10¾	6,355	234,466	8	0½	103,558	18	5¼ .28
Nevis	39	3	11¾	8,722	341,893	6	3½	151,007	2	11¾ .31
St. Christopher's....	36	6	10¼	20,660	750,840	7	1	331,630	10	7¼ .88
Dominica..........	43	8	7½	14,384	624,715	2	0	275,923	12	8½ .38
Barbadoes	47	1	3½	82,807	3,897,276	10	0½	1,721,345	19	7½ .57
Grenada	59	6	0	23,536	1,395,684	16	0	616,444	17	7½ .89
St. Vincents	58	6	8	22,997	1,341,491	13	4	592,508	18	0¼ .50
Tobago	45	12	0½	11,621	529,941	16	2½	234,064	4	11¾ .23
St. Lucia	56	18	7	13,348	759,890	10	4	335,627	15	11¾ .39
Trinidad	105	4	5¼	22,959	2,352,655	18	0¾	1,039,119	1	9½ .11
British Guiana......	114	11	5¾	84,915	9,729,047	13	5½	4,297,117	10	6½ .20
Cape of Good Hope..	73	9	11	38,427	2,824,224	7	9	1,247,401	0	7½ .74
Mauritius..........	69	14	3	68,613	4,783,183	15	3	2,112,632	10	11¾ .68
				780,993	45,281,738	15	10¼	20,000,000	0	0

(Signed) JOHN BONHAM CARTER.

JAMES LEWIS.

JAMES STEPHEN.

SAMUEL DUCKWORTH.

THOMAS AMYOT.

HASTINGS ELWIN.

HENRY FREDERICK STEPHENSON.

Office of Commissioners of Compensation. 'Inter-colonial Apportionment' document, 7 July 1835

To secure abolition, the British government negotiated a deal with the powerful pro-slavery lobby, allocating £20 million of public money to 'compensate' former enslavers for their loss of 'property'. This document, issued by the Office of Commissioners of Compensation in July 1835, outlines the process to would-be claimants and the amount of compensation allotted to each of the nineteen British Caribbean colonies, determined by the number and 'relative value of the slaves'.

Amongst the 4,000 claimants was Thomas Greg of Belfast, who may himself have callously annotated this copy with sums calculating the amount he could claim for 128 enslaved people living on Hillsborough (his plantation in Dominica; for which also see [28]) and eighty-three enslaved people living on Cane Garden (his plantation in St Vincent). Records show that the Hillsborough claim was submitted first, on 7 December 1835, and that, with interest, Greg was paid £2,830 15s. 9d. The Cane Garden claim, submitted on 22 February 1836, resulted in a further payment of £2,250 14s. 10d. — in total, the equivalent of well over £500,000 today. Not a single penny was paid to any of the 211 formerly enslaved people on either plantation.

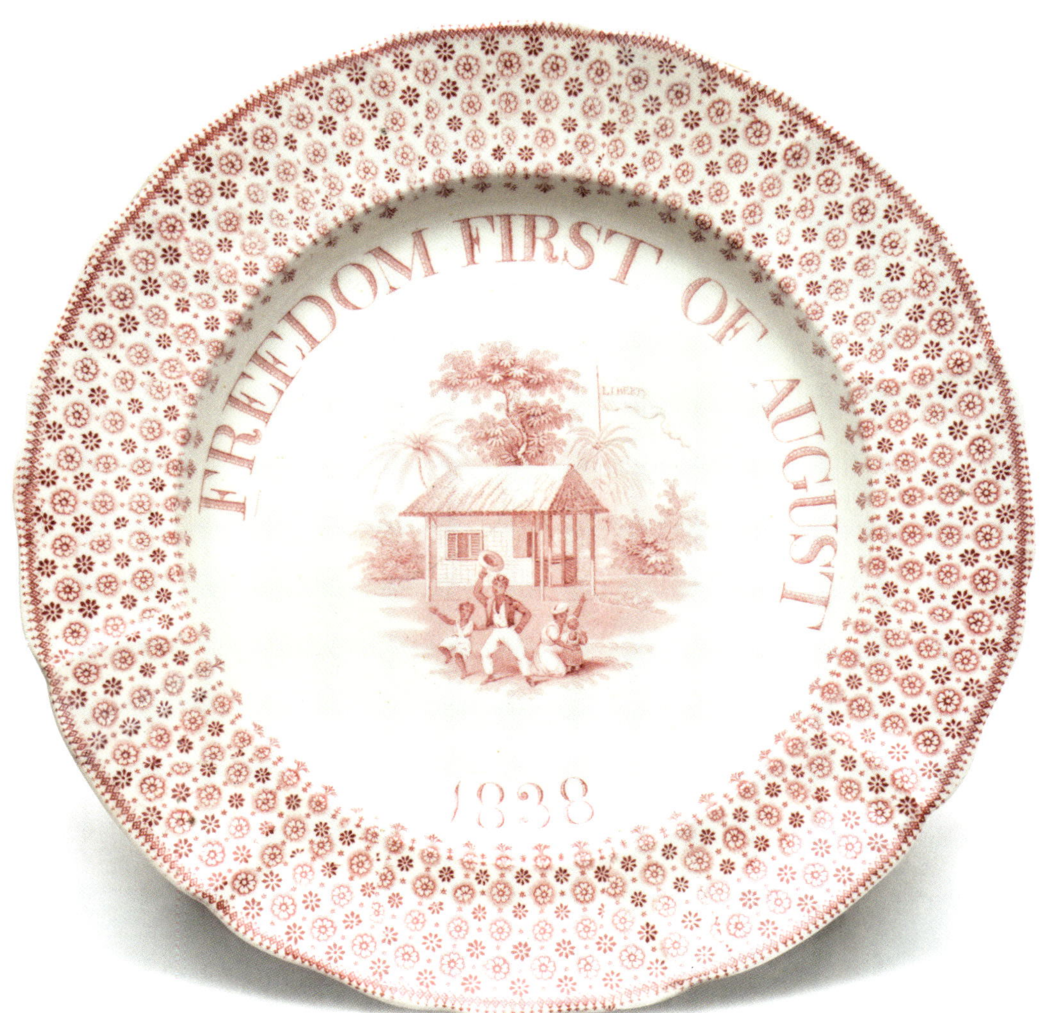

116

Unidentified English factory,
probably Staffordshire.
**Apprenticeship abolition
dinner plate**, *c.*1838. Lead-
glazed pearlware, transfer
printed in underglaze puce
enamel, diam. 27 cm.

Inscribed 'FREEDOM FIRST OF AUGUST
1838', with flag inscribed 'LIBERTY'.
Fitzwilliam Museum, Cambridge (C.7-2021).
Given by the Friends of the Fitzwilliam
Museum, 2021. Purchased at auction
(Woolley & Wallis, Salisbury, *The Robin
Simpson Collection of Commemorative
Ceramics*, 8 September 2021, lot 516)

The compulsory apprenticeship system was promoted across the British Caribbean as an allegedly benevolent scheme to assist the more than 800,000 people liberated from slavery on 1 August 1834 into new 'freed' lives. However, in reality, it only benefited former enslavers. Apprenticeship was therefore seen by many as simply another form of slavery and a perpetuation of exploitation. Lobbying by anti-apprenticeship campaigners in Britain and sustained resistance by enslaved people across the Caribbean finally paid off: following pressure from Parliament, the legislative assemblies in the British West Indies finally abolished apprenticeship, and complete emancipation (freedom without apprenticeship) was rolled out across British Caribbean colonies on 1 August 1838. This enactment allowed Britain to recast itself from oppressor to saviour: the nation responsible for enslaving more Africans in this period than any other now promoted itself as defender and liberator of African and African-descended people in bondage.

Manufacturers were quick to market objects with images and slogans celebrating each of Britain's newly legislated abolition milestones. This plate is one example of the triumphalist ceramics made by British factories to commemorate the formal abolition of the apprenticeship system in 1838. It shows a Black family in the Caribbean rejoicing outside their home, under a flag proclaiming 'liberty'. Also printed in blue, it was intended for moderately wealthy homes. Many freed people dreamed of owning and cultivating their own land but the most viable terrain still lay in the hands of their former enslavers. Consequently, many had no choice but to continue working on the same plantations as they had during enslavement, for low wages, and under oppressive conditions.

Celebrating Black Cambridge history

Black people made major contributions to the performing arts, intellectual culture and sporting life of nineteenth-century Britain, but these are all too often forgotten. Here we commemorate and celebrate the newly researched contributions of a small selection of Black people who spent time in Cambridge.

Virtuoso violinist George Bridgtower and campaigning clergyman Alexander Crummell studied at Cambridge. Champion boxer Bill Richmond tried to establish a boxing academy in the town in 1807, but was prevented from doing so by the University; and Shakespearean actor Ira Aldridge performed here during the 1850s. Several influential African American authors spoke in Cambridge and other nearby towns about the ongoing evils of American slavery, including Zilpha Elaw in the mid-1850s and Moses Roper, who was recorded as living in Cambridge in the 1861 census.

117

Unrecorded maker.
George Augustus Polgreen Bridgtower, 1805.
Watercolour on paper,
10.2 × 8.1 cm

Inscribed (verso): 'G. Bridgtower a present to C Hague 1805'; Department of Music Manuscripts and Books, The Morgan Library & Museum, New York (CMP B851). Bought with the Cary Fund from auction (Christie's, London, 20 December 1972, lot 95) through Haas

Eleven-year-old African—Swabian violin prodigy George Bridgtower fled Revolutionary Paris for London in summer 1789, and was informally adopted by the Prince of Wales (future George IV) and brought up in his household from 1791. Until recently, Bridgtower's connections to Cambridge University were believed to be limited to his music degree of 1811, when he graduated from Trinity Hall, the college of his friend and mentor Charles Hague, the University's Professor of Music. However, new research reveals that Bridgtower was well acquainted with Hague, his wife and their daughters, by the later 1790s, and was invited regularly to make guest appearances in the University's annual Commencement Concerts, which Hague had to organise. Letters in the Vienna archives reveal their deep friendship, as does Bridgtower's gift of this portrait of himself to Hague in 1805.

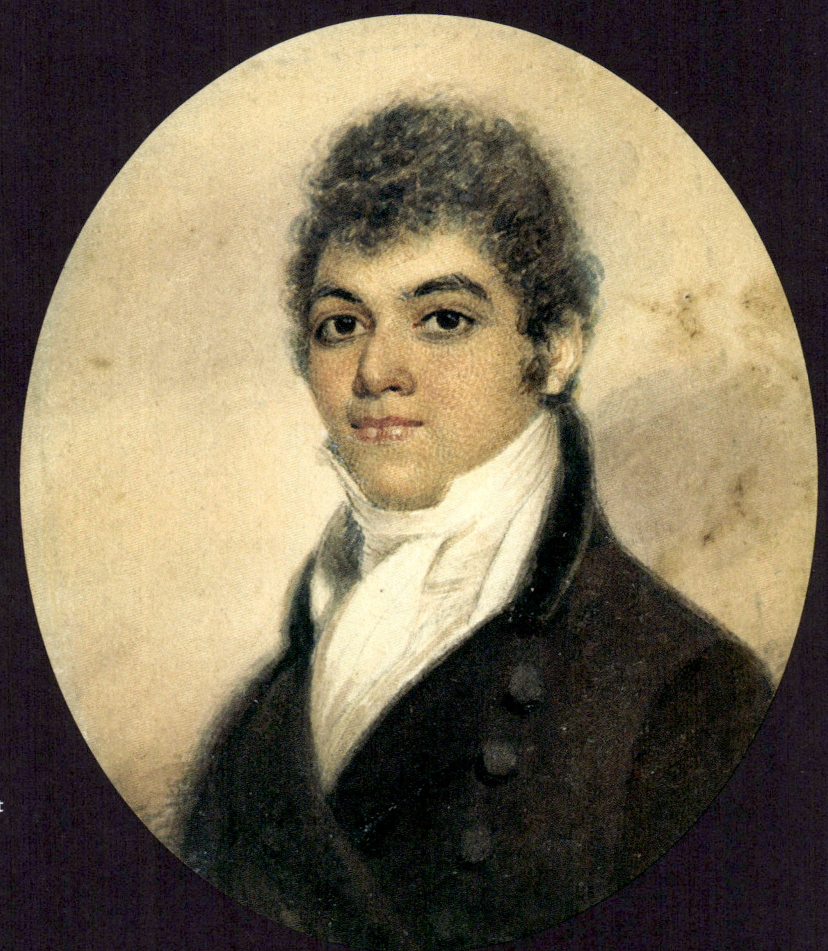

Unrecorded maker. **Tuning fork**
for note A above middle C (with
455.4 Hertz frequency), about
1800. Steel, in walnut-veneered
wooden storage box, h. 12 cm

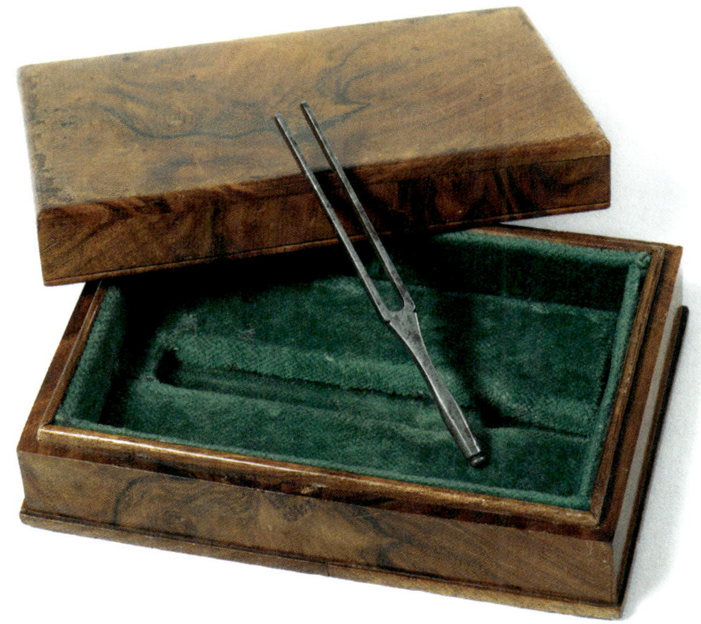

In 1803, George Bridgtower met the famous German pianist and composer Ludwig
van Beethoven in Vienna. Beethoven dedicated his latest violin-piano sonata to
his new friend, and they premiered it together on 24 May 1803. Still unfinished,
Bridgtower improvised an ending, which reputedly delighted Beethoven so much
that he gave his tuning fork to Bridgtower. After a falling out with Bridgtower,
Beethoven re-dedicated his unusually long and difficult composition to French
violinist Rodolphe Kreutzer: Beethoven's 'Kreutzer Sonata' is now world famous
but its original dedication and connections to Bridgtower are long forgotten.

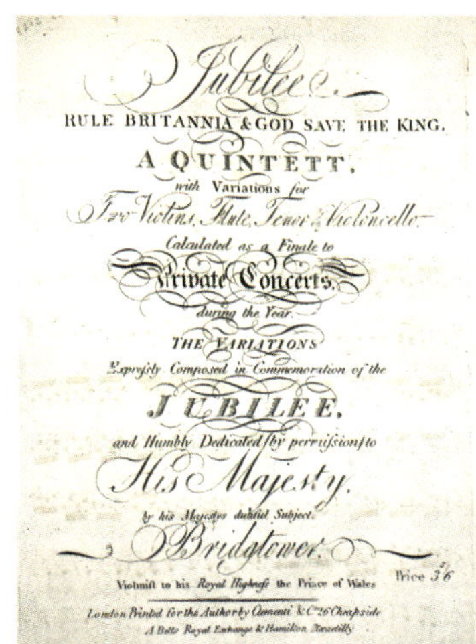

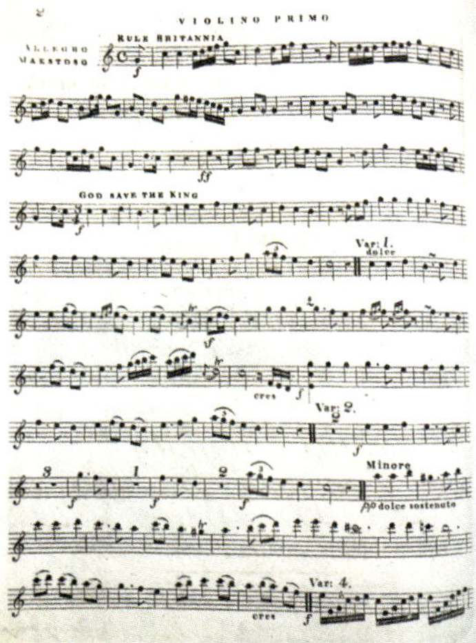

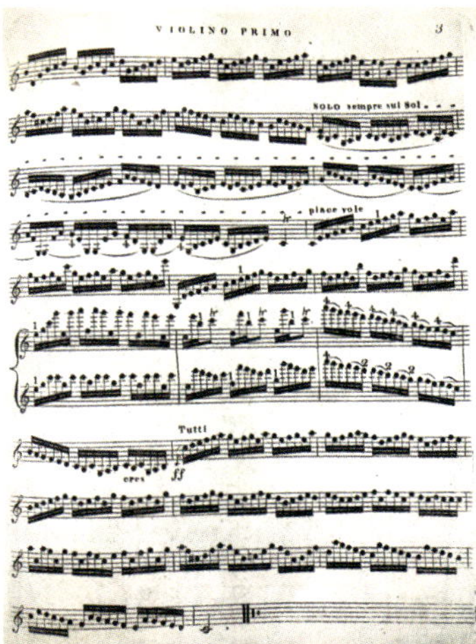

George Bridgtower
(1778–1860).
*Jubilee: Rule Britannia
& God Save the King ...*,
about 1809.

George III's Golden Jubilee was celebrated on 25 October 1809, prior to its actual
fiftieth anniversary in 1810, and Bridgtower 'expressly composed' his Jubilee quintet
'as a finale to private concerts during the year'. Bridgtower, who had been raised in
the Prince of Wales's household and held the title Violinist to the Prince of Wales,
was understandably keen to show his loyalty. He stated that this composition 'was
humbly dedicated (by permission) to His Majesty by His Majesty's dutiful subject'.
Brigtower also wrote numerous scores for piano and voice, piano exercises for
students, compositions for small string groups and larger orchestral works but
only a handful are known today.

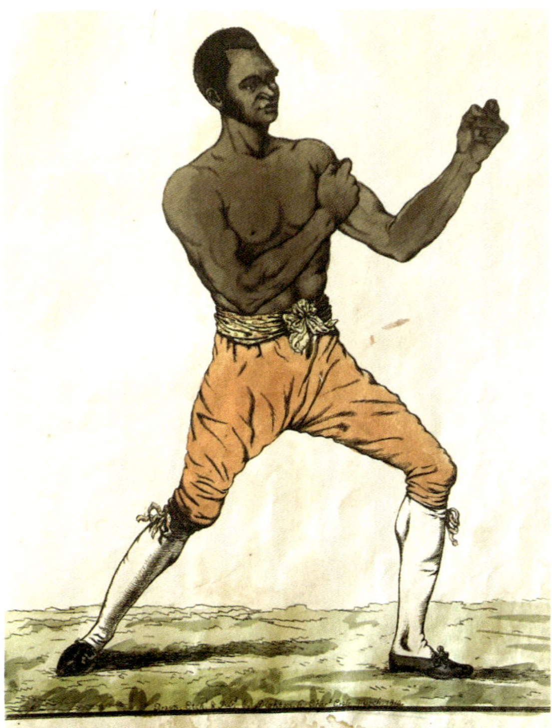

120

Robert Dighton (*c*.1752—1814).
A Striking View of Richmond, March 1810.
Hand-coloured line engraving, 36.5 × 23 cm

The Card-Reynolds Collection, London. Bought from Grosvenor Prints, London, 2019

Born into slavery in Staten Island, New York, African American Bill Richmond was taken to London as a servant of Lord Percy, 3rd Duke of Northumberland, and began boxing in his forties. He quickly became a celebrity champion-fighter, as proven by Robert Dighton's popular print, whose punning title contains wordplays on 'striking' and 'Richmond'. Richmond's earnings from a record-breaking seventeen wins in nineteen fights enabled him in 1810 to buy a tavern near Leicester Square, which became a hub for London's Black community. A member of the Pugilistic Society, Richmond mixed with the highest levels of British society, including the future George IV (Bridgtower's protector), who invited him to be one of eighteen celebrity-status ushers at his coronation in 1821.

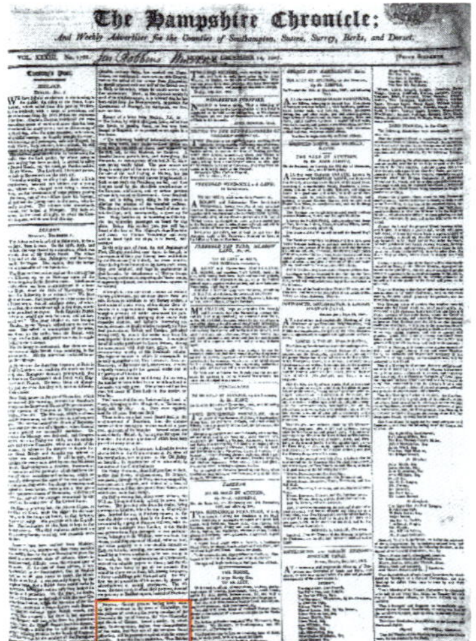

121

The Hampshire Chronicle,
vol. XXXIII, no. 1762,
14 December 1807, p. 1

British Library, London, via the British Newspaper Archive

BOXING.—Several persons having lately taken up their residence in the town of Cambridge, for the purpose of teaching the young members of the University the art of boxing, the Vice Chancellor and Heads of Houses, issued a notice, in which they, in strong terms, declare their disapprobation of the same, and that any of the members found offending, will be proceeded against with the utmost severity. Since the above resolution, Tom Belcher and Richmond the Black, have left the place.

A long-forgotten notice published in both the *Hampshire Chronicle* and the London *Morning Herald* on 14 December 1807 reveals how Bill Richmond and his white fellow-boxer Tom Belcher spent time in Cambridge in Michaelmas term 1807 trying to establish a boxing academy. However, the Vice-Chancellor and college masters banned it from being set up, because they were worried it would distract University students from their studies. Richmond and Belcher returned to London, where Richmond eventually saw his dream fulfilled when he opened a gymnasium in the 1820s. This was frequented by many white noblemen, including Cambridge graduate, poet and boxing enthusiast Lord Byron.

Moses Roper (1815—1891).
Narrative of the Adventures and Escape of Moses Roper ...,
2nd edn, Berwick-upon-Tweed
1848

University of North Carolina, UNC-Chapel Hill Library (CCB R784n). [Version in exhibition: 2nd edn copy (London, 1838): Cambridge University Library (X.29.44.)]

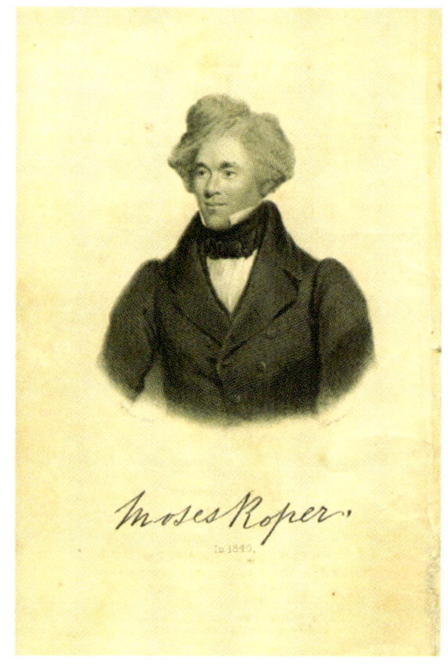

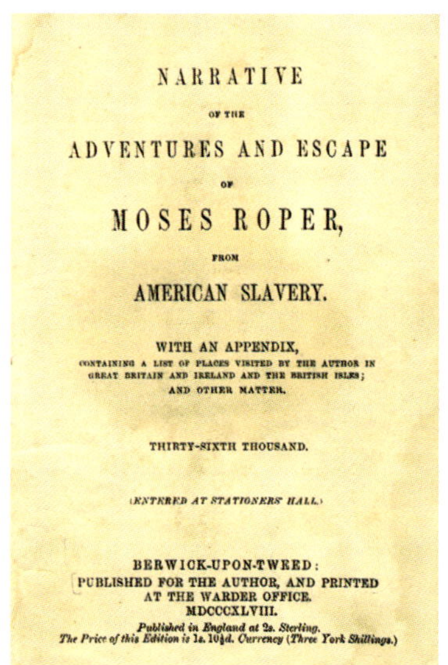

Born into enslavement in North Carolina, Moses Roper escaped after indescribable sufferings and moved to England in 1835. Having published his autobiography in 1838, he tirelessly promoted it, and the abolition of slavery in America, in churches across Britain for over two decades. In 1839, Roper lectured in Wisbech, and the following year in Cambridge and St Ives. He also spoke in Clavering, Essex, and must have met Equiano's surviving daughter, Johanna Vassa, whose husband was a Congregationalist minister there. By 1848, over 38,000 copies of his autobiography had been sold. In the 1861 census, Roper was recorded as 'Lecturer on Slavery', lodging in Cambridge at the junction of Hills Road and Regent Street. Local papers record him lecturing in early 1861 in Ashley, Bottisham, Cheveley, Horningsea and Soham.

Zilpha Elaw (*c.* 1790—1873).
Memoirs of the Life, Religious Experience ...,
London 1846

British Library, London (4986.de.38)

African American preacher Zilpha Elaw is little known today but in the 1850s and 1860s, she created a huge stir in British Methodist circles by her radical presence on the non-conformist preaching circuit. This elderly Black female evangelical refused to be silenced. She delivered hundreds of sermons and talks in churches across Britain, simultaneously promoting her 1846 spiritual autobiography. Local newspaper reviews reveal the long-forgotten fact that Elaw, now in her late sixties, visited Cambridgeshire in 1856, preaching in Elm, Wisbech, Cambridge and Chatteris. She returned in 1857 to preach in Ely.

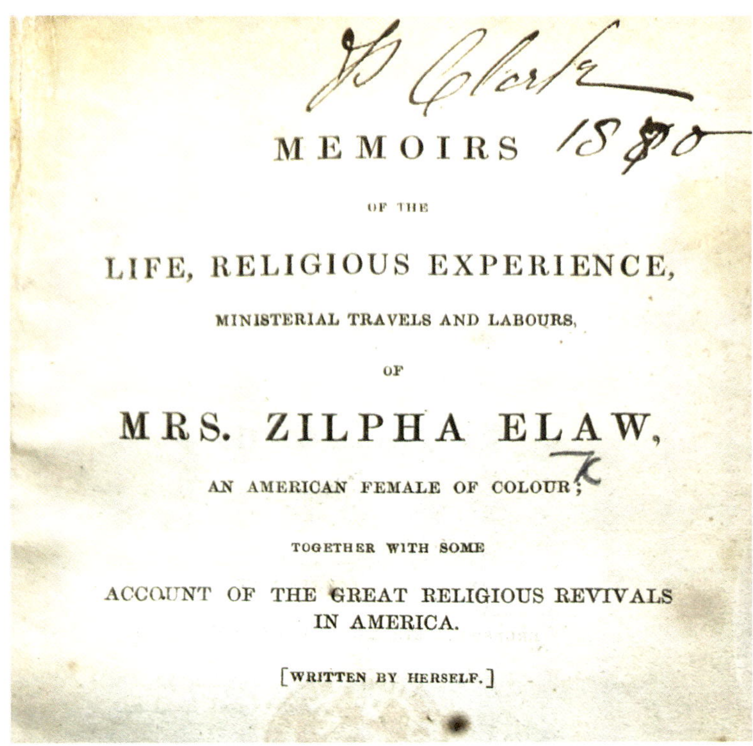

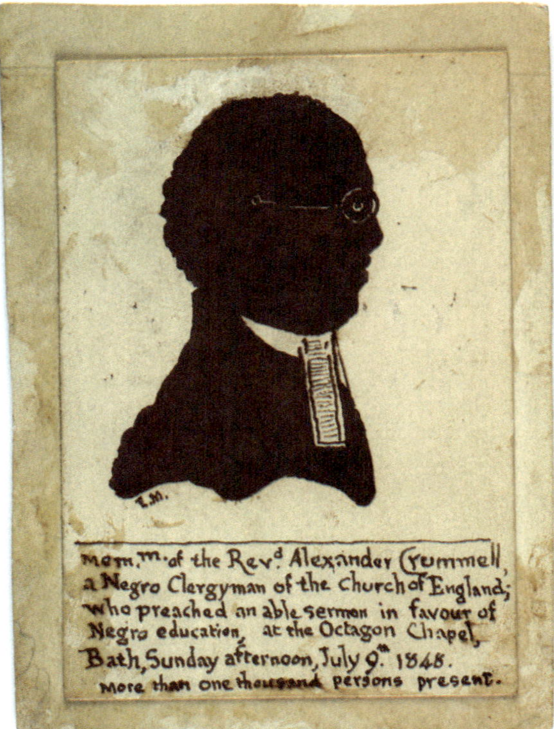

124

Unidentified amateur artist with initials 'F.M.'.
***Alexander Crummell**, Bath, 9 July 1848.*
Black ink on card, 10.3 × 7.5 cm

Inscribed: 'Mem.m of the Rev.d Alexander Crummell, a Negro
Clergyman of the Church of England; who preached an able sermon
in favour of Negro education, at the Octagon Chapel, Bath, Sunday
afternoon, July 9th, 1848. More than one thousand persons present.'
Private collection of Prof. Sarah Meer, Selwyn College, Cambridge.
Given to her by Alison Lloyd, 2013; inherited from Lloyd's father,
Alan Sabourin, 1992, who found it in a bag of discarded paperwork
outside an abandoned Somerset vicarage, about 1987

On 15 April 1848, New York born Alexander Crummell
delivered a well-attended speech at Cambridge Town Hall
promoting the education of Black Americans. He then went
to Bath for tutoring in Greek and Latin to prepare him for
university study in Cambridge. It was in Bath, on 9 July 1848,
when Crummell delivered his Octagon Chapel lecture to over
1,000 people, that this tiny portrait was made. It gives a
unique insight into his appearance just before he started
his degree at Queens' College, Cambridge, in 1849.

125

Alexander Crummell (1819–1898).
***Hope for Africa. A Sermon ...**, London 1853*

Cambridge University Library (6.21.24. UkCU)

Crummell deliberately chose to study at Cambridge University
because of its renown as an abolitionist centre of learning
in the 1780s, and his unwavering admiration for Thomas
Clarkson, whom he had eulogised in a lecture delivered in
New York in 1846. After four years of intense study, Crummell
graduated on 16 February 1853, a fact he was keen to promote
in subsequent publications, such as this sermon on increasing
access to education for the people of the African diaspora,
on whose front cover he records himself as 'Rev. Alexander
Crummell, B.A. Cantab.'. He also records himself as author
of Clarkson's eulogy.

126

James Northcote (1746–1831).
Ira Aldridge as Othello, the Moor of Venice,
1826. Oil on canvas, 76.2 × 63.5 cm

On 11 May 1825, seventeen-year-old New Yorker Ira Aldridge
became the first Black actor to play Shakespeare's 'Othello,
the Moor of Venice' on an English stage, a role previously
played by white actors in 'blackface' make-up. Aldridge quickly
established himself as one of the greatest Shakespearean
actors of his day and was in demand in theatres across Britain
and Europe. In 1827, Aldridge debuted in Manchester, and
afterwards the newly formed Royal Manchester Institution
for the Promotion of Literature, Science and the Arts (which
became Manchester Art Gallery) purchased this portrait of
him, as its first acquisition. Established to counter accusations
that Manchester was an industrial city devoid of culture, the
Institution's inaugural purchase was designed not only to show
aesthetic sensibilities but also to demonstrate its anti-Black-
racist credentials and its support of abolitionism. This brilliant
and sensitive portrait shows Aldridge mid-performance, his
sideways glance suggesting the flawed hero's jealousy.

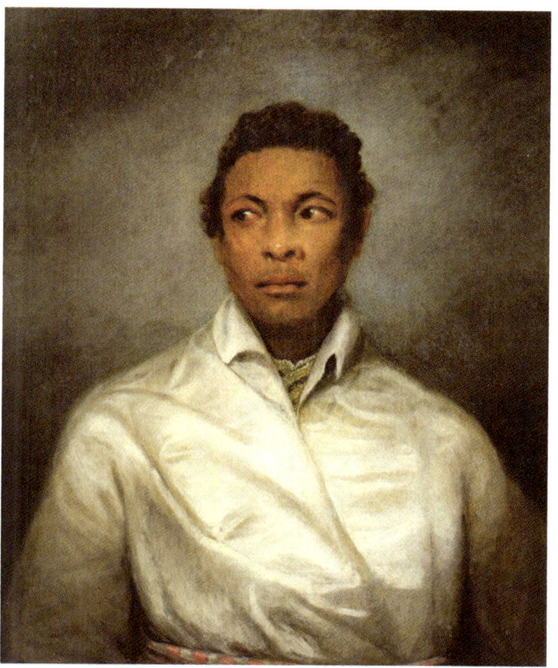

127

Playbills, Theatre Royal, Cambridge, recording some
of Ira Aldridge's performances,
September 1850 and
September 1859.

Cambridgeshire Collection, Cambridge
Central Library (no accession numbers
allocated)

These playbills celebrate long-
forgotten evening performances
starring Ira Aldridge on two separate
tours to the Theatre Royal, Barnwell,
Cambridge. Aldridge's first tour (9–21
September 1850) saw him perform
a staggering twelve different tragic
and comic roles, including Othello,
Shylock and Mungo in *The Padlock*
and Man Friday in *Robinson Crusoe*.
Brought back by popular demand,
Aldridge performed nine roles during
his shorter second tour (19–24
September 1859), which included the
title roles in *Macbeth* and *King Lear*.
Billed as 'The African Roscius', after
the ancient Roman manumitted-slave-
actor Quintus Roscius Gallus, Aldridge
used his performances to contradict
prevailing racist stereotypes. Aldridge
died on tour in Poland, where he was
honoured with a celebrated funeral
and marked grave.

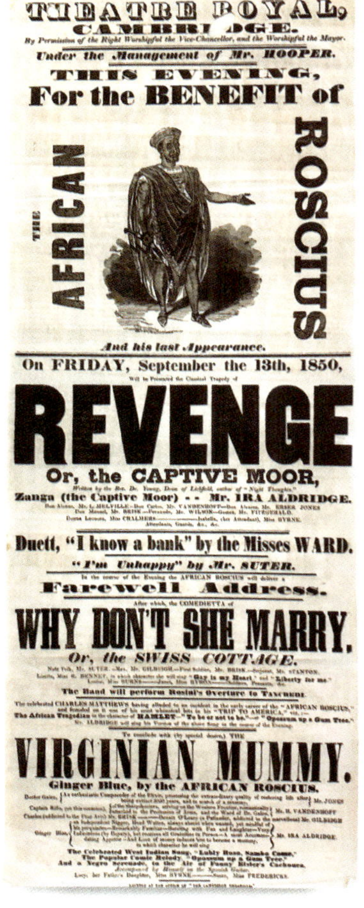

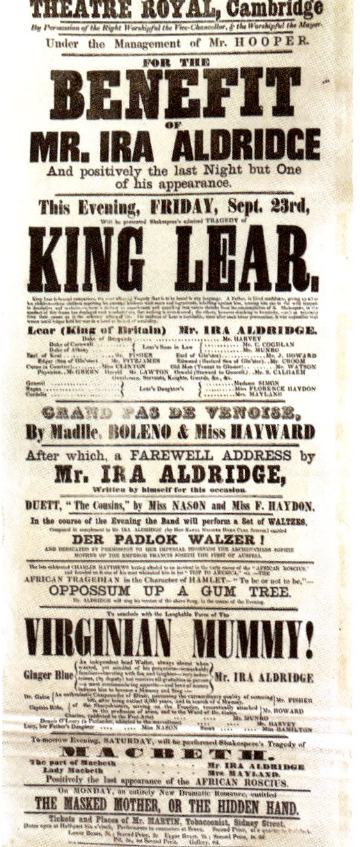

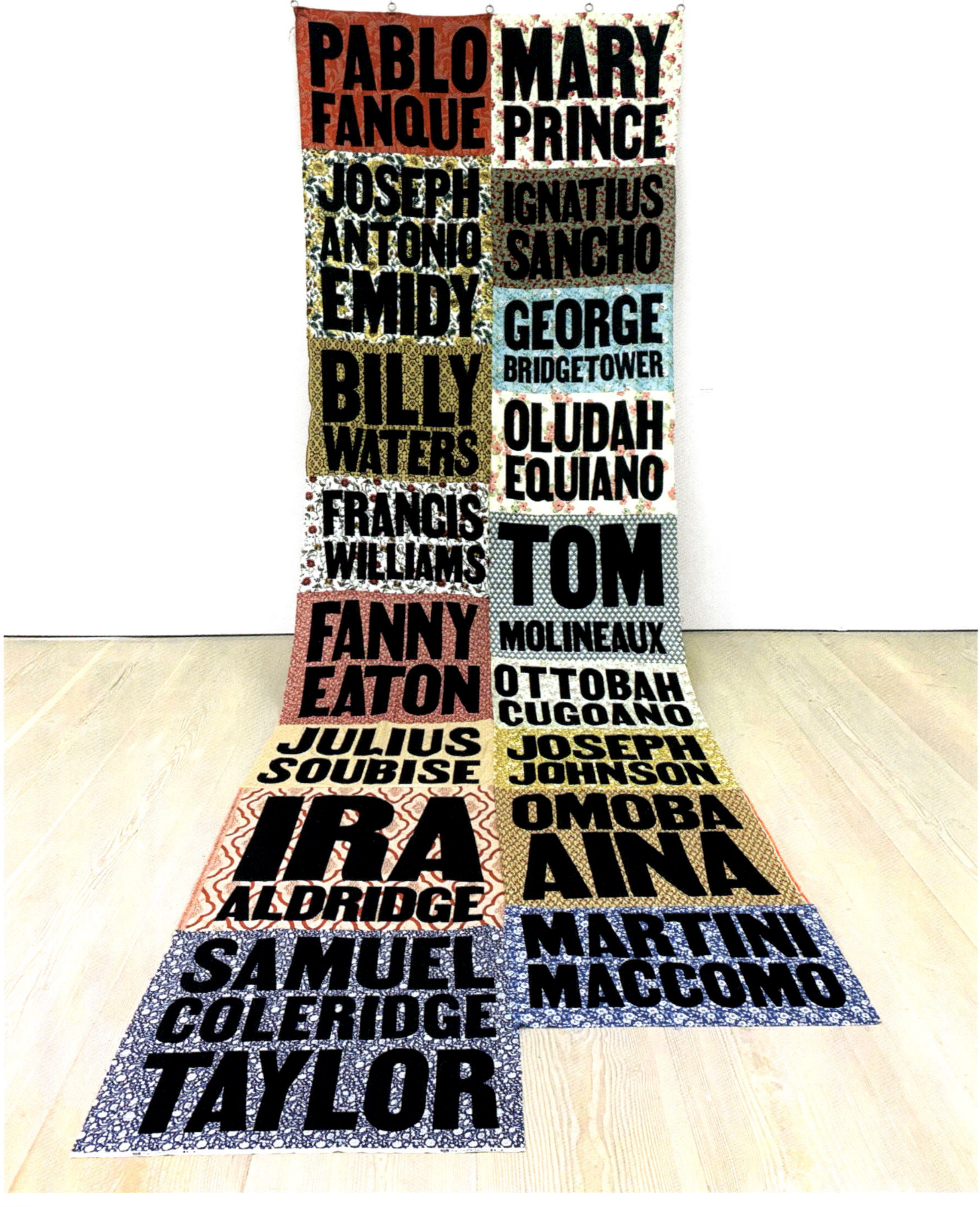

Jahnavi Inniss (born 1998). *Representation: Black British History Quilt*,
2020 and extended with additional names, 2024.
Different fabrics including cotton, polyester and sateen, 11.78 × 1.74 m

Collection of the Artist © Jahnavi Inniss

Re-presentation: Black British History Quilt

Jahnavi Inniss

More than half of Britons know so little about Black British history that they cannot name a single historical figure.[1]

Reflecting on *Can Graphic Design Save Your Life?*, an exhibition at the Wellcome Collection in 2017, I was reminded of the power of graphic design in its ability to 'persuade, inform and empower' whilst simultaneously 'shaping our environment, our health and our sense of self'.[2] This influence was echoed in my discovery of the racist imagery produced during the Jim Crow era in the southern states of the US [129]. I observed how these distorted representations fixed harmful stereotypes upon Black people and have helped to maintain systems of 'racial superiority' and marginalisation.[3] I came to understand that although visible representations can create prejudices, the lack of visible representation can have an equal, if not, worse effect. Using cultural theorist Stuart Hall's Representation Theory as a contextual framework, I began exploring different design methods to create visibility for Black British history.

Whilst volunteering at the Black Cultural Archives in Brixton in 2019, I was often overwhelmed by the extent of largely untold histories that I discovered whilst engaging with the archival material.[4] Reflecting on the various access restrictions and relative obscurity of archives, I was motivated to create a more accessible means of sharing these stories with a wider audience. I noticed frequent, silent gaps in the chronology of the Black experience and existence in Britain and came across *Black Victorians, Black Victoriana*, a book which aims to 'dispel [the silent gaps] by carefully combining the records to locate Black Victorians and put them back into the national picture.'[5] This inspired me to investigate and surface the lives of Black people in Britain between the seventeenth and nineteenth centuries. In doing so, I aimed to dismantle the common misconception that Black people only arrived in Britain during the late 1940s wave of immigration known as the 'Windrush Period', and to high-light the historic presence of Black people in Britain. I began compiling a list of names of the people I found and explored the best ways to present them.

After experimenting with a variety of design methods and artistic mediums, I was drawn into the vibrant and dynamic world of quilting. I learned how quilting became a means of creative expression, communication, survival and liberation for enslaved African women in the deep American South.[6] Quilting became a catalyst in the formation of communities such as Gee's Bend and the Freedom Quilting Bee Cooperative in Alabama, and it has become a long-standing tradition amongst African American women in the South [131]. I evaluated modern approaches to quilt-ing through artists and organisations such as Faith Ringgold, Bisa Butler and the Social Justice Sewing Academy.[7] I was encouraged by their bold adaptation of quilting and the power of quilts, in their

1. Dalya Alberge, 'Half of Britons can't Name a Black British Historical Figure, Survey Finds', *The Guardian,* 26 October 2023, https://www.theguardian.com/uk-news/2023/oct/26/half-of-britons-cant-name-a-black-british-historical-figure-survey-finds (accessed 23 July 2024).
2. *Can Graphic Design Save Your Life?*, Wellcome Collection, 7 September 2017 – 14 January 2018, https://wellcomecollection.org/exhibitions/WZwh4ioAAJ3usf86 (accessed 23 July 2024).
3. bell hooks, *Black Looks: Race and Representation*, New York 1992, p. 2. For an online version, see: https://aboutabicycle.wordpress.com/wp-content/uploads/2012/05/bell-hooks-black-locks-race-and-representation.pdf (accessed 23 July 2024).
4. *Black Cultural Archives*, https://blackculturalarchives.org/ (accessed 23 July 2024).
5. Gretchen Holbrook Gerzina, *Black Victorians, Black Victoriana*, New Jersey 2003, p. 2.
6. Floris Barnett Cash, 'Kinship and Quilting: An Examination of an African-American Tradition', *The Journal of Negro History*, 80, no. 1 (Winter 1995), pp. 30–41.
7. For further information about the Social Justice Sewing Academy, see: https://www.sjsacademy.org/ (accessed 23 July 2024).

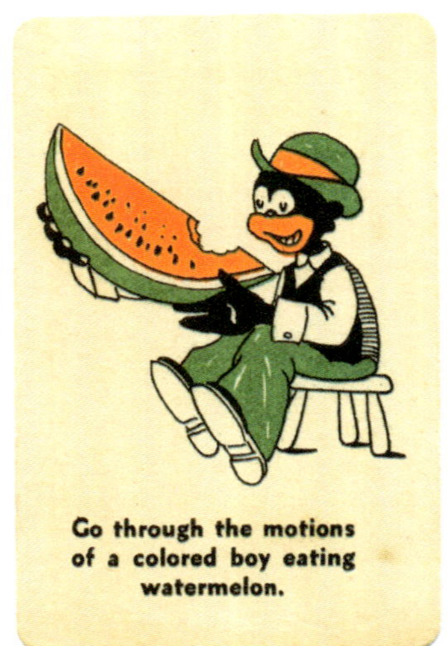

129

Whitman Publishing Company. 'Go through the motions of a colored boy eating watermelon' card, 1935. One of '72 Pictured Party Stunts' from a 1930s party game with racial and ethnic stereotyping

Austin History Center, Austin Public Library (AR-A-001-box239-item1) [not in exhibition]

ability to tell stories and create visibility and empowerment for African Americans in their fight for justice and equality [132].

Whilst considering the different design elements of my quilt [128], I was able to embed meaning and further reiterate themes of empowerment through my use of typography and fabric. I discovered *Martin,* a typeface designed by Vocal Type and inspired by the Memphis Sanitation Strike of 1968. Members of the strike carried visually striking posters declaring 'I AM A MAN' — a slogan that 'challenged centuries of dehumanisation' [130].[8] This slogan originates from the abolitionist movement in which Ignatius Sancho and Olaudah Equiano (both featured on my quilt) were directly involved.[9]

As the time period was a crucial message within my quilt, I specifically chose fabric with patterns that were relevant to each period. For example, Pablo Fanque was a successful circus proprietor in the Victorian era, so I used a fabric with a Victorian damask pattern for his segment. The decision not to hem the fabric at the end of my quilt was to emphasise the fact that there are still gaps in this history, and so there are undoubtedly still many more people to be discovered and added. As an attempt to facilitate this discovery, I adopted an interactive approach whereby viewers can learn about the people featured on the quilt and submit the names of anyone relevant that they feel

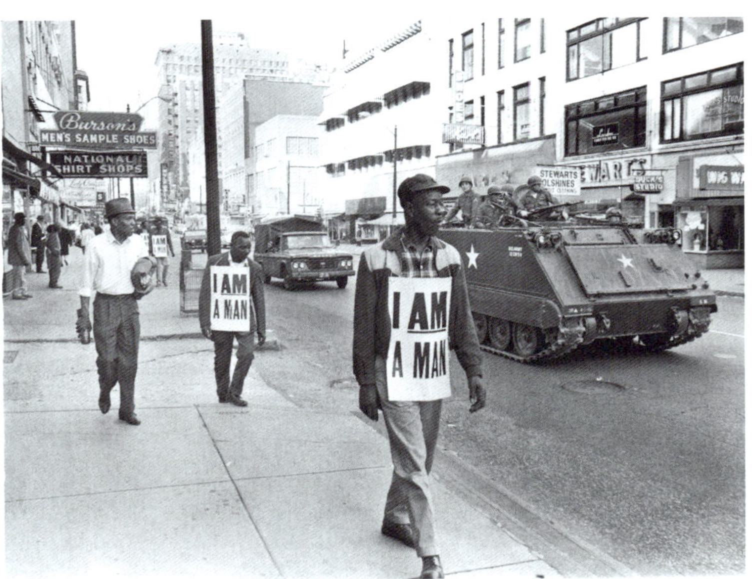

130

Ken Ross. Marchers with 'I AM A MAN' sign, Memphis, 1968. Taken during Memphis Sanitation Workers' Strike, Main Street, Memphis, March 1968.

Memphis Press-Scimitar newspaper morgue, Special Collections Department, University of Memphis Libraries (sc.0475.90012_01.014) [not in exhibition]

8. Lisa Wade, '"I Am a Man": Black Men's Claims to Humanity', *The Society Pages*, 15 July 2023, https://thesocietypages. org/socimages/2013/07/15/i-am-a-man-fighting-dehumanization-in-the-civil-rights-era/ (accessed 23 July 24).
9. 'The Wedgwood Anti-Slavery Medallion', *V&A*, https://www.vam.ac.uk/articles/the-wedgwood-anti-slavery-medallion (accessed 23 July 2024).

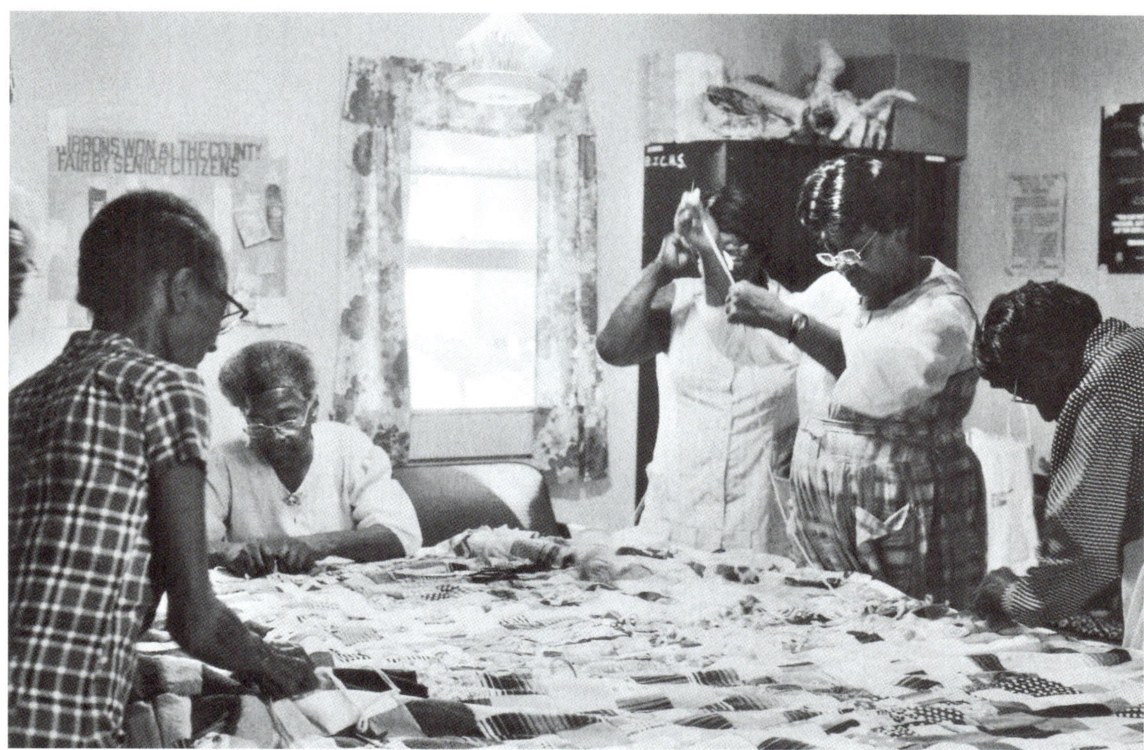

131
Doris Derby (1939—2022).
**Quilting Cooperative,
Beaufort, South Carolina**,
1972. Gelatin silver print.
High Museum of Art, Atlanta, Gift of
David Knaus (2023.324) [not in exhibition]

should be added via my website.[10] Following on from discussions with the *Rise Up: Resistance, Revolution, Abolition* exhibition curators at the Fitzwilliam Museum about my quilt's inclusion in the show, I've been able to add three additional names, giving further recognition of the Black presence in Britain during this period.

Through documenting Black lives and celebrating our collective history, I hope to encourage a sense of pride, empowerment and self-worth in Black Brits. I believe that we are all living histories and through self-documentation, we have the power to tell our own stories and redefine our identities. History can be an emancipatory tool for liberation, and we must document and preserve our stories for ourselves and future generations.

10 'Projects'. www.jahnavi-inniss.com
(accessed 3 September 2024).

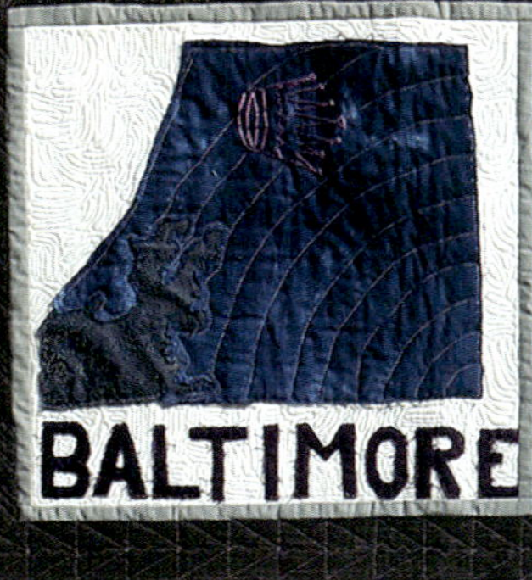
BALTIMORE

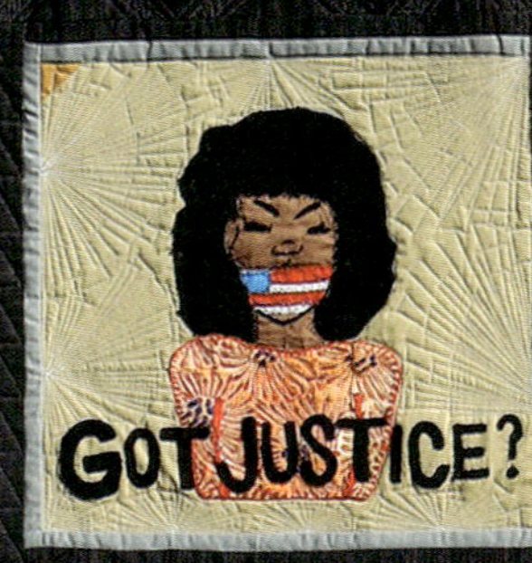
GOT JUSTICE?

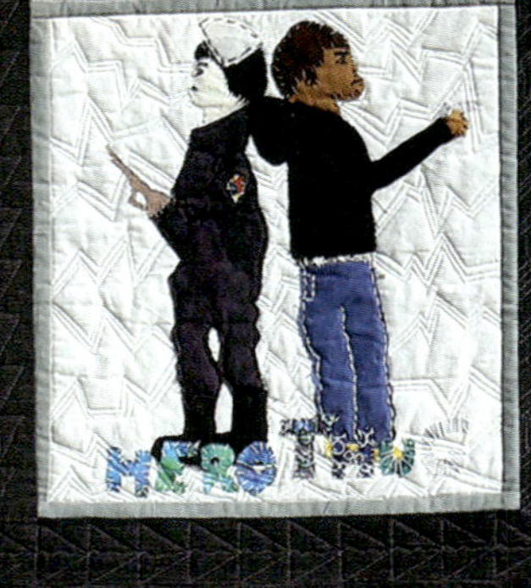
HERO THUG

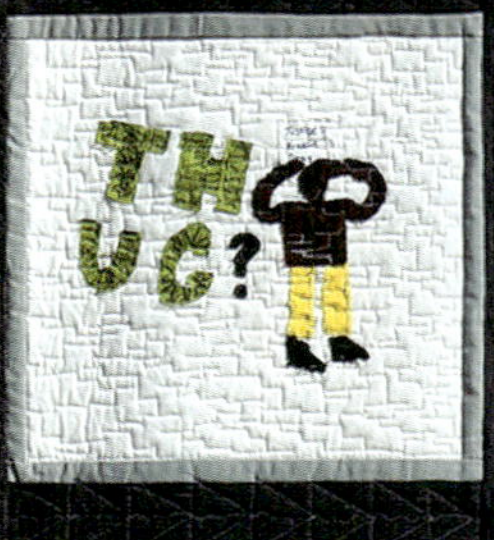
THUG?

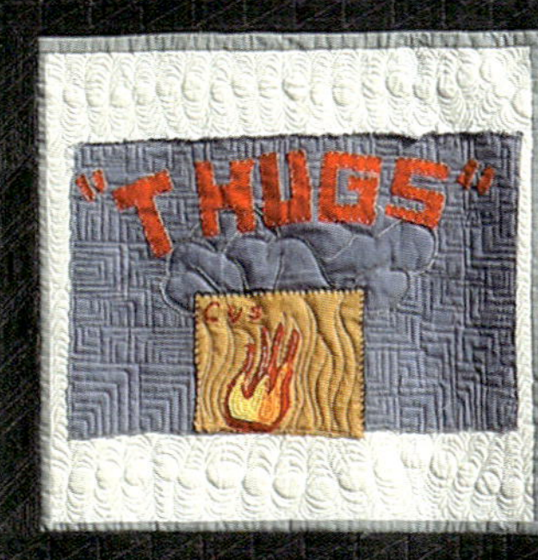
"THUGS"

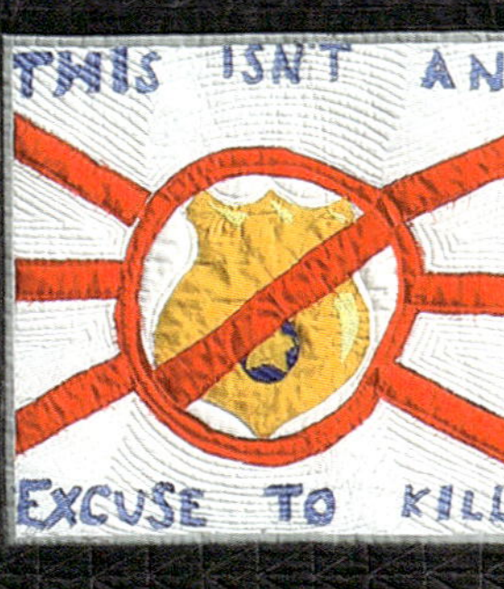
THIS ISN'T AN
EXCUSE TO KILL

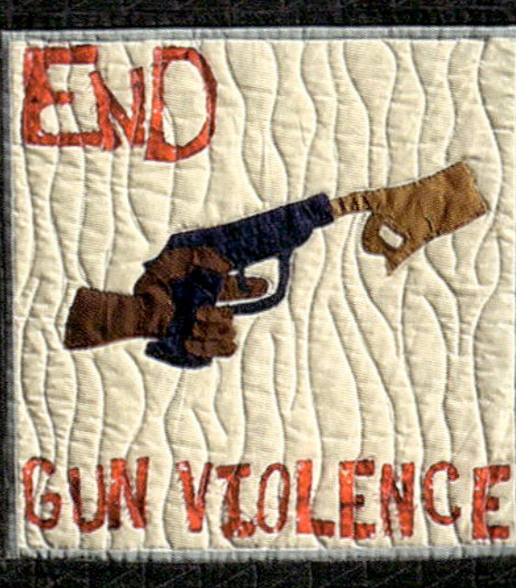
END
GUN VIOLENCE

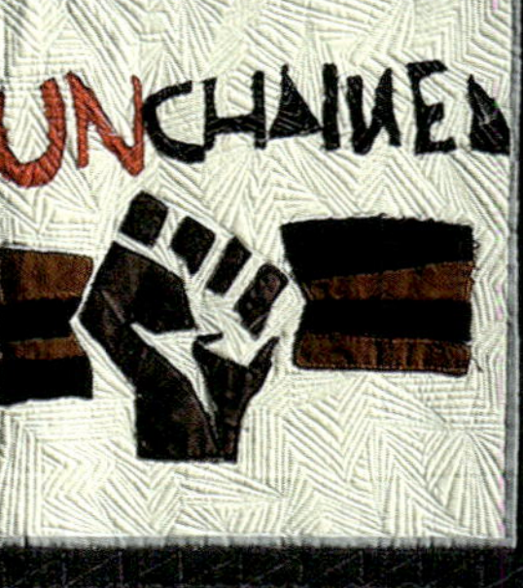
UNCHAINED

The System was BUILT this way

BLACK
LIVES
MATTER

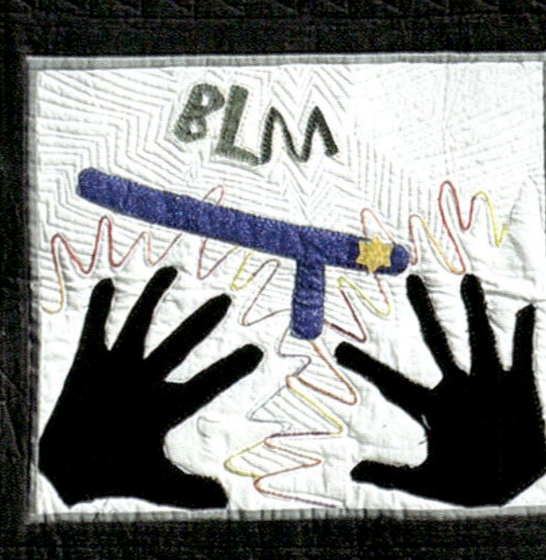
BLM

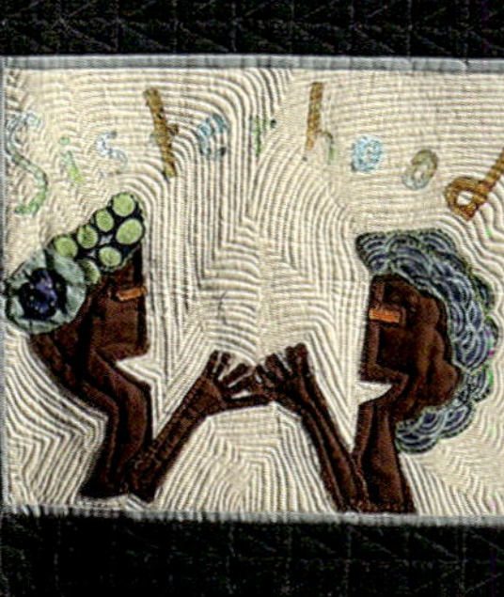

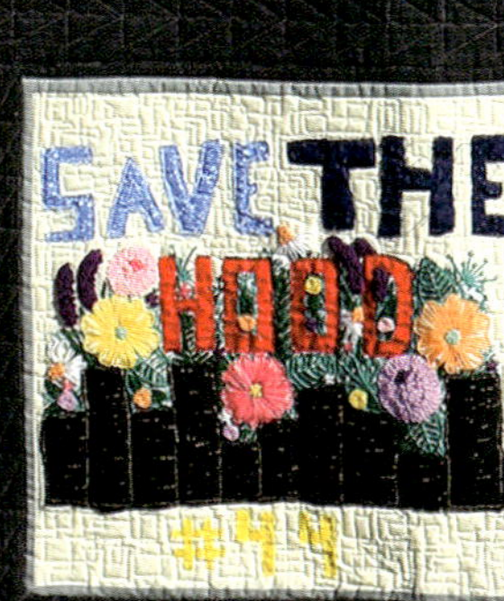
SAVE THE HOOD
#44

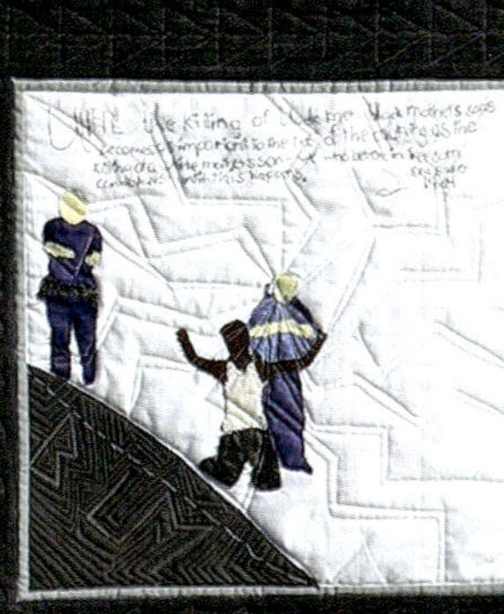

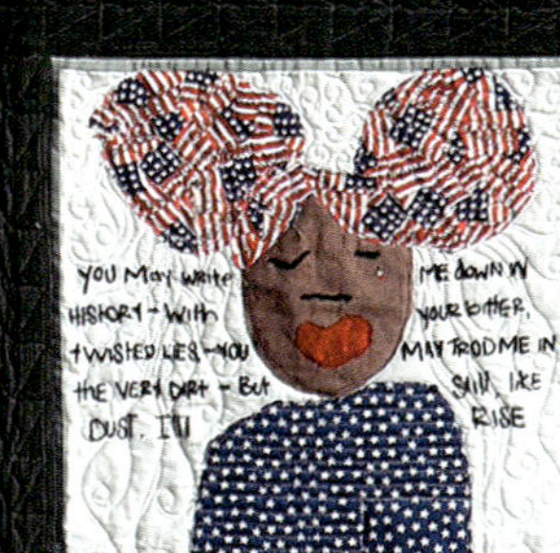
You may write me down in history with your bitter, twisted lies — you may trod me in the very dirt — but still, like dust, I'll rise

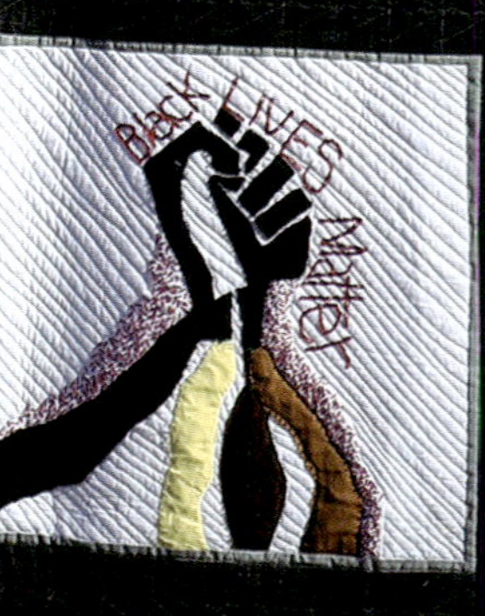
Black Lives Matter

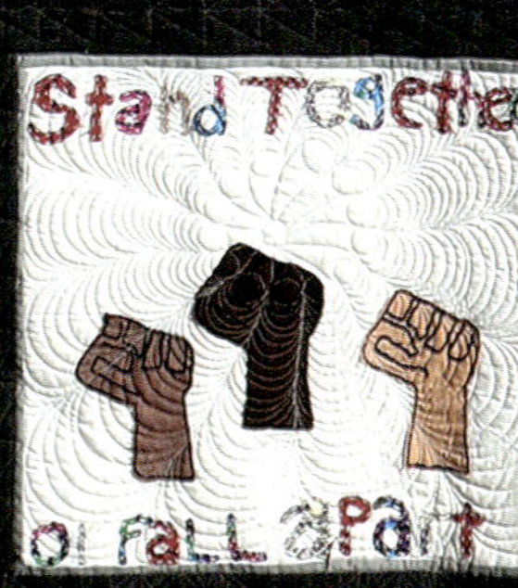
Stand Together or fall apart

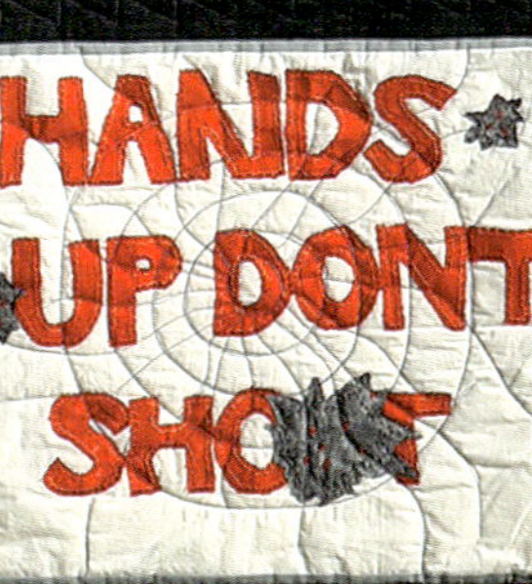
HANDS UP DON'T SHOOT

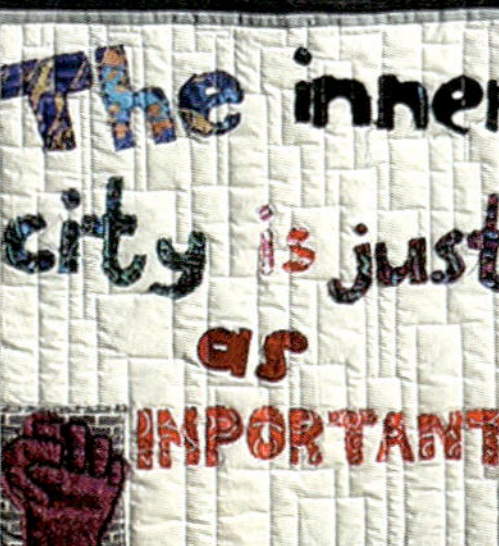
The inner city is just as IMPORTANT

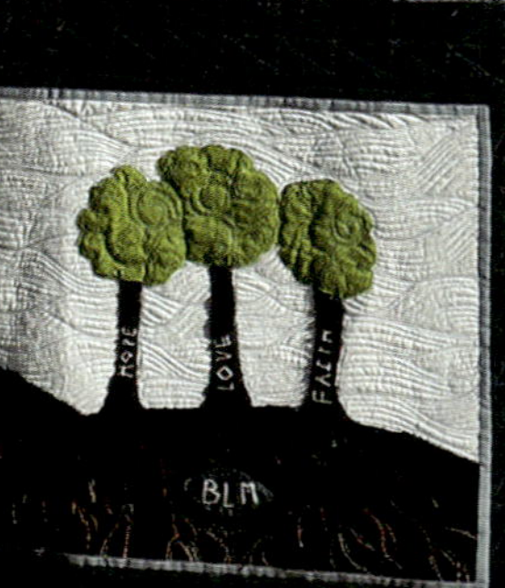
HOPE
LOVE
FAITH
BLM

Moving forward

The extractive and inhumane economies of enslavement that privileged Britain, Europe and settler societies in North America at the expense of Africa and the Caribbean in the eighteenth and nineteenth centuries have continued ever since in different guises, with far-reaching global consequences today.

Despite the passing of almost two centuries since Britain outlawed slavery in its empire, the struggles for autonomy, equality and social justice that characterised the Age of Abolition are deeply familiar and just as pressing today. Further humanitarian gains have been made along the way, and the process of change and repair continues. But if we're still having conversations about the intergenerational and present-day harms caused by racism, unsafe or exploitative circuits of migration and entrenched societal inequalities today, then how much has really changed in over 200 years?

When Olaudah Equiano published his autobiography in 1789, his voice became one among many anti-slavery campaigners in Britain. Together with millions of captive African and Indigenous men, women and children in British colonies in the Atlantic sphere who resisted their enslavers day in and day out, they drove nations to change.

The lives of these courageous activists, abolitionists and revolutionaries brought an end to the institution of slavery and paved the way for a better world. Those who fought for freedom, justice and autonomy remain a beacon of inspiration, showing us that radical individual and collective actions are vital and effective in the fight for a more equitable society.

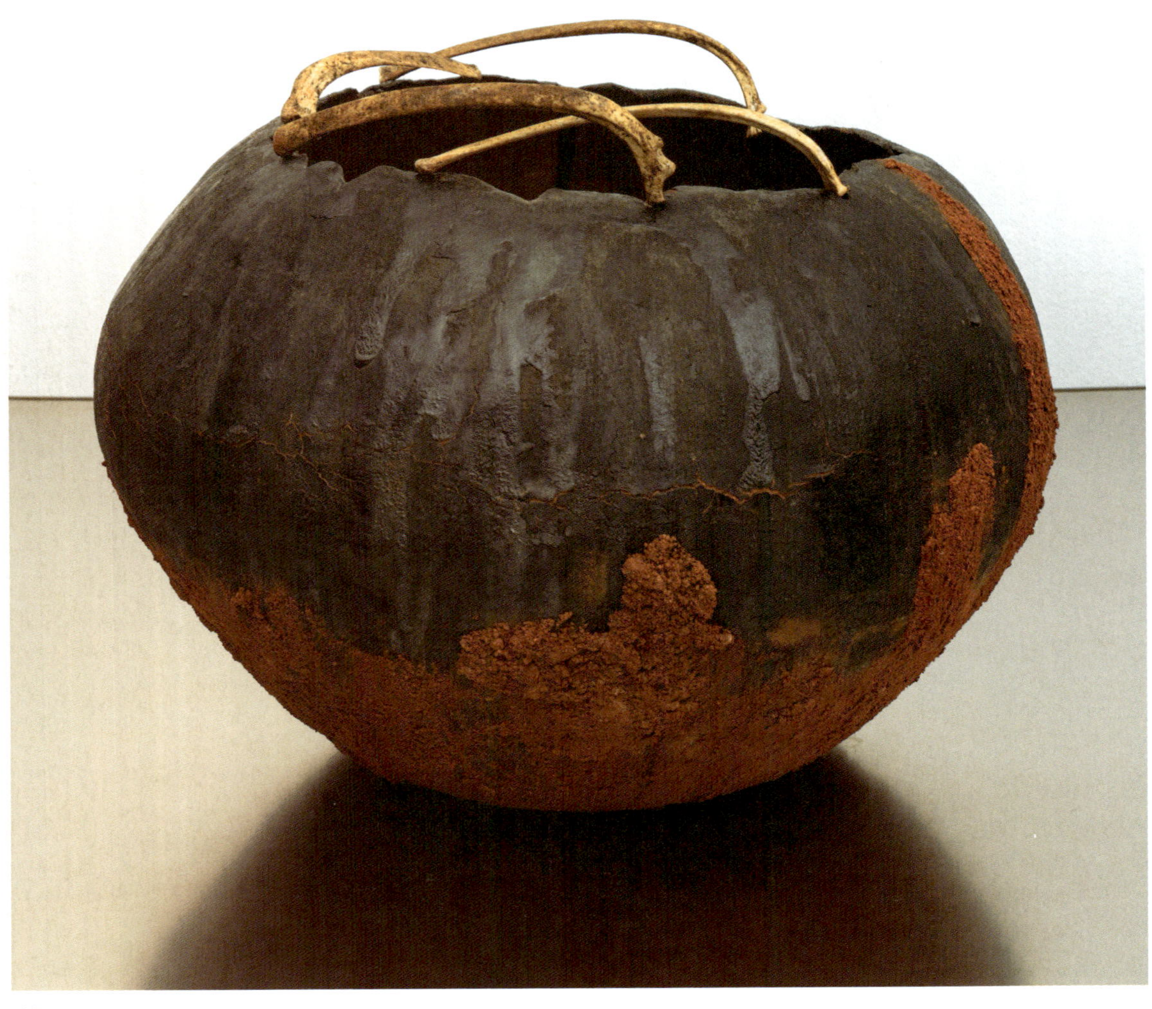

Adebunmi Gbadebo (born 1992).
In Memory of June Miller, 1871–1928, Gone but Not Forgotten, H.F.S., 2023.
Clay and animal bones from True Blue Plantation Cemetery, Fort Motte, South Carol na, USA,
on which Gbadebo's ancestors worked, gas-fired, 30.5 × 40.6 × 40.6 cm
Courtesy of the Artist and Maximillian William, London © The Artist (AG-23-02)

I'll think of a title after I write[*]

Wanja Kimani

A note to the reader

There is a delicate balance in knowing how much to share on these pages and which details should remain unwritten. This is a reflection from my perspective and experience as an artist working at the Fitzwilliam Museum as Exhibition Project Curator for *Black Atlantic: Power, People, Resistance* and Associate Curator for *Rise Up: Resistance, Revolution, Abolition* over the past two years. I do not attempt to cover the breadth of the themes I will explore within the prescribed word count. There will be citations to guide you further that can lead you to wonderful places, which I encourage you to follow.

In early October 2022, I was fortunate to attend the *Loophole of Retreat* symposium in Venice, which was part of Simone Leigh's exhibition at the US Pavilion at the 59th Venice Biennale. The three-day symposium was organised by Rashida Bumbray with curatorial advisors Tina Campt and Saidiya Hartman. Within the same week, I started my role as Exhibition Project Curator for *Black Atlantic: Power, People, Resistance* at the Fitzwilliam Museum. I begin here as a way to reflect on how these two sites have helped me think about resistance and equity.

On gathering

It's the first morning of the *Loophole of Retreat* symposium. I leave my rented apartment and make the short walk towards the San Zaccaria vaporetto stop. Three women are already there, wide-eyed and with welcoming smiles. We strike up a conversation about how we've found ourselves here; the professor who is accompanying her students, the fashion designer who made an impromptu decision to attend and a writer who was already in Milan; our collective expectation fills the cool morning air. More women join us and soon we are ushered onto a shuttle water bus heading to the Fondazione Giorgio Cini. Upon arrival, we are greeted by local staff who welcome us and direct us to register before we are shown to the large hall where over 700 black women from the African diaspora will gather for the next few days. I sit in the second row, behind several of the artists, scholars, writers, activists and filmmakers scheduled to speak. Rashida Bumbray takes

---

[*]The title for this essay is inspired by a convening of performance artists titled *London/LA LAB: We'll Think of a Title After We Meet*, curated by Suzanne Lacy and Susan Hiller, New York, 1981. Performance artist Lorraine O'Grady was in attendance and was the only black performance artist in the room. Her presence at this gathering defied the odds and my encounter with her at the *Loophole of Retreat* symposium was unforgettable. It is a reminder to create our own spaces to think, to rest and to play.

to the stage, encouraging us to our seats with the familiar sound of the tambourine, followed by her voice flowing across the room as she sings 'good morning everybody'.[1] During the next few days, we are seen, we are heard and we are held. The intentional and visible convergence of black artists, academics, activists, filmmakers and writers within the context of the Venice Biennale altered the physical landscape for those who were present, and the effects of this were felt by those who watched the proceedings online.[2]

Loophole of Retreat borrowed its title from author and abolitionist Harriet Jacobs. After her escape from enslavement, Jacobs lived in a garret — a small crawl space that measured nine feet long, seven feet wide and three feet high that was built into the roof of the shed at her grandmother's house.[3] Within that crawl space, she found a gimlet, a screw-tipped tool for boring holes, that enabled her to carve a small hole that was one inch wide and one inch high.[4] From this hole, she was able to breathe in the fresh air that floated in, steal glimpses of her children Joseph and Louisa playing outside and use daylight to read and sew.[5] At night, she would be brought food and have conversations with her Aunt Nancy or Uncle Philip at the trapdoor to the crawl space. When hundreds of little red insects pierced her skin, her grandmother made her herbal teas and medicines that cured her. For seven years, she lived in this space, which she described as a loophole of retreat, a site that physically enclosed her, but provided her mind with the freedom to strategise and imagine new ways of enacting freedom.[6]

Over the three days in Venice, five key directives shaped the presentations: maroonage, manual, magic realism, sovereignty and medicine. For this essay, I will draw on two of them, namely maroonage and sovereignty. Maroons were individuals who fled from slavery and established autonomous communities on the fringes of enslaved societies. Sovereignty refers to both personal and collective self-determination in how we theorise and act. Both of these directives expand our ways of thinking about resistance and equity. Whilst I draw on some of the presentations that have contributed to my understanding of maroonage and sovereignty, this will not be an account of the entire symposium. The content of the symposium and the conversations and connections that grew from that gathering have continued to provide me with sustenance as I operate in a space that was not built to acknowledge or accommodate my personhood. But still, we stand, speak, write and carve the bravest of spaces.

On maroonage

The act of maroonage broadly describes the act of fleeing enslavement, but there was a difference between maroons

1 Rashida Bumbray, 'Loophole of Retreat: Venice, Day 1', *YouTube*, https://www.youtube.com/watch?v= (accessed 5 June 2024).
2 Nailah Reine Barnes, *Simone Leigh's 'Loophole of Retreat' at the 59th Venice Biennale Was a Transformative Ode to Black Women*, https://www.teenvogue.com/story/simone-leighs-loophole-of-retreat (accessed 12 June 2024).
3 Harriet A. Jacobs, *Incidents in the Life of a Slave Girl. Written by Herself*, Boston 1861. Electronic edition available via *Documenting the American South*, https://docsouth.unc.edu/fpn/jacobs/jacobs.html (accessed 1 June 2024).
4 Sandra Jackson-Dumont, 'Sandra Jackson-Dumont, Loophole of Retreat: Venice', *YouTube*, https://www.youtube.com/watch?v=FOv3wWchbts (accessed 31 May 2024).
5 Thanks to Jade Monserrat for drawing my attention to the use of language throughout this essay and especially when discussing Jacobs' experience: see note 3.
6 'Loophole of Retreat', *Simone Leigh 2022 Venice Biennale*, https://simoneleighvenice2022.org/loophole-of-retreat/ (accessed 31 June 2024).

and enslaved people who were classed as runaways who lived communally. Although much literature around maroons focuses on the communities in Jamaica and the Americas, maroon communities were also found in Africa.[7] Sylviane Diouf makes the distinction between runaways who refused enslavement but wanted to be part of larger society, albeit from the margin, and maroons, who considered exile as a step towards autonomy.[8] The term 'borderland maroons' refers to those who lived in the land that bordered farms and plantations. At times, they maintained relations with those who were enslaved, visiting plantations several times a week for food, information and to connect with family members. 'Hinterland maroons' settled in places with difficult terrain that was harder to reach, including mountainous land and in elaborate and extensive underground caves.[9] The 'maroon landscape' was therefore defined by a mode of living that resisted slavery and was located in the periphery of enforced labour and driven by self-determination.[10] Written evidence of maroon communities can be traced through legal documents that mention maroons and how their lives threatened slavery, newspaper articles written following raids on their settlements, and their complicity in tracking runaways and returning them for reward money.[11] This complex relationship with enslaved people was also reflected in their relationship with abolitionists. It is believed that abolitionists tended to ignore maroons, seeing them as lost souls and an example of what slavery was driving people to rather than as an intentional mode of living that resisted slavery.[12]

Despite this limited understanding, their early pursuit of black liberation provided a blueprint for other movements that followed, whereby black people chose to voluntarily separate themselves in order to create autonomous spaces. In the African diaspora, the Black Panther Party, the Black Panther Movement and the Black Power movement emphasised self-determination, economic empowerment and racial pride. In the creative sector in the UK, the BLK Art Group, Black Ballad, Black Blossoms, Black Curators Collective, Black Curatorial, Black Cultural Archives, Shade Podcast, Museum Detox and the Collective Makers are examples of networks and organisations that facilitate knowledge exchange with an element of understanding of the realities of working within particular spaces as a black person. For instance, Museum Detox is a network for people of colour working in the heritage sector, galleries and libraries in the UK, providing professional support such as networking opportunities as well as supporting the well-being of its members.[13] This element of care is especially necessary during times of precarity.

In her presentation at the *Loophole of Retreat* symposium, Sandra Jackson-Dumont spoke eloquently about the gimlet

7. Claire Ratnon, *Unearthed: On Race and Roots, and How the Soil Taught Me I Belong*, London 2022.
8. Sylviane Diouf, *Slavery's Exile* New York 2014.
9. Sylviane Diouf, 'Slavery's Exiles', *C-Span*, https://www.c-span.org/video/?318368-1%2Fslaverys-exiles (accessed 30 June 2024).
10. See note 7.
11. See note 8.
12. See note 8.
13. The network supports its members in a number of ways, including formal and informal events that provide the opportunity to meet others and share knowledge as well providing funding for those affected by redundancies and financial challenges that arise from widespread precarious employment within the sector. See *Home: Museum Detox, Museum Detox CIC*, https://www.museumdetox.org/ (accessed 28 July 2024).

that Harriet Jacobs used to bore a hole in her crawl space. She suggested that black women ought to carry a gimlet for the precarious times in which we may be in 'need of retreat or need to retreat'.[14] In some way, Museum Detox offers this retreat for those people of colour who work within museums that are steeped in historical fallacies and imbalances of power. These opportunities to connect and share knowledge and experience reflect the liberatory nature of the 'maroon landscape' for enslaved individuals in their pursuit of self-determination.

Although little is recorded about knowledge-systems that were passed down within maroon communities because of the nature of oral history, the communities that exist today suggest that ecological knowledge played an important role.[15] At the *Loophole of Retreat*, Deborah Anzinger spoke about *Training Stations*, her living interactive sculptures that are located in Jamaica's Cockpit Country: a historic place of refuge for maroons fleeing slavery, which now hosts a number of rare and endangered species.[16] The sculptures were made using local materials and techniques to create space for gathering, sharing ancestral knowledge and fostering an equitable relationship to natures, which are under threat from ecologically harmful policies.[17] East of Cockpit Country is the Charles Town Maroon Community where Colonel Marcia 'Kim' Douglas, who recently joined the ancestors, was the acting colonel. Selected by her community, she was the leader of one of several maroon communities in Jamaica and was the first woman to hold the position.[18] She cared for the Maroon Museum and Safu Yard, ensuring that intergenerational knowledge, particularly around ecology, was shared, incorporated into daily life and passed down to the youngest generation. There is a desire to reflect the adaptability of nature and live in community with it and she was instrumental in ensuring that their way of life was legally protected whilst also providing spiritual guidance.[19] This insistence on self-governance is a key aspect of sovereignty.

On sovereignty

> To be sovereign is to not be subject to another's authority, another's desires, or another's gaze, but rather to be the author of one's own history.[20]

In the first gallery of the US Pavilion at the 59th Venice Biennale, we are greeted with *Last Garment* [134]. A black woman, bent at the waist, washes clothes against a rock. The figure is reminiscent of a photograph taken in Jamaica in 1899 entitled *Mammy's Last Garment*, which was used to promote the increasing Caribbean tourism industry. It depicted an

14 In these instances, a gimlet could be physical, metaphorical or theoretical. See Jackson-Dumont, note 4.

15 Artists and curators have also engaged with the notion of maroonage. Thanks to Barbara Asante for directing me to the work of Beatriz Nascimento and her concept of *quilombo*: historical spaces of black resistance in Brazil where formerly enslaved Africans forged communities that are still inhabiting those spaces today. Beatriz Nasciento and Abdias do Nascimento inspired the recent *O Quilombismo: Of Resisting and Insisting. Of Flight as Fight. Of Other Democratic Egalitarian Political Philosophies* exhibition at HKW in Berlin: https://www.hkw.de/en/programme/o-quilombismo (accessed 31 May 2024).

16 'Welcome to Cockpit Country!', *Cockpit Country Forest*, https://www.cockpitcountry.com/Forestnative.html (accessed 16 July 2024).

17 Deborah Anzinger, 'Loophole of Retreat: Venice', *YouTube*: https://www.youtube.com/watch?v=mH9oGYiBGNE (accessed 10 August 2024).

18 'Acting Colonel Marcia Douglas', *The Charles Town Maroons*, https://www.maroons-jamaica.com/marcia-douglas/ (accessed 16 July 2024).

19 Marcia Douglas, interview with the author, 24 July 2024.

20 'Simone Leigh: Sovereignty at the US Pavilion', *YouTube*, https://www.youtube.com/watch?v=QvTfeqnY5rs (accessed 2 July 2024).

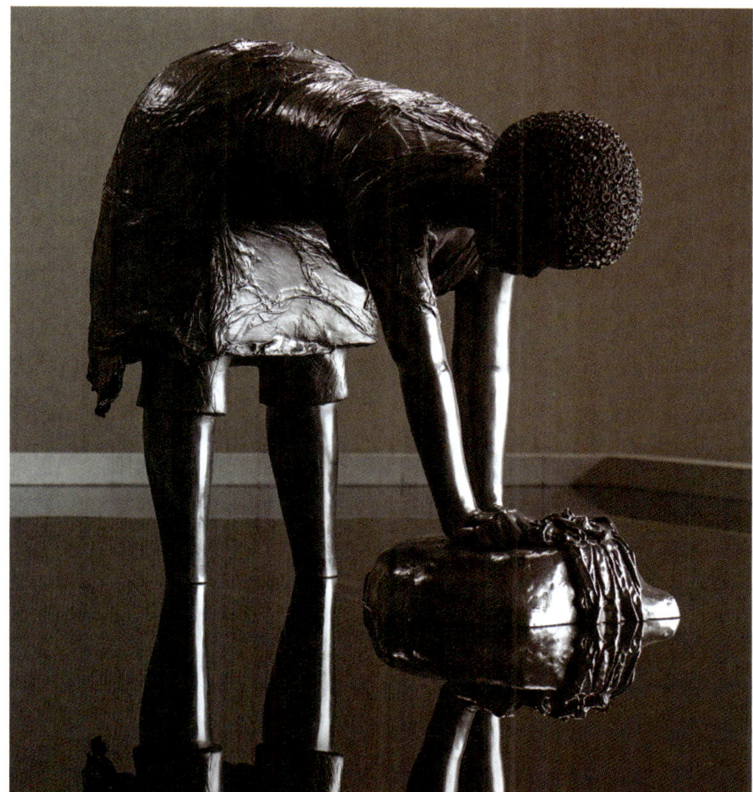

idealised view of the landscape and its unassuming inhabitants, in this case, a black woman at work, who is unlikely to have consented to the use of her image.[21] Leigh reworks this image, starting with clay to sculpt her hair from more than 800 rosettes, working from a life model in clothing similar to the period. Her attention to detail and the expansiveness of who the figure represents is emblematic of Leigh's work. As Vanessa Agard-Jones states, 'clay embodies Leigh's insistence upon remembrance, an evocative parallel to her primary work methodology: citation. Leigh's citations here are at once intimate and expansive, but always simultaneously at the macroscale of African diasporic cultural forms and at the microscale of Leigh's own life's milieu'.[22] Her labour remains etched in the work which is welded and cast into bronze. Her choice of an 'eternal material to render and memorialise black women' allows them to 'weather history and are virtually indestructible'.[23] The lineage she traces carves out a black female subjectivity that is poetic and quiet, radical and resolute.

The figure's presence and the stillness that surrounds her take up most of the floor-space, forcing visitors to think about how they navigate their own bodies around her. She is within reach but protected by the peripheral structure around her. However,

21. 'Mammy's Last Garment, Jamaica', *The New York Public Library Digital Collections*, https://digitalcollections.nyp.org/items/ 5e66b3e8-92cf-d471-e040-e00a 180654d7 (accessed 28 June 2024).
22. Vanessa Agard-Jones, 'Clay's Memory', in Eva Respini (ed.), *Simone Leigh*, New York 2023, p. 105.
23. Eva Respini, 'Introduction: Simone Leigh, Sculpting Time', in Respini 2023, p. 19.

for the many women and girls who wash clothes and tend to homes across metropolitan cities across Africa, their labour and bodies are vulnerable to unwanted attention and exploitation. They aren't elevated in the same way. The distance between this figure and those that have limited options but to remain in dangerous service to others is determined by positionality. As a black woman rooted in Kenya who grew up in England, I acknowledge the privilege I have, including access through transnational mobility, the right to work in most parts of the world, being able-bodied, the education I have received and the opportunities that are available to me as a result of these factors. As a transient daughter of empire, Leigh's work offers refuge.

The retreat that is found in Leigh's work is in part due to her process and how the work is presented. Her ability to rework aspects of the archive that have minimised or erased the image of the black woman or her intellectual labour is the praxis of Saidiya Hartman's method of 'critical fabulation'.[24] Within this methodology, elements of history are reformulated, 're-presenting the sequence of events in divergent stories and from contested points of view ... to jeopardize the status of the event, to displace the received or authorized account, and to imagine what might have happened or might have been said or might have been done'.[25] In her seminal essay, 'Venus in Two Acts', Hartman conjures up the presence of Venus, an enslaved woman on board the ship *Recovery*. Her presence is briefly mentioned as one of the victims during the trial of Captain John Kimber, indicted for murdering two enslaved women. This formulation of her presence and personhood provides us with ways to speak to illegible archives, drawing on the gift of narration to flesh out individuals and give substance to historical voids. Eva Respini argues that this rejection of linearity creates a tool to address historical absences and fallacies.[26] It allows us to move beyond categorisations that have been historically dictated within colonial histories. The durational aspect of Leigh's work — the workshops and symposiums that accompany her exhibitions — highlight the importance of gathering and collaboration in shaping history.[27] As Katherine McKittrick reflects, 'a black sense of place is not individualized knowledge; it is collaborative praxis, it assumes that our selfhood is always in tandem with other ways of being'.[28] Collaborative praxis may include thinking and working alongside others, as in the case of Museum Detox and others who convene intentionally to address and offer strategies for those attempting to shift the centre within dominant narratives inherent in museums in the UK, which are centred on white supremacy. By shifting away from individualised knowledge and towards other ways of being, we may also consider how we engage with the natural world, including the earth and the memories it contains.

24. 'Simone Leigh: Summer Series Conversation, Anderson Ranch Art Center', *YouTube*, https://www.youtube.com/watch?v=k3e9-SKH2Co (accessed 7 June 2024). Critical fabulation is also discussed by Niru Ratnam in his reflection piece on the work of Kimathi Donkor on p. 56 of this book.
25. Saidiya Hartman, 'Venus in Two Acts', *Small Axe: A Caribbean Journal of Criticism*, 26, no. 2 (2008), p. 11.
26. Eva Respini discusses the way Simone Leigh's practice collapses time and geographies and in doing so, she creates new hybrids by addressing historical gaps and absences (Respini, 'Introduction', in Respini 2023, p. 16).
27. Respini, 'Introduction', in Respini 2023, p. 20.
28. Katherine McKittrick, 'A Glossary of the Tangible and Unfettered', in Respini 2023, p. 136.

Whilst crafting her clay vessels, Adebunmi Gbadebo was aware her work would be in conversation with the work of Simone Leigh.[29] Gbadebo had previously been working with handmade rice paper, but when her mother passed away, she returned to the True Blue Plantation in Fort Motte, South Carolina, to bury her ashes among her ancestors. Whilst she was there, she was moved by the history embedded in the red earth that her ancestors had once laboured on and created new artworks that incorporated it [133 and 135]. In the process of making these vessels, Gbadebo works with others to understand how to practically and respectfully retrieve soil from the perimeters of the burial grounds so as not to disturb the ecologies within the land.[30] After transporting the soil to her studio in Philadelphia, she makes use of all she has collected, repurposing even the dust that comes from the firing process. Utilising materials from the land such as soil, rice and indigo, and techniques including the Nigerian coil technique, her body becomes a surrogate for the knowledge that enslaved people embodied when they were forcibly trafficked. She says, 'when we couldn't take anything, when things were taken away from us, we always carried our relationship with the land'.[31] She recalls early research into ceramic plantations in South Carolina where enslaved people made vessels to hold food and water. David Drake (*c.* 1801– 1874), also known as 'Dave the Potter', wrote on his vessels, inscribing his name alongside poetry and Christian proverbs, which provide us with an understanding of agency during enslavement.[32] The connection between Gbadebo's body and hand are a continuum of her thinking about lineage; both the tangible and the imagined. The ability to conceive new ways of living in the aftermath of slavery, the 'mode of inhabiting and rupturing this episteme with our known lived and un/ imaginable lives' is what Christina Sharpe refers to as 'wake work'.[33] Using names found on the headstones on the burial grounds to name the works on paper and in clay, Gbadebo engages in wake work, the results of which are both intimate and monumental.

On equity

Black geographies, including the slave ship, the 'Middle Passage' and the plantation, are difficult sites to write and create from.[34] Engaging with works that bear witness to violence inflicted on your ancestors is difficult, particularly when they are located in spaces that are entrenched in structural racism. In 2019, the University of Cambridge launched its Legacies of Enslavement inquiry, which aimed to explore how the University benefited from, shaped or challenged slavery.[35] A report by Sabine Cadeau and Nicolas Bell-Romero provides an attempt to uncover the history of racial violence and exploitation enacted on communities of

29. Chinma Johnson-Nwosu, 'A New Generation of Ceramicists Takes the Spotlight in London Show', *The Art Newspaper*, 2023, https://www.theart newspaper.com/2023/06/29/adebunmi-gbadebo-ceramics-exhibition-maximillian-william (accessed 20 June 2024).

30. Adebunmi Gbadebo, interview with the author, 29 July 2024.

31. See note 30.

32. See note 30, and Shantay Robinson, 'For the Enslaved Potter David Drake, His Literary Practice Was His Resistance', *Smithsonian Magazine*, 2 March 2023, https://www.smithsonianmag.com/smithsonian-institution/dave-the-potters-resistance-was-his-literary-practice-18C981707/ (accessed 2 June 2024).

33. Christina Sharpe, *In the Wake: On Blackness and Being*, Durham 2016, p. 18.

34. McKittrick, 'Glossary', in Respini 2023, p. 137.

35. 'Legacies of Enslavement', *University of Cambridge*, https://www.cam.ac.uk/about-the-university/advisory-group-on-legacies-of-enslavement-final-report (accessed 2 June 2024).

African descent and on the global South.[36] In the same year, Jake Subryan Richards and Victoria Avery began research into the University of Cambridge's museums, libraries and colleges and their role in the transatlantic slave trade.[37] In 2022, when I began my role as Exhibition Project Curator, Legacies of Enslavement, the exhibition was largely predefined.

As a practising artist and curator who has worked with artists from Africa and its diaspora, I was tasked with increasing the number of works by contemporary artists. Internally, there was some apprehension about the volume of contemporary art as it disrupted a largely historical, linear narrative, whereas I saw it as a way for the historic to speak to the complexity of black lived experience and as an attempt to provide reprieve for audiences whose perspectives were not recorded within the historical objects on display. A few weeks later, it was decided that there would be a number of exhibitions, displays and interventions taking place between 2023 and 2026.[38] This would enable anti-racist work to take place across the institution and provide a much-needed space for a growing list of objects, including the contemporary art that I had suggested.[39] Therefore, the initial exhibition was divided into three parts: the first part was *Black Atlantic: Power, People, Resistance*; the second part is *Rise Up: Resistance, Revolution, Abolition* (21 February — 1 June 2025); the third part, which I had hoped would feature predominantly contemporary art, does not feature in the exhibition plan for 2025–6.

The juxtaposition of historic objects and contemporary works within the bastion of the Founder's Galleries, which had never held a temporary exhibition, made for multiple readings. For some visitors, it offered a re-engagement with familiar works of contemporary art; others questioned how the exhibition would transform the rest of the Museum; and some didn't think the exhibition went far enough in holding the Museum to account. When managing over 120 objects, each with their own specific lighting, conservation requirements and conditions set out by lenders and Government indemnity insurance, there are multiple requirements to balance, in addition to considering how individuals with various access requirements navigate the space. This is challenging enough when working in an exhibition space that is used for the purpose of staging temporary exhibitions. Working within three of the five Founder's Galleries which, up until that point had largely housed paintings by white, male, European artists from the permanent collection, was an intentional disruption that brought additional challenges. There were other permanent structures that needed to be incorporated into the exhibition design. At times, these created pinch points within the exhibition and contemporary works could not receive the treatment they needed to breathe within

36. Sabine Cadeau and Nicolas Bell-Romero, *Legacies of Enslavement Report*, Cambridge 2023, https://www.cam.ac.uk/system/files/legacies_of_enslavement_report_21.09.2022.pdf (accessed 2 June 2024).
37. *Black Atlantic: Power, People, Resistance*, Fitzwilliam Museum, https://fitzmuseum.cam.ac.uk/plan-your-visit/exhibitions/black-atlantic-power-people-resistance (accessed 2 June 2024).
38. See note 37.
39. In the end, only one work that I had suggested was included in *Black Atlantic: Power, People, Resistance*, which was *Ifá*, by Alexis Peskine, 2020.

the space, particularly considering the demanding work they were doing.[40] Still, by bringing these works into conversation with historical objects, we glimpse a collapsing of time, providing a space to challenge and expand what is presented as truth.

Observing the ways in which historic objects that depict enslaved people are described, circulated and collected is disturbing.[41] The process of developing both exhibitions has highlighted the importance of equity when engaging in this work from the position of a black woman at the Fitzwilliam Museum. Sonya Renee Taylor suggests that racial equity 'acknowledges we have varying needs and seeks to provide resource and opportunity based on what will help us achieve the best outcomes based on our specific circumstances'.[42] Within the context of curating the narratives of enslavement, black bodies carry the emotional labour deeply and it is felt physically, mentally and spiritually. Therefore, equitable practices are needed to mitigate the potential harm, which I will reflect on based on my own experience. The need to retreat and take time out came after facing burn-out as a result of engaging with racist material within an environment that lacked support whilst facing instances of harm by members of staff.[43] When I returned, I prioritised my well-being, which the Museum has continued to support in recognition of the emotional labour this work entails for me. To be hyper-visible in a predominantly white sea of faces, yet invisible when it comes to listening to my perspective on race and racism at the Museum adds to the exhaustion. The Museum publicly appears to have a grasp of racial literacy, but internally, exclusionary practices continue and there remains a dangerous apathy in understanding the complexity of black lived experience.[44]

A significant proportion of Richard Fitzwilliam's wealth that was used to found the Museum came from profits from slavery, but the commitment to equity falls short of tangible change.[45] There have been two ways in which the Museum has attempted to address equity, the first being through the Collections Development Strategy 2022—2024 and Collections Development Policy and secondly, the Empowering Culture Programme.

The Collections Development Strategy 2022—2024 provides four principles that provide guidance on how the collection should be shaped in order to build an 'ambitious, distinct, relevant and inclusive' permanent collection. The Collections Development Policy assesses objects and artworks against a set of criteria to determine a number of factors, including whether they can offer new ways of telling complex narratives, enhance the range and quality of the collection and provide impact in terms of research, teaching and other public engagement.

40. Or as Jade Foster described it, the task of carrying the burden of the colonial archive in order to refashion disfigured perspectives', in Jade Foster, 'Black Atlantic: Power, People, Resistance', *Art Monthly*, 471 (November 2023), pp. 28—9 (p. 29).
41. Holly Graham, 'Be/hold/en — A Duty of Care', in S. Kivland and R. Jagoe (eds), *On Care*, London 2020, p. 82.
42. Sonya Renee Taylor, *The Body is Not an Apology: The Power of Radical Self-love*, Oakland, CA, 2018, pp. 120—2.
43. This article was published around the time that I returned to the Museum. I urge you to read it. Bonaventure Soh Bejeng Ndikung, 'Every Straw Is a Straw Too Much: On the Psychological Burden of Being Racialized While Doing Art', *E-Flux*, 29 June 2023, https://www.e-flux.com/notes/548186/every-straw-is-a-straw-too-much-on-the-psychological-burden-of-being-racialized-while-doing-art (accessed 30 June 2023).
44. For a starting point on racial literacy, please see https://theblackcurriculum.com/blog/blog-post-title-three-dx3ps (accessed 14 November 2024). In her article, *Proximity to Whiteness: Anti-Blackness, People of Color, and the Struggle for Solidarity* (https://www.drnimishabarton.com/redacted/proximity-to-whitenessnbspanti-blackness-people-of-color-and-the-struggle-for-solidarity) (accessed 14 November 2024) Nimisha Barton provides a nuanced approach to understanding how an individual's proximity to whiteness shapes their experience of white supremacy and how this contributes to the complexity of anti-black racism. Whilst she speaks about it within the American context, there are similarities in the UK.
45. *Black Atlantic: Power, People, Resistance*, Fitzwilliam Museum, https://fitzmuseum.cam.ac.uk/plan-your-visit/exhibitions/black-atlantic-power-people-resistance#:~:text=The%20original%20bequest%20used%20to,via%20routes%20linked%20to%20slavery (accessed 2 June 2024).

In June 2022, *An Eighteenth-Century Family* by Joy Labinjo [8] was the first painting by a black artist to enter the permanent collection at the Fitzwilliam Museum. It was acquired with this series of exhibitions in mind as it captures abolitionist Olaudah Equiano and his family, with their strong connections to Cambridgeshire. Since its acquisition, there have been a number of other works by black artists that have entered the permanent collection. However, in my experience, there is a level of gatekeeping at multiple stages of discussion that potentially excludes some of those with lived experience in attempting to contribute to the Museum's understanding of how these works can be part of a wider institutional shift towards reparative inclusion. By failing to incorporate what I believe to be a full diversity of experience — both personal and professional — the works that are likely to be considered for acquisition is limited. In doing so, the Museum feeds into Stefano Harney's proposition of the asset class in which institutions such as museums inflate the value of artworks by elevating a handful of artists, which influences the art market. Such exclusive practices can never achieve equity.[46] Furthermore, the small number of permanent staff with the racial literacy to facilitate and support critical discussion may mean that the contributions of black artists will remain abandoned within the storage facilities that are bursting from the insatiable greed that built these collections centuries ago.

The three-year Empowering Culture Programme began in May 2023 with the intention of building a more diverse workforce, supporting the Museum to overcome systematic and individual biases and to expand individuals' mindsets and perspectives. Whilst there were a number of anti-racism staff training sessions available in the lead up to the *Black Atlantic: Power, People, Resistance* exhibition, the overall programme is led by senior management, which makes it feel far-removed from regular interactions with colleagues. When attempting to discuss the use of language around race across the Museum's didactic material for instance, there was no space to accommodate conversation and little ownership of how decisions are made. The Museum is nearly halfway through the programme, and I believe that whilst the inherent imbalance of power that is ingrained in the hierarchy at the Museum remains, nothing will change.

It requires minimal effort for institutions built with capital gained through racial violence such as the Fitzwilliam Museum to soothe their guilt by purchasing work by black artists. Similarly, it takes little effort to employ black women on fixed-term contracts to carry out work that requires emotional labour but limit their ability to effect tangible change. The lack of permanent roles that offer the possibility of radical transformation shows the lack of commitment to equity and a complacency with the continuation of erasure and entrenched racism. In my experience, discussions around blackness and anti-racism fall short of the potential work that could have been done in the two years I have been working at the Museum. Discussions around equity and racial justice among predominantly white colleagues has been limited by white fragility.

White fragility describes the uncomfortable feelings that white people feel when faced with discussions around racism. These feelings may include guilt, fear or anger, leading to behaviours such as defensiveness, silence or the weaponisation of tears, particularly by white women.[47] Robin DiAngelo discusses the historical backdrop of black men in America being tortured and murdered because of a white woman's distress, the repercussions of which play out in different spaces today, where the attention shifts away from the harm that a white woman may have caused to consoling her when she becomes visibly upset after being criticised.[48] In the UK context, Nicola Rollock examines the ways that white women simultaneously speak against the limitations of patriarchy on career progression whilst remaining silent on the inherent power of being white.[49] White women who have been brought up on fairy tales in which the white princess is saved by a charming prince are at times ill equipped to extend their feminist ideals to black women and therefore enact white violence in ways that differ from their male counterparts, but are still as destructive. In contrast, the adultification of black children removes notions of innocence and vulnerability, which impacts their access and treatment within education, healthcare, child protection and safeguarding.[50] The manifestation of white fragility is exhausting for black people and denies white people the self-reflexivity to assess their own role in perpetuating white supremacy.[51] If we were to shift the focus on how these feelings and behaviours affected black and brown bodies, Taylor suggests that a more apt description of white fragility is white violence.[52] In such situations, care is needed with the understanding of the complexity of it in practice. Within a university museum context such as the Fitzwilliam Museum, where teaching provides another opportunity to disseminate knowledge, this would mean acknowledging different sources of expertise and giving due attention to lived experience around matters of racial justice. In my experience, the discomfort with conversations around race generally, and blackness particularly, has meant that the very people with lived experience remain excluded. It seems that it is much easier to have a conversation about black lived experience with anyone other than a black person. The perpetuation of this and other forms of white violence requires an honest look at the structures and networks that maintain the predominantly white, middle-class individuals who collectively manage the Fitzwilliam Museum.

47. Robin DiAngelo, *White Fragility: Why It's So Hard for White People to Talk About Racism*, Boston 2018, https://cl1.cuni.cz/pluginfile.php/1170336/mod_resource/content/1/Robin%20DiAngelo%20White%2CFragility.pdf (accessed 2 June 2024), p. 133.
48. DiAngelo 2018, p. 134.
49. Nicola Rollock, *The Racial Code: Tales of Resistance and Survival*, London 2022, p. 111.
50. The adultification of black children across all areas of education, health, child protection and safeguarding, welfare services and the criminal justice system is evidenced in a number of research papers including: Jahnine Davis, *Adultification Bias within Child Protection and Safeguarding*, Manchester 2022, (accessed 16 September 2024) https://www.justiceinspectorates.gov.uk/hmiprobation/wp-content/uploads/sites/5/2022/06/Academic-Insights-Adultification-bias-within-child-protection-and-safeguarding.pdf and a report of the widely reported case of Child Q can be found be found here: Jim Gamble and Rory McCallum, *Local Child Safeguarding Practice Review, Child Q*, London 2022 https://chscp.org.uk/wp-content/uploads/2022/03/Child-Q-PUBLISHED-14-March-22.pdf. (accessed 16 September 2024). For a personal exploration of black girlhood in the UK, Ebinehita Iyere and Milk Honey Bees, *Girlhood Unfiltered*, London 2022, provides a fantastic starting point.
51. Taylor 2018, p. 122.
52. Taylor 2018, p. 122.

In conclusion, equity implies radical acts of care that go beyond rhetoric and provide tangible changes. Christina Sharpe calls for 'acts and accounts of care as shared and distributed risk, as mass refusals of the unbearable life, as total rejections of the dead future'.[53] When black women seek care whilst engaging in this work, it requires everyone to be mindful of how their actions and inactions may make spaces hostile and violent; to be quiet and listen when someone has lived experience that you can only theorise; to acknowledge whiteness and the collective responsibility for perpetuating racism and reaping the rewards from social and institutional power.

The past two years have been punctuated with moments of deep insight into the role that maroonage played in the resistance to slavery and the effects of this on black liberation; the importance of self-determination in the face of white supremacy; the need for retreat and rest; and the reminder that despite the social and physical death that black women continue to face, I am sovereign.

Freedom, desire and wild imaginings are ours.

Selected reading
• Akala, *Natives: Race and Class in the Ruins of Empire*, London 2018
• Victoria Adukwei Bulley, *Quiet*, London 2022
• Akwaeke Emezi, *Freshwater*, London 2019
• Ebinehita Iyere and Milk Honey Bees, *Girlhood Unfiltered*, London 2022
• Grada Kilomba, *Plantation Memories: Episodes of Everyday Racism*, Münster 2023
• Saidiya Hartman, *Lose Your Mother: A Journey Along the Atlantic Slave Route*, London 2021
• Christina Sharpe, *Ordinary Notes*, London 2023

53 Sharpe 2023, p. 333.

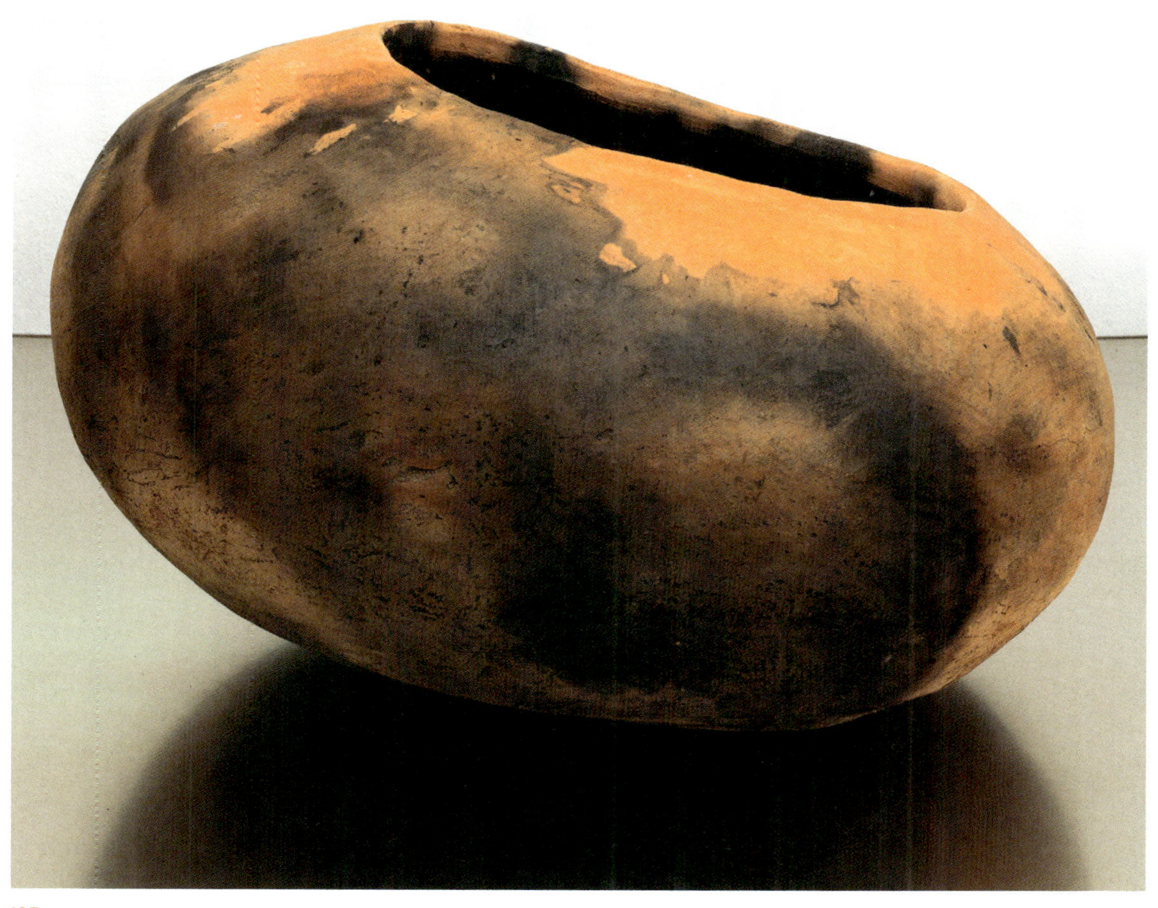

Adebunmi Gbadebo (born 1992).
In Memory of Carrie Dash, 1903—1930, Here I Lay My Burden Down, B.A.S., 2023.
Clay from True Blue Plantation Cemetery, Fort Motte, South Carolina, USA,
on which Gbadebo's ancestors worked, and Carolina Gold rice, pit-fired, 33 × 53.3 × 53.3 cm
Private collector © The Artist (AG-23-01)

Touching the void: on becoming an art historian and reckoning with slavery at Cambridge

Temi Odumosu

In this essay I want to explore in candid and plain words, how I came to study slavery images as a PhD student in the History of Art Department at Cambridge University, and why I think researchers should be cautious about the way this work continues to be done, moving forwards. I offer three broad impressions drawn from my own experiences, as field notes describing a practice and profession that has afforded me many privileges, but has also been racked with grief, ghosts, speechlessness and ongoing trepidation. The word impression is important for me as a print scholar whose research often engages with multiple versions of a source image that migrates across artworks, and sometimes onto other objects such as teapots or snuffboxes or handbags [110]. Impression is a nuanced word that concurrently explains the intentional design of an image onto a metal plate in reverse, the pressure created by the printing press that visualises that image with ink on paper, and consequentially what happens as an image is reproduced and circulates in the wider culture. I suppose the words I share here, then, are concurrently about marks, moments and aftereffects. In recollection, they are the words I needed to hear from others way back when I began to take archival and collections research seriously. Words that would have offered some comfort on this sometimes-isolating scholarly island, where curious souls 'wrestle with the angels', to paraphrase Stuart Hall describing theory.[1] Whilst these notes are somewhat of a subtext or meta-data to this catalogue, know that they are shared not only with the weight of professional concern, but also with love.

First impression: NW

I was born in north-west London at the end of the 1970s, the first girlchild of two dreamers: Nigerian settlers in Britain who were exploring what it meant to move freely as young people, after almost two decades of independence from colonial rule at home. My parents were starting a new family in a city that was a complex monument in the eyes of postcolonial travellers, particularly those who were forging new identities but still considered 'British Subjects' by virtue of their commonwealth attribution. 'London town' was iconic, and understood as the beating heart of England, as well as a beacon of prosperity, so often described in metaphorical terms as the 'land of milk and honey'. The city existed in their imaginations as an aspirational space, and thus the kind of place where one might realise professional goals, upgrade education whilst earning a living in a stable currency, transcend indigenous class and caste structures, and embolden the family name. If you asked them, the African aunties, uncles and cousins that is, who made up our cultural milieu, they did not necessarily see themselves as 'migrating', but rather taking the steps that were necessary to succeeding in a country that had enshrined itself as the pinnacle of colonial power and prestige within the Anglophone empire. A flight to London, then, was more akin to a pilgrimage to hallowed ground, with an understanding that the codes for engagement and interaction needed to shift. And for such an expensive journey (a risky life investment really), so much was at stake. If you were, eventually, going to go back to the place you were born, it needed to be on very different terms. Going to England required transformation.

I now know that the London I was born into was a space of intense racialised conflict underscored by troubled histories such as the prevalence of street riots, senseless murdering of Black and Brown people, hateful politicians, and the brand omnipresence of Robertson's gollywog.[2] However, my parents worked hard to shield me and my sisters from all this at home, and we certainly did not discuss or learn anything about it at school. That said, unusually for someone so invested in history, my memories of those early years are few, which I interpret as significant given those times, and because I deeply recognise the silences children of immigrants can harbour as they sense what is at stake for the family. Similarly, it is only now, with time and distance and a paradigm shift in the wider culture, that our communities are finding the words to explain the way things were, more fully. In recent conversations they retold that in the everyday ordinary, many immigrant communities with thick accents and/or dark skin were subject to sustained racist hostilities — some which came with the indignity of direct violence, aggression or discriminatory outcomes. Others were experienced more subtly as sleights of eye, gesture and speech. This is why living together in micro-communities was not just a matter of financial necessity or forced separatism, but it also provided some physical security. My godmother reminded us that back in 'those days', housing landlords regularly displayed signs stating: 'no Blacks, no Irish, and no dogs'.[3] She felt that such segregation tactics were no different from the Jim Crow laws and signage that codified everyday life

2. Some critical events include: the 1919 Race Riots around the UK, after the First World War, due to anxieties around immigrant visibility and employment scarcity; the Notting Hill Race Riots instigated against the African-Caribbean community by white nationalists in late summer of 1958; Enoch Powell's anti-immigrant 'Rivers of Blood' speech on 20 April 1968; the Battle of Lewisham, which saw violence erupt between the police and counter-protesters reacting to a National Front march through London's multicultural borough on 13 August 1977 — an event that saw the UK's first deployment of plastic riot shields by police; and the fascist petrol bomb that started a fire killing thirteen Black teenagers celebrating a birthday party at home on New Cross Road in south-east London, on 18 January 1981. That event has come to be known locally as the 'New Cross Massacre', and it was followed in March by uprisings and protests that quickly became violent. For further scholarship and context see Paul Gilroy, *There Ain't No Black in the Union Jack: The Cultural Politics of Race and Nation*, London 2002.
3. For an archival reference to the UK's housing segregation, see the public information film, *Race Relations Board*, 1969, on BFI Player: https://player.bfi.org.uk/free/film/watch-race-relations-board-1969-online (accessed 22 August 2024).

in the United States from the late nineteenth century until the 1960s. They also mirrored similar practices by British colonists in Nigeria, where places like Victoria Island in Lagos displayed signs stating, 'no horns and no natives'.[4] In one of her first retail jobs, another aunt mentioned how British people would approach her describing the colour of brown garments using the 'N-word'. This was done without reflexivity and very casually — habituated, embedded, naturalised.[5] But it was hard to explain these details to their parents and extended family back home in Africa, who saw the opportunity to live in Britain as highly advantageous, and therefore had unwavering expectations that their children's independence in the West would be realised. Elders' letters of enquiry on blue airmail paper, and the prayerful weekend phone calls across time zones, served as a constant reminder that upward social mobility was both important and the ultimate end goal.

Nigerians love education and see it as central for thriving in life. Becoming a lawyer or doctor is even sung to babies in lullabies and praise songs. However, a story that is rarely told is that back in the 1970s those who were able to pay for schooling would respond to annual advertisements from England to send their young ones over temporarily for summer 'holiday jobs'. Parents would pay for the flight and organisations would arrange a short travel visa plus basic accommodation upon arrival. Those African students expecting something of a British grand tour arrived to conduct low-paid manual work in factories and farms (work that is now done by other communities from places like Eastern Europe). My parents were not sent on those exclusive trips, but they did eventually come to England as young adults with the same kind of hopeful expectation — that they too would explore new possibilities, live well on different terms, or at least live with more resources at hand. However, imagination and reality were often out of sync, and those who relocated and then managed to stave off the deep melancholy and disappointment of England's true lived experiences, placed some of their energies towards integration — not only for themselves, but also their children. All kinds of material and emotional efforts were made to ensure that African children were seen as respectable, orderly, disciplined, well-behaved and indeed model citizen-subjects, despite a history of stereotyping. I understand so clearly now the intensity of childhood scolding around grades, or use of words, or not speaking back to the teacher, or maintaining the clarity of your cursive writing. This was counter-image work.

With these few words I am only lightly touching the tender edges of transgenerational wounds. For now, they are offered as *intimations* — hints, signals, emotional citations that will need to be returned to at another time. But I start here with origin stories and postcolonial memory work in the family,

4. For the Nigerian context see Bright Alozie, 'Space and Colonial Alterity: Interrogating British Residential Segregation in Nigeria, 1899–1919', *Ufahamu: Journal of the African Activist Association* (Online), 41, no. 2 (2020), pp. 1–26.
5. For an example of this naturalised racist language, see Mets and Soon Ltd. Furniture advertisement in *Nash's Pall Mall Magazine*, 91, no. 482 (July 1933), p. 85.

because it is the only real way to respond to questions I am regularly asked by people, and which I similarly ask myself: why this? why now? why art history? why British art and visual culture? why the eighteenth century? why slavery? why racialised things?[6]

Second impression: posh boys

It was the final parents' evening of the year, and I sat quietly in the school hall alongside my mother as she talked with the A-level art history teacher about my progress, and the possibility of taking up art history at degree level. Whilst there was supportiveness for me pursuing further education, the teacher was visibly horrified at the idea of me entering this kind of training. They said (with a tone that implied their own personal aggrievement) that 'art history is for posh boys from Eton' and not the kind of environment that I should set my sights on entering. In some respects, they were right. I had become enamoured with the teacher's storytelling and the ways the art they shared opened all kinds of world views. But it did not occur to me that our grammar school version of art history for beginners would take on a very different shape when it came to a degree. Neither I nor my parents were prepared for the ensuing accoutrements and hidden curriculum of such an education — the trips, the languages, the Corinthian columns and endless time spent in museums with varnished wooden floors; the snobbery, the pre-installed references, the Europeanness of taste-making, the whiteness of it all. Still, back in that school hall, my teacher's dismissal of the idea certainly lit a fire under the both of us, and whilst the journey there took a detour via applications to English literature courses, I eventually found my way in.

Technically, I could have studied any genre, period or artist in my work, but over the years, as I began to whittle my interests towards a specialism, I noticed that I was drawn to the representation of African people in British art and material culture between the seventeenth and nineteenth centuries. Some of this curiosity had to do with addressing historical gaps and finding visual evidence for an earlier Black presence than the post-war African-Caribbean migration to England, depicted in mainstream media through black and white films and photographs of arrivals at Tilbury docks on the HMT *Empire Windrush*. This period of intensive migration by Black people who helped to supplement the British workforce was often explained as a definitive moment when the nation visibly diversified. So, I wanted to go back and find other records, older images that showed how *we* had a longer presence here, too, even if the terms of our being here were tangled up with other histories. That was one reason for my curiosity with finding a Black presence in art. But, if I am honest, I think this work

6. In this text and with these questions, personalising history, I follow a lineage of Black scholarship that invokes the 'autobiographical example', which Saidiya Hartman explains as a personal story that is 'trying to look at historical and social process and one's own formation as a window onto social and historical processes, as an example of them', thereby 'countering the violence of abstraction' and the notion of the universal. See Patricia J. Saunders, 'Fugitive Dreams of Diaspora: Conversations with Saidiya Hartman', *Anthurium*, 6, no. 1 (2008), p. 5; also, Dionne Brand, *A Map to the Door of No Return: Notes to Belonging*, Toronto 2002.

was also motivated by a deeper need to understand what ideas about blackness and African people informed the collective British imagination; and by extension every teacher, playground bully, employer, salesclerk or stranger on the bus who went out of their way to let us know that we were not wanted in this/their space. So, I needed to know about the ghosts in the cultural algorithm, which is to say the invisible but potent notions that showed up in rooms ahead of us, before we even had a chance to speak, and which had concrete outcomes impacting the way we lived our lives.

Little did I know that this curiosity, which morphed into an obsession, would lead me to a PhD at Cambridge, where I interrogated the most primal and direct form of visual communication in Britain, the caricature. It might seem like a contradiction to study 'low' culture when you are immersed in an elite learning environment with ancient rituals, secret codes and a structural format for learning created to suit the needs of 'posh boys' who went to Eton. But eighteenth-century, Georgian-era caricatures thrived in such settings of English male sociability, or put more simply, bro-zones, where joking at other people's expense was the norm. These crass, gossipy, but still literary, images were made for them, and featured their peers in ways that echo the early in-club days of social media around 2006. The kind of jokes that Georgian caricatures made served as a cultural mirror during radically changing times that included national unification with Scotland and Ireland, acceleration followed by abolition of the transatlantic slave trade, the American and French Revolutions, the intellectual Enlightenment, war, crop crisis, money problems and recession, in addition to empire building in multiple countries abroad. Caricatures pierced through the pretentions of the privileged by telling some truths, whilst also providing rudeness a public platform. So, they toyed with posh boy taboos, revealed some of their shady activities, and articulated their politics with that decidedly British form of humour that I can only describe as double speak from the side of the mouth. It would be much later, in recovery from the inevitable scarring that came from looking at these visual jokes (and related documents) in the hundreds, that I realised what was at stake in accessing the inner workings (or deep code) of subversive communication. Broaching the truth of what English people really believed about themselves and others required entering history's filthy mind (the cesspit), and hoping that as you learned its languages and navigated its trickery, you did not get lost there or drown.

Third impression: candlesticks

There is a pair of George II candlesticks made in 1730, by luxury London silversmith Francis Nelme. They represent the figure of a kneeling African child holding up an ornate

7. These concerns have been taken up by scholarship in the influential multi-volume collection of books *The Image of the Black in Western Art*, 10 vols, Cambridge, MA 2010—14, republished and edited by Professors David Bindman and Henry Louis Gates Jr, and published by Harvard University Press. Black servants were also the focal point of the 2014 exhibition *Figures of Empire: Slavery and Portraiture in Eighteenth-Century Atlantic Britain* at the Yale Center for British Art. See also Catherine Molineux, *Faces of Perfect Ebony: Encountering Atlantic Slavery in Imperial Britain*, Cambridge, MA 2012; and Beth Fowkes Tobin, *Picturing Imperial Power: Colonial Subjects in Eighteenth-Century British Painting*, Durham, NC 1999. Scholar and curator Adrienne L. Childs has also worked extensively on this topic of ornamental imagery, for example in her 2017 exhibition, *The Black Figure in the European Imaginary* at Rollins Museum of Art. For writing, see Adrienne L. Childs, 'Sugar Boxes and Blackamoors: Ornamental Blackness in Early Meissen Porcelain', in Alden Cavanagh and Michael Elia Yonan (eds), *The Cultural Aesthetics of Eighteenth-Century Porcelain*, Farnham 2010, pp. 159—77.

bowled basin for collecting molten beeswax. There is a chain that links the slave collar around the figure's neck with a restraint around their ankle, making the bondage visible, incontestable and permanent. The sticks are impressed with the Thruston family coat-of-arms, which features a stork and three horns. They were prominent colonial settlers from England to Virginia in the seventeenth century and embedded in slavery. I had the opportunity to view these sticks up close before they eventually became part of the Portland Art Museum Collection in Oregon. This object encounter was one that continues to haunt my work as an art historian, since I struggled then and now to comprehend the intensity of racist and inhumane feelings that brought such objects into being. Furthermore, I needed to reckon with the complicated intentions and cultural systems driving their continued circulation as artefacts of economic, aesthetic and historical significance. Given my research on colonial imagery, I was used to seeing the employment of decorative 'blackamoor' figures in marble and porcelain, and ornamental Black servants featured regularly as both supporting and symbolic characters in many paintings and caricatures.[7] However, with the candlesticks, it is the high contrast of values — African subjugation chained and solidified in ornate precious metals — that was particularly disturbing, and no words can adequately explain or rationalise it. This is why I can describe them, but I am ambivalent about reproducing an image of them in this book. My refusal to show them here, even though they are free to view online, is an imperfect ethical negotiation around the redistribution of trauma. After all, you will see them somewhere. However, this critical standpoint and decision to say 'no, not here', comes with an understanding that these objects are particularly harmful in the ways they advocate for oppression.[8] During that first encounter with the candlesticks, I was so affected that contact with them initiated a week's long period of depression mixed with mourning. I had touched the void, the incomprehensible bankruptcy of colonial violence, and at the same time sensed the middle passage disappearance of irreplaceable African lives that Martinican philosopher Édouard Glissant described in another way through the metaphor of the 'abyss'.[9] My parents explained that in this strong reaction my ancestors were just speaking to me, and working through me, but back then I was unable to bring this sensitivity (this other way of knowing) to the foreground of my work. I was still proving myself as a doctoral student at Cambridge and trying to figure out what all this work had been for, and what I would end up doing next, when the searching and looking and writing was done.

Coming face to face with objects such as this one is integral to an art historian's work. And for the most part we tend to eagerly anticipate them, particularly when things are rare, or we are invested in them in some way. When it comes to

8. My current research is concerned with wellbeing and the responsibilites of memory work. See: Temi Odumosu, 'The Crying Child: On Colonial Archives, Digitisation, and Ethics of Care in the Cultural Commons', *Current Anthropology*, 61, no. 22 (2020), pp. 289–302; and Temi Odumosu, 'How to Deal with Distress when Working with Documents', *AM Research Methods: Interrogating Colonial Archives and Narratives*, Marlborough: AM Digital Online, 2024. The decision not to show is an ethical negotiation which I am taking up in dialogue with other scholars engaging in these issues. For example, Christina Sharpe's practice of redaction in Christina Elizabeth Sharpe, *In the Wake: On Blackness and Being*, Durham, NC 2016; and other refusals proposed in Tina Campt, 'Black Visuality and the Practice of Refusal', *Women & Performance: A Journal of Feminist Theory*, 29, no. 1 (2019), pp. 79–87; and Eve Tuck and K. Wayne Yang, 'R-words: Refusing Research', in Django Paris and Maisha T. Winn (eds), *Humanizing Research: Decolonizing Qualitative Inquiry with Youth and Communities*, Los Angeles; London 2014, pp. 223–48.
9. See 'The Open Boat', in Édouard Glissant, *Poetics of Relation*, trans. B. Wing, Ann Arbor, MI 2010, pp. 5–9. Scholar Nana Adusei-Poku theorises with Glissant's abyss, the void and the '*ohnemacht*' (detachment from self) in her essay on Black artistic practices that counter and problematise Western aesthetics of empty space. See Nana Adusei-Poku, 'On Being Present Where You Wish to Disappear', *E-Flux Journal*, 80, no. 3, 2017, pp. 1–7. She writes: 'The void appears when one sees history repeating itself … It is the void that calls blackness, in all its heterogeneity, into appearance' (p. 3).

artworks and objects linked to slavery, I have felt an added responsibility towards being with these things in real time, rather than through digital reproductions, as a more direct way to reconcile with historical evidence — heightening awareness that this object truly exists, that this painting was really made, that African stories have left tangible traces, that an actual person really did blow that overseer's whistle to run a plantation in Barbados and participated in that violent reality [27]. I think that when you are physically in the presence of such objects, you are forced to ask different questions, not only focused on content (the what, the who, the where and the when), but also on feeling (the how, the why, the who else and the what if). For example, how far did the sound of this whistle travel? For such a small everyday functional object, why was so much effort placed on the design? Was it only European lips that pursed on its gold flute? What if this object is the closest we can get to sensing the presences of silent figures who do not feature in official records?

Nigerians are superstitious about many things, but particularly signs, images and objects. Yoruba people especially are highly sensitised to the idea of impression, and what gets left behind both literally and energetically once you have witnessed something that is difficult to unsee. I brought some of this inherited hesitancy to my research at Cambridge, and the untold hours spent writing call slips and sitting quietly with leatherbound volumes in many of the University's libraries and special collections, as well as in international libraries and museums, and furthermore private collections. Those unique embodied experiences made me cognisant of the ways I was implicated in, and intimate with, historical records that were my focus of study. Although I often wore white gloves to handle these works, I also inhaled the dust and fibres and probably a little mould. Similarly, something was likely left behind from my own cellular shedding and close-quarters breathing with all that paper.[10] Beyond these material exchanges, there is the complicated work of also being implicated through understanding, by which I mean those moments of recognition with English planters and politicians and landed gentry that puts you, as the researcher, in their place — that enables you to see *how* they saw. It is empathy that hurts. To this day, I wonder about the ways this information has changed me, and how, in my willingness to be confronted with evidence of colonial crimes, I have, somehow, been actively choosing violence. As Octavia Butler so eloquently wrote in her speculative novel, *The Parable of the Sower* (1993): 'All that you touch, you change; All that you change, changes you.'[11]

Sustenance

What does it mean to inhabit a Black researcher-body whilst studying slavery in predominantly white institutions? Or,

10. I have been particularly inspired by scholars such as Tiya Miles, Ann Stoler, Carolyn Steedman and Tina Campt, who all pay attention to the subtle and embodied experiences of being in the archive, as well as the affects and effects of contact. They also offer alternative pathways for storytelling. See: Tiya Miles, *All That She Carried: The Journey of Ashley's Sack, a Black Family Keepsake*, New York 2021; Ann Laura Stoler, *Along the Archival Grain: Epistemic Anxieties and Colonial Common Sense*, Princeton 2010; Carolyn Steedman, *Dust*, Manchester 2001; and Tina M. Campt, *Listening to Images*, Durham 2017.

11. See Octavia E. Butler, *Parable of the Sower*, New York 2023, p. 3. These words begin Butler's speculative novel on the aftermath of global catastrophe, first published in 1993 but set in 2024. They are phrases from the central character's philosophy for a new religion called Earthseed. The full quote states: 'All that you touch You Change. All that you Change Changes you. The only lasting truth Is Change. God Is Change.'

leaning on Katherine McKittrick's thinking, how is a 'black sense of place' found, felt and lived out in the academy or museum?[12] These are the underlying inquiry questions posed by this essay, but responding to them is not so straightforward. At the beginning of this text, I expressed the need for caution regarding the future of slavery research, particularly for those of us whose ancestry is registered negatively in objects, artworks and archival material. We most certainly need to be doing this work, but I think new strategies for *how* are required. The discerning among you might perceive a notable absence in my reflections, which have not mentioned the additional time and emotional labour spent wrestling with the gendered nature of the research experience, and how the work of confronting boisterous images depicting Black women's pain and stigmatisation was almost too close, ricocheting ideas back and forth across time such that it was difficult to hold stable boundaries or maintain 'academic distance'. Science fiction repeatedly reminds us that time travel comes with dangers, not only because of the ripple effects of making changes, but also because the traveller inevitably ends up occupying a different, loosely defined, multiverse space — not fully present, restless in the past, cautious of the future in emergence.

Approaching a conclusion, I feel it is important to leave these pages with some sustenance — an offering for those who are moved to begin a research process of any kind, but particularly concerned with slavery and colonialism. For a start, I think we need to take seriously the fact that our skin is *in* this work, and sensitive to this work, and furthermore that this skin is permeable. Things easily pass through, and injury is possible. Whilst we might anticipate some of our reactions to colonial records (because we know these are difficult histories), it is likely other emotions, sensations and effects will lead us to unexpected insights. Make room for the unexpected. Experience has also taught me that you will not be or feel the same as when you started, and that you will need a vibrant community of careful listeners, soothsayers, party animals, healing practitioners and joy bringers, to support the wear and tear of this loaded work. Yes, at some point, you will need to be alone with your thoughts and words, and all these images, but that does not mean you need to detach completely from the social body. Contrary to what I once believed, you will not infect or ruin the good mood in the room or with your loved ones. Your knowledge, in fact, will underscore the urgency for transformation and repair.

Finally letting go of my own words, I will end by sharing a selection of inspirational statements taken from my personal archive, by Black poets, artists, musicians and writers, who continue to provide me remote and mystical mentorship for this ongoing memory work. I hope they serve you well.

12. Read the story 'Failure (My head was full of misty fumes of doubt)', in Katherine McKittrick, *Dear Science and Other Stories*, Durham 2020, pp. 103–21. In this story grappling with algorithms, interdisciplinarity and how we come to know what we know, she writes 'Part of what I am suggesting is a monumental demand — to reorder how we know, to produce a new science of black mnemonic livingness — but I think it is a meaningful demand. We might engender and honor black life as methodology — human be ng as praxis coupled with diasporic nterdisciplinarity that cannot be measured or pinned down. The demand can, therefore, be grasped on a smaller scale by posing new and different academic questions that emerge from a black sense of place (where we know from)' (p. 117).

Research is formalized curiosity. It is poking and prying with a purpose. It is a seeking that he who wishes may know the cosmic secrets of the world, and they that dwell therein.

Zora Neale Hurston, *Dust Tracks on a Road*, 1942

When I write I am trying to express my way of being in the world. This is primarily a process of elimination: once you have removed all the dead language, the second-hand dogma, the truths that are not your own but other people's, the mottos, the slogans, the out-and-out lies of your nation, the myths of your historical moment — once you have removed all that warps experience into a shape you do not recognise and do not believe in — what you are left with is something approximating the truth of your own conception.

Zadie Smith, 'What Makes a Good Writer?', in *The Writer's Reader*, 2017

One enters a room and history follows; one enters a room and history precedes. History is already seated in the chair in the empty room when one arrives. Where one stands in a society seems always related to this historical experience. Where one can be observed is relative to that history. All human effort seems to emanate from this door. How do I know this? Only by self-observation, only by looking. Only by feeling. Only by being a part, sitting in the room with history.

Dionne Brand, *A Map to the Door of No Return*, 2001

There are, forever, swamps to be drained, cities to be created, mines to be exploited, children to be fed. None of these things can be done alone. But the conquest of the physical world is not man's only duty. He is also enjoined to conquer the great wilderness of himself. The precise role of the artist, then, is to illuminate that darkness, blaze roads through that vast forest, so that we will not, in all our doing, lose sight of its purpose, which is, after all, to make the world a more human dwelling place.

James Baldwin, 'The Creative Process', in *Creative America*, 1962

When my mother taught me to read, took me to the public library when I was five, and told me that if I learned to read, I could experience a form of freedom, neither she nor I saw the magnitude of that one action in my life and the lives that my work has subsequently touched. As people push against, step away from, and shift the terms of their participation in power relations, the shape of power relations changes for everyone.

Patricia Hill Collins, *Black Feminist Thought*, 1990

This is a story within a story — so slippery at the edges that one wonders when and where it started and whether it will ever end.

Michel-Rolf Trouillot, *Silencing the Past*, 1995

Imagine a team of African archaeologists from the future — some carbon, some wet, some dry — excavating a site, a museum from their past: a museum whose ruined documents and leaking discs are identifiable as belonging to our present, the early twenty-first century. Sifting patiently through the rubble, our archaeologists from the United States of Africa, the USAF, would be struck by how much Afrodiasporic subjectivity in the twentieth century constituted itself through the cultural project of recovery. In their Age of Total Recall, memory is never lost. Only the art of forgetting. Imagine them reconstructing the conceptual framework of our cultural moment from those fragments. What are the parameters of that moment, the edge of that framework?

Kodwo Eshun, 'Further Considerations on Afrofuturism', in *The New Centennial Review*, 2003

Say something whose phonic substance will be impossible to reduce, whose cuts and augmentations have to be recorded.

Fred Moten, *In the Break*, 2003

I've always felt that emotional knowledge is an important aspect of the way that we learn and the way that we analyse what it is that we find. And I can't discount that.

Tiya Miles, *On Being Podcast*, 2012

How can narrative embody life in words and at the same time respect what we cannot know? How does one listen for the groans and cries, the undecipherable songs, the crackle of fire in the cane fields, the laments for the dead, and the shouts of victory, and then assign words to all of it? Is it possible to construct a story from 'the locus of impossible speech' or resurrect lives from the ruins? Can beauty provide an antidote to dishonour, and love a way to 'exhume buried cries' and reanimate the dead?

Saidiya Hartman, 'Venus in Two Acts', in *Small Axe*, 2008

Hard to say which way we go from here. Is it written in the stars? Do they even know where we are? / We loved a while, let go, seen nothing for miles / Now we're standing here alone / How will we ever get home? / Lay the breadcrumb down so we can find our way.

Laura Mvula, 'Bread', on *The Dreaming Room* album, 2016

See your face in the sun / Feel your nearness in the wind / I feel your face in the sun / I feel your nearness in the wind / Come to me now / I open myself to you.

Mike Odumosu, 'Chant to Mother Earth', on *BLO Phase 1* album, 1973

Readings I was in conversation with
- Nana Adusei-Poku, 'On Being Present Where You Wish to Disappear', *E-Flux Journal*, 80, no. 3 (2017), pp. 1—7
- Ruha Benjamin, *Viral Justice: How We Grow the World We Want*, Princeton 2022
- Dionne Brand, *A Map to the Door of No Return: Notes to Belonging*, Toronto 2002
- Tina Campt, 'Black Visuality and the Practice of Refusal', *Women & Performance: A Journal of Feminist Theory*, 29, no. 1 (2019), pp. 79—87
- Ekow Eshun, *In the Black Fantastic*, Cambridge, MA 2022
- Saidiya Hartman, 'Venus in Two Acts', *Small Axe: A Journal of Criticism*, 12, no. 2 (2008), pp. 1—14
- Katherine McKittrick, *Dear Science and Other Stories*, Durham 2020
- Tiya Miles, *All That She Carried: The Journey of Ashley's Sack, a Black Family Keepsake*, New York 2021
- Kei Miller, *The Cartographer Tries to Map a Way to Zion*, Manchester 2014
- Carolyn Steedman, *Dust*, Manchester 2001
- Eve Tuck and K. Wayne Yang, 'R-words: Refusing Research', in D. Paris and M.T. Winn (eds), *Humanizing Research: Decolonizing Qualitative Inquiry with Youth and Communities*, Los Angeles; London 2014, pp. 223—48

Contributors

Section texts and captions

Victoria Avery (Co-editor and Lead Curator) was co-curator of *Black Atlantic: Power, People, Resistance*, the first Legacies-themed exhibition at the Fitzwilliam and co-editor of the accompanying book (2023). Vicky is Keeper of European Sculpture and Decorative Arts at the Fitzwilliam Museum and Professor of European Sculpture at Cambridge University. She has curated numerous research-based interdisciplinary exhibitions and is co-editing a multi-author volume, *The Pineapple from Domestication to Commodification: Representing a Global Fruit*, for the Proceedings of the British Academy. Her research into the presence of key Black figures in Cambridge, such as Olaudah Equiano and George Bridgtower, is ongoing.

Wanja Kimani (Co-editor and Associate Curator) was Exhibition Project Curator for *Black Atlantic: Power, People, Resistance*, having previously been Research Associate on the *Art and Work in East Africa: New Engagements in Art Curating Project* at Newcastle University. Co-founder of *Guzo Art Projects*, Wanja has worked on international exhibitions with numerous artists based in East Africa. Her research interests lie in the intersection of art, evolutionary ecology and the politics of gender and sexuality, which inform her visual practice. In 2022, she represented Kenya at the 59th Venice Biennale. She is a recipient of the Literature Matters Award 2023 from the Royal Society of Literature and is part of the Emerging Curators Group 2024 (British Art Network and Tate). She is currently a PhD candidate in Fine Art at Chelsea College of Arts, University of the Arts London.

Steven Swaby (Interpretation Consultant) is a writer and interpretation specialist with twenty-five years' experience working across an eclectic mixture of museums, visitor experiences and cultural attractions in the UK, Europe, the Middle East, Asia and North America. He wrote and co-curated *Nelson Mandela: The Official Exhibition*, exploring the life and legacy of South Africa's first democratically elected president, and the fight against apartheid. Steven has also worked on several temporary exhibitions with Black Cultural Archives, London, and co-created *Nobody's Listening* — a touring exhibition that provides an international platform for the Yazidi people of Iraq, who were targeted in the campaign of genocide launched by ISIS in 2014.

Lila O'Leary Chambers (Academic Consultant) is a historian of slavery, race and commodification in the early modern Atlantic. Currently a research fellow at Gonville & Caius College, Cambridge, she completed her PhD at New York University (2021) before joining the *Register of British Slave-Traders* project at University College London. Her work explores how women, men and children hailing from Africa, the Caribbean, North America and the British Isles made and contested value during the growth of Atlantic slaveries. She has published in *Past & Present* (2024) and is finishing her first book, *Liquid Capital: Alcohol and the Rise of Slavery in the British Atlantic*.

Essays

Sabine F. Cadeau is Associate Professor in History at McGill University, Canada. In 2023, her book *More than a Massacre: Racial Violence and Citizenship in the Haitian Dominican-Borderlands* (Cambridge University Press 2022; paperback 2024) was awarded the Bryce Wood Book Award from the Latin American Studies Association and the Raphael Lemkin Book Award from the Institute for the Study of Genocide. Her manuscript *Bonds and Bondage: Financial Capitalism and the Legacies of Atlantic Slavery at the University of Cambridge* is forthcoming with Cambridge University Press. She was a research fellow for the Legacies of Enslavement Project at the University of Cambridge.

Mathelinda Nabugodi is a lecturer in Comparative Literature at University College London, having previously been Research Associate in the Literary and Artistic Archive at the Fitzwilliam Museum, Cambridge. Her current research explores the connections between British Romanticism and the Black Atlantic through the archives of the Romantic poets. Her critical memoir, *The Trembling Hand. Reflections of a Black Woman in the Romantic Archive*, is forthcoming with Hamish Hamilton (UK) and Alfred A. Knopf (USA), samples from which won the Deborah Rogers Foundation Writers Award (2021) and a Whiting Foundation Creative Non-Fiction Grant (2022).

Temi Odumosu is Assistant Professor at the University of Washington Information School in Seattle, USA. She is the author of *Africans in English Caricature 1769—1819: Black Jokes, White Humour* (2017), which was the topic of her doctoral research at Cambridge. For over a decade she has been interrogating the visual politics and legacies of colonialism, activating collections as sites of memory and conscience and collaborating with contemporary artists, designers and cultural heritage professionals to communicate unfinished histories more sensitively. Her current research and curatorial work centres wellbeing, considers the ethics of digitisation in the age of AI and big data, and engages histories and future manifestations of Black archives.

Contemporary artwork texts

Jacqueline Bishop is an award-winning writer, academic and visual artist, born and raised in Jamaica, who now lives between Miami and New York City. She has had exhibitions in Belgium, Morocco, Italy, Cape Verde, Niger, the US and Jamaica. In addition to her role as clinical full professor at New York University, Jacqueline was a Dora Maar/Brown Foundation Fellow in France (2020); a UNESCO/Fulbright Fellow in Paris (2009—10); and a Fulbright Fellow in Morocco (2008—9). Jacqueline has received several awards from the Jamaica Cultural Development Commission, as well as others including the OCM Bocas Prize for Non-Fiction for her book *The Gymnast and Other Positions: Stories, Essays, Interviews*; The Canute A. Brodhurst Prize for short story writing; the Arthur Schomburg Award for Excellence in the Humanities from New York University; and a James Michener Creative Writing Fellowship. Jacqueline's recent ceramic work consists of brightly coloured bone china plates, such as are often used symbolically in Caribbean homes, and explores how their designs hid the violent legacy of slavery and colonialism in the Atlantic world.

Kimathi Donkor makes work that re-imagines mythic, legendary and domestic encounters across Africa and its global diasporas. Bournemouth-born Donkor studied at Goldsmiths, University of London, and subsequently worked with community initiatives in Brixton before returning to making art at the start of the 2000s. Donkor has become known for work that features Black history figures who have been written out of history as well as works that focus on police brutality against members of the Black British community. Donkor has exhibited in major international biennials such as São Paulo (2010), Venice (2017) and Sharjah (2023). Institutional exhibitions have included *War Inna Babylon: The Community's Struggle for Truth and Rights* (ICA, London, 2021), *Untitled: Art on the Conditions of Our Time* (Kettle's Yard, Cambridge, 2021), *Artists Reframe the Black Figure* (National Portrait Gallery, London, 2024) and *Soulscapes* (Dulwich Picture Gallery, 2024).

Jahnavi Inniss is an award-winning graphic designer and creative producer whose practice is focused on celebrating untold stories within Black British history. Through her adaption of the culturally rich medium of quilting, she documents history through a critical lens, challenging distorted historical narratives and creating representation and empowerment for Black Brits. As a creative producer, Inniss has facilitated artistic workshops for a number of organisations including Crafts Council England, Tate Britain and Lewisham Council. Her workshops engage participants with stories of joy and empowerment to celebrate, reframe and document our collective and personal histories. Whilst experimenting with a variety of different artistic forms including sculpture, collage and portraiture, she emphasises the power of documenting history and creative expression as tools for empowerment and liberation.

Born in Essex in 1994, **Joy Labinjo** holds a BFA from Newcastle University (2017) and an MFA from Ruskin School of Art, University of Oxford (2022). Her contribution to contemporary figurative painting is guided by a unique visual language informed by her British-Nigerian heritage and diasporic perspective, which guide her thoughts about the social, cultural and political contexts that shape her everyday life. Labinjo's work is included in public and private collections internationally, including in the UK (the Fitzwilliam Museum, Cambridge; the Government Art Collection, London; Soho House, Brixton; HSBC, London; and Harry David Art Collection, JP Morgan, London) and the US (Pizzuti Collection, Columbus, Ohio; Green Family Art Foundation, Dallas, Texas; Perez Art Collection, Miami, Florida; and Minneapolis Institute of Art, Minneapolis) as well as the Walter Vanhaerents Collection, Belgium; the Museum of Contemporary Art Al-Maaden, Marrakech, Morocco; Yemisi Shyllon Museum, Lagos, Nigeria; and MARe Museum, Romania.

Keith Piper is a British-based artist and academic. His creative practice responds to specific social issues, historical relationships and geographical sites. An examination of the legacies of empire and imperialism has resurfaced as a recurring theme within his practice alongside an interest in the ways in which narrative, both recalled and imagined, can be articulated through artwork. Adopting research-driven approaches, and using a variety of media, his work ranges from painting, through photography and installation, to a use of digital media, video and computer-based interactivity. He currently works in the Fine Art Department at Middlesex University, London.

Niru Ratnam is an art dealer, writer and gallery-owner known for his efforts to champion diversity and underrepresented voices in the contemporary art scene. He is the director of Niru Ratnam, which he founded in 2019 in London. The gallery focuses on promoting emerging and mid-career artists, particularly those from minoritised backgrounds, reflecting Ratnam's commitment to inclusivity and representation in the art world. Before founding his own gallery, Ratnam worked on a number of projects that emphasised issues of race, identity and globalisation. His writings have often explored the impact of these themes on contemporary art, and he has published widely, including in *ArtReview, Frieze, Third Text, The Observer, The Spectator* and *The Guardian*.

Orlando Reade studied at Cambridge and Princeton, where he received his PhD in 2020. He is now an assistant professor of English at Northeastern University London. He writes about Renaissance literature, contemporary art, and political history. His first book, *What in Me is Dark: The Revolutionary Life of Paradise Lost*, is published by Jonathan Cape.

Acknowledgements

We are fortunate to have had expert help and sustained input from many individuals and institutions in the planning, researching and realisation of this book and the associated exhibition, and we are truly grateful to every single person for their belief in the project and for sharing in, and supporting us with the intellectual and emotional labour this has entailed over the past three years.

We extend our thanks to colleagues at the Fitzwilliam Museum, especially Sophia Patel (Exhibitions Project Manager) and Elena Saggers (Registrar), and to the Exhibition Project Team: Andrew Bowker (Internal Projects Manager), Jo Dillon (Lead Conservator), Natalie Duff (Head of Digital Content), Tracy Hall (Marketing Coordinator), Elaine Holder (Photographer), Joanna Johnson (Marketing Coordinator), Mike Jones (Head of Photography), Andrew Maloney (Lead Technician), Amy Marquis (Documentation), Emma Shaw (Press and Social Media Manager) and Katie Young (Photographer). We thank numerous curatorial colleagues, especially Carol Humphrey, Richard Kelleher, Elenor Ling, Olivia Majumdar, Jane Munro, Eva Namusoke, Julia Poole, Adi Popescu, Habda Rashid, Suzanne Reynolds, Helen Ritchie, Helen Strudwick and Henrietta Ward; and equally the Museum conservators, especially Edward Cheese, Richard Farleigh, Harry Metcalf, Sophie Rowe and Monika Stokowiec. We remain grateful to many other Fitzwilliam colleagues, including Richard Carpenter, Michael Corley, Emma Darbyshire, Rosanna Evans, Alex Fairhead, Amy Foulds, Jacqueline Hay, Emilie Herrbach, Nadine Langford, Timothy Matthews, Holly Morrison, Florencia Nannetti, Kate Noble, Mary Paltridge, Adrian Shaw, Jacqui Strawbridge, James Tortise-Crawford, Jo Vine, Philip Wheeler and William Wilson. Heartfelt 'thank yous' are also due to our fantastic Visitor Experience Hosts led by Grant O'Brien, and to the Curating Cambridge team, especially Len Dunne, Ruth McPhee and Sara Haslam. Finally, we gratefully acknowledge support, guidance, input and encouragement from Ruth Queen (Head of Human Resources) and Bimmy Rai (former Programme Manager, Empowering Culture); the Museum's Senior Leadership Team, above all Luke Syson (Director), Lucy Perman (Chief Operating Officer) and the Deputy Directors, especially Claire Alfrey, Jennifer Grindley, Karen Livingstone, Carey Robinson and Neal Spencer, and the Museum Syndics.

We remain grateful to Niki Hughes for overseeing the University of Cambridge Museums (UCM) *Celebrating Black People in Cambridge Project* and its two interns Jade Pollard-Crowe and Selena Scott for creating such wonderful visual resources. For input into exhibition design decisions, we thank the members of our Black Atlantic Community Group who, in addition to Jade and Selena, are Tyra Amofah-Akardom, Isaac Ayamba, Carol Brown-Leonardi, Ila Chandavarkar, Anasuya Chattopadhyay and Shahida Rahman; and its chair, David Farrell-Banks (Practitioner Research Associate: Collections & Participation). We thank all the members of the *@tlantic Xplorers* youth collective (made up of Soham Village College pupils, aged fourteen and fifteen) led by Sandra Shakespeare and *Future/Power Project* Coordinator Harriet Vickers, for their creative responses to their exploration of place, identity and the complexities of British history through a Black British history lens. We also want to acknowledge our former UCM colleagues Danika Parikh, Shereese Peters-Valton and Ruchika Gurung for their earlier Legacies-related academic and community outreach work.

Beyond the Museum, we extend heartfelt thanks to Steven Swaby (Interpretation Consultant) and Lila O'Leary Chambers (Academic Consultant) for their invaluable expert input and dedication; Jake Subryan Richards for having conceived the original *Black Atlantic* exhibition narrative from which this emerged; Michael I. Ohajuru for content critique; and Dawnanna Kreeger for archival and historical input with additional help from Eleanor Stephenson. We are grateful to our former University of Cambridge colleagues Sabine Cadeau, Mathelinda Nabugodi and Temi Odumosu for their invaluable essays included here; and to our external peer-reviewers for insightful feedback: Barbara Asante, Vincent Carretta, Jareh Das, Holly Graham, Paul E. Lovejoy and Jade Montserrat. Thanks to Adebunmi Gbadebo and Colonel Marcia 'Kim' Douglas, who recently joined the ancestors, for their input into Wanja's essay. An enormous thank you, too, to our artist and gallerist contributors for their texts on selected contemporary artworks: Jacqueline Bishop, Jahnavi Inniss, Keith Piper, Niru Ratnam and Orlando Reade. Sincere thanks to all the other contemporary artists and gallerists for generously agreeing to their works being included: Errol Ross Brewster, François Cauvin, Kimathi Donkor, Joscelyn Gardner, Adebunmi Gbadebo, Grada Kilomba, Joy Labinjo, Rosemarie Marke, Karen McLean, Russell Newell and Julien Sinzogan.

For early input into content and themes, we thank Alissandra Cummins (Director, Barbados Museum and Historical Society), Susana Guimarães (Curator, Musée d'archéologie de Guadeloupe), Christelle Lozere (Associate Professor of Art History, University of the Antilles) and Marsha Pearce (Faculty of Humanities and Education, University of the West Indies, Trinidad and Tobago) who participated in the *Caribbean & Cambridge Collections: Collaborative Research Futures* workshop, supported by the Collections-Connections-Communities Strategic Research Initiative and the Global Humanities Initiative. We are also grateful for insightful discussions with Lisa Anderson, Ebory Bamber, Paul Goodwin, Joseph Ijoyemi and Sandra Shakespeare.

For the exhibition design, we thank Stuart Sang (Spatial Planning Consultant), Philip Hughes and Seun Oduwole and the Living Object team (3D design) and Helen Eger of Studio Eger (2D design) for their creative flair, dedication and vision. For this book, we are keen to acknowledge equally brilliant help from Susannah Lawson (Editorial Consultant), Jo Walton (Picture Researcher), Clare Martelli (Senior Commissioning Editor, PWP), Russell Butcher (Commissioning Editor, PWP), Victoria Hume (copy editor), Margaret Haynes (proofreader) and Ian Parfitt (book designer).

We are grateful for financial and other support received from the Fitzwilliam Museum's Marlay Group, the Fitzwilliam Museum Development Trust and the British Art Network's Emerging Curators Group.

We are indebted to the institutional and private lenders to the exhibition and to the curators, conservators, technicians and registrars involved in the often complex loan negotiations. For Cambridge and Cambridgeshire lenders, we are particularly grateful to Jacqueline Cox, Sally Kent, Mark Purcell and Liam Sims (Cambridge University Library); Katy Green, Simon Stoddart, and Catherine Sutherland (Magdalene College); Adam Crothers (St John's College), Nicolas Bell (Trinity College); Jonathan Soyars and Helen Weller (Westminster College); Mark Elliott, Stephanie De Roemer and Rachel Hand (Museum of Archaeology and Anthropology) and Sarah Meer. We are most grateful to Robert Bell and Stephen McGregor (Wisbech & Fenland Museum) and Sarah Coleman, former *Articles for Change Project* Lead, which resulted in new research on the contents of Thomas Clarkson's campaign chest. The *Articles for Change* research team included Lauren Gardiner (Cambridge University Herbarium), Margarita Gleba (University of Padua), Malika Kraamer (Leicester Arts and Museums Service), Zachary Kingdon (National Museums Liverpool) and Mark Nesbitt (Royal Botanic Gardens, Kew). At our request, Amira K. Bennison (Faculty of Asian and Middle Eastern Studies, Cambridge University) and Shady H. Nasser (Harvard University) provided transcriptions and translations of the Arabic manuscripts.

Our sincere thanks to the following colleagues in numerous UK archives, galleries, libraries, museums and private collections for particularly valuable assistance with research-based queries into their loans: Alexandra Ault, Catriona Gourlay, Tom Harper, Jeff Kattenhorn, Fiona McHenry and Chris Scobie (British Library, London); Laura Housden (Cambridgeshire Archives, Ely); Heather Forbes (Gloucestershire Archives, Gloucester); Anna Bonsink, Kemi Sanbe and Jo Sawicka (Goodman Gallery, London); Tobi Ajayi, Phoebe Cripps and Maximillian William (Maximillian William, London); Hannah Jones, Kate Narewska, Jess Nelson and Ishwant Sahota (National Archives, Kew); Claire Greenaway and Lucy Peltz (National Portrait Gallery, London); Niru Ratnam and Georgia Griffiths (Niru Ratnam Gallery, London); Gerard Houghton (October Gallery, London); Libby Adams and Melissa Atkinson (Religious Society of Friends, London); Allison Derrett (Royal Archives, Windsor) and Carlotta Barranu and Stella Panayotova (Royal Collection Trust); Clive E.A. Cheesman, Christopher Harvey and James Lloyd (College of Arms, London); Stephen J. Brannigan and Viscount Stormont (Scone Palace, Perth); Desmond Crone and Bridget Hanley (Suffolk Archives, Bury St Edmunds); Adelaide Bannerman, Martina Mei, Gabriele Vakare Taraseviciute and Maria Varnava (Tiwani Contemporary, London); Jenny Gaschke, Claudia Heidebluth, Joanna Norman, Amber Redican and Florence Tyler (Victoria and Albert Museum, London); and Ruth Frendo (The Worshipful Company of Stationers and Newspaper Makers, Stationers' Hall, London). We are also very grateful to Haja Fanta, Jean-Pierre Eleady-Cole and Gerard Houghton for heir timely assistance and Father Charles Card-Reynolds and Stephanie Waibel for their generous loans.

For loans from non-UK institutions, we would like to acknowledge especial help from: Christopher Etheridge (National Gallery of Canada, Ottawa, Canada); Aura M. Diaz Lopez (José M. Lázaro Library, University of Puerto Rico, San Juan, Puerto Rico); Josh Feldstein, Emily C. Nice and Simon Stock (Desroches painting, USA); and Julie Golia, Meredith Mann and Michelle McCarthy-Behler (New York Public Library, NYC, USA). We are hugely grateful to Jean Claude Legagneur and Daniel Supplice for their enormous efforts with a potential painting loan from the Musée du Panthéon National Haïtien (MUPANAH) and sincerely sorry that, in the end, we were unable to achieve the desired outcome due to ongoing civil unrest in Haiti. We are so grateful to Jacqueline Bishop for generously creating *Nana* for the exhibition and for her passion, dedication and ongoing collaborations; we extend thanks to embroiderer Leonie Edmead and gallerist Leslie Ferrin for their help with this artwork project.

For vital academic, archival and artistic input and interpretation, we would also like to thank: Matthew Abel, Susanna Avery-Quash, Freddie Beare, Esther Bell, David Bindman, Jenny Blackhurst, Sam Blade, Carol Brown-Leonardi, the late Trevor Burnard, Helen Burton, Sabine Cadeau, Melissa Calaresu, Father Charles Card-Reynolds, Vincent Carretta, Esther Chadwick, Nicole Cherry, Paul Clammer, Tim Craig, Anna Crutchley, Fara Dabhoiwala, Gloria Daniel, Jennifer Davis, Robin Diaper, Inge Dornan, Mark Eccleston, Simon Fairclough, Margaret Faultless, Miriam Franchina, Hank Gonzales, Genny Grim, Catherine Hall, Bill Hern, Brandon High, John Hill, Mary Hockaday, Jennifer Hopkins, Joanne Ichimura, Emma Jones, Michael Joseph, Leah Kharibian, Dawnanna Kreeger, Eve Lacey, David Lambert, Victoria Lane, Sarah Lea, Jenni Lecky-Thompson, Meriel Lees, Hester Lees-Jeffries, Ayla Lepine, Holly Maples, Patricia Mcguire, Kathryn McKee, Karen McLean, Mary-Ann Middelkoop, Frieda Midgley, Kayleigh Miller, Reggie Mobley, Kathleen Morris, Tom Nichols, Dot Price, David Prior, Rochelle Rowe, Katie Sambrook, Eleanor Stephenson, Silke Strickrodt, Sarah Thomas, Sarah Turner, Arthur Torrington, Brett Trynor, Marco Valle, Edric van Vredenburgh, Nicole Willson and Pam Woolliscroft.

We end by thanking our families, friends and mentors for their steadfast support throughout. For Wanja, this means: Mellissa Gyimah, Memory Gyimah, Moses and Erica Ngugi, Lorna Roxburgh, Mathelinda Nabugodi, Eva Namusoke, Temi Odumosu, Kemi Oguntoye, Leine-Marie O'Kenze, Priscellia Robinson, Sylvia Theuri, Victoria Avery, Anna Freij and cherished family members Sally and Richard Tann, John Mungai, Maureen, Maxwell, Isabel, Nathaniel and Gabriel Labi, Fasil Elias and especially Anaya and Ayla Kimani who are a constant reminder that other futures are possible. For Vicky, this means: Jacqueline Bishop, Carol Brown-Leonardi, Melissa Calaresu, Monica Cameron, Nicole Cherry, Sarah Coleman, Alissandra Cummins, Inge Dornan, Jessica Heeb, Victoria Johnson, Leah Kharibian, Wanja Kimani, Dawnanna Kreeger, Susannah Lawson, Miriam Lynn, Holly Maples, Sophia Patel, Ruth Queen, Steve Swaby, Eleanor Whalley; and beloved family members Charles and Mary Avery, Charlotte Avery-Pillett, Susanna Avery-Quash, Roberta Avery-Jones and, above all, my beloved wife and soulmate Emma Jones.

Picture credits

1. By permission of the Master and Fellows of Magdalene College, Cambridge; 2. Card-Reynolds Collection, London; 3. The Stationers' Company Archive; 4. Cambridge University Library/Photograph Amélie Deblauwe; 5. Photo © The Fitzwilliam Museum, University of Cambridge; 6. Courtesy of the Artist and Tiwani Contemporary. Photo Deniz Guzel; 7. Courtesy of the Artist and Tiwani Contemporary. Photo Stuart Whipps; 8. Photo © The Fitzwilliam Museum, University of Cambridge. Courtesy of the Artist and Tiwani Contemporary; 9. Museum of Archaeology and Anthropology, Cambridge; 10. Photo © The Fitzwilliam Museum, University of Cambridge; 11, 12, 13. Courtesy of the Artist; 14. Gloucestershire Archives, D3549/13/3/27. Reproduced with Permission; 15. Museum of Archaeology and Anthropology, Cambridge; 16. Photo © The Fitzwilliam Museum, University of Cambridge; 17, 18. Museum of Archaeology and Anthropology, Cambridge; 19. Yale Center for British Art, Paul Mellon Collection; 20, 21. Museum of Archaeology and Anthropology, Cambridge; 22. Reproduced and used with the permission of the Trustees of the Wisbech and Fenland Museum; 23. Photo © The Fitzwilliam Museum, University of Cambridge; 24. Reproduced and used with the permission of the Trustees of the Wisbech and Fenland Museum; 25. MAHLR/Photo Max Roy; 26. Private Collection. Courtesy the Artist and October Gallery, London Photo © Jonathan Greet; 27. Photo © The Fitzwilliam Museum, University of Cambridge; 28. Cambridge University Library/Photograph Amélie Deblauwe; 29. Courtesy of the Artist and Niru Ratnam, London. Photo Tim Bowditch; 30, 31. Courtesy of the Artist and Niru Ratnam, London. Photo Studio Damian Griffiths; 32. Courtesy of Karen McLean (page 60 below left Photo Mark Hinton); 33. Photo © The Fitzwilliam Museum, University of Cambridge; 34, 35, 36. Courtesy of the Artist; 37, 38, 39. Photo © The Fitzwilliam Museum, University of Cambridge. Courtesy of the Artist; 40. Photo © Living Object, 2024. Courtesy Jacqueline Bishop; 41, 42. Courtesy Jacqueline Bishop. Photo © The Fitzwilliam Museum, University of Cambridge; 43. © Britain Yearly Meeting of the Religious Society of Friends (Quakers); 44. © Victoria and Albert Museum, London; 45. National Gallery of Canada, Ottawa. Photo NGC; 46. Cambridge University Library/Photograph Amélie Deblauwe; 47. Reproduced with the permission of the Trustees of the Cheshunt Foundation, Westminster College, Cambridge; 48. Cambridge University Library/Photograph Amélie Deblauwe; 49, 50, 51. Reproduced with the permission of the Trustees of the Cheshunt Foundation, Westminster College, Cambridge; 52, 53. © Royal Collection Enterprises Limited 2025/Royal Collection Trust; 54. Earl of Mansfield, Scone Palace, Perth; 55. Wilberforce House Museum/Bridgeman Images; 56. Reproduced and used with the permission of the Trustees of the Wisbech and Fenland Museum; 57. Photo © The Fitzwilliam Museum, University of Cambridge. Courtesy of the Artist and Tiwani Contemporary; 58. Cambridge University Library/Photograph Amélie Deblauwe; 59. By permission of the Master and Fellows of St John's College, Cambridge; 60. Cambridge University Library/Photograph Amélie Deblauwe; 61. By permission of the Master and Fellows of Magdalene College, Cambridge; 62. Cambridge University Library/Photograph Amélie Deblauwe; 63. Cambridgeshire Archives, P142/1/11; 64. The Moorland Spingarn Research Center Collection, Howard University Library, Washington DC; 65. Cambridgeshire Archives, K132/B/10; 66. Cambridgeshire Collection, Cambridge Central Library; 67. St Andrew's Chesterton. Photo Philip Lockley; 68. Photo © The Fitzwilliam Museum, University of Cambridge; 69. © National Maritime Museum, Greenwich, London; 70. Courtesy the Artist and Goodman Gallery; 71. © Britain Yearly Meeting of the Religious Society of Friends (Quakers); 72. The Trustees of the British Museum; 73. National Museums Liverpool. Courtesy of the Artist and Niru Ratnam, London; 74. The National Archives; 75. Photo © The Fitzwilliam Museum, University of Cambridge; 76. Rare Book Division, The New York Public Library; 77, 78. Photo © The Fitzwilliam Museum, University of Cambridge; 79. From the British Library archive/Bridgeman Images; 80. Photo © The Fitzwilliam Museum, University of Cambridge; 81. Card-Reynolds Collection, London; 82. Courtesy of the Artist; 83, 84. Courtesy François Cauvin; 85. Private Collection. Courtesy of Sotheby's; 86. College of Arms MS J.P. 177, fol. 1r, 2r, 4r, 8r, 10r, 17r, 51r, 64r, 67r, 73r. Reproduced by permission of the Kings, Heralds and Pursuivants of Arms; 87. © Victoria and Albert Museum, London; 88. Alfred Nemours Collection, Library System, University of Puerto Rico, Río Piedras Campus; 89. By permission of the Master and Fellows of Pembroke College, Cambridge; 90. Collection of Sabine F Cadeau. Courtesy the Artist; 91. The National Archives; 92. Courtesy François Cauvin; 93. Wilberforce House Museum/Bridgeman Images; 94. Alfred Nemours Collection, Library System, University of Puerto Rico, Río Piedras Campus; 95. Photo by Daniel L Berek; 96. Builders of Barbados stamp, Barbados Post. Courtesy Akyem-i Ramsay; 97. The National Archives; 98. Manuscripts and Archives Division, The New York Public Library; 99. Courtesy of the John Carter Brown Library; 100, 101. Courtesy Errol Ross Brewster; 102. Maggs Bros. Ltd; 103, 104. © Bank of Jamaica. Photo The Fitzwilliam Museum, University of Cambridge; 105. Cambridge University Library/Photograph Amélie Deblauwe; 106. Courtesy of the Artist and Niru Ratnam, London. Photo Studio Damian Griffiths; 107. From the British Library Collection: (8156.c.71.(7)); 108, 109. Photo © The Fitzwilliam Museum, University of Cambridge; 110. © Britain Yearly Meeting of the Religious Society of Friends (Quakers); 111. Photo © The Fitzwilliam Museum, University of Cambridge; 112. Wilberforce House Museum/Bridgeman Images; 113, 114. Photo © The Fitzwilliam Museum, University of Cambridge; 115. Cambridge University Library/Photograph Amélie Deblauwe; 116. Photo © The Fitzwilliam Museum, University of Cambridge; 117. The Morgan Library & Museum. CMP B851. Purchased on the Cary Fund, 1972; 118. From the British Library archive/Bridgeman Images; 119. From the British Library Collection: h.3212.cc.(2.); 120. Card-Reynolds Collection, London; 121. The British Library Board. All Rights Reserved. With thanks to The British Newspaper Archive (www.britishnewspaperarchive.co.uk); 122. Documenting the American South, UNC-Chapel Hill Library; 123. From the British Library Collection: (4986.de.38); 124. Private Collection of Professor Sarah Meer, Selwyn College, Cambridge; 125. Cambridge University Library/Photograph Amélie Deblauwe; 126. Manchester Art Gallery/Bridgeman Images; 127. Cambridgeshire Collection, Cambridge Central Library; 128. © Jahnavi Inniss; 129. AR-A-001-box239-item1, Austin History Center, Austin Public Library; 130. High Museum of Art, Gift of David Knaus; 131. Memphis Press-Scimitar newspaper morgue, Special Collections Department, University of Memphis Libraries; 132. Courtesy Social Justice Sewing Academy; 133. Courtesy of the Artist. Photo Deniz Guzel; 134. © Simone Leigh, Courtesy Matthew Marks Gallery; 135. Courtesy of the artist. Photo Deniz Guzel.

Index

Page numbers in *italics* refer to illustrations;
page numbers in **bold** refer to tables.

abolition of slavery 11, 16—18, 19, 22, 25,
    45, 58, 75, 76, 78, 82, 88, 94, 98—100,
    108—10, *109*, 113, 131, 133—8, 143, 154,
    156, *156*, 158, 160, *160*, 161, *161*, 175
    1807 Abolition of the Slave Trade Act
        11, 27, 64, *64—7*, 74, 84, 108,
        108, *111*, 119, 123, 153
    1833 Slavery Abolition Act
        64, 84, 123, 136, 151, 153,
        160, *160*, 161, *161*
    boycott of commodities
        108, 110, *110*, 154, 156, *155*
    compensation 19, 133, 136, 161, 162, *162*
    see also individual abolitionists;
        Cambridge/Cambridgeshire;
        University of Cambridge; women's
        activism and resistance
Adams, John 21
Aelane, Yahne (aka Joseph Sanders) 21
African art/cultures
    35, *36*, 38, 40, *42*, *43*, *45*, *46*,
    48, *48*, 49, *49*, 85, *85*, 184
African diaspora
    43, 45, 49, 53, *111*, 168, 177, 179,
    181, 184, 190—2, 193, 199
'Africa Trade'
    38, 50—3, *50—3*, 84, *84*,
    85, *85*, 88, 108, 109, *109*
    see also Atlantic slave trade
        (under enslavement)
Agard-Jones, Vanessa 181
Alderman Ind's Club 94
Aldridge, Ira *152*, 164, 169, *169 170*
Almaze, Joseph 21
Ammere, Cojoh (aka George Williams) 21
Annesley, Arthur (5th Earl of Anglesey) 17
Anti-Slavery Society 58, 84, 154, 156, 158
Anzinger, Deborah 180
Apostool, Cornelis: *New Settlement*
    119, *119*
apprenticeship 45, 136, 161, 163, *163*
Aristide, Jean-Bertrand 136
art history/ artistic conventions
    (European) 11, 25, 28, 30, 33, 37—40,
    45—6, 56, 58—9, 64, 66, 68, 83, 108,
    111, *111*, 124, 146—7, 150, 190—9
    see also African art/cultures;
        Black music and dance
Ash, William 116
Atkinson, Law 26, 27
Atkinson, Susannah 26—7
Atlantic slave trade *see under* enslavement
Audley, John 87, 93, 94, 106

Babbage, Charles 14
Bailey, James 21

Baldwin, James 198
Bank of England 13—14
Barbados
    17, *42*, 54, *54*, 90, 133, 142,
    143, 144—7, *144—7*, 196
    see also rebellions and uprisings
Bartolozzi, Francesco: *Ignatius Sancho*
    78, *78*
Beethoven, Ludwig van 165, *165*
Bélair, Sanité *10*, 124, *124*
Belcher, Tom 166
Belisario, Isaac Mendes 45
    'Koo, Koo, or Actor-Boy' 45—6, *47*
Belle, Dido Elizabeth 83, *83*
Belle, Maria 83
Bermuda 58
Bhalla, Anshuman 78
Bilby, Kenneth 46
Birch, Samuel *114—15*, 115
Bishop, Jacqueline: *Nana*
    2, 69, *69*, *70*, 71, *72—3*
Black Ballad 179
Black Blossoms 179
Black British history
    11, 30, 31, 75—84, 87—107, 154—5,
    164—9, *170*, 171—3 190—7
Black Cultural Archives 171, 179
Black Curatorial 179
Black Curators Collective 179
Black empowerment and self-determination
    61, 62, 69, 138, 146—7, *146—7*, 161,
    172, 173, 175, 178—80, 186
Black Georgian people
    20, 21—8, 30, 33, 56—8, 75—83,
    76—83, 84, *86*, 87—107, 116—17, *116*,
    154—5, *155*, 164—5, *164*, 166, *166*, 194
Black music and dance
    26, 35, 40—6, *42*, *43*, *44*, *47*, 48,
    48, 53, 125, 164—5, *164—5*
Black Panther Movement/Party 179
Black Poor, the 82, 113, 119
Black Power movement 179
blackness 185, 186, 194, 196—7
Bland, Francis 96, 99
BLK Art Group 179
Bonsu, Osei: *Male drummer 43*
Booth, William
    Figure on horsedrawn sled 118, *118*
    Winter view 118, *118*
Boyer, Jean-Pierre 135, 136, 137
Brand, Dionne 198
Brewster, Errol Ross
    Amba Gladstone 149, *149*
    Jack Gladstone 149, *149*
Bridgtower, George 164—5, *164*, *170*
    Jubilee: Rule Britannia 165, *165*
Britain
    11, 25, 64, 68, 76—83,
    110, *110*, 111, *111*, 190—4

Haiti and
    122, 128, *128*, *130*, 131—6, 140—3
Parliament
    11, 13, 19, 75, 84, 88, 89, 90, *92*, 94,
    95, 108, 110, 134, 160, 161, 163
pro-slavery stance
    17, 27, 88, 97, 99—100, 108,
    109, 140, 153, 160, *160*, 162
    see also abolition of slavery; Atlantic
        slave trade (under enslavement)
British and Foreign Anti-Slavery Society
    (Anti-Slavery International) 84
British empire *see* Britain
British Museum 159
Broodhagen, Karl: *Emancipation 144*
Brooke, Henry 23
Bryant, Joshua: *Bachelor's Adventure*
    148, *148*
Buck-Morss, Susan 141—2
Bumbray, Rashida 177, 178
Bussa (uprising leader)
    144, *144*, 145, *145*, 146—7
Butler, Bisa 171
Butler, Octavia 196
Byron, George G. (Lord) 166

cacao 50, 54
Cambridge/Cambridgeshire 54, 164—9
    abolitionism and
        16, 21, 33, 75, 84, 87—107, 131—43
    see also University of Cambridge
Cambridge Chronicle 94, *95*, 99, 104
Caribbean, the
    11, 17, 35, 39—44, *39*, *42*, *44*, 50, 52,
    75, 88, 123—51, 153, 160, *160*, 161,
    162, *162*, 163, *163*, 175, 180, 193
    plantations
        15, 19, 35, 54—9, *54*, *55*,
        60, 61, *61*, 64—8, *64—8*,
        69, *69*, *70*, *72—3*, 73, 128,
        132, 133, 142, 162, 163
    see also specific Caribbean countries
Cauvin, François 124
    Marie Jeanne Lamartinière 125
    Sanité Bélair 10, 124
    Toussaint L'Ouverture 139
Cavendish College, Cambridge 133
Chalon, Alfred E.: *Thomas Clarkson 84*
Chapman, Thomas 19
Charlotte (Queen) 108, 110, *110*
Christophe, Henry (Henry I of Haiti)
    123, 124, 128, *128—9*, *130*,
    131, 135, 137, 138—41
    Sans-Souci palace
        126—7, 127, 128, *128*, 140
Christopher, John 21
Christ's College, Cambridge 17
Church of England
    16, 19, 80, 88, 94, 121, *124*

Clarkson, Thomas
16, 38, 84, *84*, 85, 87—8, 91, *91*,
92, 93, 96, 110, 113, 119, 131, 138,
140—1, 142, 143, 156, *161*, 168
'Cabinet of Freedom' (campaign chest)
38, *51*, *84*, 85, *85*
Essay on Slavery 16, 87—8, *88*
Clinton, Sir Henry (General) 114
coffee 41, 54, 128, 132
Collective Makers, the 179
Collins, Patricia Hill 198
Cooper, Thomas 21
Cosway, Maria (née Hadfield) 25, 82, *82*
Cosway, Richard 25, 82, *82*
cotton 41, 48, 146, 148
Coulthurst, Henry William 90
Crewe, Frances (Lady) 78
critical fabulation 56, 182
Cromwell, Oliver 133
Cruikshank, Isaac R.: *John Bull* 160, *160*
Crummell, Alexander 164, 168, *168*
Cudjoe, Captain 62, *62*
Cugoano, Ottobah
21, 25, 75, 79, 82, *82*, 170
Thoughts and Sentiments 22, 82, *82*
Cullen, Susannah (Equiano's wife)
32—3, 33, 84, *86*, 87,
94—5, 96—106, *100*

D'Aquin family 133
Darwin, George 14
De Vastey (Baron) 140
Decker, Matthew 15, 16, **16**, 38
daughters of 15, 37, *37*, 38—9, *38*
Demerara Uprising
see under rebellions and uprisings
Denton, William 24—5
Olaudah Equiano 20, 24, 30
Derby, Doris *173*
Desroches, Numa 127
Sans-Souci palace *126—7*, 127, 140
Dessalines, Jean-Jacques
123, 124, 131, 134—5, *135*, 136, 137—8
Dickson, William *42*
Digges, Thomas Attwood 102—4, *103*
Dighton, Robert: *Richmond* 166, *166*
Diouf, Sylviane 179
Dominica 15, 55, *55*, 143, 162
Dominican Republic 132
Donkor, Kimathi 56—9, 124
Bacchus and Ariadne 56, *57*
Life of Mary Prince 56, 58—9, *58*, *59*
Mary Prince dictating …
56, 58—9, 155, *155*
UK Diaspora 111, *111*
Downing, Philadelphia 17
Downing College, Cambridge 16, 17
Drake, David 183
Dundas, Henry 99
Dunmore, Lord 114
Duperly, Adolphe
Roehampton Estate 150, *150*
Dutty, Boukman 132

East India Company
13, 14, 15, 16, 18, **18**, 160
Eaton, Fanny *170*
Eddington, Arthur 14

Edwards, Susannah: sampler 120, *120*
Effeong, Egboyoung 51, *51*
Elaw, Zilpha 164, 167, *167*
Emidy, Joseph Antonio *170*
Emmanuel College, Cambridge 89
enslavement
6, 14—15, *26*, *36*, *39*, *42*, *44*,
50—5, *60—1*, *63—8*, 109, 120,
137, 138, 144—51, 161, 175
Atlantic slave trade
11, 13—19, **16**, **18**, 22, 30, 38, 40,
50—4, *50*, *51*, *63*, 64, 108, 111
brutality and death
11, 13, 35, 40, 48, 50, 52, 53, 54—5,
58, *58*, *60—1*, 71, 75, 76, 85, 97, 108,
109, *109*, 123, 132, 155, *155*, 195, 197
enslaved people as commodities
15, 22, 40, 50, 51, 55, 132, 153
slaving ships
30, 40, 50, 52, *52*, 75, 119,
119, 120, 131, 153, 182, 183
see also East India Company;
maroonage/maroons; 'Middle
Passage' voyage; plantations;
rebellions and uprisings; resistance;
Royal African Company; South Sea
Company; University of Cambridge
Equiano, Olaudah (Gustavus Vassa)
17, *20*, 21—8, *24*, *29*, 30, *32—3*, 33,
48, 51, 75, 76, *76*, 79, 80, 84, *86*,
87—107, *91*, *93*, *95*, *100*, *103*, *105*,
107, 113, 119, 143, *170*, 172, 175
Interesting Narrative
21—7, *23*, *24*, 30, 48, 76, 79,
87, 90, 91—104, 107, 175
correspondence to and from
26—7, 76, *76*, 87, 93, *93*, 94,
95, 96, 98, 101—4, *103*
marriage
33, *33*, 84, 87, 94, 96—104, *100*, 106
portraits
20, 23—7, *24*, 28, *29*, 30,
32—3, 33, *86*, 104
equity 177, 178, 183—8
Eshun, Kodwo 198—9
Evans, Richard 127, 141
Henry Christophe, King of Haiti 130
Prince Royal 122, *143*

Fanque, Pablo *170*, 172
Female Society for Birmingham
see Ladies' Society
Ferrar, Martha 90
Finch, Charles 90
Fitzwilliam, Richard (6th Viscount) 15
Fitzwilliam, Richard (7th Viscount)
15—16, **16**, 185
Fitzwilliam Museum
15—16, 18, 37, 38, *86*, 173, 177, 184—7
Folkes, Martin 77
Forbes Bonetta, Sarah (Omoba Aina)
120, 121
Fox, William 110
France
56, *56*, 79, 101, 132, 133, 135—8, 140—3
Franklin, Benjamin 81
French Revolution 19, 101, 123, 133, 194
Frend, William 89

Gaffield, Julia 141
Gainsborough, Thomas
Ignatius Sancho 78, *78*
Gardner, Joscelyn
Creole Portraits 6, 39—40, *39*
Gbadebo, Adebunmi 183
In Memory of Carrie Dash 189
In Memory of June Miller 176
Gegansmel, Boughwa (Jasper Goree) 21
Geggus, David 132
General Evening Post 99
George (1st Duke of Montagu) 78
George II 194—5
George III 82, 110, *110*, 165, *165*
George IV 82, 164, 165, 166
Ghana *43*, 61, 69
Gillray, James: *Anti-saccharrites* 110, *110*
Girton College, Cambridge 16
Gladstone, Amba (uprising leader) 149, *149*
Gladstone, Jack (uprising leader) 149, *149*
Gladstone, William 149
Glissant, Édouard 195
Gonville and Caius College, Cambridge
18, 89
Gray, Thomas 18
Greek, William 21
Greg family 55, *55*, 162, *162*
Grenada 138, 142, 143
Griffiths, Bernard Elliot 21
Gronniosaw, Betty (Gronniosaw's wife)
79, *79*
Gronniosaw, Ukawsaw (James Albert)
17, 79, *79*, 80
Groome, John (Revd) 18, **18**
Gustavus Vasa (King of Sweden) 23
Guyana 143, 144, 148—9, *148—9*
see also rebellions and uprisings

Hackwood, William: badge *26*
Hague, Charles 164
Haiti
122, 123, 124, 125, 127, *126—7*, 128, *128*,
129, *130*, 131—43, *135*, *138*, *139*, *143*
Haitian Revolution
19, 56, *57*, 75, 123, 124, *124*, 125, *125*,
131—8, *135*, *138*, *139*, 141—3, 144
see also Bélair, Sanité; Christophe,
Henry; Dessalines, Jean-Jacques;
Lamartinière, Marie Jeanne;
L'Ouverture, Toussaint
Hakewell, James 150
Hall, Stuart 171, 190
Halley, Edmund 77
Halliday, Thomas: medal 161, *161*
Hampshire Chronicle 166, *166*
Haraden, Colleen and Nancy Williams
Liberation 174
Hardy, Lydia 101—2
Hardy, Thomas 101—2
Hartman, Saidiya 56, 177, 182, 199
Harvey, William Woodis 141
Hastings, Selina (Countess of Huntingdon)
17, 79, *79*, 80, 90, 81, 116, 117
Hatton, Mary (Lady) 90
Hawking, Stephen 14
Hegel, Georg W.F. 141—2
Heyrick, Elizabeth 154, 158
Immediate … abolition 25, 154, 156, *156*

Hickel, Karl A.: *William Wilberforce 141*
Hinchliffe, John 89
Hispaniola 71, 131, 132, 133, 137
Hodson, Francis 94, *95*
Holy Trinity Church, Cambridge 93, 94
Holy Trinity Church, Clapham 94
Holy Trinity Church, Ely 96
Hopkinson, Benjamin 148
Hopkinson, Thomas 148
Hugo, Victor 141
Hurston, Zora Neale 198

Igbo people *36, 46*, 48—9, *48, 49*, 51
Ind, Edward 87, 93—4, 106, *107*
indentured labour 11, 61, 120, 161, 163
Ingham, Mary 56, 58, *58*, 155
Inniss, Jahnavi: *Re-presentation 170*, 171—3

Jackson-Dumont, Sandra 179—80
Jacobs, Harriet 178, 180
Jacques-Victor Henry Christophe
(Prince of Haiti) *122*, 124, 123, 141, *143*
Jamaica
19, 40—1, 43, 44, *44*, 45—6, *47*,
56, *60*, 61, 62, *62—3*, 69, *70*, 71,
77, *77*, 133—4, 136, 143, 179, 180
maroons
60, 61, 62, *62—3*, 119, 151, *151*, 180
see also rebellions and uprisings
James, C.L.R. 137
James, Daniel (Mary Prince's husband)
154, 155
Jesus College, Cambridge 89
Jones, Thomas (Son of Africa) 21
Jones, Thomas (Cambridge academic)
89, 90, *91, 91*, 92
Jowett, Joseph 93

Kilomba, Grada: *Untitled Poem 109, 109*
Kimber, John (Captain) 182
King's College, Cambridge 14

Labinjo, Joy 28, 30, 33, 124
An Eighteenth-Century Family
32—3, 33, *86*, 104
Olaudah Equiano 28, 29, 30
Phillis Wheatley 30, 31
Ladies' Society for the Relief of Negro Slaves
(later Female Society for Birmingham)
157—9, *157—9*
Lamartinière, Louis Daure 125
Lamartinière, Marie Jeanne 125, *125*
Leclerc, Charles (General) 56, 138
Leigh, Simone 177, 183
Last Garment 180—2, *181*
Leith, Sir James 145, 147
Lindsay, Sir John 83
Lines, Samuel *157—9*, 159
Lloyd, Nathaniel 133
Long, Edward: *History of Jamaica* 77
Lonsdale, Sarah 134
Loophole of Retreat symposium
(59th Venice Biennale) 177—8, 179, 180
Louis XVI (King of France) 101
L'Ouverture, Toussaint
56, 123, 132, 133, 135,
136—8, *139*, 142, *161*
Lowther, James (Earl of Lonsdale) 142

Lucas, David 160
Lynch, Thomas, Jr 17—18

Mackenzie, Charles 142
Madiou, Thomas 124
Magdalene College, Cambridge
13, 16, 17, 18, **18**, 19, 87, 89, 93, 134
Pepys Library 17, **18**, 19
Mandeville (Mandevil), George Robert 21
Marie-Louise (Queen of Haiti) 141
Marke, Rosemarie: *Which One …*
112, 121, *121*
maroonage/maroons
35, 56, 60, *60*, 61, 62, *62—3*,
119, 131, 151, *151*, 178—80, 188
Marrant, John 80, 116, *116*, 118
Narrative 117, *117*
Martin, David: *Dido Elizabeth Belle … 83, 83*
masks/masquerades
36, 37—8, 42—4, 45—6, *46, 47*, 53
McKittrick, Katherine 182, 197
McLean, Karen: *Ar'n't I a Woman! 60*, 61, *61*
Memphis Sanitation Strike (1968) 172, *172*
'Middle Passage' voyage
30, 52, 109, 183, 195
Middleton, Arthur 17
Miles, Tiya 199
Milner, Isaac 18, **18**
Moorhead, Scipio 30
Morland, George: *Slave Trade* 109, *109*
Morning Post 142
Mortlock, John 93
Moten, Fred 199
Murray, Elizabeth (Lady) 83, *83*
Murray, William (1st Earl of Mansfield) 83
Museum Detox 179—80, 182
Mvula, Laura 199

Nanny of the Maroons (Grandy Nanny)
56, *60*, 61, *61*, 62, 71, 151, *151*
Napoleon Bonaparte 56, 137—8
Nelme, Francis 194—5
Nelson, Thomas, Jr 17
Neville-Grenville, George 19
New York Times 136
Newell, Russell: *Hair combs* 62, *62—3*
Newnham College, Cambridge 16
Newton, Sir Isaac 77
Nigeria
28, *36*, 46, *46*, 48, *48*, 49, *49*,
50, *50*, 183, 190, 192, 196
North, Frederick (Lord) 78
Northcote, James: *Ira Aldridge* 169,
169
Nova Scotia (Canada)
80, 113, 114—18, *114—15, 117, 118*, 119

Obeah 44, *45*
Odumosu, Mike 199
Okorafor, Nnedi 49
Old Calabar 51
Olusoga, David 76
Orme, Daniel 24—5
Olaudah Equiano 20, 24, 26, 28
Oxford 91
Oxford, Thomas 21
Oxford Journal 91
Oxford University 19

Parliament *see under* Britain
Payas (Pierre S. Augustin)
Jean-Jacques Dessalines 134, *135*
Peckard, Peter
12, 13, 16, 17, 18, **18**, 19, 84, 87,
89—90, 93, *93*, 95, 96, 134
Peckover, Jonathan 88, 90
Pembroke College, Cambridge 96, 134, *134*
Pepys, Samuel 17, 18, 19
Perkins, Cato 116
Peterhouse 89, 142
Pétion, Alexandre 135, 137
Phillips, James 88
Pickering, Sir Henry 17
Piper, Keith
Lost Vitrines project 64—8, *64—8*
Pitt, William (the Younger)
88, 131, 134, *134*, 140
plantations
15, 17, 19, 35, 41, 54—5, *54, 55*, 58, *58*,
60, 61, *61*, 66, 68, *64—8*, 69, *70*, 71,
72—3, 75, 80, 90, 109, 125, 128, 132,
133, 136, 137, 138, 140, 142, 144, 145,
146, 147, 148, 149, 150, *150*, 162,
162, 163, *176*, 183, *189*, 196
Prince, Mary 56, 58, *58*, *59*, 154, 155,
155, *170*
History of Mary Prince
58—9, *59*, 154, *154*, 155, *155*
Pringle, Thomas 58, 154
Privy Council inquiry (1788—9) 85

Quakers (Society of Friends)
21, 51, 75, 76, *76*, 88,
110, *110*, 154, 160, *160*
Queen Anne's Bounty 16, 17
Queen Nanny *see* Nanny of the Maroons
Queens' College, Cambridge 18, 141, 168
quilting *61*, *170*, 171—3, *173, 174*

race
15, 33, 41, 96—7, 100, 179, 185, 186, 187
racism
21, 22, 26—7, 45, 61, *67*, 68, 79, 82,
90, 97, 100, 106, 114, 142—3, 145,
161, 169, 171, 175, 183—8, 191—2
Rainsford, Marcus (Captain) 142
Ramsay, James 97
rebellions and uprisings
35, 41—2, 44, 52, *52*, 56, 60, 61, 62,
62—3, 65, 66, 76, 123, 131—43, 144—51
Barbados 143, 144—7, *144—7*
Demerara Uprising (Guyana)
143, 144, 148—9, *148—9*
Jamaica
60, 61, *62—3*, 136, 143,
144, 150—1, *150—1*
see also Haitian Revolution; resistance
Renard, Édouard-Antoine
Rebellion … 34, 52, *52*
Renny, Robert 40—1
reparation/repair
11, 19, 30, 33, 136, 175, 197
representation of Black people (non-racist)
2, 6, 10, 20, 23—5, *24, 29*, 30, *31, 32—3*,
33, *34*, 39—40, *39, 43, 45, 52, 53*, 56,
57, 58—9, *58, 59, 60*, 61, 64, 66, 68, *70*,
71, *72—3, 77, 78, 81, 86, 113, 116, 121, 122*,

124—5, *124—5*, *130*, *135*, *139*, *143*, *144*,
   145, *146*, *147*, 149, *149*, *150*, *151*, *152*, 155,
   155, *156*, *164*, *166—9*, 180—2, *181*, 183
representation of Black people (racist)
   25, *26*, *47*, *67*, 82, *82*, 83, *83*, *109*, *148*,
   157, *157—61*, 161, 171, *172*, 194—5
resistance
   11, 22, 25, 27, 35, 40—1, 44, *52*, 58,
   60—2, *60—4*, 66, 75, 76, 108, *121*, 123,
   124, 131, 143, 154, 167, 175, 178, 179
   see also maroonage/maroons;
      rebellions and uprisings;
      women's activism and resistance
Reynolds, Joshua 82
Richmond, Bill 164, 166, *166*
Ringgold, Faith 171
Rippingille, Alexander 160
Robinson, Robert 92, 94, 96
Roper, Moses 164, 167, *167*
Ross, Ken: *Marchers 172*
Rowlandson, Thomas
   Richard Cosway ... 82, *82*
Royal African Company
   13, 15, 16, **16**, 17, 19, 50
Royal Navy
   13, 27, 30, 79, 83, 113, 117,
   119, 120, *146*, 147, *147*
rum 50, 54, 110
Russell, John
   Countess of Huntingdon ... 80, *80*

St Catharine's College, Cambridge 89
Saint-Domingue 123, 131—8, 140, 142, 143
St John's College, Cambridge
   16, 87, 88, 89, 91, *91*, 142
St Vincent 50, 162
Sancho, Ann (Sancho's wife) 78
Sancho, Ignatius
   26, 78, *78*, 84, 90, *170*, 172
   Letters of ... 78, *78*
Sancho, William (Sancho's son) 78
Santo Domingo 131, 132, 133, 137
Scarlett, James 90
Scarlett, Kitty 144
Scott, David 19
Scott, Julius 44—5
Seven Years' War 30, 79
Shade Podcast 179
Sharp, Granville *42*, 87, 88, 89, 94, 119, *161*
Sharpe, Christina 183, 188
Sharpe, Samuel 144, 151, *151*
Sidney Sussex College, Cambridge 89, 90
Sierra Leone
   82, 113, 114, 119—21, *119*, *120*, *121*, 140
Sierra Leona Company 106
Simeon, Charles 93, 94
Sinzogan, Julien: *Land Ho!* 53, *53*
slavery *see* enslavement
Sloane, Hans: *A Voyage* ... 41—2, *44*
Smallwood, Stephanie 15
Smith, John Raphael
   Slave Trade 109, *109*
Smith, Robert 14
Smith, Zadie 198
Social Justice Sewing Academy 171, *174*
Society for Effecting the Abolition
   of the Slave Trade (SEAST)
   25, 75, 76, 84, 85, 88—93, 98, 158

emancipation badge and logo
   25, *26*, 89—90, 91, *91*, 156, *156*, 161, *161*
Sons of Africa 21—2, 75, 76, *76*
South Sea Company 13—14
   Annuities/securities
   13—14, 16, **16**, 17, 18, **18**, 19
   Fitzwilliam Museum and 15—16, 18
   University of Cambridge and
   13—14, 16—19
sovereignty 49, 136, 138, 178, 180—3
Spode Ceramic works 128, *128*
Stackhouse, Thomas, 51
   'Africa Antiqua' and 'Present Africa' 51, *51*
Stevens, William 21
Stevenson, William 78
Strickland Moodie, Susanna
   58, *59*, 154, 155, *155*
sugar/sugarcane cultivation
   2, 37, 41, 50, 54, 69, 71, *72—3*, 75,
   110, 128, 132, 133, 149, *157—9*
   boycott 108, 110, *110*, 154, 156, *156*

Taylor, Sonya Renee 185
Thomas, Northcote Whitridge 46, 48
Titian: *Bacchus and Ariadne* 56
tobacco 25, 41
Tobin, James 97
Trelawny, Edward 62
Trinidad and Tobago 42
Trinity College, Cambridge
   14, 89, 90, 91, 92, 133, 142, 148
Trinity Hall, Cambridge 15, 17, 93, 133, 164
Trouillot, Michel-Rolph 138, 198
Trousdall (Trousdale), John 50

UK Measuring Worth project 15, 16, 18
United States (US/North America)
   17, 25, 27, 80, 111, 113, 114, 115,
   117, 136, 138, 141, 164, 166, 167,
   168, *169*, 171, 175, 192, 195
   Jim Crow laws 171, 191—2
   South Carolina
   17, 80, 117, *173*, *176*, 183, *189*
University of Cambridge
   141, 144, 148, 183, 190, 194
   abolitionism and
   16—17, 87—96, *88*, *91*, *92*,
   93, *95*, 131—2, 133—4, 168
   Haitian Revolution and
   131—2, 133—4, 138, 141, 142
   Legacies of Enslavement inquiry
   13, 183—4
   slave trade and
   13—19, 54, *54*, 55, *55*,
   84, 88, 131—4, 184
   see also individual colleges; Cambridge/
      Cambridgeshire; enslavement
University of Cambridge Museums
   11, 37, 184
   see also Fitzwilliam Museum
University Library (Cambridge) 15

Van Meyer, Jan
   Daughters of Sir Matthew Decker
   15, *37*, *38*, 37—9
Vassa, Anna Maria (Equiano's daughter)
   32—3, 33, *86*, 96, 101,
   102, 104, 105—6, *107*

Vassa, Gustavus *see* Equiano, Olaudah
Vassa, Johanna (Equiano's daughter)
   32—3, 33, *86*, 96, 102, 104, 105—6
Vassa, Susannah (Equiano's wife)
   see Cullen, Susannah
Venice Biennale (59th) 177, 178
Venn, Henry 94
Verley, Bertie Louis 133
Verley, Vincent Everard Louis 133
Victoria (Queen) 121
Victoria and Albert Museum 64—8, *77*

Wakelin, John and William Taylor
   lidded tureen 134, *134*
Walker, George 98—9
Wallace, George 21
Watson, Richard 89
Watson, Sir Brook 81
Webb, Thomas: medal *74*, 108, *108*
Webber, Henry: badge *26*
Wedgwood, Josiah 25, *26*
West Africa
   30, 44, 46, 48, 52, 64, 69, 71, 113, 135
West India Committee 27, 99, 100, 108
Westminster College 17, *79*, *80*, *81*
Wheatley, John 30
Wheatley, Phillis
   17, 26, 30, *31*, 80, *80*, 81, *81*, 84, 90
   Poems on Various Subjects ...
   30, 80, *80*, 81, *81*
Wheatley, Susannah 81
white/whiteness 37—8, 185—8, 195
white supremacy 37, 182, 185, 187, 188
Wilberforce, William
   74, 75, 84, 88, 94, 99, 108, *108*, 131,
   138, 140, 141, *141*, 142, 143, 156, *161*
Wilder, Craig 131
Williams, Francis 77, *77*, *170*
Williams, Nancy and Colleen Haraden:
   Liberation 174
'Windrush Period' 171, 193
women's activism and resistance
   11, *39*, 40—1, 44, 58—9, *59*, 60,
   60, 61, 62, *65*, 66, 68, *68*, 69—73,
   69—70, *72—3*, 110, 123, 124, *124*, 125,
   125, 134, *135*, 144, 149, *149*, 151, *151*,
   154—9, *154—9*, 161, *161*, 171, 175
Woodward, John 14
Wordsworth, Christopher 142
Wordsworth, John 142
Wordsworth, William 142—3
World Anti-Slavery Convention 84
Wright, James: boycott of sugar 110, *110*

Yoruba people 53, 121, 196
Young West India (African trader) 50, *50*